EDUCATION AND POLICY IN ENGLAND
IN THE TWENTIETH CENTURY

By Peter Gordon

The Victorian School Manager (1974)
Philosophers as Educational Reformers (1979) with J. White
Selection For Secondary Education (1980)
The Study of Education: Inaugural Lectures 3 vols. (1980–8)
The Red Earl. The Papers of the Fifth Earl Spencer 1835–1910 2 vols.
(1980, 1986)
HMI (1987) with D. Lawton

By Richard Aldrich

Sir John Pakington and National Education (1979)
An Introduction to the History of Education (1982)
Education: Time for a New Act? (1985) with P. Leighton
Dictionary of British Educationists (1989) with P. Gordon

EDUCATION AND POLICY
IN ENGLAND IN THE
TWENTIETH CENTURY

PETER GORDON,
RICHARD ALDRICH and DENNIS DEAN
University of London Institute of Education

THE WOBURN PRESS

First published 1991 in Great Britain by
THE WOBURN PRESS
Gainsborough House, Gainsborough Road,
London, E11 1RS, England

and in the United States of America by
THE WOBURN PRESS
c/o International Specialized Book Services, Inc.
5602 N.E. Hassalo Street, Portland, Oregon 97213

Copyright © 1991 Peter Gordon, Richard Aldrich and Dennis Dean

British Library Cataloguing in Publication Data

Gordon, Peter *1927–*
    Education and policy in England in the twentieth century.
    1. England. Education. Political aspects
    I. Title.   II. Aldrich, Richard   III. Dean, Dennis
    379.42

ISBN 0 7130 0181 X (cased)
ISBN 0 7130 4016 5 (pbk)

Printed in Great Britain by
Antony Rowe Ltd, Chippenham

Contents

PART FOUR
TEACHERS AND TEACHING

APPENDIX

Introduction

The aim of this book is to provide a clear introduction to education and educational policy in England in the twentieth century.

The work is divided into four sections. The first, which focuses upon central politics and education, begins with an account of the nineteenth-century legacy, and then proceeds to follow a broadly chronological framework through to the 1980s.

The second section provides an overall consideration of the relationship between education and society, and then deals in more detail with two particularly important areas of twentieth-century development. This thematic approach is continued into the third section, which examines a range of educational institutions from the primary school to the university.

The final section concentrates upon the providers and provisions of education, with chapters on teachers, curriculum and examinations. In conclusion the 1988 Education Reform Act is taken to mark both the end of the period under consideration and the beginning of a new era.

For those readers wishing to follow up some of the themes mentioned in the text there are suggestions for further reading at the end of each chapter.

The authors consider that an historical study of the period covered by this book is both valid in its own right, and has much to offer in informing the current educational debate.

In writing this book the authors have benefited from the help of many individuals. We are especially grateful to Sue Bailey, Ros Greenbaum, Deborah Hines, Jane O'Sullivan and Patricia Thomas for their help in preparing the manuscript for publication.

October, 1990

PART ONE
Politics of Education

CHAPTER ONE

The Nineteenth-Century Legacy

This chapter provides an overview of the legacy of nineteenth-century politics in respect of education. That legacy is considered under four headings: the politics of central government, the politics of local government, the politics of Christianity and class, and a conclusion. The relationship between politics and the whole sphere of formal and informal educational provision is too broad to be summarized in a single chapter; attention here is principally confined to mainstream politics and to elementary schooling but other areas will be taken up in introductory sections to subsequent chapters.

CENTRAL POLITICS

The politics of central government and education has a long history. Personal interventions by medieval and Tudor monarchs, parliamentary legislation of the mid-seventeenth century, and the very representation of the universities of Oxford and Cambridge in the House of Commons from 1604, are episodes in that history. The major nineteenth-century legacy, however, dates from 1839. In that year a Whig government assumed a new responsibility for education by establishing a Committee of Privy Council on Education. This was created by Order in Council because the Conservative majority (which included Anglican bishops) in the House of Lords ensured that at this time no bill to establish a central government authority for education would be successful. The new Committee was composed of four politicians: the Chancellor of the Exchequer, the Home Secretary and the Lord Privy Seal, presided over by the Lord President of the Council himself. A new section was set up in the Privy Council Office and Dr Kay (later Sir James Kay-Shuttleworth) was placed at its head. John Allen and Hugh Seymour Tremenheere were appointed the first two inspectors.

Those who opposed the principle and the fact of a central government authority for education did so on a number of deeply-held political and religious grounds. Some believed that this would be a step on the way to tyranny, it was un-English, an assault on freedom. Others believed that national education was the responsibility of the national (i.e. Anglican) church. Others again, opponents of the Established Church, feared that the new body would discriminate against the schools of other Christian denominations. In 1839 itself there was great political controversy. The Whig government, with the support of the Radicals, narrowly carried the day against the Conservatives in the Commons, by 280 votes to 275. The House of Lords, furious at being bypassed in this fashion, resolved by 229 votes to 118 to present a formal address of protest to the monarch. This was written by Sir Robert Peel, but the Duke of Wellington declined to lead a mob to the palace, whilst the young Queen Victoria was not particularly impressed by the deputation, although she did later remark to Lord Lansdowne that she had never seen so many Tories all together before.

In 1841, however, when Sir Robert Peel and the Conservatives came into office, the Committee of Privy Council on Education was continued. Indeed, although from its inception it was considered to be but a temporary expedient, the Committee lasted until 1899 when the Board of Education Act brought together the Education Department of the Privy Council, the Science and Art Department (established in 1853 at South Kensington as a direct outcome of the Great Exhibition) and the educational responsibilities of the Charity Commissioners. The new Board of Education, however, was a complete fiction. Whereas the old Committee of Council had met occasionally, the Board never met at all.

From 1856 the Lord President of the Council was assisted in his educational duties by a Vice-President who, though having other responsibilities, was principally concerned with education and would represent this concern in the Commons. This appointment, though welcome in itself, only further confused the issue of where ultimate responsibility was to lie. Such confusion was shown in 1864 when the Conservative, Lord Robert Cecil's, resolution, which deplored the mutilation of inspectors' reports and the exclusion from them of statements and views adverse to the educational policies of the Committee of Council, was approved by 101 votes to 93. Robert Lowe, the Vice-President, resigned, whilst Lord Granville, the Lord President, who had earlier offered his resignation, withdrew it. Lowe's explanation was indeed accepted after investigation by a Select Committee, and the original resolution was rescinded, but his resignation stood, whilst Granville, and Lingen who had succeeded Kay-Shuttleworth as Secretary in 1849 and who was probably most to blame, remained in office.

For those who believed that education was not primarily a concern of central government the Committee of Privy Council indeed might seem to be a perfect instrument. Though it provided encouragement for the training and remuneration of teachers and the building and equipping of schools, it did so by grants in support of individual or institutional initiatives. The Committee of Council itself rarely met, perhaps once or twice a year, and much of its work passed into the hands of administrators. Too much indeed in the early years, for in 1849 Kay-Shuttleworth resigned after a breakdown brought on by overwork, whilst one of his successors, Patric Cumin, died in 1890 after but six years of strenuous toil. Ralph Lingen, secretary to 1870 (the others were Sir Francis Sandford, 1870–84 and Sir George Kekewich, 1890–99), survived by adopting a more rigorous control and simplification of procedures which restricted rather than encouraged central initiatives.

Nevertheless the weaknesses of the system were well known, and particular attention was drawn to them by Sir John Pakington's Select Committee of 1865–66 whose draft report recommended the abolition of the Committee of Council and the role of the Lord President, and their replacement by a Ministry and Minister of Public Instruction with a seat in the Cabinet. Conservative minority governments 1866–68 prepared a bill to establish such a Minister, but it failed to reach the Statute Book, thus leaving the way open for the 1870 Act, the Liberal solution, which introduced local education authorities in the shape of school boards. In 1884 another Select Committee, the Childers Committee, proposed that the Committee of Council should be replaced by a board headed by a President who should be the real rather than the nominal minister. By this time the Vice-President undertook nearly all the business of education and yet was still subordinate to the Lord President. Once again, however, nothing was done. In 1895 the Bryce Commission put the issue into a rather different focus by emphasizing the need for a more unified rather than a more powerful central authority. Lord Salisbury's Conservative administration of 1895 exemplified the dangers of division, for the Duke of Devonshire as Lord President, and Sir John Gorst, the Vice-President, held widely-differing attitudes towards the subject of the education of the poor.

Finally in 1899 a Board of Education was established which united the Education Department, the Science and Art Department and the educational work of the Charity Commissioners. In future there would be only one minister, the President of the Board of Education, but his status and office would be of second rank, like that of the President of the Board of Agriculture or the President of the Board of Trade. The

Board of Education was 'charged with the superintendence of matters relating to education in England and Wales', a general statement which might have presaged more had the new office been on a par with those of the principal Secretaries of State. Even in 1944 the first formulation of the new bill proposed that the title and role of President of the Board of Education should continue.

LOCAL POLITICS

Local politics in the nineteenth century found expression in a variety of ways. In the counties elaborate hierarchies of a feudal nature persisted throughout the nineteenth century. Such a hierarchy might comprise: 'The Lord Lieutenant; the Master of Foxhounds; the Agricultural Landlords; the Bishop; the Chairman of Quarter Sessions; the Colonel of the Yeomanry; the Members of Parliament; the Dean and Archdeacons; the Justices of the Peace; the lesser Gentry; the larger Farmers' (Allsobrook, 1986, p.24). The great county families exercised power over the political, social, religious and sporting life of the shires. Conflict and compromise coexisted. In some areas there was an amicable division of spoils between Tory and Whig families, in others fierce political feuding was the order of the day. Not until 1888 was a system of county councils which provided for election by ratepayers established.

Although in the rural areas, both in the countryside itself and in cathedral and market towns, power tended to lie in the traditional hands of squire and parson, in other urban areas new political forces were emerging. Even prior to the 1832 Reform Act relatively democratic constituencies like Preston and Westminster returned Radical MPs. Chartist petitions received significant support in the House of Commons. Municipal government was reformed in 1835, and this provided the opportunity for members of the Dissenting communities, and those who had made their way by industry, trade, commerce and profession, to achieve power and status in the local councils and in the offices of alderman and mayor.

There were many proposals to use the county as a basis for educational organization – county schools, county examinations, county boards, county rates, county colleges, county degrees. Some of these proposals were concerned with levels of education above the elementary school. The issue of rate-aided elementary schooling featured more strongly in the towns and cities, with Manchester to the fore in the 1840s and 1850s. Private bills were promoted in Parliament to achieve this end, and in 1857 the various contending Manchester parties – Anglicans, Dissenters, Secularists, Conservatives, Liberals, Radicals – threw their combined weight behind a general but permissive bill to enable boroughs and cities to establish education committees, and to raise money for education from the poor rate. The most important recommendation of the Newcastle Commissioners who reported in 1861 was that elected boards for education, empowered to levy rates and to pay grants, should be established both in counties and in large boroughs.

Neither of these schemes was successful and rate-aided elementary schooling was finally introduced by the Elementary Education Act of 1870. *Ad hoc* school boards were established wherever there were gaps in elementary school provision. Their role was to remedy the deficiency. Apart from London with some 50 members, boards had between five and 15 representatives, elected triennially by the ratepayers. Women were entitled both to vote and to stand as candidates, and a secret ballot was employed. In 1900 London had eight women out of a total of 55 members, Bradford three, and Birmingham, Leeds, Manchester and Nottingham two apiece. In 1903, the final year of the school boards, there were some 370 women members (Hurt, 1979, p.97). School board areas varied greatly in size. Many rural school boards controlled but one school. At the other end of the scale, by the turn of the twentieth century, half a million pupils were attending London's board schools, at which date there were some 2,500 school boards scattered across the country. This administrative nightmare was further complicated with the creation of county councils and county boroughs from 1888. An Act of 1889 empowered these new authorities to raise a penny rate for the purposes of technical education, and to establish technical instruction committees to oversee this work. From 1890 'whisky money', raised from a duty on beer and spirits, could also be applied to this purpose. On occasion school boards and technical instruction committees came into conflict over the definition of their respective powers, and the Cockerton judgements of 1900–01 which prohibited expenditure by the London School Board on the North London School of Art, on the grounds that it was expenditure neither on elementary education nor on children, brought these issues into sharp relief. The large urban school boards had become associated in Conservative eyes with the growth of extravagance, radicalism, unsectarianism (indeed the British and Foreign School Society handed over many of its schools to the boards), and even secularism. The new county and county borough authorities, on the other hand, seemed to be more disposed towards financial restraint, conservatism, denominational education and traditional values. The principle of large multi-purpose local authorities, moreover, was a logical one, and the technical instruction committees had shown that education could be incorporated into the general provision of local services. Thus in 1902 some 318 local education authorities were created for England and Wales, comprising 63 county councils, 82 county boroughs and 173 non-county boroughs and urban districts. These latter bodies (the Part III authorities) were given contol over elementary education only. County councils and county boroughs were additionally required to 'take such steps as seem to them desirable to supply or aid the supply of education other than elementary'. A political storm, however, arose over those clauses which required local education authorities to meet certain costs (including the teachers' salaries) of voluntary schools.

Education was a local political issue of great importance throughout the nineteenth century, both in rural and in urban areas. It became particularly prominent in the larger cities as municipal growth and reform allowed hitherto excluded groups to break traditional authority patterns (Reeder, 1977, pp. 11–25). Thus in 1835 in Tory, Anglican Liverpool, following the municipal corporations' reform, Liberals and Nonconformists gained power and opened the Corporation's schools to children of all denominations, including Roman Catholics. Clergymen of the several communions were allowed to provide instruction to their adherents at specific times in the school day, but otherwise only the reading of Bible extracts was allowed. Education thus became the local political issue of the hour. In 1841 the Tories regained control and restored the schools to the Protestant fold. In the 1840s local educational issues, fired by such campaigners as W.F. Hook, the vicar of Leeds, and the Congregationalist Edward Baines, editor of the *Leeds Mercury*, spilled over into the national scene and played a significant part in the West Riding parliamentary elections of 1847. Hook himself, a thoroughly controversial figure who appointed Chartists as his churchwardens, promoted the construction of 28 schools and four churches in Leeds during his 22-year ministry. Reference has already been made to the educational controversies of Manchester in the 1840s and 1850s which centred upon the rivalry between the Lancashire (later National) Public School Association and the Manchester and Salford Bill Committee. In 1869 the Manchester-based National Education Union was ranged against the Birmingham-based National Education League, and indeed on one occasion fighting broke out between rival groups of supporters in the Manchester Free Trade Hall.

The school board era, 1870–1902, though heir to a considerable history of education and politics at the local level, provided an immediate and indeed a unique relationship between the two. Since voters had as many votes as there were candidates, sophisticated political organization was required to enable these votes to be used to the best advantage. Thus in a 15-seat school board it was preferable for a party to put up eight candidates and return them all, rather than to allow 15 to stand and to gain only seven seats. In Birmingham, for example, the 'Liberal Eight' controlled the School Board from 1873, and pursued consistently radical and secular policies. In 1900 the 'Church Seven' defeated the 'Liberal Eight' (renamed the 'Education Eight') and, with Roman Catholic and independent support, Bishop Knox became chairman of the School Board and introduced religious instruction into Birmingham's board schools. Those, however, who stood as independents or representatives of minority parties – the Fabian Society, the Social Democratic Federation, the Independent Labour Party – encouraged their supporters to 'plump' for them with all their votes. For example, Henry Payne, a trade unionist and building worker, who stood as an ILP candidate in the Leicester School Board election of 1897, concluded his printed election address with the advice 'PLUMP FOR PAYNE! 15 VOTES NO CROSSES' (Simon, 1974a, p.153).

In 1861, in *Considerations on Representative Government*, John Stuart Mill had argued for multi-purpose local authorities on the grounds that people of ability would not be willing to serve on *ad hoc* boards. Whilst it would be dangerous to generalize about the membership of school boards overall, important members of the religious and civil establishments, including bishops and even a former governor-general of India in the shape of Lord Lawrence, first chairman of the London School Board, did seek and secure election. Newer political forces were represented by Keir Hardie, first chairman of the ILP founded in 1893, and Philip Snowden, Chancellor of the Exchequer in the Labour governments of 1924 and 1929. Female members of distinction included Mill's own stepdaughter Helen Taylor, Lydia Becker, Emily Davies, Margaret McMillan, and Elizabeth Garrett Anderson who subsequently became the country's first woman mayor at Aldeburgh in Suffolk in 1908. School boards and technical instruction committees also necessitated the creation of a corps of local educational administrators, many of whom continued in office after 1902 with the new educational authorities.

Overall, however, the conclusion to be drawn from this section is that in 1902 English education was characterized by local diversity. Local differences in respect of social and economic structures, religious and party politics, had produced significant local differences in educational provision. Such differences were compounded rather than reduced by the school boards. Some schools provided religious teaching, others did not. Some had large playgrounds and apparatus, pianos and other musical instruments, others were run on lines of the strictest economy. Differences were also apparent in local attitudes to further and higher education. Cities like Manchester and Birmingham, as the result of the actions of wealthy and influential citizens, and of municipal councils, were to the fore in the later nineteenth-century movement to establish civic universities.

CHRISTIANITY AND CLASS

The religious politics of nineteenth-century education took many forms, and reference has already been made to the connections which existed between political and religious groupings at both central and local levels. For example the British and Foreign School Society which favoured non-denominational teaching, and University College, London which had no religious teaching at all, had firm connections with Whig, Liberal and Radical politicians. On the other hand the National Society and King's College, London, promoters of Anglicanism at elementary and higher levels of education, were assured of Tory and Conservative support. Such affiliations, however, were neither absolute nor unchanging, nor was there any simple conflict, as occurred in other countries, between Church and State. Indeed in England the head of state was also head of the Anglican Church, whilst bishops, whose appointments were often made on political grounds, sat in the House of Lords.

Politicians and administrators found themselves assailed from all sides. Anglicans believed that governments were not doing enough to preserve the historic rights of the Established Church in education, non-Anglicans argued that governments were doing too much. Anglicans could point to the legislation of 1854, 1856 and 1871 which required the universities of Oxford and Cambridge to open their degrees and fellowships to those who would not subscribe to the 39 Articles. On the other hand, although the Religious Census of 1851 showed that only half of the nation's church-going population were Anglicans, prior to 1870 Anglican schools received some three-quarters of government grants for elementary education. Faith and expediency appeared to go hand in hand. In Ireland where adherents of the Established Church were in a distinct minority, a scheme of 'united education' and a supervisory board which included Roman Catholics and Protestants were established in the 1830s. Between 1843 and 1867 the 'Voluntaryists' in England, principally Baptists and Congregationalists, eschewed all state aid for education on the grounds that such aid was principally designed to further the interests of the State Church. In the latter year financial necessity occasioned a change of policy, and government grants were accepted. Hostility of Protestants towards Roman Catholics was another important theme. In 1847, for example, the Wesleyans in accepting state aid for their schools did so on condition that such acceptance did not imply their approval of grants to Roman Catholic schools. In 1902 Protestant Dissenting fury was particularly directed at the prospect of local finance for Roman Catholic schools – 'Rome on the rates'.

Contrary to popular opinion the 1870 Act did not provide a clear solution to the problem of religious instruction in board schools. School boards could forbid all religious instruction during normal school hours in their schools, as was done in Birmingham between 1873 and 1879, or could sanction denominational instruction as long as a catechism or formulary as such was not employed. In practice, however, most board schools, as in London, provided non-denominational religious teaching. Nevertheless, the whether and how of religious teaching in board schools, the existence of single school areas (usually Anglican), and the power of boards to pay the school fees of poor children to attend denominational schools, were continuing sources of controversy.

The most fundamental political legacy, however, concerned the declining religious influence in education. At the end of the nineteenth century although over 70 per cent of elementary schools were controlled by voluntary bodies, such schools contained only just over half of all elementary school children. Board schools were not only larger, but often better resourced and in many ways more efficient. In 1870 the main problem was how to fill up the gaps in voluntary school provision. In 1902, and during the twentieth century, the main problem was how to ensure the financial survival of voluntary schools, whilst enabling them to retain their religious or denominational identities.

Throughout the nineteenth century there was an alternative political perspective on education which was located outside central and local government and the churches. In the early nineteenth century it found expression in such movements as Owenism and Chartism. By 1900 it received trade union support. This alternative legacy began from an interpretation of a capitalist, class-based society, in which ordinary people were subject to various forms of political and economic exploitation. Elementary schools of the type provided by the National Society were seen as agents of social control, financed by a corrupt church and a tyrannical government to teach the children of the poor to be grateful and humble, and to accept their poverty in this world with the promise of salvation in the next. This alternative vision embraced schools which taught really useful knowledge, knowledge of how to overcome the iniquities of the existing social, economic and political system. It envisaged a radical free press (the *Poor Man's Guardian* and *Northern Star* of the 1830s were two examples) and a range of new educational institutions for children and adults – schools, libraries, institutes, reading rooms, discussion groups – free from state and church control.

By the end of the nineteenth century, however, the alternative ideal commanded less support than the doctrine of thorough reform of the provided system. Compulsory age-specific schooling, for all its faults, was seen as the best means of preventing the evils of child labour, an experience shared by many of the labour, socialist and trade union pioneers of the late nineteenth century. For example Will Thorne had left school at six years of age, Keir Hardie at seven, Will Crooks and Ben Tillett at eight. Thus, by the 1890s, the alternative political legacy had become a reform programme which comprised: equality of opportunity for all children in education, an equality guaranteed by maintenance grants and free school meals; the raising of the school-leaving age to 16; the financing of education directly from taxation; and the exclusion of all but secular subjects from the school curriculum (Griggs, 1983, p. 259).

SUMMARY

Four concluding points may be made in respect of the political legacy.

First: throughout the nineteenth century governments were aristocratic and (apart from Queen Victoria) exclusively male. True, some women, and male members of the working classes, had gained a toehold in the school boards, but in respect of central government, even in the 1860s, half of the members of the House of Commons were themselves members of the peerage or baronetage or connected with these orders. For most of the century patronage rather than election was the principal means of determining who should represent a particular constituency in Parliament. Thus although the term 'National Education' was often used by politicians in the nineteenth century, it did not imply common schools, equality of gender or class, or a state-controlled system, but rather separate education for separate groups of society. Indeed there was widespread political concern lest free or assisted schooling for children of the working classes should enable them to receive a better education at the state's expense than that available to children of the 'superior' classes. At the turn of the century this concern found particular expression in attacks on higher grade schools, and on the general use of money by school boards for non-elementary purposes.

Second: three broad political attitudes may be determined. Radical politicians were keen for educational advance. Free, compulsory, unsectarian (or even secular) schooling was their goal, and many of them were prepared to see considerable government intervention to achieve this end. But the political failure of the Radicals, the existence of so many denominationally-controlled and private schools, and the considerable cost, made such a solution unlikely.

Tory and Conservative politicians were identified with the Anglican and landed interests. Initially they opposed government intervention and a central authority, but when it became apparent that the Church would benefit greatly from the grants system, and could veto the appointment of the inspectors of its schools, they became more supportive of the Committee of Privy Council. Conservatives supported the 1870 Bill because it offered a period of grace in which denominational schools might be built to fill up the gaps, and because free, compulsory, unsectarian education was not to be imposed upon the country as a whole. In the last 30 years of the century, however, Conservatives became concerned to prevent denominational schools from being eased out, as the working-class private schools had been, by the new board schools, which relied not only upon grants from central government but also upon support from the rates. Solutions were no longer sought at central level and the Board of Education Act of 1899 aroused little interest. On the other hand the Education Act of 1902, which ended the school boards and enabled denominational schools to receive aid from the rates, provoked a political and religious furore.

The basic political and administrative framework of English education was created by the Whigs and Liberals in the middle years of the nineteenth century. They were a compromise party, a party of Church and Dissent, a party of country and town. Had they controlled the House of Lords they might have achieved more. But the basic tenets of Liberalism included freedom from state interference, administrative efficiency, and leaving money to fructify in the pockets of the people. Moreover as a coalition party the Liberals could not propose extreme measures for fear of suffering the same fate as had befallen the Conservatives in 1846 over the repeal of the Corn Laws, and consigned them to minority politics for nearly 30 years. Indeed the main parliamentary opposition to the 1870 Education Act came not from the

Conservatives but from the government's own Radical and Noncon-formist supporters who, as in 1833 on the occasion of the £20,000 grant to education, pressed for a more adventurous policy.

Third: most politicians shared the general belief that education was primarily the responsibility of parents, the churches and the work place. Children of the upper and middle classes, and indeed many children of the working classes, attended schools financed by fees paid by the parents. From the early nineteenth century the National Society for promoting the education of the poor in the principles of the Established Church, other denominational societies, and the non-denominational British and Foreign School Society provided many elementary schools. William Gladstone, prime minister in four Liberal governments in the second half of the nineteenth century, whose first government produced the 1870 Act, firmly believed that in education, as in other spheres of life, voluntary effort was preferable to state interference. The central government, therefore, did not seek to establish its own schools but rather to assist others in so doing. It thus built up considerable experience of distributing funds, and a determination that such funds should be used efficiently. From 1862, under the terms of the Revised Code, most of the grant was disbursed on the principle of payment by results – success rather than need was the basic criterion for assistance. Thus many (but not all) of those engaged in the central superintendence of education, from Lords President, Vice-Presidents, Secretaries, Examiners through to Her Majesty's Inspectors, believed that state-aided schools were but a second best, and that the work in which they were engaged was not only mundane but even demeaning to men of quality.

In conclusion, therefore, although by the end of the nineteenth century central government had adopted a role in respect of education which it had not held in 1800, no principal department of state had been established. In 1870 when the choice lay between centrally-controlled or locally-controlled schools to fill up the gaps and to eliminate the private working-class schools, W.E. Forster chose the latter alterna-tive. He did so on the grounds that the existing central body, the Committee of Privy Council, did not have sufficient power to achieve this objective, and that to grant it the authority to cover the country with its own schools would be to create an excessive and dangerous power. That decision was not reversed, and in 1900, as in 1870, the main thrust of parliamentary politics was still further to increase local rather than central government powers in education.

FURTHER READING

A. Bishop, *The Rise of a Central Authority for English Education*, 1971, which covers the administrative dimension may be supplemented from the political side by such studies as D. Paz, *The Politics of Working-Class Education in Britain, 1830–50*, 1980, and G. Sutherland, *Policy-Making in Elementary Education, 1870–1895*, 1973. Radical perspectives are examined by H. Silver, *English Education and the Radicals, 1780–1850*, 1975, and the work of the Labour movement by C. Griggs, *The Trades Union Congress and the Struggle for Education, 1868–1925*, 1983, and B. Simon, *Education and the Labour Movement, 1870–1920*, 1974. Studies of the religious dimension include J. Murphy, *Church, State and Schools in Britain, 1800–1970*, 1971, whilst D. Reeder (ed.), *Urban Education in the Nineteenth Century*, 1977, and D. Allsobrook, *Schools for the Shires*, 1986 provide useful starting points for insights into urban and rural politics. Finally D. Wardle, *Education and Society in Nineteenth-Century Nottingham*, 1971, gives a good overview of education at all levels in one locality in the later nineteenth century.

CHAPTER TWO

The Foundations of Twentieth-Century Politics, Administration and Social Policy, 1900–1944

The period of time dealt with in this chapter was one of great importance in the development of educational and social policies. The first half of the present century saw Britain involved in three wars, the emergence of a welfare state and a major upheaval in politics. These factors are reflected in the national debate on the nature of education, which took place in various forums.

POLITICS AND EDUCATIONAL POLICY 1900–1914

The extension of the franchise to rural workers in 1884, following that of their urban counterparts in 1867, introduced a new element into political life. Both the Conservative and Liberal parties henceforth would ignore such issues as poverty and education at their peril. The Fabian Society was established in 1884 to persuade intellectuals to work towards the goal of state socialism. By 1900, a Labour Representation Committee, consisting of the Fabians, the Independent Labour Party and the Social Democratic Federation, signalled the beginnings of the Labour party, though it did not become a national political body until the second decade of the century. The programme of social policy embarked upon by successive governments in the late nineteenth century was an acknowledgement of this new force. Indeed, Sir William Harcourt, the Liberal Chancellor of the Exchequer who introduced the 1894 death duties budget, demonstrated this in his famous remark, 'We are all socialists now' (Fraser, 1984, p.141).

Following the return of the Liberals to power in the 1906 election, there was a large programme of legislation aimed at improving the lot of the needy. These dealt with unemployed workmen (1905), old age pensioners (1908), poor law (1908), and national insurance (1911). It is significant too that the legislation allowing local authorities to provide meals for poor children (1906) was introduced by one of the 30 Labour Members of Parliament elected that year.

There were other issues of policy which can be more closely identified with political philosophies and parties. From the 1890s, the organized Labour movement campaigned for greater access by working-class children to secondary schools. True, the need was officially acknowledged by the Liberals in 1907 with the introduction of the Free Place Regulations, which made possible the offering of up to 25 per cent of a secondary school's places to pupils without payment and without a test of ability. It should be remembered, however, that it was not until January 1914 that the Labour party issued its first educational programme (Barker, 1972, p.25).

By the beginning of the present century, the deficiencies in the education system called for action. The provision of secondary education was inadequate and was unequally distributed. In elementary education, the 1870 Education Act made the State responsible for the first time for filling the gaps left by voluntary effort. Such schools were administered by locally-elected school boards. The religious bodies who sponsored voluntary schools often regarded the school boards with hostility, as their power to levy a rate for building schools placed them at an advantage. Another issue was the teaching of religion, which in board schools was considered by their critics to be inadequate. Voluntary schools provided education for about half the school population by 1900. Financially, the various denominational bodies responsible for the schools were finding it difficult to offer a reasonable level of education. The need for the reform of the dual system was urgent.

A further stimulus for action was the growing acceptance in Britain of the 'national efficiency' ideology which attracted adherents from a broad spectrum of beliefs. This ideology sprang from an admiration of the German model, where the State was seen as the creative and moral agency. The highly-centralized machinery of government and the organization of welfare and education had resulted in impressive military, industrial and economic advances. In contrast, the British emphasis on personal liberty and piecemeal reform could be held to account for the country's inability to match the growing military and economic superiority of Germany in Europe and Japan in the Far East. The humiliating setbacks experienced by the British Army against the Boers during the South African War (1899–1902) confirmed their worst fears. Education was one of the areas which called for action.

17

Among the group of people subscribing to this doctrine were Haldane, Milner, Rosebery, the Webbs and Morant (Searle, 1971, pp.51–60). Whilst working as assistant to Michael Sadler at the Education Department's Office of Special Inquiries, Morant wrote an article on Swiss education, published in 1898, setting out his opinions on the deficiencies in English education at the time. His solution was to establish 'a really expert Central Authority for the whole of our National Education, a localized "guidance of brains", which will watch, consider and advise upon *all* our national arrangements of all grades, of every type, *as one whole*' (Allen, 1934, pp.125–6).

Morant was able to give rein to this notion in 1901 when, as private secretary to Gorst, the Vice-President of the Committee of the Council on Education, he was invited by Balfour, who was shortly to become the Conservative Prime Minister, to assist in drawing up an ambitious Education Bill. Its major aim was to replace the *ad hoc* school boards for elementary education by a single Education Authority responsible for all forms of education in an area. The new Local Education Authority (LEA) would be able to co-opt 'educational experts' to advise on local policy, in place of democratically-elected school boards.

Fabian support for such a measure came in the form of a pamphlet by Sidney Webb, *The Education Muddle and the Way Out* (1901), which advocated the demise of school boards in favour of LEAs whilst preserving the variety of church schools. On the other hand, the Liberals, at a time when the Balfour administration was flagging, saw the 1902 Education Bill as a good opportunity to rally its supporters in opposing the proposed abolition of school boards. They were helped by church opposition to a single authority, thus making the new LEAs the masters of secular education, and by the fury of Nonconformists at the prospect of giving rate aid to denominational boards. As one Opposition Member of Parliament stated during a debate on the Bill, 'If you could eliminate the religious difficulty, your Education Bill would pass the Second Reading in a single night and the Committee stage would not take a week' (quoted in Lowndes, 1937, p.82). In fact, the final measure was a compromise: the managers of voluntary schools were to be responsible for religious education and the appointment of teachers, who would be paid by the LEA. Similarly, the managers were to run the school but the LEA directed the provision for non-religious instruction. The dual system, with Church and State schools existing alongside each other, in essence, continued.

Although Balfour and Morant were forced to retreat from their bold vision, nevertheless by the passing of the 1902 Act much had been achieved. The major LEAs which were created were responsible for the provision of both elementary and secondary education in their areas. It was from this time that a national system of secondary schools, locally administered, was established.

When the Liberals came into office following Balfour's resignation in November 1905, they fared even worse than the Conservatives in their attempts to abolish the dual system. Augustine Birrell, President of the Board, introduced an Education Bill in the Commons in April 1906 which would have transferred all rate-aided voluntary schools to the LEAs from 1 January 1908. The Cowper-Temple clause of the 1870 Act, by which no teacher was bound to give religious instruction, was to be enforced. However, denominational teaching was to be allowed on two mornings a week in transferred schools, with extra provision if four-fifths of the parents requested it. Birrell, in his autobiography (1937, p. 188), states that he was shocked by the response of MPs to the Bill: 'I have freely consorted all my life with Catholics, Roman and Anglican, with ardent Evangelical English churchmen, with Nonconformists of every shade, with Modernists, Agnostics and Atheists, but never have I drawn my breath in so irreligious and ignorant an atmosphere as that of the House of Commons when debating religion.'

The measure, described by Campbell-Bannerman, the Liberal Prime Minister, as 'an undenominational Bill, setting up an undenominational system', was aimed particularly at breaking Anglican monopoly in single school areas. Not only was the Church of England incensed, but the Nonconformists, whose passive resistance to the 1902 Act had taken the form of withholding rates, attacked once more the principle of rate aid to denominational schools. When the Bill was debated in the Lords, it was amended to allow denominational teaching in every type of school. Balfour, who led the Conservative onslaught on the Bill, was successful in ensuring that it did not reach the Statute Book. In many ways, the Bill anticipated the religious settlement of the 1944 Act (Cruickshank, 1963, p. 102).

McKenna, Birrell's successor, made another attempt in February 1908, though as it was a more ruthless assault on denominational schools there was little likelihood that it would overcome opposition. Voluntary schools were invited to transfer their schools to LEAs and facilities would be given for denominational teaching, but not during school hours. Where a voluntary school was the only one in the parish, the managers were to be allowed to 'contract out', receiving a direct Exchequer grant of up to 47s. per child annually if efficient; fees of up to 9d a week would be allowed to be charged. Unlike Birrell's Bill, McKenna's was destructive, as it would have undone the work of the

1902 Act in establishing LEAs for areas and reintroduced fee-paying in elementary schools.

In the same year, following Campbell-Bannerman's death and a Cabinet reshuffle, Runciman replaced McKenna in April 1908. Looking at the problem afresh, Runciman hoped to negotiate with both the Anglicans and Nonconformists; the Anglicans were to accept that the majority of their schools would be transferred to LEAs in return for a relaxation of denominational teaching in 'Council' schools, and the Nonconformists were to be assured of a limitation on the number of contracting out schools. The Bill was introduced on 20 November, Birrell having carried on negotiations previously with both groups. The Roman Catholics, who had not been party to the negotiations, voiced their protest and were joined by Nonconformist MPs who disliked the prospects of denominational teaching in schools, a view shared by many teachers. After a brief life of 17 days, the Bill was dropped.

No fewer than three successive Presidents of the Board of Education between 1906 and 1908 had to admit defeat in their endeavours to achieve a religious settlement. The issue did not play a prominent part in educational politics again until the Butler Act was being shaped. Meanwhile the 1902 Act had laid the foundations for building a national system but without settling the problem of dual control.

MORANT AT THE BOARD

As the architect of the 1902 Act, Robert Morant was, as Permanent Secretary to the Board of Education, from the following year responsible for its implementation. To a large extent, he was successful in setting his seal on the education system in England and Wales during the following eight years. He supported the establishment of LEAs which would co-ordinate all forms of education in their areas, but saw the Board's role as being 'to prevent variety from degenerating into competition, or elasticity into formlessness'. In the Elementary School Code of 1904, Morant set out what has been called a programme of 'education for followership' and in the Secondary School Regulations that same year promoted 'education for leadership' (Eaglesham, 1967, pp.51–5). To complete the picture, Morant attempted to bring the universities within the scope of the Board's policy-making ambit. A University Branch was set up in 1910 to win control of the administration of Treasury grants to universities. This move met with resistance from both the universities and Lloyd George, the Chancellor of the Exchequer. Although the Board was responsible from 1911 for administrative grants, the Treasury retained control over expenditure

(Sherington, 1981, p. 12). However, Morant was more successful in plotting wth Haldane and the Webbs to launch a higher technological institute in London, the Imperial College of Science and Technology (Ashby and Anderson, 1974, pp. 45–58).

Initially unsympathetic to technical and vocational education, Morant had turned his attention to these areas. He instigated an investigation into the possibility of promoting commercial education and accepted the Report in 1909. The following year, with the assistance of two like-minded colleagues, E. K. Chambers, one of his Assistant Secretaries, and F. Pullinger, the Chief Inspector, Technological Branch, he set about the replanning of technical and further education. Morant's departure from the Board in 1911 delayed the implementation of these plans. He supported the notion of continuing education as a means of widening the educational opportunities of working people. He increased grants for university tutorial classes in 1906 and encouraged Mansbridge in developing the Workers' Educational Association by addressing the Oxford Conference on Working Class Education in 1907 (Mansbridge, 1940, pp. 166–7).

Morant was eager to implement the social welfare aspects of education contained in parliamentary legislation and recommended by commissions. He assisted Margaret McMillan in establishing nursery schools and was aware of the need for the physical well-being of children. In Circular 576 issued in November 1907, Morant stated, 'The broad requirements of a healthy life are comparatively few and elementary, but they are essential, and should not be regarded as applicable only to the case of the rich'. Regulations covering topics such as school meals, the employment of children and continuation classes were aimed at promoting improvements in educational welfare. Perhaps Morant's greatest achievement in this field was the creation of the School Medical Service in 1907. The first medical officer, George Newman, vigorously pursued a scheme to provide for the medical inspection of school children administered by local education authorities.

Morant's role in the development of educational policy has attracted both admirers and critics. Whatever the verdict might be on Morant as a person, it is undeniable that it was he who was responsible for shaping the school system into a pattern which was to endure for the next half century.

THE BOARD OF EDUCATION

The need to streamline the central administrative structure of education had been noted by the Bryce Commission in 1895. The separate entities of the Education Department, the Science and Art Department and the Charity Commission, each with its own staffs and policies, placed obstacles in the way of, amongst other matters, the development of secondary education. By the Board of Education Act (1899) these departments were eventually merged, but not without opposition from various interest groups. For example, protests were made by the headmasters of well-known schools against the possibility of their being placed under the same branch of the new Board as that of technical schools (Gosden, 1966, p.91).

The new Board came into being in 1900. A President and his Parliamentary Secretary, its political heads, replaced the posts of Lord President and, on the latter's retirement from office, the Vice-President of the Privy Council. Three branches – Elementary, Secondary and Technological – were created but the Board had only one Permanent Secretary. Many of the senior staff, such as E.K. Chambers and W.N. Bruce, were dedicated to the cause of national education, even if their own backgrounds, typically, of public school and Oxbridge, hardly provided them with first-hand knowledge of the problems. All five Permanent Secretaries up to the end of the Second World War were Oxford men: Morant and L.A. Selby-Bigge had attended Winchester School, A.V. Symonds Bedford, H.P. Pelham Harrow and M. Holmes Wellington. Selby-Bigge, Morant's successor in 1911, also pointed out in his history of the Board that until 1919, unlike other government departments, the higher staff was recruited by direct appointment by the President (Selby-Bigge, 1927, p.78).

Haldane's Machinery of Government Committee (1918) had scrutinized the administrative efficiency of departments. In the following year, the Board lost responsibility for making grants to universities: this power was now given to the newly-formed University Grants Committee. A partial reform of the Board was effected in 1922 when an officer at Principal level became responsible for the work of all three Branches – Elementary, Secondary and Technological – within each of the seven territorial divisions in England. This move simplified the liaison between LEAs and the Board. Territorial officers, up to the rank of Principals and Assistant Principals, carried out the day-to-day work at the Board. Important questions affecting policy were referred to the appropriate Assistant Secretary or Principal Assistant Secretary.

To ensure co-ordination at the higher levels within the Board, conferences were held between the Principal Assistant Secretaries and the Secretary or Deputy Secretary.

With the increase in its responsibilities, the need to lighten the administrative burden carried by the Board was recognized. In 1925, the Board changed the rules concerning staffing of schools so that problems were considered from the standpoint of an area rather than from that of the individual school. The Board's 1926 Regulations, consisting of nine pages as against the previous year's 78, affected many aspects of education. The elaborate Code of Regulations for public elementary schools was replaced by key grant regulations and similar changes were made for secondary schools, further education, adult education and teacher training. Elementary schools were now free to offer their own curriculum (see Chapter 19) and official advice on the syllabus in future was to be confined to the publication, *Suggestions for Teachers in Public Elementary Schools* (see p.25 below).

ADVISORY BODIES AND THE BOARD

One of the many tasks soon facing the Board was the implementation of the 1902 Act. The relationships with the new LEAs had to be negotiated, requiring much tactful handling, as will be seen later in this chapter. Consultation rather than direction was necessary for the system to work (Armytage, 1964, p.204). The Board set up advisory bodies and interdepartmental committees, but the main channel for the gathering of information was the Consultative Committee. The Committee had two functions: to advise the Board of any matters referred to it and to frame regulations for a teachers' register. The latter function was dropped after 1907, but the Committee's role as an advisory body had an important bearing on educational policy until its demise in 1944. Membership was to consist of 'not less than two-thirds of persons qualified to represent the views of universities and other bodies interested in education'. The chairman was chosen by the President of the Board, after which a search was made for appropriate experts. Arthur Acland, a former Vice-President of the Council, was its first chairman and there were 18 members in all. The position of the Committee was a curious one as the relationship between its recommendations and the policy-making functions of the Board was unclear. After two decades of experience, Selby-Bigge was favouring Departmental and Interdepartmental Committees rather than Consultative Committees as the appropriate vehicles for inquiring into particular problems (Kogan and Packwood, 1974, pp.11–12).

Nevertheless, an impressive range of work on educational issues was undertaken by the Committee and its published findings attracted public attention. Among the better-known are the Hadow Reports on the Education of the Adolescent (1926), on the Primary School (1931) and on the Infant School (1933), and the Spens Report on Secondary Education (1938). The recommendations of these Committees will be dealt with in subsequent chapters. In considering the outcomes of these Committees' deliberations, a number of factors must be borne in mind. Much depended on the character of the chairman, and the backgrounds of members of the Committee. The composition of the Consultative Committee on the Adolescent was unusual, as it contained representatives of institutions ranging from the primary school to the university (Selleck, 1972, p.133). Where sub-committees were appointed to draft the report, as happened with the last-named Committee, such distinguished people as R.H. Tawney, Cyril Burt and Percy Nunn were invited to help. It is not difficult to detect their stamp on the outcome.

Another important source of advice to the Board was Her Majesty's Inspectorate (HMI). Established by the Privy Council on Education in 1839, HMI were appointed by the Queen in Council. Inspectors, such as Matthew Arnold, reported freely on the state of schools and on occasion were publicly critical of the permanent officials on such issues as the introduction of 'payment by results' in 1862. Up to the end of the nineteenth century, HMI devoted the majority of their time to inspecting elementary schools.

One other consequence of the Board of Education Act was that the inspection of secondary schools came within the Board's jurisdiction. Fortunately, the experience of the Inspectors of the Science and Art Department in endowed grammar schools was a useful basis for this new task. When the three branches of the Boards were established in 1903, the Inspectorate was reorganized to correspond to these groupings. Some of the Science and Art Department Inspectors became part of the Secondary Inspectorate which was set up in 1904, with its own Chief Inspector (Boothroyd, 1923, p.61). The 1902 Act, as we have seen, led to the growth of secondary schooling. To carry out this task, the Inspectorate developed the 'full inspection', whereby a team of HMI examined many aspects of a school's curriculum and organization over a number of days.

The Elementary Inspectorate was also faced with a problem. Following the ending of 'payment by results' from 1895, teachers were freer to devise their own approaches to teaching. HMI were now in a position to encourage them, though the means whereby this could be done was left to individual Inspectors. Some guidance was provided by the Board of

Education's publication, written largely by Inspectors, *Suggestions for the Consideration of Teachers* (1905); this was updated at intervals and from 1927 was renamed *Handbook of Suggestions for Teachers*.

The three branches of the Inspectorate operated within their own sectors of education. A separate Women Inspectorate was formed in 1904 by Morant: this followed the publication of the Interdepartmental Committee on Physical Deterioration which highlighted the poor physique of many potential Army recruits at the time of the Boer War. Morant seized the opportunity to recruit particularly Women Inspectors qualified in domestic subjects. Their position in terms of salary, working conditions and responsibility was inferior to that of their male colleagues. Recruitment to the Women Inspectorate ceased from 1934 when men and women were given equal responsibilities, but equal pay was not achieved until 1961 (Lawton and Gordon, 1987, pp. 88–99).

Following the disappearance of the three separate branches of the Board in 1926, the Inspectorate was also unified in its higher branches, from Divisional and Staff Inspectors upwards. Nine Divisional Inspectors were appointed and were responsible for co-ordinating the work of HMI at each stage of education within their regions. A Senior Chief Inspector (SCI), chosen from one of the three Chief Inspectors, was henceforth the head of the Inspectorate, though still retaining responsibility for his phase of education. From 1944, the SCI became a full-time post. Senior Inspectors were especially influential in their roles as assessors to important committees. For example, Francis Duckworth, SCI between 1941 and 1943 and one of the assessors to the Norwood Committee on Secondary School Curriculum and Examinations and the Fleming Committee on Public Schools, played a prominent part in the final shape of the Committees' Reports (Wallace, 1981, p. 284).

The size of the Inspectorate remained almost constant between 1900 and 1944, with 349 at the earlier date and 355 at the later. Meanwhile, LEAs, particularly the larger ones such as London, had developed their own school inspectorates. A Board of Education survey in 1922 concluded that there was little duplication of the work of the two inspectorates (Rhodes, 1981, p. 108), though the relationship between the bodies remained unclear in some areas. This balance was to change after the 1944 Education Act. HMI were given the task of ensuring a degree of national uniformity in educational standards. In order to carry this out, a further 200 HMIs were immediately recruited and a large-scale programme of inspections was undertaken. The number of Inspectors has remained at about 500 since this time.

THE BOARD AND LOCAL EDUCATION AUTHORITIES

One of the important provisions of the 1902 Education Act was the establishment of 318 LEAs in place of more than 3,000 school boards and school attendance committees. The division between elementary and secondary education was made clear by the creation of Part III authorities who were responsible for elementary education only, and Part II authorities, who were given powers for secondary and higher education.

County councils and county boroughs were to be the new LEAs and constituted Part II authorities. There were also non-county boroughs with a population of at least 10,000 and urban districts of over 20,000 people. The latter two were limited to becoming Part III authorities, though even then it was by no means automatic that they would be granted LEA status. Anomalies arose from the beginning out of the fact that though county borough status required a population of at least 50,000, there were a number of old boroughs, particularly cathedral towns, which fell well below this figure. Conversely, there were many large towns with populations well above this figure which were not county boroughs. A further weakness stemmed from opposition encountered during the passage of the 1902 Bill from MPs who considered that special local knowledge would be lost in an area as large as a county. The resultant 160 Part III authorities which came into existence weakened the LEA system administratively and were expensive. The Act also set out the constitution of managing bodies of elementary schools, both voluntary and provided. With secondary schools, the position was much less clear than with elementary schools. Where a new school was built by the LEA, it was easy to lay down rules as to its management: with existing and voluntary schools, only general guidelines could be suggested (Gosden, 1966, p. 181).

Finally, the Act stipulated that LEAs should discharge their work through an education committee of the council with a majority of council members but also allowing for the appointment of people with experience in education at different levels. In practice, the committee exercised the full powers of the council, with responsibility for control, management and the sanctioning of expenditure. The committee was advised by a full-time paid official, often bearing the title of Director of Education or Chief Education Officer, who had his own staff. A number of Directors of Education were former school board clerks. Their new task was to liaise with the chairman of the committee, the Board of Education and the Inspectorate.

The tensions which could arise from uncertain boundaries in decision-making between the Board of Education and LEAs were soon obvious. The Board had, in a Prefatory Memorandum to the 1904 Regulations, stressed the importance it attached to preserving the independence and freedom of action for governors of secondary schools and the headteacher in exercising control over teaching, organization and discipline. Model articles were drawn up by the Board in 1908 for this purpose.

Some of the more powerful Directors of Education, such as James Graham of Leeds, firmly resisted what they regarded as the inter-position of a body which diminished the powers of an LEA. Graham's defiance of the Board was supported by ten other authorities; in consequence, grants were withheld for a short time though soon afterwards the Board capitulated on this issue (Baron and Howell, 1968, pp. 24–8). Graham was one of the triumvirate of great educational administrators, known as 'The Three Musketeers', who were alternately consulted by, and in violent collision with, the Board of Education. The other two were Percival Sharp of Sheffield and Spurley Hey of Manchester. Hey, who was Director for some 16 years, dominated his education committee, promoting central schools and at one stage providing more nursery school places in his authority than in all the nursery schools in England and Wales (S.D. Simon, 1938, p. 268). Other influential education officers included the arch-administrator Robert Blair of the LCC (Thoms, 1980), and the erratic visionary Henry Morris of Cambridgeshire (Ree, 1985). Overshadowing them all, however, was William Brockington, who served as Director of Education for Leicestershire from 1903 to 1947. Amongst Brockington's several achievements were his personal inspections of schools throughout the county, his development of a policy of senior schools which foreshadowed the Hadow reorganization, his status as joint founder of Loughborough College, and service on the Burnham Committee, on the Consultative Committee of the Board of Education, and on the Secondary School Examinations Council (Seaborne, 1968).

One of the most important features of the relationship between the central authority and LEAs was, and is, the policies formulated by government and their financial implications for LEAs. Before 1902, grants were paid to individual schools: now, as far as possible, they were paid to the LEA. But expenditure increased rapidly for several reasons. Voluntary schools which were transferred to LEAs often required improvements in buildings and equipment to bring them up to the standard of other schools. The Board's *Suggestions for Teachers* in 1905 encouraged and stimulated improved teaching methods and educational developments which had financial implications. LEAs were authorized to spend money on providing dinners under the Education (Provision of Meals) Act 1906. Expenditure was limited to the product of a halfpenny rate, but many LEAs felt compelled to put the Act wholly or partly into operation. By 1911–12, expenditure under this head was £143,486 (Corlett, 1929, p.69). The Education (Administrative Provision) Act 1907 authorized expenditure on scholarships, play centres and recreation during holiday times, and the provision of medical inspection in the following year increased spending: no grant was given for this function until 1913. Serious inequalities in the rates levied in different areas often reflected the economic conditions existing locally. The elementary education rate in England varied from 2s 3d to 5d and the rateable rate per pupil from £13 to £106.

Complications in calculating income arose from the variety of headings which had accrued. In 1911–12, there were Annual, Aid, Fee, Small Population, Special Subject, Special Schools and Necessitous Area Grants. The Report of a Departmental Committee on Local Taxation (Kempe) on the matter, published in 1917, three years after finishing its deliberations, led to the Supplementary Grant which increased State assistance as LEA expenditure increased. The 1918 Education Act made provision for a Government grant of 36s. per pupil plus two-fifths of the local expenditure of education less the product of a 7d rate. Selby-Bigge believed that this change 'substituted for the relation of paymaster and recipient of subsidies a relation of advice and constructive partnership' (Selby-Bigge, 1927, p.98). In 1921, a new Education Act introduced a single consolidated grant, called the Substantive Grant, payable annually to LEAs in respect of elementary education in April each year. The economic crises of the inter-war years were to bring LEAs and the Board into dispute on a range of services which were being offered, as well as on teachers' pay. Disparities between LEA expenditure continued to reflect the problem of financing education (see table opposite).

An opportunity to examine some of the financial and other problems of LEAs was lost when a Royal Commission on Local Government was set up in 1923. This led to the Local Government Act of 1929 which introduced profound changes in the system of local government and established Block Grants. However, the Commissioners omitted education from its remit. The Commissioners reported in 1929, 'In our view the questions arising at this stage in the development of the Education service are mainly matters of policy involving decisions of Your Majesty's Government', and recommended that a further committee should examine the problem. Before action could be taken,

ELEMENTARY EDUCATION EXPENDITURE 1920–21

Average = 100

	Lowest Percentage	Highest Percentage
1. L.E.As. net expenditure per child	58.9	164.9
2. Produce of penny rate per child	40.0d	280.0d
3. Grants per child	64.4d	152.5d
4. Percentage of net expenditure met from Grants	81.1	139.0
5. Grants – expressed as a rate in the £	33.5d	293.1d
6. Expenditure falling on rates expressed as a rate in the £	40.1d	289.6d
7. Expenditure from rates per child	33.8d	183.7d
8. Details of line 1 above: L.E.As. net expenditure per child on:		
(i) Teachers' Salaries	62.2d	179.3d
(ii) Loan Charges	Nil	263.8d
(iii) Administration	14.5d	216.9d
(iv) Other Expenditure	38.2d	178.2d
(v) Special Services	10.9d	358.8d

Source: Memorandum submitted by the Meston Committee on Exchequer Grants in respect of locally administered services 1926, Cmd. 2571.

the Labour Government was out of office and no further action followed. Percentage Grants continued to be paid.

Throughout the period between the 1902 and the 1944 Education Acts, dissatisfaction was expressed with the structure of local educational administration and, to a lesser extent, the activities of the Board in relation to LEAs. One criticism was the remoteness from the locality of the area of education represented by county councils. The 1906 Education Bill, introduced by the new Liberal Government, proposed that counties with populations exceeding 60,000 should prepare schemes for delegating their functions to district authorities: boroughs and urban districts were also to be given greater autonomy. This attempt at reform was unsuccessful. A Consultative Committee on the same topic, reporting in 1908, found that few counties had taken advantage of the power to set up district committees, which were responsible to the county education committee. The Report pointed out the advantage of this form of organization on the grounds of economy of administration, educational efficiency and administrative efficiency (Gosden, 1966, p. 192). Fisher's bid after 1918 to remove the administration of elementary schools from inefficient Part III authorities to county councils also failed in the face of the combined opposition of Part III authorities. In 1938, the Spens Report recommended that the whole problem of these authorities should be remitted to a Departmental or Interdepartmental Committee.

The Board of Education had meanwhile taken steps to ease their ever-growing burden of administrative detail. As we have seen, in 1926, the Board sought to widen the field of discretion of LEAs, at the same time replacing the elaborate regulations with their Prefatory Memoranda with a series of basic grant regulations; freeing itself from much administrative detail, the Board delegated, for example, school staffing problems, subject to agreed staffing levels. At the same time, increasing burdens were being placed on LEAs as a consequence of the recommendations of the series of Consultative Committee Reports between 1927 and 1939, particularly the Hadow reorganization (see Chapter 11).

A later chance to effect reform of the LEAs and shift the balance of power towards the central authority arose during discussions by Board officials in compiling the Green Book of 1941 on post-war reconstruction. The need for co-ordination between primary and secondary education and the lack of flexibility in the LEA system led to the proposal for the abolition of Part III authorities. The 1944 Act gave county and county borough councils, 146 in all, responsibility for organizing education within their areas into primary, secondary and further stages. As an acknowledgment of the opposition of the former Part III authorities, county authorities were required to set up divisional executives which paid regard to local interests and responsibility for educational provision within their districts. Boroughs and urban districts with a population of over 60,000 people or 7,000 pupils in 1939 could also claim excepted district status and, if granted by the Ministry, operated their own schemes of divisional administration. Almost a quarter of the 200 divisional executives established by the Act were excepted districts (Gosden, 1966, p. 199).

The new Ministry inherited a pattern of LEAs which differed substantially from the pre-1944 situation. Its hand was strengthened by the provisions of the Act in several ways. The duties of LEAs were more strictly defined in terms of sufficient and satisfactory provision of education at all three stages. All schools were to have either a body of managers in the case of primary schools, or governors in the case of secondary schools. Voluntary schools were to have LEA representation on their managing or governing bodies. Modifications in the dual system applied to schools at primary and secondary levels. One concession to Church pressure was the introduction of religious worship and instruction as a compulsory element in all schools. The implementation of many of these changes will be discussed in the next chapter.

SUMMARY

The first half of this century can be characterized as a period of the development of a national system of education administered by the Local Education Authorities. Morant's plan for a *centralized* system which accorded with the principles of 'national efficiency' was never fulfilled.

Educational policy-making within the Board of Education was tempered, and in many cases influenced, by the advice and findings of Consultative Committees. The Inspectorate was rendered a more effective force with its specialist recruitment for elementary, secondary and technical institutions. There were also tensions between the newly-created Local Education Authorities and the Board of Education over policy-making matters.

Of greater consequence, however, was the effect of the movement towards a welfare state which gathered momentum during the early part of this century. In education, this took the form of free meals, school medical inspection and maintenance grants. The impact of welfare upon politics was enhanced by the emergence of the Labour Party and later, the opportunity to take office. Differences between the parties centred mainly on attitudes towards the provision and organization of secondary education.

Finally, it has been shown that the religious issues in education which emerged in the nineteenth century were carried forward unchanged into the present one: this led to many compromises where reforms were attempted, as can be witnessed in educational legislation ranging from 1902 to the 1944 Acts.

FURTHER READING

A useful background to the period is provided in G.A.N. Lowndes, *The Silent Revolution*, 1937 edn. For the administrative changes following the 1902 Education Act, see B.M. Allen, *Sir Robert Morant*, 1934 and E.J.R. Eaglesham, *The Foundations of Twentieth Century Education in England*, 1967. The story is brought up to 1944 in P.H.J.H. Gosden, *The Development of Educational Administration in England and Wales*, 1966.

An account by a former Permanent Secretary of the Board, L.A. Selby-

Bigge, *The Board of Education*, 1927, is of some interest. Biographies of Presidents of the Board such as A.J.A. Morris, *C.P. Trevelyan, 1870–1958*, 1977, and autobiographies such as Lord Eustace Percy, *Some Memories*, 1958, should be consulted.

The part played by the Inspectorate in the administration of education is described in H.E. Boothroyd, *A History of the Inspectorate*, 1923, D. Lawton and P. Gordon, *HMI*, 1987 and J. Leese, *Personalities and Power in English Education*, 1950.

Attempts to settle the religion question in education are explained in M. Cruickshank, *Church and State in English Education*, 1963.

Two books which give a full picture of policy-formation in education are G. Sherington, *English Education, Social Change and War, 1911–1920*, 1981 and B. Simon, *The Politics of Educational Reform, 1920–1940*, 1974.

CHAPTER THREE

War, Society and Education: The Experience of Two World Wars

INTRODUCTION

In the closing years of both World Wars two major pieces of educational legislation were passed. The earlier, 1918 Education Act, partly because many of its important sections were not implemented, but also because it did not visibly alter the structure of the system of education, has remained more hidden from history. Nevertheless its importance ought not to be minimized. The school-leaving age was finally fixed at 14, and all forms of exemption before that age, particularly the long challenged half-time system, were swept away. Powers were given to local authorities to improve medical and welfare services and to secure playing fields. Even the clauses relating to the introduction of a form of compulsory continuation schooling for those over 14 who were no longer in contact with educational establishments, though discarded by 1922, meant that the issue remained firmly on the agenda of later ministers. Access to secondary, technical, and central schools, though still restricted, was widened. Moreover the legislation was accompanied by a series of measures that improved teachers' pay and conditions of service, and ensured equality of treatment between localities. Much more attention has been directed at the 1944 Education Act, described in glowing terms by the commentator H. C. Dent in his 1968 preface. 'It is a very great Act which makes – and in fact has made – possible as important and substantial advance in public education as this country has ever known' (Dent, 1968, p. 1). If duration meant success, this measure clearly succeeded. Unlike the 1918 Act, it not only changed significantly the structure of education, but also streamlined local authorities. Since most of secondary, higher and further education was freed from the imposition of fees, significant sections of the population found their career expectations and personal prospects

33

altered substantially. In attempting to provide a coherent explanation of these changes, social and educational historians have not been slow to attach great significance to the experience of total war.

In both wars service considerations outweighed all others, and some schools, colleges and universities were either requisitioned or forced to share their premises with a variety of military installations. An unnamed diarist recorded one intrusion into his school life: '2nd November 1942. The Headmaster arrived to find the Army in command. An AA gun was in position in the playing field, five large tents with troops in occupation and a large hole in the fence through which the gun had been dragged' (Westall, 1985, p.189). Only in the final years did dismantling and moving out begin to take place. Moreover, in time of war all replacement work on buildings ceased, since materials were too scarce and the labour force was engaged in the more urgent demands of war. At this stage similarities between the two wars ceased. There was civilian destruction in the Great War, but the devastation wrought by aerial attack was much more extensive and total in the period of the Blitz in 1940–41. Loss of teachers, disrupted classes and makeshift buildings all, however, made politicians uneasy and susceptible to mounting press campaigns.

Even more alarming was the encouragement of practices which had been increasingly criticized in official circles in pre-war years. In agricultural areas, for instance, where seasonal employment of the schoolchild had remained firmly entrenched, pupils now found themselves working for longer hours in harvesting, weeding or fruit-picking as part of the war effort. Employers in urban areas, faced with shortage of labour, also turned to the wider use of juveniles. The destructive impact of the struggle was forcefully put by Sidney Webb:

> What with the very extensive transfer of school buildings for military or hospital use, the premature withdrawal from school and college of at least one hundred thousand children and young persons, the exclusion at the other end of many tens of thousands under five, the taking of tens of thousands of teachers into the fighting forces ... peace will involve almost the remaking of the nation's educational machinery. (Webb, 1916, p.584)

If war had severely disrupted schooling throughout 1914–18, its impact in the early years of the 1939–45 War was much more extensive. In September 1939 one of the most striking illustrations that the nation had embarked on a new kind of war was the streams of teachers, parents and children arriving at the main urban railway stations to be transported to the countryside or smaller towns. The impact of evacuation soon became a topic of controversy. Arrangements in the reception areas were often far from satisfactory. The Board of Education and the teachers had been anxious to keep the identity of the school on arrival in the evacuated area, but this proved so difficult that in many cases teachers, classes and individual pupils found themselves separated, and many soon returned home. One returning evacuee not only recorded his profound delight but also described the remains of schooling available in an area of London. 'There were no schools open, but the local vicar arranged a class in his house, using local retired people with some teaching experience to help out. I joined this class which at least kept us off the streets' (Westall, 1985, p.55). The Cabinet faced a dilemma, since a full reopening of schools would immediately encourage an even greater exodus from the safe areas. However if schools persisted in remaining closed in areas of danger children were deprived of much-needed schooling. Despite the destruction in the winter months of 1941 local authorities increasingly favoured the reopening of their schools. In their turn the reception areas suffered under the impact of evacuation, as schools found themselves merged together, or were forced to operate on a shuttle system.

THE CASE FOR WAR AS A CATALYST FOR CHANGE

In 1914 war had an immediate effect upon the educational system, as upon other established institutions. By 1915 there was a crisis in munitions for the western front which nearly brought down Asquith's government. One of the results was the formation of a vigorous campaign under the umbrella title the 'Neglect of Science' group. It started by bemoaning the low status of scientific teachers in many schools and colleges, but by 1916 had moved on to challenge the whole of the training given to those in government and senior administrative posts. The senior officials of the Board of Education, a very tight-knit group, drawn almost entirely from public schools and the older universities, were sensitive to such criticism and set in motion a series of inquiries into the teaching of a whole range of subjects in the secondary curriculum. Another response to such pressures was the creation, in 1915, of the Department of Scientific and Industrial Research which used government funds to develop industrial projects.

In the opening months of the Second World War, the speed of the German advance exposed shortcomings in Britain's defences that were once again attributed to inadequacies of scientific and technological training. The answer on this occasion was to move quickly to draw leading scientists and technologists into the war effort. By the 1930s, under the influence of figures such as J.D. Bernal and J.B.S. Haldane, the scientific community was more politically conscious, and Churchill himself relied heavily for advice on Professor Lindemann, his pre-war scientific counsellor. Demands were heard for the employment of a more scientific approach to problems of government, and this was supported strongly in left-wing circles and the planning movement. Calls were made to universities to direct their energy and resources to the teaching and production of scientists. Attention was also given to the need for an appropriate education for technologists and technicians. It was hoped that the provision of wider educational opportunities would stimulate the expansion of science and technology, the necessary instruments to win the war and to secure a long and lasting peace.

War also promoted the values of collectivism and co-operation. Success in war was attributed to planning, identification of needs, and the proper ordering of priorities. Failure, on the other hand, was the product of indecision, acting in isolation, and dealing with large problems in a piecemeal fashion. Stephen Spender was one writer who insisted that the lessons painfully learned in war could be applied to the problems of peace. 'In spite of our hatred of war, in spite of its monotony and boredom it is possible to find a reality in it which is lacking in peace; because in war people are able to co-operate in order to face the enemy threatening the nation' (Spender, 1945, p. 16).

Demands were made that governments, heavily involved in every aspect of life in the war period, ought not to withdraw in peacetime. Indeed, both in 1916 and 1940, pre-war governments were swept aside because it was felt that too many of the older leaders were unwilling to accept the new demands. Ministries that had often defined their role in the narrowest sense, confining their operations solely to the close supervision of public expenditure, found themselves criticized for their lack of vision. The issue of education was widely discussed. Thus it could be argued that the Education Bill drawn up in 1917 indicated that the Board of Education was finally prepared to take on hostile industrialists, suspicious smaller local authorities and entrenched religious denominations.

Similarly, in 1944, the wartime spirit has been used to explain much of the Butler Education Act. The determination to streamline the structure of education to secure a more orderly and fairer passage through the system for the majority of the population, which might mean tackling the dual system and Part III authorities, could be seen as a sign of a new direction in government. Local authorities were specifically asked to present development plans within a year of the Act coming into operation, and the Minister had to be satisfied that sufficient primary and secondary schools and a range of other services were being provided. Indeed, fears were expressed that the new Ministry, which replaced the Board of Education, was assuming extensive powers that threatened the localities.

Collectivism was linked with co-operation, particularly during the Second World War. Underground shelters, canteens, even rescue operations gave the civilian population a new sense of shared identity. Rationing came early in the war and was widely welcomed. People began to dress alike in the same utility style, listen to the same music and plays and share the common experience of war. The gulf between soldiers and civilians, so apparent in the previous Great War, was much less marked. Indeed in some ways the vast conscript force built up by 1940 resembled a citizen army. Politicians and generals feared boredom and apathy which might lead to insubordination. In response a programme of adult education, discussion and current events programmes was introduced by the Army Bureau of Current Affairs (ABCA) which ranged over war aims, the future of society and political participation. Claims have been made that these activities made radicals of servicemen. Its founder certainly believed that it was a model that could be used to broaden the boundaries of democracy throughout British society and he proclaimed, 'If wartime conditions can produce even a rude and approximate education in citizenship then ABCA is the pattern which might also be attempted in factory and dockyard as well' (Williams, 1942, p.259). On the home front the BBC attempted to carry out a similar function. The earlier war had not brought out the best in communications. A veil of secrecy had made news and discussion very scarce, and to fill the gap sensation, rumour and lurid journalism, supplied by notorious figures such as Horatio Bottomley, became a feature of daily life. The 1939–45 War saw great changes in communication. Writers, artists and musicians took their products to new audiences who were often enclosed for long hours in their places of work. Artists like Henry Moore insisted that the only way to withstand the horrors of war was for the nation to encourage the production and dissemination of great works of art through the whole community.

Out of all this ceaseless jostling together, the broadening of horizons for rich and poor alike, came, it was claimed, an impatience with much of the life of pre-war society with its barriers and divisions. In this situation sections of the wealthier classes were, it was believed, becoming radicalized. Shrewd Labour strategists such as Herbert Morrison became aware that sections of the middle class, previously

Conservative or Liberal, were moving to the Left. The victory by Labour in 1945 was not only won by the successful mobilization of the aroused working-class and trade union vote, but by a significant proportion of suburban areas switching their allegiance to Labour. On the Conservative side, Eden and Macmillan, themselves the product of the trench warfare of the earlier struggle, emerged with a deep sense of the 'One Nation' philosophy which made them very hostile to some of the harder forms of Conservatism. Education was likely therefore to become an issue. It offered the opportunity for a freer, more mobile society. Too often in the past, it was argued, separate educational institutions and schools had kept classes apart. Any move towards a common sense of citizenship was likely to be reflected in a broadening of access to hitherto-restricted places such as universities or secondary schools, and the freeing of large areas of the educational system from their fee-paying basis. It was also likely to make public opinion very hostile indeed to older vested interests such as the various churches or industry which might, for their own ends, seek to hold back the course of educational progress.

In both wars the work undertaken by women on the home front seemed to overturn traditional views in society about the capabilities of women. Losses suffered in war focused the attention of politicians and administrators on labour shortages and the need to find a substitute by using more women. The young, in all their age groups, were singled out for consideration. In both World Wars a wide range of infant welfare schemes, fully supported by politicians, administrators and physicians, were introduced to counteract shortages of food, loss of morale and, on occasions, fears of population decline. The poorest sections of the community were able to give their infant children a more balanced diet because of steadier employment and the opportunity to take up over-time. At school age, in wartime, other changes took place. During the First World War the obligation to provide school meals for the needy was strengthened, and this was endorsed in the 1918 Education Act. There was concern about the physical fitness of the school child, and educational advance began to be measured not only in terms of the improved supply of teachers and buildings, but also in the provision of more playing fields, gymnasia and swimming pools. At the end of the 1939–45 War local authorities were compelled, in presenting their reconstruction plans, to ensure the development of these facilities. Even more strikingly, free school milk and cheap, subsidized meals were now being provided in all maintained schools.

Finally, in the educational legislation at the end of both wars, there was a determined attempt to deal with the difficulties likely to be encountered by the juvenile population, and particularly by those who had left school at the earliest opportunity to enter the world of adult work. War conditions appeared to bring out fears about increasing delinquency among this group, and the inadequacy of voluntary organizations to look after their leisure needs. In planning his 1918 legislation H. A. L. Fisher, President of the Board of Education, was able to exploit uneasiness about this whole generation of juveniles, to overcome the strong resistance from many employers, and some of the labour movement, to the introduction of compulsory part-time continuation schools. On occasions harsh language about the attitudes of these young people was used to gain support for changes. Sidney Webb made the provision of extended education almost an issue of national survival, berating 'the "hooliganism" characteristic of so much town youth – the uncouth animalism of so much of our rural youth' (Webb, 1916, p.584). Continuation schools, in taking into account these wartime fears, were encouraged to promote programmes of social education rather than of vocational training. Again, in the 1939–45 War, this group of juveniles, often discovering the world of work amid shattered communities and extensive devastation, found their life style and recreations under constant scrutiny. Alarm grew at stories of mounting crime and street violence among this part of the population, and even led to proposals for the introduction of some kind of compulsory wartime service. Fears were raised that this looked too close to the creation of fascist militia-style youth movements. Instead young people were encouraged to register on a list so that they could be put in touch with existing voluntary organizations. Compulsory part-time education in county colleges under the 1944 Education Act, however, was never achieved.

THE CASE AGAINST WAR AS A CATALYST FOR CHANGE

The failure of such schemes as continuation schools and county colleges can be cited as evidence of the strength of existing institutions and their ability to divert the forces of wartime radicalism. Change, as a result, came about in an orderly fashion and in accordance with procedures already defined by decisions taken within government departments in periods before war had broken out. This has led to a revision of the reasons why extended welfare services in the schools had been brought in. From the early part of the century welfare provisions had primarily been restricted to the very necessitous children. The definition of necessitous was steadily extended as the century had progressed. By 1944 the scope of provision had become so widened that services like free milk became universal. Evacuation, introduced in the period 1939–40, was seen as only one episode in this process, and no longer the crucial factor that had forced governments to bring in this range of services.

In 1981 Geoffrey Sherington maintained that much of the agitation about youth and adolescence which eventually led to the introduction of continuation schools in Fisher's educational legislation of 1918 was the product of the Board's own concern about what they saw as the moral deterioration of the juvenile population in the Edwardian period. Similarly it has been argued that the plans for county colleges in the period after the Second World War had their origins in the work of Henry Morris in Cambridgeshire in the 1930s. There had also been schemes in depressed areas to provide for the needs of the unemployed school leaver. All this could be seen as giving the impetus for the later proposals in the 1944 Education Act.

Even one of the most significant reforms in education, the introduction in 1944 of free secondary education for all, has been put into a longer historical perspective. One of the major political parties had placed it on the educational agenda very early in the present century. In the inter-war period a stream of recommendations on primary and post-primary education, all of which undermined the existing elementary school system, proceeded from the Consultative Committees. Politicians of all parties had been pressing for reorganization throughout the 1930s, and a major education measure was being urged from many quarters in the later part of that decade.

In the decades before 1939 there were reforming ministers at the Board of Education, particularly Lord Eustace Percy and Sir Charles Trevelyan, who were urging their colleagues to attend to educational needs. They found themselves struggling against the power of a Treasury dominated by senior politicians such as Churchill, Neville Chamberlain and Snowden who were determined to pursue retrenchment policies, and used their considerable authority to block suggestions of increased expenditure on education. Moreover, although it has been accepted by the revisionists that the Treasury was less likely to be able to assert its influence during the duration of long wars, once wars ended and the costs had to be met, the Treasury found itself in a very powerful blocking position. This had been the case at the end of the 1914–18 War when the implementation of Fisher's legislation soon met with strong and successful Treasury resistance.

It has often been argued that in the wartime conditions of coalition governments and national unity, politicians were likely to abandon their adversarial stances and work for the promotion of the common good. In neither war was this wholly true. Lloyd George, in late 1916, came to power as Prime Minister after intense political activity. He needed to build up his power base after dislodging a successful party leader of great standing. Many of his reconstruction activities and the recruitment of figures from outside the mainsprings of political life could be attributed to this factor. Thus H.A.L. Fisher, a distinguished Oxford historian and vice-chancellor of Sheffield University, was brought to Education for that purpose. Kevin Jeffreys (1984) has argued strongly that, even after 1940, political manoeuvring continued and was kept up until the war ended. By 1941 R.A. Butler, Under-Secretary of State for Foreign Affairs since 1938, was worrying about Conservative prospects in a future election. His own political fortunes were in decline as all his mentors were dead, or displaced by Churchill's men. Sir John Colville, Churchill's private secretary, commented on Butler's isolation, indicating that he was a person 'who has somewhat reluctantly come to admire the PM though he still clearly does not think much of his own Secretary of State' (Colville, 1985, p. 367). A move to the Board of Education would revive Butler's flagging fortunes and, if he could get a major educational measure enacted, might well improve the Conservative electoral fortunes.

In both wars new ministers gave their departments fresh leadership at a vital stage. Thus, in 1916, the senior officials at the Board saw themselves faced by a hostile pressure group comprising progressive opinion such as the WEA, and disaffected politicians like Haldane. They feared that they were about to lose control over the pace of change. A weak political head, too deeply involved in matters outside the department, made matters worse. Indeed Arthur Henderson had asked to be relieved of the post because he thought that he ought to be pursuing the work of educational reform with more vigour. A letter to Asquith confirmed his misgivings. 'This being so, I was strongly of opinion that someone should be placed in charge of the Board of Education who could make the necessary enquiries and preparation for the introduction of a comprehensive and far-reaching scheme of reform.' (Quoted in Hamilton, 1938, pp. 105–6.) The appointment of Fisher strengthened the senior officials. He worked well with Selby-Bigge, his Permanent Secretary, and one of his former students. Although he was in favour of change his enthusiasm was tempered by caution, and pessimism about the future. All this made him sympathetic to the evolving proposals within his own department, and opposed to the more extensive programme coming from outside sources. He declined to take on powerful vested interests such as industrialists, churches and local authorities, preferring to conciliate and persuade rather than cajole.

R.G. Wallace has described a similar situation facing the tight-knit group of permanent officials at the Board of Education in 1941. They faced great anger from a broad coalition of educational reformers, left-wing activists and a powerful science lobby, about the restricted way in which the debate on educational reconstruction was being conducted. There was a clamour, in much of the educational world and beyond, for common schooling, the demise of independent schools and extensive curriculum reform. It was at this critical stage that Butler arrived at the Board. He defused these major issues by appointing carefully selected committees which could be expected to move very slowly. He accepted the need for free secondary education but was careful to avoid specific recommendations which would stir up controversy. Butler correctly assumed that local authorities would fall back on well-tried procedures that were likely to favour an evolving tripartite system.

The outcome of wartime legislation in education has been seen as limited, contained and conservative. Pent-up radicalism in both wars had been skilfully diverted by careful handling, and reforming zeal was brought under control. Part of the problem was that the more radical reformers in both wars had never worked out their own strategy of change. Thus, in 1916, the 'Neglect of Science' committee demanded that much greater attention must be paid to scientific needs in education. They were less sure about what subjects would have to be dropped to meet these demands. Moreover, there was little indication where the emphasis on more science teaching was to be placed. Some members of the committee were anxious that the public schools, where the majority of the governing élite continued to be educated, must be their main target. Others insisted that the diffusion of science throughout the nation was the greatest priority. A final group was more concerned about the supply of scientists and the creation of more appropriate, better funded institutions where they could be more satisfactorily trained.

Examples of this kind were repeated in the Second World War. A call for common secondary schooling was heard in progressive circles. Labour representatives were now in government and ought to have been able to influence the course of events. However their most influential thinker, R.H. Tawney, was at his best when denouncing what he disliked about the existing elementary system, particularly its low expectations and sense of inferiority. On issues for the future such as selection for the new types of secondary education he was to pursue a cautious course. He maintained, 'Selection is necessary, and provided the penalties of not being selected are not excessive, is innocuous. But it should be selection between alternate paths, not as in the past, between educational opportunities and the absence of it. It should proceed by differentiation, not by elimination' (Tawney lecture draft, BLPES, Tawney MSS, undated). Few Labour politicians at that time believed that this approach was likely to extend a stratified, meritocratic secondary system. Too many of them were limited by their own background and experience. Attlee and Dalton were products of public schools and the older universities, and remained attached to these institutions. Such views were in sharp contrast to those of self-educated figures like Aneurin Bevan who were suspicious of all state-provided schooling. Ernest Bevin and George Tomlinson, the products of shortened or half-time education, wanted more schooling for the masses as an act of social justice. Butler's legislation was fulfilling this and seemed to embody what Labour had been advocating throughout the century. It was, for them, a measure that demanded unswerving support, particularly if the minister found himself faced with criticism and suspicion from some of his own party.

Increasingly doubts have been raised about the levelling-off process that total war was supposed to create. Claims that wartime experiences generated fellowship, understanding and closer co-operation between hitherto antagonistic groups have been challenged. Episodes in both wars demonstrated that the social distance between all classes remained as wide as ever. By 1915 class conflict had erupted in the Clydeside area on a scale that equalled that of the period 1911–14. Any manifestations of a new spirit remained in most areas at a surface level. As the Great War drew to its close the ranks of organized labour gathered to meet the revived threat of employers who considered that the trade unions had too successfully exploited conditions in war to secure excessive wages. It was hardly a situation in which the promise of educational advance was likely to prosper.

Even more expansive claims have been made about the new spirit abroad in the People's War of 1939–45, with its broader coalition government, the experience of rationing and the shared destruction that affected all sections of the population. Yet harmony was not always created in wartime Britain. Evacuation revealed divisions between classes and regions. The Fabian Evacuation Survey indicated the gulf between social groups as urban working-class children found themselves coming to terms with more suburban middle-class households. The researchers argued, 'a middle-class home is a stranger to the close-packed share-and-share everything, of the working class, so that a poor child is apt to feel cold and lonely in a middle-class home and his hosts to find him a nuisance' (Padley and Cole, 1940, p.74). By contrast, children from the wealthiest homes, accustomed to periods away from the family, found the evacuation experience much less distressing.

The Blitz often demonstrated the continuation of privilege. An American journalist described part of a night spent in the squalor of the Isle of Dogs in East London, in which he maintained, 'It was impossible to take in the whole room. ... You cannot take in the concept of thousands upon thousands of people sleeping in a dim-lit cave'. It was in marked contrast to his return to the shelter in his West End hotel equipped 'with a neat row of cots, spaced about two feet apart, each one covered with a lovely fluffy eiderdown' (Longmate, 1981, pp. 77–8). Government and local authorities failed frequently to come to the aid of the masses and people more often decided to use their own initiatives to protect their lives. Thus, at the height of bombing, underground stations were taken over by the crowds, while the Home Office attempted, in the first instance, to keep them clear. The new collectivist spirit was far from evident at these times. Even the highly proclaimed rationing scheme to ensure that scarce resources were fairly distributed, was sidestepped by those able to dine at favoured restaurants.

Memories of common effort and equality of sacrifice could not hide the fact that at the end of both wars the gaps between rich and poor had not altered too markedly. Few in the working class owned their own houses or possessed bank accounts or investments. They had little say in what happened at the workplace. Nevertheless after the 1939–45 War most of the long-term unemployed of the 1930s were absorbed into industry and did not return to the dole. The old, the young mother bringing up a family on service pay, and those with large families continued to struggle to make ends meet. It could be argued that both wars ended with most of society as stratified as ever and locked into highly separate life styles in work, leisure and residence. In this sense the major legislation in education, which sifted the child population rather than threw open doors to all, reflected the uneven nature of income, expectations and status.

Questions about widening opportunities in wartime for women will be examined in a later chapter. At this stage it will be sufficient to note that in neither war did they enter into vital policy-making or strategic decisions. The nation's leaders and commanders were male. Throughout the wars women remained a substitute labour force, trained and directed by males. Politicians, administrators and clergymen never ceased to express deep concern about the grave danger to society of too many women pursuing permanent careers outside the home.

SUMMARY

Much of the Fisher and Butler legislation was the result of processes that had their origins in debates and investigations which occurred long before the coming of war. It could be accepted that for most of the population at the time the experience of total war was the most abiding landmark in their lives. What they chose to make of that experience is more difficult to evaluate. There is little consensus, for instance, on the impact of total war on religious feeling. Heightened possibilities of sudden death might be expected to turn people to a religious awareness. On the other hand the prospect of indiscriminate killing and haphazard death could equally lead to scepticism and doubt. In this respect, the emphasis on the corporate act of worship and religious instruction in all schools written into the Butler Act could allow two explanations. Some would acknowledge that it was a recognition of strong feelings about religion in time of wartime crisis. Others could see the clauses as the attempt of a beleaguered, if influential group, to fight a rearguard action against the growing indifference and secularism that war had done nothing to reverse.

Wartime legislation could lead to outcomes that were not anticipated. The Butler Education Act was widely considered to be part of the centralizing process encouraged by war. The decision to phase out Part III authorities, the opening preamble of the Act, and indeed the insistence on each authority producing a development plan for the new ministry appeared to presage the opening shots of a new relationship between a stronger centre and the localities. Larger local units meant, however, a more powerful career structure at that level, and the creation of a more vigorous bureaucracy. While central government became increasingly overwhelmed by the most immediate problems, the real thinking in education often came from local levels. Finally Corelli Barnett has drawn attention to the fact that outward success in both wars encouraged a complacency that made it very difficult for politicians to grapple with the urgent underlying problems of the economy. There was much talk in both wars about the need for more technical education, more relevant courses at university level and the expansion of further education. It could be argued that, too often, this ran side by side with a belief that, as the United Kingdom was emerging as the victor in war, established institutions and procedures had stood the supreme test and justified themselves. In this respect, as events in the 1950s were to show, such optimism proved to be sadly amiss.

FURTHER READING

A. Marwick, *War and Social Change in the Twentieth Century*, 1974 and H.L. Smith (ed.), *War and Social Change*, 1986 provide very differing views on the impact of total war. On the Great War there are the studies by L. Andrews, *The Education Act 1918*, 1976; G. Sherington, *English Education, Social Change and War, 1911–20*, 1981; and D.W. Dean, 'H.A.L. Fisher, Reconstruction and the Development of the 1918 Education Act', *British Journal of Educational Studies*, Vol. 18, No. 3, 1970. For the 1939–45 World War, the most important contributions are P.H.J.H. Gosden, *Education in the Second World War*, 1976; R.G. Wallace, 'The Origins and Authorship of the 1944 Education Act', *History of Education*, Vol. 10, No. 4, 1981; K. Jeffreys, 'R.A. Butler, the Board of Education and the 1944 Act', *History*, Vol. 69, No. 227, 1984; and B. Simon, 'The 1944 Education Act: A Conservative Measure?' *History of Education*, Vol. 15, No. 1, 1986. W.H.G. Armytage, 'Battles for the Best: Some Educational Aspects of the Welfare–Warfare State in England' in P. Nash (ed.), *History and Education*, 1970, and D.H. Akenson, 'Patterns of English Educational Change: the Fisher and Butler Acts', *History of Education Quarterly*, Vol. 11, No. 2, 1971, are both stimulating approaches.

CHAPTER FOUR

Stagnation or Progress?
Education in the 1920s and 1930s

POLITICAL PARTIES

In 1916 David Lloyd George ousted his fellow Liberal, Herbert Asquith, as leader of the wartime Coalition government, and in December 1918 his position as Prime Minister was confirmed in the 'Coupon' election. Some 335 of the Coalition's 478 MPs, however, were Conservatives. The Labour party with 59 representatives in the House of Commons became the official opposition, whilst the Asquithian Liberals achieved only 26 seats. Never again would there be a Liberal government. The Conservatives were to dominate the inter-war years, in office under Andrew Bonar Law from 1922 to 1923, and with Stanley Baldwin as Prime Minister, 1923–24 and 1924–29. The first Labour government of James Ramsay MacDonald, 1924, had 191 seats to the Liberals' 159 and the Conservatives' 258, and survived a mere nine months. The second, with 288 MPs to the Conservatives' 260 and the Liberals' 59, lasted from 1929 to 1931 when MacDonald formed a National government, a decision which split both the Labour and Liberal parties. National governments under Baldwin (1935–37) and Neville Chamberlain (1937–40) finally gave way to another wartime coalition, led by Winston Churchill.

Conservative education policy in the inter-war years was essentially conservative. Conservatism meant the championing of traditional values: the energy of empire, the calm of the countryside, the security of suburbia. There was a widespread fear of those revolutionary upheavals which had occurred in so many parts of post-war continental Europe and had led to the rise of totalitarian regimes. All of the nation's children were entitled to a basic elementary education, but extension of compulsory schooling beyond the age of 14 could be opposed as being an unwarranted infringement of the individual rights of young people and their parents. It would also lead to extravagant educational expenditure. Cost-effectiveness and cost-cutting were ever present features of the inter-war years, and Conservatives were to the fore in schemes for reducing the expenses of education at both central and local levels. Social control rather than social liberation was seen as the primary purpose of elementary schooling, although scholarships to enable the very brightest of elementary school pupils to proceed to secondary education, and even beyond, would provide a useful safety valve.

Unlike the Conservatives who dominated the inter-war years, Liberals could only look back ruefully to the world they had lost, or perhaps even had thrown away. Some indeed harked back to the school board era and argued for single-purpose local authorities for education again. Old hostilities toward the 1902 Act and the dual system found expression in opposition to the teaching of doctrinal religion in schools, and to the exclusion of teachers from certain posts on religious grounds. The themes of civil, religious and educational liberty remained at the centre of Liberal philosophy, and defence of the 1918 Act provided a rallying call across the decade of the 1920s, but by the 1930s Liberal educational policy had much in common with that of Labour moderates.

Moderate Labour policy, the policy of MacDonald and of Labour in government, envisaged gradual educational reform within the traditional framework. This would require more educational expenditure rather than less, more access to secondary schooling, culminating even in secondary education for all, and a raising of the compulsory school-leaving age. Not all Labour supporters, however, were content with this gradualist approach. Some of those who had been educated in the university of life remained profoundly suspicious of the formal educational process which taught the mass of children to accept their unhappy lot in life, and made intelligent boys and girls traitors to their class, thus depriving working people of their natural leaders, by filling their heads with English literature and other seductive trappings of a liberal education. Others argued rather that the formal system must be prised away from middle-class politicians and administrators, at both central and local government levels, and placed under popular control. Specific criticisms centred upon the messages of capitalism, competition and imperialism which were to be found in classroom, curriculum and text book. Thus in 1934 when the Labour party became the majority group on the London County Council, Empire Day, which had long been celebrated in London schools, was immediately changed into Commonwealth Day.

THE 1918 ACT

The Education Act of 1918, like that of 1944, was not only an immediate product of the years of war, but also the culmination of decades of reform proposals, and a pledge for the future. It abolished all exemptions to the compulsory leaving age of 14, and all fees in elementary schools. Employment of children under 12 was forbidden, and those aged 12 to 14 were restricted to two hours' work per day. Local authorities were empowered to provide nursery schools for the under-fives, to raise the school-leaving age to 15, to allot maintenance grants to scholarship pupils in secondary schools, and to provide a much wider range of ancillary services and facilities for education than hitherto. Central government, moreover, would meet at least 50 per cent of approved local education authority costs. Children aged between 14 and 16 years not otherwise in school were to attend continuation schools for 320 hours (280 hours in special circumstances) per year. Provision was made for the subsequent extension of continuation schooling to 16–18-year-olds, and for the raising of the school-leaving age to 15.

Nevertheless, though in 1917 and 1918 there was a general feeling both in Parliament and in the country that something should be done in education, and though the denominational rivalries which had so bedevilled the 1902 Act were largely absent, there was no clear consensus on what was required. Once again the weakness of central government in respect of education – the absence of a coherent policy – was revealed. Thus regional plans to abolish the Part III authorities, and to group some authorities into provincial councils, were abandoned in the face of opposition from the smaller LEAs and from the Association of Education Committees.

Similarly, proposals for continuation education to age 18 for all young persons not otherwise in school were shelved in the face of opposition from employers, parents and no doubt many pupils themselves. The traditional employers of unskilled and child labour – the owners of textile mills and coal mines, farmers and builders – were to the fore in such opposition. In Lancashire some 30 per cent of those working in cotton mills were aged 18 or under, and there was a growing threat of cheap foreign competition. Though in 1917 H. A. L. Fisher, the President of the Board of Education, personally carried the attack into the enemy strongholds, and though his speeches outlining the bill were well received in great meetings in Manchester, Swansea, Bristol, Plymouth and London, in the end he had to concede. For it was not just groups of employers, the newly-formed Federation of British Industries and many Conservative politicians who opposed continuation education to 18. The United Textile Factory Workers' Federation was but one of several trade unions which saw Fisher's proposals as an unwarranted intrusion into economic affairs which would seriously worsen the standard of living of many working-class families. Many Labour MPs indeed were confused as to where the true interests of the working classes lay in this matter, and covered their confusion by studiously absenting themselves from the Commons during debates on the bill. Philip Snowden, Labour MP for Blackburn, indicated the depth of this unease when he advised the House of Commons that 'this proposal for the abolition of half-time employment is in advance of the opinion of the people who are likely to be most affected by it' (*Hansard*, Vol. 106, Col. 1068, 30 May 1918).

No one, however, could be unaware of the enormous logistical and financial problems which part-time continuation education to 18 would create. The elimination of half-time schooling and the consolidation of a leaving age of 14, together with an extension of other educational services and facilities, would necessitate considerable redeployment of human and financial resources – in a country which was still at war. In the event, as was soon to be shown, neither central government nor local educational authorities were even prepared to resource continuation schooling to age 16.

Finally, though Asquith and his followers were amongst the bill's most enthusiastic parliamentary supporters, it was the Liberal J.H. Whitehouse, MP for Lanarkshire, and founder and first headmaster of Bembridge School, who made the most trenchant criticism of continuation schooling. Whitehouse's amendment in favour of giving LEAs the power to require compulsory schooling to 16 was defeated by 168 votes to 24 (*Hansard*, Vol. 106, Cols. 874–5, 29 May 1918), but his message has echoed across the twentieth century until the present day. Continuation classes, he argued, would simply mean a continuation of elementary schooling, with all its meanness, for a longer period. Separate education for separate classes in society would be further enshrined in the formal school system (*Hansard*, Vol. 104, Cols. 400–12, 13 March 1918).

In conclusion, therefore, the 1918 Act, though but a rump of Fisher's original proposals, was an important piece of enabling legislation with significant potential for increasing formal educational provision. Its implementation would depend upon political will, popular support, and the commitment of substantial financial and human resources.

THE 1920S

By any standards post-war Britain faced enormous problems. There were new types of casualty figures. The public debt was virtually incalculable and the prospect of reparations proved to be illusory. In 1918 and 1919 more than 150,000 people died in influenza epidemics. Inflation was rampant, and in March 1920 the price index was 323 as against 100 in July 1914. Between 1920 and 1921 the value of Britain's overseas trade declined by nearly one half. In the spring and early summer of 1921 there were more than 2 million unemployed. An acute housing shortage belied Lloyd George's promise of homes fit for heroes to live in. Strikes occurred in essential services – the police in 1918 and 1919, the railways in 1920. Civil war erupted in Ireland and continued until 1922. Nationalist movements challenged the existence of the Empire, and in April 1919 nearly 400 people died in the Amritsar massacre when British troops fired upon an unarmed crowd of Indians.

By 1920 the Coalition government, faced with major economic and social dislocation, an overall decline in revenue and an increase in expenditure, and under attack from large sections of the press and public for extravagant use of taxpayers' money, was scrutinizing its accounts with great care. Treasury grants to education had risen from £19 million in 1918–19 to £32 million in 1919–20, and were forecast to go on increasing at more than £10 million per annum. Much of this increased expenditure (after allowing for inflation) was accounted for by arrangements for financing teachers' pay as established by the new Burnham Committee. Already in 1920 a brake was applied from the centre upon new educational expenditure, for example upon school buildings, and in August 1921 a committee of businessmen, chaired by Sir Eric Geddes, was set up to review all the proposed estimates for 1922–23. The Geddes package or 'axe', which was designed to lop £18 million from an education budget of £50 million, contained the following proposed economies.

Entry to schools should be raised from five years to six, class sizes should be increased, a figure of one teacher per 50 pupils in elementary schools was envisaged, and new building proposals should be shelved. Free places in secondary schools were to be restricted, and feepayers required to pay more. State scholarships to universities should be abolished and local authority awards reviewed. Fewer teachers would be needed, and their salaries should be reduced. The recently negotiated teachers' superannuation scheme should be overturned. The new percentage grant system introduced under the 1918

Act was judged to be an invitation to extravagance and should be ended. The Geddes Committee concluded that the provided education system was an unwarranted consumption of national wealth, a claim upon hard-pressed resources, rather than an investment for the future. A reduction in state-provided education was required, rather than the expansion envisaged under the 1918 Act. Local authorities, far from being encouraged to provide nursery schools for the under-fives and to raise the school-leaving age to 15, should concentrate upon cheap education for six- to 14-year-olds.

Opposition to the Geddes proposals came from a variety of quarters – the teachers' unions, the Association of Education Committees, from directors of education, including Spurley Hey in Manchester and Percy Sharp at Sheffield. Labour and Liberal politicians took up the cause, Conservatives were divided, and in February 1922 Labour were victorious in two by-elections, in the Clayton division of Manchester and at Camberwell in South London, with campaigns which concentrated upon opposition to education cuts. At the same time the government found itself under attack from the Admiralty which was justifying its title of the senior service by leading the opposition to Geddes' proposed cuts of some £46 million in the defence budget. Thus from the spring of 1922 a series of compromises emerged. Education cuts of £6½ million were approved, cuts achieved principally by an increase in the size of elementary school classes, by requiring teachers to contribute 5 per cent of their salaries to the superannuation fund, and by reductions in special services, including school meals and medicals.

Though the percentage grant system was continued, and though Fisher expressed the hope that once the immediate economic situation had eased it would be possible fully to implement the 1918 Act, the theme of strict economy begun in 1921–22 was to characterize education throughout the inter-war period. Indeed Fisher himself, before Lloyd George's government fell in October 1922, seriously considered a plan to make school attendance under the age of six voluntary rather than compulsory. He also came to favour voluntary rather than compulsory continuation classes, and encouraged the LCC in such a policy, a policy supported by the London electorate in the Council elections of 1922. Thus the 35 schools and 47,000 students of the spring term of 1922 had dwindled to 10 schools and 4,000 students by the autumn term (Maclure, 1970, pp. 118–19). The London experience was crucial. Only in Rugby, where there was a new school building and a group of employers of skilled labour willing to pay five days' wages for four days spent at work and one at school, did continuation classes survive.

Between October 1922 and January 1924, Conservative governments under Bonar Law and Baldwin placed a greater priority on the construction of houses than on the building of schools. Edward Wood, the new President of the Board of Education, acquiesced in a reduction of £3 million in the Education estimates of 1923–24 from those of the previous year. The year 1923 was notable for lengthy and bitter teachers' strikes, as some local authorities sought to pay lower salaries than those determined by Burnham, and to employ unqualified teachers. Ramsay MacDonald's Labour government of 1924 was totally dependent on Liberal support in the Commons, and indeed boasted a former Liberal, in the shape of Sir Charles Trevelyan, as President of the Board. Philip Snowden as Chancellor of the Exchequer followed an orthodox line, and increases in unemployment benefits meant that the education budget was squeezed once more. Nevertheless Trevelyan had more interest and experience in educational matters than his predecessor, both as a former member of the London School Board and as Parliamentary Secretary to the Board of Education, 1908–14. A 'Black List' of obsolete school premises was begun, and regulations concerning new school building were relaxed. The proportion of free places in secondary schools was increased, maintenance allowances were raised, and state scholarships reintroduced. Trevelyan was personally interested in raising the school-leaving age to 15, not least as a counter to juvenile unemployment, but would make no commitment to secondary education for all. Indeed he stated in the Commons that legislation to achieve such an end 'would be perfectly impossible at the present time' (*Hansard*, House of Commons, 174, 1435, 5 June 1924).

Between 1924 and 1929 Stanley Baldwin led a Conservative government with a large majority in the House of Commons. The election of October 1924 proved disastrous for the Liberals, who dropped from 159 to 40 seats, and became the permanent third party. Neville Chamberlain as Minister of Health (the ministry had been established in 1919 with particular responsibility for Health and Housing) produced a set of interconnected reforms in the areas of health, housing, national insurance, pensions, poor law and local government. These did something to counter the immediate social and economic distress (although there was much opposition to the hated means test), contributed towards the formation of the welfare state, and marked Chamberlain out as a future Prime Minister. The General Strike of May 1926 was a tragic affair which ended in mutual recriminations amongst union leaders, and a general weakening of the power of organized labour. Baldwin rode out the crisis and restrained his more aggressive Cabinet colleagues (notably Churchill who was Chancellor of the Exchequer) from further exacerbating the situation.

The main educational issue of these years was what to do about secondary education. Lord Eustace Percy, who became President of the Board of Education in 1924 at the age of 37, accepted the modest changes initiated under Trevelyan. The major proposal of the Hadow Report of 1926 was that all children after six years of primary schooling should go on to a further period of 'post-primary' education. Such a policy commanded general political support. Labour commitment could be traced back to *Secondary Education for All*, published in 1922, and R.H. Tawney himself sat on the Hadow Committee. But the immediate origins of this report on 'The Education of the Adolescent' lie not in their terms of reference issued under a Labour government in February 1924, nor with Tawney, but with the initiatives of Wood and Lord Eustace Percy, in the last months of 1923 (Simon, 1974b, pp. 116–17). In January 1925, moreover, the Board of Education Circular 1350, *The Organization of Public Elementary Schools*, had advised that in planning new schools local authorities should provide for a definite break at 11, wherever possible in distinct junior and senior schools. Thus Hadow's proposals for a break at 11 were broadly shared across the political spectrum, but recommendations that all pupils should have a minimum of four years post-primary education, and that the school-leaving age should be raised to 15 at the beginning of the school year 1932, were more contentious.

Percy himself, and the bulk of the Conservative parliamentary party, opposed such a policy. With Churchill at the Exchequer lavish public expenditure on education would not be possible. It was widely believed, moreover, that in 1918 Fisher had failed because he attempted to achieve too much. To commit the country to a leaving age of 15 in 1932 would, given the post-war bulge in the birth rate, place the system under intolerable strain. To force all pupils to stay at school to 15 in over-crowded classrooms, with insufficient teachers, books and equipment, would be a recipe for chaos and widespread truancy. Far better to proceed gradually by reducing class sizes and improving the quality of the education, and thus to provide real incentives and opportunities for those pupils who genuinely wished to stay on at school. Percy was later to claim, in his autobiography (Percy, 1958, p. 100), that his opposition to the raising of the school-leaving age was tactical rather than absolute – a postponement to the mid-1930s when there would have been fewer pupils in the 15-year-old cohort. Nevertheless opposition to the raising of the school-leaving age was widespread in all sections of society, including the working classes. Very few local authorities, Liberal, Labour or Conservative, had availed themselves of the power granted under the 1918 and 1921 Acts of introducing a leaving age of 15 in their own areas.

Liberals indeed were divided on this issue. Many opposed the very considerable costs entailed in providing new buildings, teachers and maintenance allowances, and feared a resurgence of denominational rivalry. Fisher himself still believed in the principle of continuation schools, with increased provision of full-time post-14 education, accompanied in appropriate cases by maintenance grants. Others in the Liberal party, however, including Lloyd George, Herbert Samuel and John Simon put their names to the so called 'Yellow Book', *Britain's Industrial Future*, published in 1928. This envisaged a school-leaving age of 16 and part-time continuing education to 18, as but two of a range of measures (which included public works and other government intervention) designed to remove unemployment and stimulate the economy. In the short term the 'Yellow Book' proposed that all local authorities should require either full-time schooling to 15 or part-time to 16.

Labour policy, as spelled out in 1928–29 by Trevelyan, was for an immediate raising of the school-leaving age to 15 with a subsequent extension to 16, coupled with maintenance grants for those in need. Labour victory in the election of May 1929 gave the opportunity for such pledges to be redeemed, particularly as Trevelyan returned to the Board of Education. In July, indeed, he announced that the leaving age would be raised to 15 on 1 April 1931, in advance of the Hadow recommendation for 1932, and a bill to effect this decision and to provide maintenance grants was accordingly introduced in December 1929. In October 1930 it was replaced by a revised bill which proceeded via amendment in the Commons to defeat in the Lords in 1931.

THE 1930S

The events of 1929–30 demonstrate the force of religion, social class and finance in matters educational. Snowden, as Chancellor of the Exchequer, viewed Trevelyan's proposals with undisguised alarm. Early in 1930 he conceded an increase of 100 in the number of state scholarships to universities, and a maximum of 50 per cent as opposed to 40 per cent of free places in secondary schools. In September 1929 an increased Exchequer grant for new school buildings of 50 per cent, as opposed to 20 per cent, had been approved for three years, in pursuance of Hadow reorganization and the raising of the school-leaving age. But the churches lacked the financial resources to reorganize their schools, whilst the immediate prospect of maintenance grants for senior pupils, and the ultimate provision of free secondary schooling for all, betokened a massive rise in the education budget at a time when the world economy was suffering an unparalleled crisis. Thus the proposed maintenance allowances were to be restricted to 14–15-year-olds and made subject to a strict means test of family income. Even so, in the summer of 1930 the bill was postponed. Trevelyan now sought to concentrate upon securing legislation to raise the school-leaving age to 15 in 1931, and to treat financial and religious issues under a separate heading. He was prevented in this strategy by the amendment of John Scurr, Labour MP for Stepney and a leader of the Roman Catholic cause. The Scurr amendment, which was approved in the Commons in January 1931 with the support of more than 40 Labour members, stated that the raising of the school-leaving age should be postponed

> until an Act has been passed authorizing expenditure out of public funds, upon such conditions as necessary to meet the cost to be incurred by the managers of non-provided schools in meeting the requirements of the provision of this Act, but that in no event shall this Act come into operation earlier than the first day of September, nineteen hundred and thirty two. (*Hansard*, Vol. 247, Col. 193, 21 January 1931)

This amendment safeguarded the position of the Roman Catholic and Anglican interests, infuriated the Nonconformists and increased the concerns of MacDonald and Snowden. In February 1931, to the probable relief of the Prime Minister and Chancellor of the Exchequer, the amended bill was defeated in the Lords by 168 votes to 22. Trevelyan resigned (to be succeeded by Lees-Smith), with little to show for all his idealism and efforts except the increased building grants. Nevertheless in spite of Trevelyan's resignation and of his conviction that the Prime Minister was the bill's major opponent, a Cabinet decision was taken to override the Lords' objections by use of the Parliament Act. Lees-Smith, therefore, continued discussions with the religious bodies (Barker, 1972, p. 63).

In the summer of 1931 a committee headed by Sir George May proposed that budget expenditure should be cut by some £100 million, with £12 million coming from education. The Labour Cabinet split over the proposed reduction in unemployment benefit, and MacDonald, supported by Snowden, formed a National Government. At the election of October 1931 the new government was confirmed in office with more than 550 supporters (mainly Conservatives). Cuts were applied to education. The minimum 50 per cent grant from the Exchequer to local authorities was abolished. Teachers' salaries were reduced by 10 per cent, with local authorities paying a higher proportion of salary bills. Free places in secondary schools were replaced by means-tested contributions. Opposition to such cuts was led by Labour and Liberal politicians, by Churchmen, notably William Temple, then Archbishop of York, by educationists and trade unionists. Their opposition was successful only in so far as it helped to prevent even larger reductions in educational finance.

Economy was the watchword of the early 1930s, but by the end of 1935 the National Government had been returned to office with another substantial majority. Baldwin had replaced MacDonald as Prime Minister, and Oliver Stanley had replaced Lord Halifax (formerly Edward Wood and Lord Irwin) as President of the Board of Education. Teachers' pay had been restored to its former levels. In 1936 Stanley introduced a bill to raise the school-leaving age to 15 on 1 September 1939, and to provide government finance to enable this objective to be achieved. Exchequer grants would be made of 50 per cent to local, and 75 per cent to church, authorities to enable them to build the extra places required. In return non-denominational teaching according to an agreed syllabus was to be provided for the children of any parents who requested this. On this occasion, however, controversy centred not on denominational issues but upon the concept of 'beneficial exemptions' included in the bill. Children would be allowed to leave school at the end of the term in which they reached their 14th birthday if they were going to be engaged in 'beneficial' employment. Supporters of this principle agreed that such exemptions reflected the best interests of pupils and parents, an interpretation made easier by the fact that no clear definition of 'beneficial' was ever provided. Ultimate decisions on this matter would be left to local authorities. Opponents pointed out that in ten local authorities where the school-leaving age had already been raised to 15 with exemptions (under the provisions of the 1921 consolidating act), exemption rates were not less than 79 per cent, except in Caernarvonshire. There the payment of 3s per week maintenance allowances (a feature excluded from the 1936 Act) had produced a situation where only 37 per cent of children were exempted from school attendance to 15. Notwithstanding the widespread opposition to exemptions the bill became law in July 1936, although events in yet another 'far off country' were to ensure that it was not put into effect in 1939.

SUMMARY

The 1936 Act has been generally condemned by historians of education. Brian Simon, for example, called it 'belated and inadequate' (Simon, 1974b, p. 224). Harold Dent dismissed it as 'that poor little pennyworth of half-baked compromise' (Dent, 1970, p. 111). Can such comments be generalized to apply to the inter-war years as a whole? Were the decades of the 1920s and 1930s in educational terms a period of stagnation and failure or rather of progress?

Certainly three of the objectives of educational reformers – secondary schools for all, compulsory schooling to 16, and part-time education to 18 – were not achieved. In fairness, however, it must be acknowledged that 20 years after 1945, in spite of a growth of democracy, more favourable economic circumstances, and the advent of majority Labour governments, two, and arguably all three, of these goals had still not been attained. The county colleges of 1944 proved to be even more of a fiasco than the continuation schools of 1918. A quarter of a century was to elapse before the school-leaving age of 15, finally achieved in 1947, was to be raised again. Only in 1965 was the first successful major move made against the ideal of tripartite secondary schooling, separate but equal.

Although the number of pupils in secondary schools in England and Wales recognized by the Board of Education grew from 307,862 in 1920 to 470,003 in 1938, much of this increase was accounted for by pupils staying on longer at school. In 1920 the annual intake of pupils was 96,283, in 1938 only 98,820. In 1920 30.3 per cent of pupils in these secondary schools had free places. By 1933 this reached a peak of 48.8 per cent but in 1938 had declined to 45.8 per cent. These figures must, however, be set against a general decline in the school population in the inter-war years which reflected a drop in the birth rate from 957,782 in 1920 to 621,264 in 1938. Thus whereas in 1920 there were nearly six million pupils in public elementary schools in England and Wales, by 1938 there were just over five million. This decline helped to reduce the ratio of pupils in average attendance to teachers in public elementary schools over the same period from 31.6 per cent to 27.2 per cent (these figures are taken from the statistical tables in Simon, 1974b, pp. 363–80). Teachers, however, suffered many difficulties in this period. Their material well-being was attacked in the reports of Geddes and May. Their worth was not enhanced by their own high incidence of unemployment, and by the unemployment of so many of their better-qualified former pupils.

Yet the inter-war years also saw a flourishing of ideas, the production of blueprints for the future. Chief amongst these were the reports of the Board of Education Consultative Committee, the Hadow reports of 1926, 1931 and 1933. The vision of an enlightened infant school operating in the tradition of Owen and Wilderspin (1933) and of a junior school in which the curriculum was to be thought of 'in terms of activity and experience, rather than of knowledge to be acquired and facts to be stored' (1931), were steps towards the development of a child-centred progressive doctrine of primary education which culminated in the Plowden Report of 1967. Indeed it was in the 1920s and 1930s that child-centred education became the intellectual ortho-doxy of the primary school and of the training college (Selleck, 1972). The Hadow Report of 1926 and the Spens Report of 1938 (Spens replaced Hadow as chairman of the Consultative Committee in 1934) established the principle of secondary education for all, implemented in 1944, though in distinct types of schools – grammar, modern and technical. Elimination of the old elementary tradition, as exempli-fied by all-age schools, proceeded steadily prior to 1939, but with considerable regional variations. For instance in Northampton all elementary schools had been reorganized along Hadow lines by this date. Amongst church schools and in rural areas, in contrast, the figure was as low as 20 per cent.

Not all rural authorities, however, could be dismissed as backward, nor was the separation of institutions the only means of educational advance. For example in Cambridgeshire Henry Morris, who had himself left elementary school in Southport at 14, before subsequent study at Lampeter, Oxford and Cambridge, became County Education Secretary (Chief Education Officer) in 1922 at the age of 33. His memorandum of 1924, entitled *The Village College*, which proposed in rural areas the grouping of all educational and social agencies into one village college, bore fruit in 1930 when the Prince of Wales opened the first such college at Sawston. The complex, which included a school, hall, adult wing, workshop, library and playing fields, represented the incorporation rather than the separation of education in terms of function, age and social groups.

In spite of such innovations, however, in structural terms the overall verdict on this period must be one of stagnation rather than progress. Some of the proposed educational reforms of the inter-war years were indeed fulfilled in the text of the 1944 Act, though that fulfilment was subsequently modified by failures in implementation. Nevertheless the 1920s and 1930s, like the 1940s and 1950s, were essentially a period of missed opportunities in education, which left the country with inadequate secondary, further and higher education, particularly in terms of science and technology, inadequacies which were soon to be reflected in her relative economic decline.

FURTHER READING

The economic, social and political backgrounds are well covered in such standard works as D.H. Aldcroft, *The Inter-War Economy: Britain 1919– 1939*, 1970, C.L. Mowat, *Britain between the Wars, 1918–1940*, 1955, and J. Stevenson, *British Society 1914–45*, 1984. L. Andrews, *The Education Act, 1918*, 1976, and G. Sherington, *English Education, Social Change and War, 1911–1920*, 1981, provide useful introductions to the educational policy issues of the inter-war period, whilst R. Barker, *Education and Politics, 1900–1951: a Study of the Labour Party*, 1972, devotes three chapters to this period. G. Bernbaum, *Social Change and the Schools, 1918–1944*, 1967, is a brief over-view, but the most detailed treatment remains B. Simon, *The Politics of Educational Reform, 1920–1940*, 1974. For more detailed studies of particular aspects of education in this era see R.J.W. Selleck, *English Primary Education and the Progressives, 1914–1939*, 1972, O. Banks, *Parity and Prestige in English Secondary Education*, 1955, and A. Kazamias, *Politics, Society and Secondary Education in England*, 1966.

CHAPTER FIVE

The Politics and Administration of Consensus, 1945–1960

INTRODUCTION

There has been a strong tendency among political commentators and historians to regard the post-war period from 1945 into the 1960s as years of relative moderation and consensus, when the major political parties sought to capture the middle ground in politics. A contrast has often been made between the apparently peaceful 1950s and the bitter, angry pre-war decade, which was marked by unemployment marches, distressed areas and clashes between extremist groups on the Right and Left. In the 1950s the term 'Butskellism' had even come to be used to describe the management of the economy by the Conservative government, a derivation from the supposed common approach instigated by the previous Labour Chancellor, Hugh Gaitskell, and largely carried on by his Conservative successor at the Treasury, R. A. Butler. A spate of recent biographies of key figures in that Conservative government, including those of Eden and Butler, has demonstrated how far they were determined to distance themselves from pre-war Conservatism and how anxious they had become to secure trade union co-operation and reaffirm their commitment to a welfare state.

The large-scale defeat of the Conservatives in 1945, the period of regrouping while in opposition, and the narrowness of their electoral victory in 1951, strengthened the resolve of moderates within the Conservative party who did not see the return of a Conservative government as an opportunity to steer the nation to the Right. Significantly this view of a moderate, consensus-minded, over-cautious party was taken up in the later 1970s by new forces within the Conservative party which claimed that the previous long period of Tory domination from 1951 to 1964 had been largely wasted by a timid leadership, which had mainly tackled short-term problems. Thus it had squandered many opportunities, provided by falling world prices in food and materials after 1953, a gradual thawing in East–West relations and a Labour opposition in disarray, to secure those fundamental changes in the economy and society which were needed.

The Labour party, too, particularly in recent studies by historians, has generally been portrayed as using the realities of power, while in government, to push through much needed reforms in industrial relations, employment and welfare provisions. Angry grass-roots protests were muted in this period, and standard-bearers of the Left from the 1930s such as Stafford Cripps, John Strachey, Ellen Wilkinson and even Aneurin Bevan, settled down to work with their civil servants to carry through post-war reconstruction. In the 1950s, particularly in the Bevanite challenge, there may have been echoes of the need to return to a more marked ideological confrontation with their political opponents, but the general picture which has emerged has been of a party moving steadily in pursuit of moderation. In highlighting early loss of nerve in Labour circles, education has been regarded as one very important area where the initiative passed to the Conservatives, even at a time when Labour ministers presided over the Ministry of Education. As a result a system of education had been built up, so deeply entrenched in the public's mind, that when the Wilson government did attempt much needed changes in the 1960s there were acute difficulties and barriers to an effective implementation of distinctive policies.

THE CONSENSUS IN EDUCATION?

If there was, in this period, common acceptance of the policies needed in education, what were the major ingredients which encouraged the impression of a broad consensus? The major political parties both presented themselves as totally committed to the implementation of the 1944 Act, because it ended older, bitter religious controversies. At the end of his life, R.A. Butler, the Bill's architect, paid tribute to William Temple, who had sacrificed some of his own Church's position for the general good. Throughout his later political career Butler had continued to involve himself, even in Opposition, in educational matters, giving an impression of bipartisanship. Ellen Wilkinson, Labour Minister of Education, 1945–47, from the first days in office, took the view that the only possible route was to keep up the momentum. Any delay on the part of central government or hesitant local authorities would rapidly destroy major sections of the Act which needed to be implemented. At first her deepest suspicions were reserved for local authorities, particularly those in the rural areas, who might not be easily persuaded to support the necessary changes. John Maud, her personal secretary, recorded that 'from the start she was determined that all children should have a better chance than she and her generation had' (Redcliffe–Maud, 1982, p.51). Thus she insisted that the local authorities pursued their development plans with speed, despite difficulties. Throughout 1946 the powerful Association of Education Committees complained of the extra demands being put on them, particularly if they included an additional year of school life

> without any further reorganisation involving as it will do in the majority of small rural schools the education of children up to 15 years of age in the same class as former pupils, and without additional accommodation or additional teachers. (AEC, PRO ED 136/797, 18 October 1946)

From the opening weeks in office, Wilkinson made clear her resolve to raise the school-leaving age at the appointed time. She wrote:

> Admittedly if the age is raised in April 1947 it will be necessary to accept very imperfect conditions. A number of children, approximately 40 per cent, will have to spend the extra year in un-reorganised all-age schools, and the additional accommodation will be temporary and makeshift. Further the problem of over-large classes will continue untouched and in some ways may be intensified for a time. I am sure however that to wait till we attain perfection would postpone the raising of the school leaving age indefinitely. (Wilkinson, PRO CAB 78/36, 27 August 1945)

Nevertheless, at the end of 1946, Hugh Dalton, then Chancellor of the Exchequer, proposed a six-month delay in raising the school-leaving age, in many politicians' minds a trifling postponement. Ellen Wilkinson, exhausted and within weeks of death, fought tenaciously and successfully to uphold what she considered a fundamental part of the Butler Act. She would also, almost certainly, have resisted very strongly the postponement of the creation of county colleges, and her own enthusiasm for them would have certainly brought her into acute conflict with the Treasury, increasingly anxious to question expenditure under the austere Stafford Cripps. She anticipated trouble from the occasional, cheeseparing Tory authority, but found irksome the doubts of ultra-progressive Labour authorities who turned their attention to issues of secondary education whilst modern schools were still at the formative stage, and a mass of all-age schools continued to exist. By and large, Conservatives accepted the extra year of school life in 1947, and they welcomed her reluctance to tinker with the emerging tripartite system. Her successor, George Tomlinson (1947–51), for his part, was content broadly to follow her policy.

In their turn, in 1951, the incoming Conservative government, after rumours that the prime minister Churchill was in favour of shortening the years of compulsory schooling, maintained the major outlines of the Butler Act. For a variety of reasons, Churchill had grave reservations about the value of the additional year at school, which he thought the majority of the population neither wished nor required. He certainly raised the issue of returning to a programme of exemptions at 14, and after meeting resistance on this, tentatively proposed raising the age of entry to six. Both proposals were fought tenaciously by Churchill's Minister of Education, Florence Horsbrugh, who was able to count on the support of Butler, the Chancellor of the Exchequer. He was far from helpful on many occasions to his hard-pressed colleague, but in this instance rallied to her aid on this matter. Another feature of Conservative policy in the 1950s, particularly after David Eccles arrived at the Ministry of Education in 1954, was the sustained pressure to eliminate the all-age school, especially in the rural areas. Though the pace might have been quicker with a Labour government there was little disagreement that this was a major priority which had been clearly laid down in the Butler Act.

A corollary of both parties' determination to sustain the impetus of the Butler Act was the overwhelming acceptance of the expansion in number of students, colleges, schools and teachers. In the 1957 Report of the Ministry of Education there was much satisfaction that 500 new schools would be built within the year and that a further 900 were in the process of reconstruction. Evidence that some young people were staying beyond the age of 17, and that the number taking various combinations of Advanced Level subjects was rising, was welcomed. In 1958, Sir Edward Boyle, then Parliamentary Secretary at the Ministry, praised the extent of the school building programme: 'there can really be no doubt that our effort in new school buildings has been one of the national achievements since the war' (Boyle, AMA, 1958, p. 231). Much of this rebuilding was the consequence of war damage and the need to provide schools in new suburbs. There was widespread shock at revelations of the squalor of older schools. The parties argued in the 1950s over delays, temporary curtailments and reluctance to push harder, but all agreed on the need for building programmes. It was Florence Horsbrugh who bore a good deal of Opposition attacks in the early 1950s over what was seen as a lack of fight in resisting Treasury pressure for delaying school building. Some of this was unfair, for the outgoing Labour Education Minister, George Tomlinson, had, from 1948, carried out a number of economies under Treasury direction. Richard Crossman, a left-wing Labour member, acknowledged that the emergency measures introduced by Butler were not too different from those likely to have been introduced by Labour. 'I checked with Stokes [a former Labour Minister] and found it was precisely what the previous Cabinet had decided on' (Crossman, 1981, p.33). Later, Labour launched their most telling attack. In the fight for scarce resources the charge was made that Horsbrugh had lost in a power struggle to a politically more accomplished Minister responsible for housing, Harold Macmillan, who had exploited the Conservative Party Conference pledge that a future Conservative government would raise the housing target to 300,000 a year. He had insisted that this pledge was carried out and the Opposition claimed that other legitimate necessities, such as the building of new schools, had been neglected. Outwardly compliant to the Housing Minister's aims, but in private expressing annoyance, she was no match for him, particularly as he could count on Churchill's total support. Macmillan was a member of a group of ministers who disliked the exhortations and cheese-paring economies favoured by Treasury ministers like Cripps and Butler. The most effective way to make people work harder was to offer them inducements: the possession of a home was the most attractive one. The Education Ministry found itself outflanked.

A rising population diverted the attention of successive Education Ministers from other urgent matters. Instead of the 1944 Act coming into operation with a stable, even declining, school population, at the end of the War the birthrate rose very sharply. By 1948 both the Minister and local authorities were very aware of the problems which this would cause. In 1947 Ellen Wilkinson had used the argument that school numbers were at their lowest, a reflection of the pre-war Depression, to support her case for the additional year at school. However, within a year, George Tomlinson saw the position reversed. Infant schools now seemed likely to be swamped. Resources needed to be switched to this sector to meet the crisis. Talk of expanded programmes to meet the problems of the 15–18 age group, including county colleges, required thorough re-examination in the light of this new necessity. The steady move of the population bulge up through the school system in the following years became a constant preoccupation of Ministers and their officials.

David Eccles, on coming to office as Minister of Education in 1954, believed that the management of rising numbers coming through the system had raised serious issues. 'As a newcomer in the field he had received the impression that there had been an increase in the scale of education but not in its quality' (Eccles, PRO ED 136/857, 22 November 1954). Ministers welcomed the prospect of this bulge eventually working its way through the system, since it was predicted, 'A survey of the resources show that "the battle of the bulge" is well on the way to being won and this makes it possible to plan ahead with complete confidence' (Ministry of Education Report, 1958, p.1). Much of the educational debate in the early 1950s, therefore, was focused on the government's success or failure in coping with numbers and matching demand with resources in the educational system. It was only at the end of the 1950s that debates in Parliament returned to wider issues. At the same time the piecemeal progress in ridding the nation of all-age schools, and the glaring inadequacies of so-called modern schools still based in older, unsuitable sites was now an important issue.

In seeking to sustain the advances anticipated in the Butler Act successive governments proclaimed the importance of the partnership value of the enterprise. Collaboration between a central Ministry, local authorities and the teaching body was regarded as a peculiarly British and unique way to run education. The fact that the Board, lowly in status in Cabinet, had been transformed into a Ministry with a more directive capacity did not mean central control. It was recognized that local authorities had their own rights and duties, and in turn, that they, too, were answerable to local electorates. Care had to be taken not to upset teachers' particular interests, though the continuing divisions within the body did not make this an easy task. This view of partnership was therefore universally held, although on occasions tussles developed between Ministers, anxious to get their way, and local authorities who believed that they were overstepping the boundaries. Thus the attitude of Ministers of Education and the level of contact with their partners was often crucial. Very early on Ellen Wilkinson had to be lectured on the subtlety of the relationship by the Senior Chief Inspector, Sir Martin Roseveare. She clearly had strong views on teacher training, but her attention was drawn to the need for discretion. 'I explained that in schools and all other educational establishments, although HMI uses his influence and the general influence of the Inspectorate unobtrusively but none the less vigorously, he is always most careful to avoid giving the impression that we are laying down the law' (Roseveare, PRO ED 143/2, 3 September 1945). There had been protest in the George Tomlinson era about the way in which the Minister had used his powers to prevent closure to thwart the plans of the Middlesex Education Committee for school reorganization. While the Association of Education Committees tried to avoid being drawn into the controversy over the particular plans for reorganization, they demonstrated that they were deeply concerned about the way the Middlesex proposals had been handled, stating: 'That this Association welcomes experiments in the organisation of secondary education and urges the Minister of Education that each LEA be left full autonomy in the determination of its schemes for the organisation of secondary schools in the area' (AEC, PRO ED 136/799, 17 June 1948). In reply, the Ministry reasserted its own position:

> We have also made it quite clear, and this is important because of the Minister's overall responsibility, that we cannot leave LEAs full autonomy in the matter, that our only concern is that these proposals which are adopted should be consistent with sound educational practice and principles and that the best existing standards should be maintained and indeed raised. (Heaton, PRO ED 136/799, 17 August 1948)

The warning issued here was a clear one. National policies and standards were clearly prescribed from the centre. George Tomlinson, in this case, won his battle, possibly because in 1949 political control in Middlesex changed hands, and probably because of doubts too in the local authority lobby and teacher associations about the wisdom of the proposed reorganization. Moreover, in spite of rumblings about interference, he was a figure whose own roots were in the local authority world. The charge was often raised that Labour, in these years, was more likely to prefer to be the centralizers and interferers and seek to advance the boundaries of central government. Significantly, in this respect, however, his actions found approval on the Conservative benches, while the organ of the National Association of Labour Teachers bitterly attacked what they saw as excessive control.

Florence Horsbrugh's partnership with local authorities and teachers was clouded from the beginning. Her omission from Churchill's Cabinet in 1951 was seen by the other parties as an affront and a downgrading of education's importance. She never really recovered from this, and was continuously under fire from the local authorities who saw her losing the battle with other Ministers for scarce building resources. In their 1952 resolutions, the Association of Education Committees expressed disquiet about her position, 'It would be a poor reflection of the anxiety expressed by the Association to inform the Minister that we are in fact without necessary evidence to see that the general principles which she has enunciated are implemented' (AEC, PRO ED 136/903, June 1952).

Although she was eventually included in the Cabinet in 1953 and, on occasions, earned praise for her defence of government policies on building programmes, the standing of the Ministry among the parties was not high when she was replaced in 1954. It was left to her successor,

David Eccles, to improve this reputation. One of his first acts was to call together representatives of local authorities and the teacher associations to emphasize the need for a continuing pattern of partnership and consultation. Throughout 1955 he embarked on a campaign of exhortation and encouragement, typically opening his speech to the delegates at the Assistant Masters' Conference with the words, 'You ought to be talking to me. How badly I need your advice' (Eccles, AMA, 1955, p.20). In the period 1955–57 there was the impression of a strong minister in search of new ideas and new initiatives.

During the opening years of the Macmillan government, his successors fared less well in cementing this partnership. There was discontent during the short time that Lord Hailsham was at the Ministry in 1957, mostly on the grounds that his presence in the Upper Chamber freed him from the more searching enquiries to which ministers were subjected in the Commons. Geoffrey Lloyd (1957–59) ran into difficulties because of the anxieties expressed by local authorities at the proposed reorganization of rate support grants, which, it was claimed, would affect education adversely. Throughout the 1950s Conservative ministers played on the fact that they were more likely to respect partnership in education than a potential Labour government too inclined to move towards uniform treatment of children, particularly in the secondary sector. On the other hand, throughout the 1950s pressure was mounting for more central management through financial monitoring. Education was regarded as a very expensive service requiring ever increasing funds; this was seen as the result of inadequate control at local authority level. Shortages of teachers seemed to be unevenly spread, giving rise to the belief in Ministry circles that the local authorities in more attractive areas were recruiting too easily, while the areas of real need suffered. David Eccles had moved quickly to settle this problem by persuading each authority to accept a quota of new teachers. A further indication of the growing attention being paid to planning and management of resources was the creation of the Architects and Building Branch within the Ministry. Partnership was accepted by both parties, but was, because of the very vagueness of much of the legislation, never uniformly upheld.

A marked feature throughout the period was the debate about the most suitable ways to provide scientific, technological and technical education, and the need to highlight the importance of science in the fight for Britain's continuing industrial and international standing. At first sight, full employment and steadily rising standards of living, fuelled by the need to reconstruct not only at home but within a shattered Europe, created an impression of continued progress and energy. By the early 1950s Butler was able to take advantage of improved East–West relations and general world recovery to carry through tax-reducing budgets and end much of rationing and control. Britain therefore appeared to be prospering, and apart from occasional anxieties about trade balances, was enjoying improved productivity and full employment. Nevertheless, there was concern that sustained economic growth, the cornerstone of both the Conservative policy for a fiercer, more competitive, society and for Labour's renewed push to a more egalitarian Commonwealth, might not continue into the next decade.

Conservative commentators often denounced the lack of adaptability of the work-force, bolstered by growing trade union power which used restrictive practices to maintain over-manning and slackness. As a result costs were pushed up and British goods became less competitive. For its part Labour tended to concentrate its attention on the shortcomings of management and its inability to adapt to a changing world. Herbert Morrison was one Labour politician urging the full mobilization of scientists and technicians in British industry to sweep away many practices and customs holding back change. Throughout his period as Lord President of the Council (1945–51) he pressed at one level for more scientists in the major areas of government, and at another level for the positive promotion of science and technical studies in the school. In this respect he did not always secure total support from his colleagues, such as Ellen Wilkinson, who always suspected any form of studies that too closely directed pupils into prescribed employment patterns. Both political parties, however, had advocates of the advance of science and technical education.

There was no agreement about the best way in which this could be done. Two solutions emerged in the post-war period. One group argued that a distinctive strand, stressing scientific, technological and technical education, equal in resources, staff and prestige to other comparable spheres of education should be built up throughout secondary, further and higher education. If this separatist strand were not developed, they maintained, it would be subsumed by the more strongly entrenched academic subjects. In the post-war era, as a result of this philosophy, the role of the technical school received much attention. Nevertheless, in spite of wide publicity, by the end of the 1950s less than five per cent of the secondary population went to these schools. Conservative ministers therefore began, for a variety of reasons, to move towards an integrationist position whereby the modern school might increase its standing if it developed more technical streams. This was to be achieved by setting up bilateral schools. Moreover, perhaps as an answer to the problems of early leaving in the grammar schools, an important topic in the 1950s, there were suggestions of technical streams being added to the more academic ones to stem this drift of dissatisfied, if potentially able, pupils. Also, it was hoped that more laboratories and workshops in all types of secondary schools would make their pupils more aware of industry's demands.

As for higher education, the debate over separation or integration became shrouded in bitter debates over the purpose of this kind of education, who was to administer it, and what resources should be allocated. The older universities resented any pronouncement that, in future, because of increased government funding, they ought to turn their attention more to the training of applied scientists and technologists and thereby exclude other disciplines. Some politicians, Herbert Morrison on the Labour side, Lord Cherwell and Lord Woolton on the Conservative, argued that if science and technology continued to be located exclusively in the existing university sector, these disciplines could be starved of teachers and resources. Their conclusion was that the nation required the creation of highly prestigious, separately-funded and award-giving institutions of repute similar to those prevalent in European countries and the USA. These would be at the summit of a whole network of regional, area and local institutions which would provide for full-time lower level work, sandwich courses, part-time and evening programmes and feed in to the highest level.

Many Ministers, both Conservative and Labour, were unhappy at these kinds of suggestions. R. A. Butler believed strongly that any kind of scientific élite needed to be educated within a liberal atmosphere, and deplored the notion of separate institutions for this purpose. Even in 1946, Ellen Wilkinson had been wary of the technical and vocational lobby which she felt threatened other more worthwhile educational aims. Amid these debates surrounding higher technological education was a power struggle over control, for if this kind of education was wrested from the technical colleges it would ultimately diminish the authority of the Ministry of Education. The White Paper on Technical Education of 1956, a five-year plan, was in a sense a compromise. A number of colleges of technology, still remaining with the local authorities, were set up. Salary scales and the general conditions of the teachers working in further education were improved. Building programmes were instituted to expand all sections of further education, from the colleges of advanced technology to the local technical colleges. Generally this was a period of great expansion in numbers in this sector. The path had clearly been set for the separate development in higher education of the mid-1960s.

It was generally agreed by the mid-1950s that the emerging educational system was increasingly providing wider educational opportunities for the majority of the population. For Labour and progressive opinion much-needed changes in society depended on this aim being achieved. Limitation of education led to poor wages and diminished the prospect of promotion; it also impaired cultural horizons and leisure activities. In a society which openly expounded the virtues of democracy and pluralism it was essential that the vestiges of a more class-based educational system had to be swept away. The elimination of a fee-paying secondary system therefore appeared to be the opening up of new opportunities and fresh prospects. Conservatives too, particularly the younger element, strongly upheld the concept of increased educational opportunity. It was hoped that its results would lead to a freer, more mobile society in which the working classes as well as other groups in society would be able to take advantage of the wider prosperity and employment prospects, particularly in new industries. They also freely admitted that too many barriers against the working-class pupil had existed in the earlier part of the century.

There was also evidence that any young person of talent could now successfully pass through the system and secure a share of the most prestigious positions. None believed this more strongly than David Eccles who saw these educational opportunities in much the same way as he saw expanded home-ownership, a wider range of domestic goods, and even the possession of a motor car, by a much greater proportion of the population. All generally signified that the days of confrontation and suspicion between the battalions of capital and labour were at an end. For Conservatives there were limitations to these adjustments in education. Barriers had been taken down, but governments could not make all people equal at the start of their lives. A certain amount of inequality and disadvantage was a fact of life, and attempts by the school system to eradicate all differences could lead to dangerous and totalitarian innovations. People had the right to use their wealth in whatever way was legally acceptable, and this included making provision for the education of the young.

CHALLENGES TO CONSENSUS IN THE 1950s

In the 1950s what was happening in the educational system to further equality of opportunity came under intense scrutiny. A number of reasons have been given for this. Certainly there had always been a section of the Labour party at national and local level who had expressed very strong reservations about the tripartite system of secondary education. Within the universities, the building up of research groups in sociology and allied disciplines led to investigations into the workings of society at large. In this respect the work of D.V. Glass and Jean Floud, used extensively by Tony Crosland in his book *Future of Socialism* (1956), indicated that the expansion of secondary education disproportionately benefited the already advantaged sections of the nation. As Himmelweit wrote: 'Success within the grammar school is partly determined by the boy's social class membership' (in Glass (ed.), 1954, p.159). The educational system, therefore, was at least maintaining, or even strengthening, rather than diminishing, class inequality. From this kind of investigation, Crosland was to make the charge that the school system remained the most divisive and unjust aspect of social inequality. In his examination of the claims made for the 1944 Education Act he emphasized the failures: 'The intention was, since it was recognised that the grammar schools would retain their superior quality and hence their differential advantage as an avenue to the better occupations, to throw open this advantage, by abolishing fees and standardising entry procedures, to all social classes on equal terms' (Crosland, 1956, pp.258–9).

That this appeared not to be happening brought education to the forefront of future policy-making. In search of a fairer system of education he hoped that the twin aims of building a more cohesive, happier society and securing more effective industrial performance could be achieved. Politicians' dissatisfaction was reinforced by the more impressionistic cultural critics. Playwrights like John Osborne in *Look Back in Anger* (1956) reflected with bitterness that the advances since the War, including wider educational opportunities, had not seriously diminished the snobbery and prejudices so prevalent in earlier decades. Richard Hoggart, particularly in his book *The Uses of Literacy* (1957), expressed the anguish of a group of writers who saw working-class values and a community outlook gradually eroded by metropolitan values, advertising and mass entertainment, and regretted the loss of its most articulate members as a result of receiving higher education.

By the late 1950s growing affluence, consumerism and rising expectations competed with deeper feelings of alienation, missed opportunities and wasted talent. It pushed the political parties to new approaches in education. The Labour party was committed, since its policy statements issued in 1951, to a programme of comprehensive education. In reality major political figures on the Right, such as Hugh

Gaitskell, and the Bevanite Left, such as Richard Crossman, had strong reservations about the electoral impact of this commitment. Crosland himself reflected some of the difficulties. He was unclear whether the first step towards greater equality should be changes in the independent system, or reforms in the maintained grammar schools. On the Conservative side, spokesmen such as David Eccles and Edward Boyle were aware of rising public uneasiness, particularly over early selection for secondary schools. In 1958, in a new educational drive to build up their third electoral victory, the Conservatives issued a White Paper, *Secondary Education for All*, cleverly plundering R.H. Tawney's pioneering socialist slogan for their own purpose. The White Paper acknowledged public disquiet about selection. Action therefore was needed. Towards the end of the 1950s, academic streams grew in modern schools, which were encouraged to experiment with a range of leaving examinations and to enter larger numbers for the external examination system. Entry to grammar schools was to be relaxed by later admission at 13 or 16, and wider provision of courses in sixth forms. This kind of activity did not always lead to the reassurance that all was well within the system. A broad consensus of parents and educationists not always agreed on ends, but united in their condemnation of a system which, they claimed, harmed their children, was building up. A fluid class system threatened established groups who believed that they already possessed a higher status but were uneasy about their own position. Considering themselves as middle-class, they were throughout the 1950s under threat from the growth of 'the affluent worker', a group intensely concerned with their children's future.

Although the grammar schools were largely attended by children of the middle class, selection at eleven made their prospects of entry to the schools more precarious. There was no longer the possibility of entrance through fee-paying, and rising costs at independent schools might make it difficult to protect their young from failure. Increasingly this powerful group was tempted to favour grammar school education with all its trappings but without the selective process at eleven. Selection on intellectual merit alone, it was insisted, was not sufficient: character, hard work and good manners ought to count more. Dissatisfaction at the limitations in numbers at grammar schools, as well as anger at the unevenness of distribution of places, made them often strong supporters of changes in the educational system. There was also growing public concern about wastage and disadvantage in education, which were attributed to low expectations and failure in the school system. The school, rather than reinforcing existing handicaps, ought to work to bring out potentialities by new approaches, new teaching methods, and above all by building up wider social relationships within a common school. Thus a diffuse coalition with significantly different aims and aspirations was now eager for change in the existing system.

SUMMARY

The year 1959 is a convenient point at which to reconsider the educational 'consensus' which had always been more fragile than in other areas of social policy. Indeed the Crowther Report (1959), which was subsequently overshadowed by Robbins, Newsom and Plowden, anticipated issues of the 1960s. The Committee had directed attention to those groups in society who benefited least from the expanding educational services – the children of manual workers, those in larger families, and, because of deeply entrenched prejudices, the female section of the population. While not endorsing comprehensive education, it pointed out that the population bulge of the 1950s had given rise to doubts on all forms of selection procedures which had once been held to be fair. The Report looked at the needs of society at a point of economic change, and emphasized the role of education in developing the potential skills required for the new technological world.

Throughout its field of research with young people the Crowther Report detected a substantial shift of opinion in society about many aspects of family life, marriage and social behaviour, and indicated to the politicians the need to consider these changes in outlook in their approach to policy-making. The population bulge which had haunted successive education ministers on its path through primary and secondary schooling was now poised to move into adult life. There had already been glimpses in the mid-1950s of tensions between parents and older children, and much talk of the generation gap. Much of this generation had grown up better fed, educated and housed than their parents. This had made them more restless, more radical. One constraint on this radicalism was about to be revised. National Service, which detached most young men of 18 to 20 from active participation in everyday life was drawing to an end. At the beginning of the 1960s leading Conservatives, at the centre of politics since 1951, detected a changing mood, that they could not wholly grasp. Lord Kilmuir, the Lord Chancellor from 1957 to 1962, wrote:

> The Conservative Party had done marvels to raise the standard of living of the nation since 1951, but subsequently the appeal of 1959 had lost its impact. We were dimly aware, at least a few of us

were, of a new cry among the younger people for a new standard to gather round. (Kilmuir, 1964, p. 302)

The country was now moving towards a period that left the pattern of education significantly different from that of the earlier post-war decades.

FURTHER READING

On the Attlee governments the two most recent, and substantial works are K. Morgan, *Labour in Power 1945–51*, 1983, and H. Pelling, *The Labour Governments 1945–51*, 1984. Various aspects of policy on education are examined in C. Benn, 'Comprehensive School Reform and the 1945 Labour Government', *History Workshop*, Vol. 10, 1980; D.W. Dean, 'Planning for a Post-War Generation; Ellen Wilkinson and George Tomlinson at the Ministry of Education 1945–51', *History of Education*, Vol. 15, No. 2, 1986, and the lively debate between B. Hughes, 'In Defence of Ellen Wilkinson' and D. Rubinstein, 'Ellen Wilkinson Reconsidered', conducted in *History Workshop*, Vol. 7, 1979. There are biographies of Labour education ministers notably B. Vernon, *Ellen Wilkinson 1891–1947*, 1982 and F. Blackburn, *George Tomlinson*, 1954. On relationships with a Labour-controlled LEA there is R. Saran, *Policy-Making in Secondary Education*, 1973. The Conservative governments of the 1950s are covered in A. Seldon, *Churchill's Indian Summer*, 1981; V. Bogdanor and R. Skidelsky, *The Age of Affluence*, 1970, and B. Simon, 'The Tory Government and Education 1951–60', *History of Education*, Vol. 14, No. 4, 1985. P.H.J.H. Gosden, *The Education System since 1944*, 1983; W.K. Richmond, *Education in Britain since 1944*, 1978; G. McCulloch, E. Jenkins, D. Layton, *Technological Revolution? The Politics of School Science and Technology in England and Wales since 1945*, 1985, and R. Lowe, *Education in the Post-War Years: a Social History*, 1988, survey the period of 'consensus'.

CHAPTER SIX

The Era of Expansion: The 1960s

INTRODUCTION

In order to cope with the speed of change, historians, including those of education, have been forced to confine their attention to decades rather than centuries. Almost every decade since the end of the First World War has been described in ways marking it off very sharply from its predecessor or its successor. Thus the so-called Roaring Twenties, a reaction against the horrors of that war, eventually gave way to the Age of Depression, characterized in this way because of its high unemployment figures and growing crisis in international relations. Already the 1960s has begun to acquire its own particular ethos, and the term Swinging Sixties has often been used to describe its permissiveness and excitement. Later decades have frequently condemned its waywardness and failure to tackle fundamental problems. Criticism came very early, and an instant appraisal, Mackie and Cook's *Decade of Disillusion*, published in 1972, was an indication that many of the early hopes for that period had already been dashed. Some of the leading political figures, Harold Wilson, Richard Crossman and Barbara Castle, have not been slow to record their attempts to modernize government, industry and social services, but their memoirs and diaries portray failure and frustration rather than success, and a growing realization of how deep the crisis had become.

These volumes describing the lengthy negotiations and disappointing breakdowns have an aura of excitement, impatience with older habits, and an urge for change, innovation and modernity. The scene was almost set in 1960 for the clash between older and newer values in the challenge mounted on the obscenity laws by the publication of the unexpurgated text of D.H. Lawrence's *Lady Chatterley's Lover*. There was a determination to expose the chaotic contradictory laws which often appeared to prevent the public at large from reading what many critics regarded as highly moral and important works of literature, while doing little to stem the double standards and hypocrisy contained in modern entertainment. The High Court's decision, together with revelations of scandal in high society that for weeks in 1962 destabilized the hitherto impregnable Macmillan government, led to an outburst of sharp social criticism of the Establishment. The retirement of Harold Macmillan, 'the last Edwardian', in 1963 and the subsequent defeat at the polls of his successor, Sir Alec Douglas-Home, in 1964 seemed to augur a new kind of politics. New political figures emerged, presided over by Harold Wilson, who appeared supremely at ease with the world of communications in a way that none of his predecessors had ever been. Many of the new MPs arriving in 1964 and 1966 were eager to take up causes that older Members regarded as wholly inappropriate for debate, or politically dangerous to espouse. Particularly during Roy Jenkins' years at the Home Office there was a determination to tackle issues such as divorce, homosexuality and abortion, which had been shrouded in assumptions fitted more for the Victorian age. As if to confirm Britain's change of direction as it reluctantly retreated from its East of Suez role and imperial commitments, the nation assumed a hitherto uncharacteristic leadership in popular entertainment and fashion. The virtues of self-denial and self-control, usually featured as a constant factor in British society, seemed to be destined for oblivion.

These events, often seen in documentaries and newsreels, contrasted sharply with the frequent appraisals of Britain's direction and its low economic growth, bad industrial relations, inadequate managers and workers, and waste of talent. External upheaval such as the retreat from Empire and older markets and the difficulty of coming to terms with a revived Western Europe, created this atmosphere of vulnerability. From 1966 the government struggled with deflation and devaluation, and this served to heighten fears about urban decay, the ill effects of poverty and disadvantage, and the apparent deterioration in race relations. In many ways what is most striking about the 1960s is that the political agenda for later decades was already set. The education service and its reform was regarded as a vital weapon in the alleviation of many of these acute difficulties. Widening access, changes in the structure of parts of the secondary system, and later, specific programmes to meet identified needs were all pressed vigorously as essential for the nation's survival and ultimate well-being.

THE POLITICIANS AND THE EDUCATIONAL SYSTEM

This growing awareness was seen in the range of reports from various commissions of enquiry during the period which covered, among other fields, the youth service, higher education, all aspects of primary schooling and the education of the majority of the school population in secondary schools. Moreover, whenever the various bodies presented in their recommendations a case for increased expenditure, they were not slow to relate them to the needs of society. In their plea for a speedy implementation of an extra year in the school life of all pupils, the Newsom Committee in its Report *Half Our Future* (1963) stated, at the outset, the strong economic grounds for this step:

> Briefly, it is that the future pattern of employment in this country will require a much larger pool of talent than is at present available, and that at least a substantial proportion of the 'average' and 'below average' pupils are sufficiently educable to supply that additional talent. The need is not only for more skilled workers to fill existing jobs, but also for a generally better educated and intelligently adaptable labour force to meet new demands. (HMSO, 1963, p.5)

Most of the members of these committees were drawn from professional groups with long traditions of public service. Their line was cautious, reformist and committed to progress by orderly stages. They chose to start their enquiries at the point education had reached by the early 1960s. As a result of this approach the message which was conveyed to the politicians and the general public was that the Butler Act and its aftermath had already transformed the expectations of large sections of the population, and that in the future it was most unlikely that the pace would slow down. Thus the Plowden Report, *Children and their Primary Schools*, in 1967, predicted a future 'marked by rapid and far reaching economic and social change' (HMSO, 1967, Vol. 1, p.185). The underlying message was that the earlier assumption, of a limited pool of talent having to be dredged through a battery of selection tests, needed revision. Mounting evidence indicated that some form of secondary reorganization needed to be considered urgently. A marked feature of the 1960s reports was the depth to which research was taken and opinion was consulted. Examples given of good practice, sensible teaching and rising standards, often refuted the voices of those who had preached that unregulated expansion would undermine all of these. Nevertheless examples of success brought into sharp focus those sections of society who appeared to be by-passed in these advances. As a result the government found itself presented with fresh areas of investigation. There was a growing confidence that if unsuccessful groups could be identified, classified and dealt with by specific programmes then the educational standards of these groups could be improved. In many of their suggestions for improvement the reports insisted on the urgency of drawing neighbourhood, school, teacher and home into close contact, and one of the significant impacts of the reports was to focus attention on the 'permanent working class' who because of multiple deprivation appeared to remain outside the rising tide of affluence. The Plowden Report acknowledged that in recent years awareness had developed of the importance to the individual of friends and social background generally; the direction of attention in this period became firmly fixed on this working-class element.

Governments of both political complexions stressed the fact that policy decisions would depend on the findings of these reports. However, both Conservative and Labour governments responded very patchily and by the end of the decade there was evidence of growing uneasiness with these committees of enquiry which were seen to generate further problems. Significantly, after the 1960s conventional official committees were replaced by internal, narrower enquiries. Moreover many of the recommendations had little chance of implementation. The Public Schools Commission (1965) was seen by Crosland as an opportunity for integrating the public schools with the maintained sector. His Cabinet colleagues held out little prospect of this occurring and acquiesced in its appointment reluctantly, probably as a concession to party activists who had been pressing for the demise of public schools.

Political responses were often influenced by electoral considerations. Expansion of university provision by creating a network of new universities in varied centres of population, and the upgrading of colleges of advanced technology, which were part of the Robbins Committee on Higher Education (1963) recommendations, were almost instantly accepted by a Conservative government approaching the end of its term of office. Any unfavourable reaction was calculated by the governing party to lose votes in a period when the pressure on scarce university places was intense. But other proposals in the Report, which, for instance, supported the closer integration of the colleges of education with the universities, met with a more muted response. At best, the move was unlikely to gain the government much popularity, and at worst, might enrage the powerful local authority lobby who saw the colleges as part of their territory. While the colleges were granted greater autonomy they continued, for all their dramatic expansion, to remain on the outer margins of higher education. Powerful ministers could block even the strongest recommendations in spite of apparently strong Cabinet support for them. Both the Crowther and Newsom Reports had come down very heavily in favour of the speedy implementation of the additional year at school. There were pressures throughout the 1960s, particularly from the Treasury, to postpone raising the school-leaving age. In 1968 Roy Jenkins, then Chancellor of the Exchequer, facing up to post-devaluation, urged that there ought to be a delay. Barbara Castle's diary reveals the intensity of the debate in Cabinet: 'The first item was education where Roy was demanding a three-year delay in raising the school-leaving age. Patrick Gordon Walker's reaction was very equivocal; it was hard to say at the end of his pros and cons where he stood, but I suspect he secretly favours postponement' (Castle, 1984, 5 January 1968, p. 350). Other Cabinet ministers however quickly joined in, the more working-class Labour ministers, supported by Lord Longford, who eventually resigned on the issue, urging immediate implementation. 'George [Brown] said he would rather accept any cut at all from the Chancellor than this. None of the rest of us, he said, knew what it was like to be denied a proper education – not only at University but also at school. It rankled all one's life' (Castle, 1984, 5 January 1968, pp. 350–1). A determined Chancellor got his way and it was not until 1972 that all secondary schoolchildren stayed on until they were 16.

Before the mid-1960s higher education referred exclusively to university education, almost entirely full-time, degree awarding, and mainly residential. After 1964, accompanying the dramatic rise of the student population, nine new universities (including colleges of advanced technology) and 30 new local authority polytechnics reshaped the higher sector of education. It took the general public many years to take in the full impact of these changes. They were, however, much more aware of the transformation of the secondary sector, where the older grammar, technical and 1944 modern schools declined in numbers, to be replaced by schools with new designations such as comprehensive, or high schools, and in some places sixth form colleges. From 1963, straddling uneasily the primary and secondary sector, there was a network of middle schools. It has been argued that these changes ended the political consensus on education as Conservative and Labour divided on the merits of comprehensive education, selection and streaming. There was indeed much wrangling, but a closer examination at national and local level reveals a more complex pattern. From the early 1960s leading Conservative ministers such as Sir David Eccles and Sir Edward Boyle were shifting the party's position on these issues. In his discussions with Maurice Kogan, the latter revealed how close he was to his successor, Crosland's, position: 'One of the historical myths is that comprehensive reorganisation all started with Circular 10/65. It didn't. It started a number of years before' (Sir E. Boyle in Kogan, 1971, p. 78).

In his own mind Crosland had little doubt that early selection and the continuation of a rigid tripartite system were neither educationally sound nor politically popular, and his task was to persuade some of his more reluctant party colleagues to accept the need to change the policy. At the local level he was helped by the activities of some scantily populated Conservative shires which, anxious about the costs of rigid tripartitism, pushed ahead, from the late 1950s, with secondary reorganization. On the other hand even if powerful sections of the Labour party were heavily committed to total comprehensive education as a major plank in policy, there were signs of divisions about timing, the degree of pressure to be brought on recalcitrant local authorities and how extensively the new schools should differ from the old. Even Edward Short, Labour's Minister of Education at the end of Wilson's government (1968–70), often used arguments in its favour that denoted a degree of confusion and ambiguity in the party.

In a speech opening a new comprehensive school in the north of England, quoted in the Ministry of Education Report 1968, Short, while he maintained that these schools would be able to promote a much wider range of courses for the whole ability range, added, perhaps to satisfy his critics, 'This certainly meant preserving what is best in the grammar schools and making it more widely available' (Ministry of Education Report, 1968, p. 11). For all Harold Wilson's attacks on segregation at schools and colleges, there were doubts among his colleagues about the extent of his commitment. Crosland's wife and biographer commented, 'Tony was never certain that Wilson had a great interest in equality' (S. Crosland, 1983, [ed], p. 169), and Crossman was blunter: 'Every really radical solution makes Harold shiver, especially in the educational field, where I know he feels, "Thank God I didn't put Richard Crossman in" ' (Crossman, 1982, Vol. 3, 28 November 1968, p. 275).

At the local level some of the older party politicians were reluctant to see the demise of *their* grammar schools. Moreover if it was intended during the Wilson administration to bring about the ending of grammar school education, there were many signs of half-heartedness. At the secondary level comprehensive reorganization ran alongside a gathering coalition of the public schools, schools on the direct grant list and the grammar schools, uneasy bedfellows in the past, but now all fighting to maintain an ascendancy at the top of the secondary sector. So varied were the comprehensives in organization, origin and catchment areas, that an unofficial league table quickly emerged. Rhodes

Boyson described the part played by origins in retaining a successful reputation: 'If a comprehensive school is made from the expansion of a highly respected academic school then there is every likelihood that the local populace will associate the new school with its predecessor' (Boyson, 1970, p.60). In the school reorganization of the 1960s many of the key posts and more prestigious positions were allocated to former grammar school teachers while the secondary modern teachers found themselves in subordinate positions. Even among the pupils the demands of external examinations, grouping the older children into Ordinary level and CSE sets, often encouraged division. Thus although there was much talk of clearing away the divisions in education, barriers not only continued to exist but may have been strengthened in this decade.

In seeking to explain the extent of changes in education at this time, the role and the style of key politicians were important. On the Conservative side both Sir David Eccles and Sir Edward Boyle were major figures within their respective parties. However the prime example of the policy-maker and pace-setter has often been seen as Anthony Crosland, Labour's appointment to the post in 1965, who had long immersed himself in issues that called for the reform of education. In spite of pressure from some backbenchers to enforce comprehensive schooling, Crosland adopted a moderate course.

In 1946 Ellen Wilkinson in the Labour Cabinet had raised the issue of transferring responsibility for higher education to her Ministry. University vice-chancellors were soon engaged in an intensive lobbying campaign to prevent the takeover by a Ministry which they believed was not competent to deal with universities. If they hoped that the issue had been settled, events in the 1950s brought the matter back to the surface. First of all, government poured more funds into the university sector, making the rather informal structure of the less expansionist era appear to be dated. The exclusion of the Ministry of Education from any involvement in the universities appeared more and more untenable as the evidence mounted that university growth depended on sixth form provision and the opportunities being created in the secondary system. The endless debates of the 1950s about the need for examinations again demonstrated the link between the secondary sector and the universities. Finally, if higher education was to be expanded through the transformation of certain technical colleges into colleges of advanced technology, this again raised the issue of jurisdiction.

THE DEPARTMENT OF EDUCATION AND SCIENCE
AND CHANGE

A new Department of Education and Science was created in 1964, responsible for all branches of education. If the Department of Education secured a higher profile in the 1960s this was the result of the dramatic expansion in expenditure. As the range of services provided by the local authorities widened, they depended for their funding on the central paymaster. In future it was unlikely that this would decrease, particularly as the local electorates were concerned with rising expenditure on rates.

There was a price to pay for this more generous funding, for the Department found itself forced to justify its claims for increased allocations from the Treasury, which insisted that the Department define its objectives and more clearly establish priorities and anticipate needs. This required changes in style, intelligence-gathering and awareness, and there were indications that the Department was moving in this direction. The Inspectorate, threatened by the range of local authority advisers, now began to look for new roles. Nevertheless, in the 1960s central government continued to proclaim its intention to work alongside its partners.

Nothing demonstrated the government's determination to work with its partners more than the initiatives undertaken in curriculum development in the early 1960s. Eccles had always been impatient about the time spent in the Ministry on resource allocation, teacher supply and building priorities. This did not mean that the Ministry had not its own views on the content of education. Over-specialization in the grammar schools, low status for technical studies and a lack of purpose and direction in the modern schools had caused much uneasiness within its ranks. Some of the remedies too, including wider provision of academic courses in modern schools and specially devised leaving certificates, had their shortcomings in the view of officials at the Ministry. At the beginning of 1960, some kind of action seemed necessary. Influential figures in the local authority world such as Sir William Alexander, reversing their previous position, put their weight behind the recommendations of the Beloe Committee (1960) for the proposed Certificate of Secondary Education for average secondary school pupils. Pressure from the Crowther and later the Newsom Report also fuelled the campaign to add an extra year to school life and this made the search for curriculum initiatives even more urgent. Finally, in spite of official disapproval of the stress on examinations, parents showed few signs of abandoning their demands for external examinations. The response of the Ministry was to set up a Curriculum Study Group in 1962, consisting mainly of Ministry officials and senior HMIs. Its main task was to demonstrate that examination needs should not dominate the curriculum, that broader based courses must take their place in the secondary school and that the curriculum should take more account of the needs of society.

News of its establishment without extensive consultation aroused opposition among teachers and local authorities. The exact intention of the Ministry still awaits the release of official records, but its effect was to act as a spur to curriculum development. Opposition from LEAs and teachers' unions to this initiative led to a recommendation in the Lockwood Report of 1964 that there should be new co-operative machinery in the curriculum field. A Schools Council, consisting of Ministry, LEA and teacher representatives, was to be established to supervise and encourage development in curriculum and examinations. The Schools Council, with its large committee structure, teacher majorities and the Department itself somewhat inadequately represented, looked a very different creation. The implementation of the new programmes suggested by the Schools Council and the teaching methods and materials required were not fully worked out. After setting an agenda, the Council found it difficult to secure its ends; as a result its proposals frequently ran into trouble with both conservative and radical educationists. Attempts to reform sixth form courses were denounced from one side because they destroyed standards, and from the other for their compromising nature. For its part the Department, after having generated action, did little to forward new developments. When they did not happen the senior officials, too, grew restless, and joined the rising tide of criticism.

In the official explanation of the explosion of educational activity throughout the 1960s much emphasis was placed on the rising population figures. A reading of the yearly reports issued by the Ministry in the early 1960s confirms the attention paid to numbers. Thus in 1963 the opening paragraphs reported:

> The year opened with 700,000 more on the registers of maintained primary and secondary schools than a decade earlier. To this increase both the higher birth rate and the desire of parents to keep their children longer at school had contributed – broadly in the ratio of 4 to 3. A new Malthus might see in this a tendency for the school population to expand to the very limit of the educational facilities available. (Ministry of Education Report, 1963, p. 1)

The pattern of the 1950s was repeated. As the rising school population moved through the system, shortcomings in that part of the structure became obvious. At the beginning of the new decade, attention became focused on the final years of secondary schooling, while two or three years later, with schools bulging with 18- or 19-year-olds anxious to continue their studies, the need for more higher education places came to the forefront. What made the problem of numbers even more acute in the early 1960s was that the government was now being forced to turn its attention to the primary sector of education.

If this sector received major attention there was a real fear that it might endanger progress in other sectors. From 1965, too, there was growing anxiety about the way in which primary schools had almost passed from notice. It was partly as a result of these concerns that the Plowden Commission was set up. *Black Paper* critics were ever vigilant against what they termed unthinking expansion, Sir Cyril Burt, for instance, arguing that 'It would surely be more realistic to press ahead with the reforms of the primary schools which, as the Plowden Report has demonstrated, are long overdue (a reduction in the size of classes, for example) than to embark on costly schemes of reorganization or expansion at the higher stages' (Burt, 1970, p.24).

These views were not lost on members of the Labour Cabinet. Crossman, a far from predictable politician on education, expressed his own misgivings about educational planning according to numbers. Barbara Castle recorded an intervention by him while cuts were under discussion: 'Tentatively but courageously he argued that postponement might do as much educational good as harm but agreed that it would be wrong to concentrate our education cuts on schools and that we ought to cut back the Universities, particularly on the postgraduate side' (Castle, 1984, 5 January 1968, p.351). Crossman himself recounted the Prime Minister's horror at a similar suggestion: 'Harold was also deeply shocked when I said we really should start cutting down the number of students admitted to universities and expanding other sorts of further education instead' (Crossman, 1982, Vol. 3, 28 November 1968, p.275). In coping with facilities to provide for rising numbers at this level, politicians justified their actions by stressing the returns to the nation in highly trained expertise and technical skills. It was a powerful argument that could quieten Treasury officials, or push education estimates ahead of other spending ministries. The price was that politicians wanted quick returns in the shape of a booming economy, industrial harmony and a more productive, capably led workforce. In the late 1960s none of these conditions was forthcoming as devaluation, deflation and industrial conflict haunted the Labour government's second term of office between 1966 and 1970. At the very height of these crises, the most expensive sector, higher education, began to experience a wave of student sit-ins. Although there was relief that the disturbances were less extensive than in parts of Europe or the USA, the government's reaction was a strong one. Edward Short denounced the troubles at LSE, and even the urbane Richard Crossman was bewildered by the antagonism of the student body. He recorded his own and younger Labour members' inability to come to terms with the student body, Paul Rose, a recruit in the 1960s telling him: 'There's an absolute barrier now between those who are over 28 ... and those who are under 28. We have no feeling or contact with these modern students at all' (Crossman, 1982, Vol. 3, 13 May 1968, p.61).

Outwardly politicians insisted that these disturbances made little impact on the priorities on education. However the closing years of the decade began the process of reconsideration. In 1970, the Conservatives replaced the much criticized and accommodating Edward Boyle with a new tougher figure, Margaret Thatcher, who insisted that the broad, general advances of recent years involving huge increases in expenditure should be replaced by measures with very specific targeting. She made clear the prime requirements for the educational system: 'The earning capacity of the nation depends on the highest level of achievement in the professions, in science and technology, industry and commerce. This is the wealth of the nation, coming from those who have the most talent' (*Hansard*, Vol. 790, Col. 596, 31 October 1969). It was a signal that the nurturing of talent, particularly scientific and technical skills, would be regarded as a major objective in the educational system. On the Labour side there was uneasiness as evidence mounted that more expansion in education, far from securing a more egalitarian society strengthened the prospects of those already in influential positions. The falling birth rate now became significant. There was no need for a decline in the birth rate to lead to extensive cutbacks within the service if the politicians and administrators remained convinced of its importance to the economy and society. Indeed throughout the 1950s and the early 1960s it had been widely argued that what the planners needed was a suspension of pressure in numbers so that they could bring down class size, use resources more adequately and enable the changes to be implemented more fully. Disillusion and falling numbers created a climate in which the Treasury was able to insist on more stringent economy, and other spending departments mounted campaigns for a change of priority in expenditure.

In assessing why certain changes arose in the 1960s, ministers of education were inclined to represent themselves as reflecting opinion in the education world. Sir Edward Boyle had discounted Cabinet, party political and parliamentary opinion in creating policy, and argued that the Ministry was rather distinctive from other departments of state in this matter. 'I would say, mostly, the starting point for educational questions was the educational world itself' (Kogan, 1971, p.90). This world had grown in the post-war period with university departments conducting research, a wider range of educational institutions involved in teacher training, and an expansion of education officers, advisers and architects within local authorities. Between them, they generated debate and a wider public interest. Ultimately the press, radio and the television documentary gave prominence to education, and throughout the 1960s new agencies such as the Campaign for the Advancement of State Education, founded in 1963, came into being as pressure groups and disseminators of information. It was asserted that parents, more affluent and leisured than ever before, would involve themselves in educational issues.

On the whole, the Ministry was reluctant to respond to this mounting pressure. The DES preferred to work through well-tried groups, such as the Nuffield Foundation or the Rowntree Trust, and relayed decisions rather than initiated debate. This was abundantly clear in policies regarding immigrant children and the encouragement of a dispersion policy drawn up in Circular 7/65. The Circular stated:

> It will be helpful if the parents of non-immigrant children can see that practical measures have been taken to deal with the problems in the schools, and that the progress of their own children is not being restricted by the undue preoccupation of the teaching staff with the linguistic and other difficulties of immigrant children. (Circular 7/65, 14 June 1965, p.5)

Thus immigrant children began to be 'bussed', often against parents' wishes. Schools were at the forefront of race relations in the 1960s. They were, after all, the first direct contact for many children with the host society. An initial, simplistic response was that by attending school with 'British' children these new groups would rapidly assimilate with the receiving community. There was little attempt to define this process, particularly in the period of change within British society. Accordingly in local authorities such as Ealing, in 1965, it led to the introduction of the bussing programme to prevent concentrations of immigrant children. It was also considered important that young children should be discouraged from using their native language, particularly in the classroom.

In the later 1960s this approach changed. Roy Jenkins at the Home Office argued that immigration controls needed to be accompanied by a more positive programme encouraging good community relations and eliminating the worst features of discrimination in jobs, housing and places of entertainment. Ever-increasing controls had not led to a diminution of tensions between white and black.

There were fears in the late 1960s that large sections of the young black population were joining the ranks of the alienated. Within the schools the black schoolchild's 'underachievement' received much attention. This led to a range of patchy, ill-coordinated and piece-meal initiatives. First of all there was an attempt made to raise the self-esteem of black pupils, who were felt to under-estimate their potentialities. Courses in Black Studies and World History became common in the attempt to build confidence. Second, there was aware-ness that any attempt to improve community relations involved all groups, white and black. Multi-cultural education emerged, stressing interdependence and the contribution to be made by all to the well-being of the local community. Frequently these programmes were introduced only in those areas where the immigrant population had settled. Some individual schools and LEAs were beginning to be aware that the real problem was often in the schools themselves. Here the black children were presented with textbooks and material that gave a most unfavourable image of their places of origin. Teachers were prone to display their prejudices, usually by low expectations. In the corridors, the playground and the classroom black children often suffered racial abuse or even physical bullying from their peer group. In the face of all this some schools initiated anti-racist policies in the curriculum and attempted to forestall signs of racist behaviour among pupils. On the other hand, there were those who argued that such policies might be counter-productive.

EDUCATION AND 'PERMISSIVENESS'

To the critics of the 1960s many of the changes called for in education were the results of a climate of permissiveness, which, it was claimed, became almost overwhelming in that decade. This had an effect on the schools and teachers. Teachers lost confidence in the task of trans-mitting the values held by society for centuries. The young, for their part, however, grew up with many difficulties as they moved towards adulthood. In the view of the *Black Paper* critics, much of the problem could be located in the primary school, influenced by 'progressive' thinking and encouraged by the Plowden Report, to practise child-centred education; the result was that in many areas habits of work and discipline were no longer inculcated. In the 1960s these ideas had spread to the secondary schools, where, aided by reorganization which destroyed the older schools, it was claimed, habits of learning and discipline were breaking down.

Evidence of this breakdown was seen in the student crisis of 1968, in which the most articulate sections of the population now appeared to have thrown off all restraint in the universities and the colleges. Brian Simon has indicated some of the fallacies of this kind of attack, since many of the students involved in college unrest at the end of the 1960s were the products, not of the freer atmosphere of that decade, but of the highly segregated, selected 1950s. The writers of the Plowden Report, certainly 'progressive' in outlook, and frequently criticized by leading figures in teacher training for their unqualified enthusiasm, clearly indicated that their own research, undertaken after 1965, demonstrated that the majority of primary schools had scarcely been touched by the revolution which had supposedly encompassed them. The schools were, in Plowden's estimation, upholders of traditional values in a society permeated by materialism, marital breakdown and commercial influences. In essence the schools were urged to take up a strong supervisory role to bolster up the family. Other remedies suggested five years earlier by the Newsom Report represented an even more traditional attitude, particularly the recommendations covering the 'natural interests' of the older girls where advice was given: 'But older girls can be brought to see that there is more to marriage than feeding the family and bathing the baby, and that they will themselves have a key role in establishing the standards of the home and in educating their children' (HMSO, 1963, p.137). There was little to suggest in official reports of the time that this was a decade in which pressures were mounting to use the education system to disturb the social order.

SUMMARY

Many of the issues raised in the 1960s such as the relationship between industry and schooling or the kind of curriculum needed for school resistant groups among the population have remained with us to the present. Other issues have come to the forefront as a result of the changes in that decade.

The prospect of expansion in colleges, student numbers and the educational world as a whole had caused uneasiness among cultural conservatives. In the early 1960s both major political parties felt it would be electorally unwise to hold back on growth. The Ministry of Education Report for 1962 began: 'When the year opened there were seven million children on the registers in maintained schools. By 1980 there may well be nearly two million more' (Ministry of Education Report, 1962, p. 1). A declining birth-rate and the rise in the number of pensioners all coincided with signs of economic stagnation and social strife which redefined the situation. The *Black Paper* publications were only part of the growth of many pressure groups attributing a sense of crisis in the later 1960s to a breakdown of authority in society. Teachers and local authorities were heavily blamed for encouraging an atmosphere of 'permissiveness' in the schools. What was now needed at the centre was for the Department of Education and Science, stiffened by other Ministries such as Labour, to reassert order and provide realistic supervision. At the local level a network of industrialists, ratepayers and parents needed to be given more power to break the hold of progressivism in education.

As the 1970s emerged the supporters of the 1960s changes appeared to find difficulty in mounting a spirited defence. Officials at the Department, most of the leading politicians in both parties and much of the educational world, had accepted the innovations in the decade as a much needed boost to a system showing signs of wear after 20 years of the Butler Act. More radical voices wanted these changes to be quickened in the next decade to ensure a more decisive weakening of the class structure. This meant much greater attention to the need for resources to be shifted to the educationally deprived, notably the inner city poor, women and the various ethnic groups. Disagreements of this kind enabled conservatives turned reformers to seize the initiative and force the pace, which they continued to do into the 1980s.

FURTHER READING

R. Rogers, *Crowther to Warnock*, 1980, contains summaries of the major official reports of the decade. Sir William Pile, *The Department of Education and Science*, 1979, reveals some of the 'official thinking'. M. Plaskow (ed.), *Life and Death of the Schools Council*, 1985, adds valuable information to curriculum development in this decade. D. Lawton, *The Politics of the School Curriculum*, 1980, has become the major work in this field. M. Kogan, *The Politics of Education*, 1971, searches out the thinking of two leading ministers of the decade, Sir Edward Boyle and Anthony Crosland. There is the biography, S. Crosland, *Tony Crosland*, 1982. E. Fearn and B. Simon (ed.), *Education in the 1960s*, 1980, is a pioneering collection. A most stimulating and controversial interpretation of the whole decade is contained in the Centre for Contemporary Cultural Studies, *Unpopular Education*, 1981.

CHAPTER SEVEN

The Politics of Intervention: The 1970s and 1980s

THE ECONOMY AND POLITICS, 1970–76

Although, as will be seen, the 1970s proved to be a decade which signalled great changes with lasting significance for the future of education, the early years of the decade showed little sign of what was to follow. The White Paper, *A Framework for Expansion*, issued in 1972, was optimistic in tone. It began: 'The last ten years have seen a major expansion of the education service. The next ten will see expansion continue – as it must if education is to make its full contribution to the vitality of our society and our economy.' It also described the pressures of the 1960s, where educational expenditure was determined by demographic factors which would be less intense in the 1970s. New choices therefore would be available in a number of aspects of education which required close attention: nursery education, school building and staffing, teacher training and higher education.

During the first two years of the new Conservative government, 1970–2, the Secretary of State for Education, Margaret Thatcher, had been reviewing the objectives and priorities in the education service. She remained in that office throughout the four years of the Heath ministry, a sharp contrast in continuity with her seven predecessors who had occupied the post in the previous decade. Optimism in planning looked ahead to 1981, with nursery provision closely following the Plowden recommendations, a school building programme to replace unsatisfactory premises, and an increased teaching force was promised. Places in higher education, then standing at 463,000, would expand to 750,000 by the target date. Teacher-training colleges would diversify or combine with other institutions and the James Committee's recommendations on teachers' in-service training were especially welcomed. Universities, included in an overall education plan for the first time, were to continue to grow. The number of university students would rise from 236,000 in 1971–72 to 375,000 by 1981.

Shortly after the publication of the White Paper, the 1973 oil crisis and the world-wide economic recession demonstrated the need for a reappraisal of these plans. Economy on education expenditure could also be justified because of a declining birth rate in Britain. Politically, too, the picture had changed. In January 1974, the Heath government, weakened by the three-day working week and the threat of an all-out miners' strike, went to the country. The following month, a Labour ministry under Harold Wilson was returned without an overall majority, necessitating a second general election later in that same year.

The disillusionment with many aspects of the education system which had begun in the 1960s now took a more positive form. Given the somewhat tentative approach to reform displayed by the Labour governments between 1974 and 1979, the initiative passed into the hands of right-wing critics. Harold Silver (1980, p. 33 ff.) has shown how, for instance, the concept of equal opportunity was attacked in the 1970s by writers of the *Black Papers* who challenged the meaning of the phrase, and those on the left, such as A.H. Halsey, who in 1975 considered that positive discrimination, as attempted through the Educational Priority Areas, had failed: 'the majority of disadvantaged children are not in disadvantaged areas, and the majority of children in disadvantaged areas are not disadvantaged.'

Contributors to the *Black Papers* also raised the issue of standards in schools. They emphasized that the task for teachers was to concentrate on teaching rather than to act as social workers. More formal teaching methods were advocated and the need to select clever working-class children in order to realize their academic potential was stressed. Evidence provided by an NFER study of standards of reading comprehension in 1972 indicated that standards had declined since 1964. Within a month of the study's publication, Margaret Thatcher had set up an inquiry into standards of literacy chaired by Alan Bullock, then Master of St. Catherine's College, Oxford. This report, *A Language for Life*, published in 1975, whilst finding that overall reading standards had not fallen, admitted that the poorer readers were to be found mainly in the lower socio-economic groups. Bullock recommended a 'language across the curriculum' policy for all teachers and a national system of monitoring of achievement in reading and writing. A national centre for language in education and a working party on capitation allowances and resources would help to improve the situation.

The Report was issued when Labour was once again in office.

The new Secretary of State, Reg Prentice (March 1974–June 1975), announced the ending of direct grant schools, but did not implement the main recommendations of the Bullock Report. As one writer has remarked, the new government seemed to be generating few new ideas but rather concentrated on completing the unfinished business of the 1964–70 government (Judge, 1984, p.164). Whereas the Conservatives in opposition were challenging many long-held beliefs about education, there was little urgency within the Wilson Labour government in initiating a debate. Harold Wilson's own substantial account of this period, *Final Term. The Labour Government 1974–1976*, makes passing reference only to the 1976 Education Act which dealt with the abolition of selection for secondary schools (1979, p.189). In February of that year, Prentice's successor, Fred Mulley (June 1975–September 1976), was present at the Cabinet which dealt with the White Paper on Public Expenditure. In contrast with Barbara Castle, Minister of Health and Social Security, who successfully defended her department's proposed spending initiatives at a Cabinet meeting, Mulley, according to her, goaded by the summary at the end of his section which showed a list of nothing but reductions, protested against the draft. ' "You are just handing our critics their speeches in the House, ready written," he moaned' (Castle, 1980, p.641).

THE 'GREAT DEBATE', 1976

If it seemed likely that education was not a high priority on the government's agenda, events conspired to give it great prominence. There was already lively public concern on educational issues and the previous consensus between the political parties no longer existed. James Callaghan, who succeeded Harold Wilson as Prime Minister in April 1976, was determined not to be seen as a stop-gap Premier until the next general election. In May 1976 he sketched a programme 'Objectives for 1980' which looked to resolving the worst aspects of the existing economic crisis and carrying out reforms in the fields of health and welfare, housing and education.

As one of the two Prime Ministers this century who had not attended a university, Callaghan wrote in his memoirs, 'I have always been a convinced believer in the importance of education, as throughout my life I have seen how many doors it could unlock for working-class children who had begun with few other advantages, and I regretted my own lack of a university education' (Callaghan, 1987, p.409). There are slightly different versions now in print of how the so-called 'Great Debate' of 1976 originated. According to Callaghan, on 21 May, only a few weeks after taking office, he summoned Fred Mulley to investigate four areas of concern which had arisen from his (Callaghan's) visits to schools: basic teaching and the three Rs, the curriculum for older pupils in comprehensive schools, especially mathematics and science, the validity of the examination system and further education for 16- to 19-year-olds (ibid., p.409). It was as a result of this interview that the 'Yellow Book' was compiled within the DES (see below). Another version of events has been given by Bernard Donoughue, Senior Policy Adviser to both Wilson and Callaghan and Head of the Downing Street Policy Unit. Donoughue claims that during Easter 1976 he drafted a paper suggesting to Callaghan that 'it would be no bad thing if he were to identify a few areas of policy of genuine interest to himself where he could try to make an impact, and I put forward education as a leading candidate' (Donoughue, 1987, p.111).

Accordingly, the Policy Unit drafted the speech which Callaghan delivered at Ruskin College, Oxford in October 1976. It called for a debate on educational trends and set an agenda which was to be taken up thereafter with greater eagerness by politicians of all parties, not least subsequent Conservative governments. Callaghan favoured 'a basic curriculum with universal standards'. He saw the goal of education as equipping 'children to the best of their ability for a lively constructive place in society and also to fit them to do a job of work'. Questions needed to be asked on why industry was held in such low esteem by pupils and graduates from higher education, and answers provided to industry on why school-leavers appeared to be inadequately equipped to enter work. Teachers needed to explain their activities more clearly to parents, who in turn were entitled to be more closely associated with the running of schools. A series of regional conferences was held in Spring 1977 with an agenda addressed to the areas outlined in the Ruskin College speech. The DES produced a draft green paper summarizing the discussions. Both Callaghan and Donoughue considered the Green Paper to be too bland and Shirley Williams, who had succeeded Fred Mulley in 1976 after a ministerial reshuffle, personally undertook a redrafting which livened up the document published under the title *Education in Schools: A Consultative Document* in July 1977.

So far, the political initiatives have been highlighted. But the role of the DES, though receiving much less publicity at the time, was increasingly important from 1970 in influencing the formulation of policy. Even before this, as was explained in Chapter 6, the Ministry of Education had, under David Eccles, attempted to establish a unit within the Department, the Curriculum Study Group, which, together with outside representatives, would have initiated reforms in school curriculum and examinations. This move was thwarted, but the economic and political climate of the 1970s was more conducive to the DES taking a lead, especially in the curriculum field where there was broad agreement that changes were necessary.

The power of senior civil servants to formulate policy under a cloak of secrecy was noted by the Organization for Economic Co-operation and Development in their 1976 Report which reviewed the work of the DES. Whilst praising the integrity of the civil servants who operate on a non-political basis, it warned:

> A permanent officialdom possessing such external protections and internal disciplines becomes a power in its own right. A British Department composed of professional civil servants who have watched the Ministers come and go is an entity that only an extremely foolish or powerful politician will persistently challenge or ignore.

The veil of secrecy behind which the DES operates was also commented upon by the House of Commons Expenditure Committee in the same year. Its suggestion of a permanent standing commission with representatives from a spectrum of interests to make recommendations on educational planning was coldly received by the Department (Lawton, 1980, p.37).

Even before these two Reports, the DES had been preparing the way for new moves. In August 1974, the Assessment of Performance Unit (APU), financed by the DES and led by an HMI, was established. Originally intended as a means of assessing the special needs of the disadvantaged, it developed into a vehicle for assessing and monitoring the achievement of school children on a national scale. Initial fears expressed, particularly by teachers, that the testing in a number of subjects would be used for political purposes, proved unfounded. Some of the dangers of using test results to support or refute ideologies were well set out in an APU publication *Occasional Paper 3 Standards of Performance – Expectations and Reality* (1981, pp.19–20).

A more direct intervention in policy-making resulted from Callaghan's request to Mulley in April 1976, mentioned earlier, to produce a DES briefing document, now known as The Yellow Book, in preparation for the Ruskin College speech. The exact authorship of the document has now been established: it was clearly from the hands of officials and possibly HMI. The Yellow Book was critical of child-centred approaches to teaching and of the secondary school curriculum; its contents were leaked to the Press shortly before the Prime Minister's Oxford speech.

In the remaining years of the Labour ministry, little direct intervention in curriculum matters was attempted by the DES. Circular 14/77 was issued in order to obtain information from LEAs about their policies and practices in curriculum arrangements. HMI were also active in producing documents on the curriculum and carrying out national surveys of primary schools (1978) and secondary schools (1979). The three years following the Ruskin College speech marked the ending of a period of debate on and diagnosis of the ills of the education system. Firmer and more direct action was soon to follow.

THE MOVE TO CENTRALISM, 1979 ONWARDS

Salter and Tapper in their book *Education, Politics and the State*, published in 1981, surmised that the DES had succeeded in giving the Great Debate the status of an ideological form where certain battles about the condition and future of education should be fought out (p.219). This view, whilst in essence correct, does not give sufficient regard to the shift in political philosophy which followed the return to office of the Conservatives in 1979. There was now a determination to reshape education in accordance with the political will. Some instances can be seen in the boosting of the independent sector by the Assisted Places Scheme, the dismantling of the Schools Council, the revival of the selective principle and the hard line taken on teachers' pay and conditions of service. It has recently been pointed out that in the last 20 years there has been a spate of intellectualizing about Conservative philosophy as the occupational composition of the party has changed in Parliament. The value of education has figured prominently, as the reports emanating from such bodies as the Hillgate Group and the Centre for Policy Studies indicate. Significantly, Sir Keith Joseph, later to be Secretary of State for Education, attacked the notion of equality in education in a book published in 1979, the year the Conservatives took office. He was also a strong advocate of reducing the participation of the State and restraining public expenditure (Sanderson, 1987, p.105).

Nevertheless, it can be argued that there is a tendency amongst analysts of educational change during the period covered by this chapter to ignore the fact that some of the policies pursued by the Conservatives in the 1980s had their origins in the period when Labour was in office in the 1970s. A good example of this would be the attitudes of governments to teachers during the last two decades. Donoughue

97

mentions that the three Labour Ministers of Education (1974–79) were increasingly concerned that educational policy was being conducted by LEAs and the teachers' unions, 'with the Department of Education, as Harold Wilson once commented to me, being little more than a post-box between the two.' Donoughue claims that 'in all my dealings with the NUT at that time I never once heard mention of education or children. The union's prime objective appeared to be to secure ever decreasing responsibilities and hours of work for its members' (ibid, p. 110). Besides the criticism made of teachers by the 1976 Committee on Expenditure, the William Tyndale School affair raised questions on the potential conflicts between teachers' views on children and those of parents and the LEA (Kogan, 1978, p. 125). At the 1977 NUT Annual Conference, the priority motion made plain the Union's determination to exercise control over the curriculum. Shirley Williams' move to reduce teacher power on the Schools Council in the same year was one indication of the concern which had been generated.

The 'consumerism' movement, participation in community affairs and demands for value for money and accountability, gathered pace in education during the 1970s and became one of the main planks of Conservative policy in the 1980s. Education institutions, it was argued, should become more open and the quality of teaching and learning be made more widely known. One manifestation of this openness has been the publication since January 1983 of HMI reports on schools and colleges. In 1977, the Taylor Report, *A New Partnership in our Schools*, emphasized the need to investigate the best way in which a governing body of a school could reflect its special character and at the same time improve the school's relationship with parents and the public. This, the Report stated, could be achieved by creating individual governing bodies for each school, consisting of equal representatives of LEAs, staff, parents and the community. Such a proposal roused the opposition of teachers and LEAs, and the 1980 Education Act did not settle the issue, merely requiring schools to have two parents as governors.

During the two years in office of Mark Carlisle as Secretary of State for Education (1979–81) and particularly during Sir Keith Joseph's long tenure of this office (1981–86), the right of parents to be fully represented on governing bodies was encouraged by publications such as the Green Paper *Parental Influence at School*, issued in May 1984, which promised legislation on the subject. The 1986 Act, following closely the Taylor recommendations, set out a national framework for school government. LEAs no longer enjoy a majority and parents had a right to see all curriculum documents: no school employee could be chairman. Powers included sharing responsibility for the curriculum with LEAs and headteachers, and parents taking part in making decisions on the school's budget. Even greater powers are contained in the 1988 Education Act which allows governors to be responsible for financial management and to initiate moves to 'opt out' of maintained status.

An acceleration in a centralist approach to the school curriculum, which is described in Chapter 18, also had its beginnings during a Labour government. DES Circular 14/77 requested details of LEA arrangements on the school curriculum. Four years later, following the government document *The School Curriculum*, Circular 6/81 asked LEAs to review their own policies in the light of it. The failure of the DES to publish LEA responses to the Circular raised suspicions that government policy was being formulated without regard to LEA practices (Stubbs, 1986, p.52). With the Conservatives' bid for office for a third successive term, the 1987 party election manifesto, *The Next Move Forward*, included the intention to introduce a national core curriculum. This promise was followed up and enshrined in the 1988 Education Act, which was piloted through Parliament by Sir Keith Joseph's successor, Kenneth Baker. A National Curriculum Council has been established to ensure that elements of the statutory national curriculum fit together into a coherent whole.

The decline in the role of LEAs has been a notable feature in this period. It was argued in the Redcliffe-Maud Commission on Local Government (1969) that larger LEAs would result in more efficiency and improve the quality of service offered. This recommendation was accepted and in 1974 the number of LEAs was reduced from 146 to 104. The new LEAs, coming into being at a time when the economic crisis was at its height, were faced with a number of difficulties. Many of the new authorities adopted the concept of corporate management, which tended to weaken the position of Chief Education Officers and local education committees. Exhortations by politicians for LEAs to expand their work in the newer fields of special needs, minority and ethnic education, equal opportunities and health education were not matched by the provision of funds to carry out these activities. The Annual Surveys on LEA expenditure published by HMI since 1981 have shown that low spending by authorities results in inadequate provision of teaching services. In 1984, HMI were under pressure from Conservative politicians to moderate or suppress such evidence (Lawton and Gordon, 1987, p.20). The 'Morton's Fork' effect was brought into play when in 1983 the government sought to limit expenditure on education within authorities by the process known as rate-capping.

The 1980s have seen the diminishing of the position of LEAs in the education system as a result of governmental pressures. We have already outlined the outcomes subsequent to the Taylor Report which gave LEAs a smaller role in the governance of schools. There is also the conjecture that the DES was not able to secure sufficient funds to finance LEA expenditure: as a result, additional sums for training, because of growing unemployment, were allocated to the Manpower Services Commission (MSC) through the Department of Employment rather than to LEAs through the DES (Stewart, 1986, p. 183). A recent example of the competition for funds was the £3 billion programme of urban regeneration announced by the government in March 1988 in a document called *Action for Cities*. It promoted a scheme by which inner-city employers guaranteed jobs to school leavers who had met targets of behaviour and achievement. Local groups of employers, schools and colleges and LEAs would bid for support to develop the proposal. The initiative, stemming from the Department of Employment, sought 'the full co-operation of the Department of Education and Science and the Department of Trade and Industry' (*The Times*, 8 March 1988, p. 5).

This duality of provision represents another feature of the educational situation of these decades, the emphasis on the relationship between school, college and work. From the time of the Great Debate, prominence was given to three deficiencies: the shortage of a skilled and flexible workforce; the alleged low attainment of pupils entering industry; and the paucity of students sufficiently well qualified in science and mathematics. The Conservative ministries of the 1980s seized the opportunity to introduce the work ethic into the curriculum, at the same time shifting the target group to include 14- to 19-year olds. The Department of Employment's document, *A New Training Initiative*, issued in 1981, stated the need for pupils and teachers to gain a closer understanding of industrial, commercial and economic aspects of society: this could be achieved through remodelling of the school curriculum. The Youth Training Scheme (YTS), for unemployed 16-year-olds, initiated in 1983, was designed to put this philosophy into action. As a response, the DES launched the Certificate of Pre-Vocational Education (CPVE), whilst the Technical and Vocational Initiative (TVEI), for preparing pupils for the world of work, was piloted in a limited number of LEAs; by 1986 it was operating in 73 authorities. How far the development of two competing systems of financing and administration is justifiable and whether the conflicting philosophies embodied in their curricula can be reconciled are still a matter for debate.

Given the many changes in education brought about by government policy, DES Circulars and legislation, LEAs have become involved in a keener scrutiny of administrative performance. Examples are the Tameside High Court case of 1977 where the Secretary of State challenged an LEA which proposed to retain selective schools, the rights given to individuals for the redress of grievances, such as the Local Government Act 1974 (Local Ombudsman), the Sex Discrimination Act, 1975, the Race Relations Act, 1976 and admission appeals which were set out in the 1980 Education Act (Fenwick, 1985, p.144).

Other developments which indicate the diminution in the future role to be played by LEAs are the dismantling of the Inner London Education Authority, the largest LEA in the United Kingdom, on the grounds of its political stance, and the growing number of Chief Education Officers who are being relieved of their posts (*Education*, 11 March 1988, p.200). The setting up of city technology colleges, a new breed of secondary schools with a strongly vocational bias, was announced by Kenneth Baker at the Conservative Party Conference in 1986. These are independent of LEA control with sponsorship from industry and provide an alternative pattern to existing schools. More fundamentally, as already noted, the 1988 Education Act struck at LEAs by allowing governors of schools, in consultation with parents, to opt out of LEA control. The plans to bring about greater central control of education and the encouragement at the same time of the privatizing of the service presents a paradox (Chitty, 1987, p.23).

Higher education underwent a similar transformation during this period, though the full and complicated story is traced in Chapter 16. Consisting in the main of three areas, the universities, polytechnics and colleges of education, each of these institutions was reshaped by political and administrative actions, some deliberate and some fortuitous.

The colleges of education, formerly training colleges for teachers, had been much praised by the Robbins Report and looked to full integration into the higher education system. It seemed as if the James Report in 1972 would fulfil at least some of these expectations. Such expansion did not take account of LEAs, one of the traditional providers, many of whom in discussion with the DES rejected the colleges' aspirations to be more closely linked with universities. The DES, whose officials, together with HMI, drew up plans for reorganization, were often equally unsympathetic. Lionel Elvin, then Director of the University of London Institute of Education, recounts the reception given to a small delegation to the DES on a suggested exchange of ideas about reorganization plans. 'There was no exchange. We put forward our ideas. They did not come forward with theirs except in so far as they are already known. We were received with courtesy but with something very near disdain' (Elvin, 1987, p. 188). In the end, there were no fewer than ten different patterns of teacher-training reorganization, with monotechnic institutions being the least favoured and with the majority firmly in the public sector. The large expansion of colleges of education in the post-war years was the main cause of their vulnerability from the time of the falling birth rate in 1964. Three successive Labour Secretaries of State made cuts in the non-university sector of teacher education. Reg Prentice in 1975 announced a reduction to 60,000 places and the loss of 30 colleges. A year later Fred Mulley limited the 1977 entry because of the likelihood of the oversupply of teachers. Shortly after this, Shirley Williams stated that a further contraction to 45,000 by 1981 was necessary (Gosden, 1983, pp. 117–18).

One of the achievements of the 1964–70 Labour government was the establishment by Tony Crosland of some 30 polytechnics to provide vocationally-orientated courses not fully provided by universities. Courses were validated by the Council for National Academic Awards (CNAA); by 1982, there were 150,000 students taking CNAA degrees in institutions outside the university. The creation of the binary system was to be the source of conflict between polytechnics and universities throughout our period.

The advent to office of the Conservatives in 1970 coincided with the arrival of a new Permanent Secretary to the Department, William Pile, who, unlike his two predecessors, had spent most of his career within the Education Department. Pile sympathized with the universities in their desire to retain their autonomy. The student troubles at universities, starting from 1968, did grave damage to the public image of these institutions and remained long in the memory of politicians. Max Beloff, in *Black Paper 3* published in 1975, headed his article 'Can the Universities Survive?' Student intake to polytechnics, as was noted, was increasing at an impressive rate and the 1972 White Paper announced a massive increase for polytechnics to 335,000 by 1981, a three-fold increase in ten years. The economic crisis, resulting in cuts in public expenditure from 1974–5, led to a large reduction in university income. This policy was maintained with the new Labour administration, who also took into account public opinion which remained unsympathetic to universities. The quinquennium target number of 306,000 full time students was reduced by the University Grants Committee (UGC) by some 8 to 11 per cent, an unprecedented action (Carswell, 1985, p. 147). Economies in staffing, building and equipment followed; morale was not helped by the terms of the Report of the Houghton Committee of Inquiry into the Pay of Non-University Teachers (1974) which led to increases of between 20 and 25 per cent. In 1976, after an intervention from Downing Street, Pile was replaced as Permanent Secretary by James Hamilton, who had a background in science and engineering (Donoughue, op. cit., p. 154). Disillusionment with higher education by school-leavers who, like others, were now questioning the value of a degree, made further financial cuts easier.

Politically, neither Labour nor the Conservatives had shown any determination to tackle the policy issues involved in dealing with higher education. An interesting attempt to explore various alternative strategies was contained in a discussion document, *Higher Education in the 1990s*, produced by Gordon Oakes, the Labour higher education minister, in 1978, though begun earlier under Fred Mulley. Whilst endorsing the 'Robbins Principle', it set out five models for dealing with future increased demand for higher education in relation to demographic trends. It also suggested that student demand would stagnate, a forecast which was admitted later by the DES to be incorrect (Scott, 1984, p. 215). Participation in higher education was 2 per cent higher in 1982 than ten years previously. Within a year, in May 1979, the Conservatives were once more in office. Rhodes Boyson, junior minister for higher education under Mark Carlisle, favoured cuts in university funding (Kogan and Kogan, 1983, p. 33). Two important decisions soon followed: the imposition of a policy of level funding on universities which was then abandoned at the end of the 1980s, and an increase in the fees of overseas students to the full economic costs of their courses. The resultant loss of income was dramatic and made future planning for institutions difficult. These policies were put into action by a new team of ministers, Sir Keith Joseph and William Waldegrave.

The task of dealing with the effects of governmental decisions fell on the UGC. It decided, in July 1981, as a means of saving money, to make selective cuts in departments and in student numbers. This was followed by a university by university scrutiny. Science and technology were to be retained at the existing levels and the arts and social studies were to be reduced. Although the UGC defended its policy, the effect on universities was strongly felt. The financial cuts, amounting to 17 per cent between 1981 and 1988, fell unevenly, and led to the restriction of student admissions and to staff redundancies.

In the public sector, control of expenditure was resolved by the setting up of a National Advisory Body (NAB) in December 1981 to scrutinize academic courses and give approval to them. It was to be chaired by the higher education minister. Reductions in expenditure of 10 per cent by 1983–84 were made, but with the restriction of numbers by universities, students flooded into the polytechnics. Some criticisms of this policy are self-evident. The cuts between the two sectors were not adequately co-ordinated: good courses were closed in one sector whilst poor ones were retained in the other. The government also operated the policies with two different sets of financial machinery (Kogan and Kogan, 1983, p. 131).

Self-examination of institutions followed Sir Keith Joseph's concern with the maintenance and improvement of standards. This led to the setting up of two committees: in September 1983, one for universities (Reynolds) and in April 1984 (Lindop) for public sector institutions. Both reported in March 1985. Two months earlier another committee, on university efficiency (Jarratt), made hard-hitting criticisms and urged action to be taken. It is, incidentally, worth noting that since the Plowden investigation into primary schools (1963–67), all governments have bypassed the Central Advisory Councils as a means of seeking independent advice. The DES claims to have sufficient resources to mount public surveys and provide rapid detailed research and evidence, thus making the deliberations of the more formal bodies less necessary (Rogers, 1980, p. 280).

The continuing financial pressure on higher education during the 1980s was the main, but not the only, important feature of the decade. With the third successive Conservative general election victory in 1987 and a new Secretary of State for Education, Kenneth Baker, in office, radical reforms were undertaken. The UGC and NAB were swept away and replaced by a Universities Funding Council and a Polytechnics and Colleges Funding Council respectively. On both of these new Councils, representation includes members from the industrial, commercial and financial institutions. Polytechnics lost their local affiliations and the division of universities into three classes, according to function, was proposed.

The first attempt to provide a legal definition of further education was made in the 1988 Education Act in order to describe LEAs' role in post-school provision. Whereas the Act encouraged a diversity of provision for schools, higher education operated within a more centralist framework. Much heated debate surrounded the issue of security of tenure and the government made concessions after a defeat on the Education Bill during its passage in the House of Lords. One novel feature of the Act was the appointment by the Secretary of State of four Commissioners who were charged with the task of ensuring that university charters contained provision for allowing staff to be made redundant or dismissed for good cause. It is clear that the 1988 Education Act provided for the greatest restructuring of education since the 1944 Act.

SUMMARY

Perhaps one of the main characteristics of the 1970s and 1980s has been the increased interest by the major political parties in effecting education change. The early optimism for growth expressed in the 1972 White Paper *A Framework for Expansion* was replaced by a closer scrutiny of value for money as the economic crisis deepened in the following years. The nature of education debate, initiated in the late 1960s by the Conservatives through the *Black Papers* on such questions as standards and accountability, became more pointed as Conservative and Labour leaders put forward very different policies for improving the education system. The so-called Great Debate of 1976 can now be seen as a much milder forerunner of policies put forward by the Conservatives during their long spells of office during this period.

Another feature has been the major part played by the DES in educational policy-making. Although this development was criticized by bodies such as the OECD and a Parliamentary Select Committee, the powers of civil servants have continued to increase. The 1988 Education Act is a good example of this.

The balance between central and local government has also changed considerably during these two decades. With the implementation of the 1974 Local Government Act, the number of LEAs was reduced; stringent economies in local government finance have made for difficulties in running the service. The dismantling of the ILEA in 1990 demonstrated the strong link between the political will and future LEA organization. The 'opting out' provisions of the 1988 Education Act also illustrate this point.

In the higher education sector, there were many fluctuations of policy which made for difficulties in planning by institutions. The binary system, though modified, remained basically intact throughout the period. However, greater interference with the financial and planning aspects of both universities and polytechnics is likely to grow in the 1990s.

FURTHER READING

Politicians' memoirs provide some insights into the sources of recent educational change; see B. Castle, *The Castle Diaries 1974–76*, 1980, J. Callaghan, *Time and Change*, 1987, and B. Donoughue, *Prime Minister. The Conduct of Policy under Harold Wilson and James Callaghan*, 1987.

There are several official publications which should be consulted, such as *The Development of Higher Education in the 1990s*, 1985. *The Times Higher Education Supplement* contains a full Review of the Year section each December. The Open University Course E333, entitled 'Policy-making in education', deals with many aspects touched on in this chapter. See also the course book, I. McNay and J. Ozga (eds.), *Policy-making in Education: the Breakdown of Consensus: A Reader*, 1985.

Civil servants rarely set down the events in which they played an active part. An exception is J. Carswell, *Government and the Universities in Britain*, 1985.

Many books have been written on educational policy during this period. They include M. Kogan, *The Politics of Educational Change*, 1978, H. Silver, *Education and the Social Condition*, 1980, B. Salter and T. Tapper, *Education, Politics and the State*, 1981, S. Ranson and J. Tomlinson (eds.), *The Changing Government of Education*, 1986, and M. Sanderson, *Educational Opportunity and Social Change in England*, 1987.

PART TWO

Education and Society

CHAPTER EIGHT

Education and Social Structure

This chapter introduces some of the main elements which affect the relationship between education and social structure. Population, social class, social mobility, and employment are used as organizing themes, but the topic is a vast one, and some issues are of such importance as to be treated in separate chapters within this section.

POPULATION

In 1801 the population of England and Wales stood at just under 9 million. That figure had doubled by 1851 and doubled again by 1911. Throughout that period the rate of increase as revealed by decennial censuses was never less than 10 per cent per decade. After 1911 the rate of population growth slowed dramatically, initially as a result of the dislocation and death toll caused by the First World War. The twentieth century also witnessed a reduction in the birth-rate. In 1900 there were some 927,000 births in England and Wales. Although in 1920, in the aftermath of war, the figure peaked at 958,000, thereafter it fell steadily and in 1933 was a mere 580,000.

In 1921 the population of England and Wales was just under 38 million. It increased by just over 2 million in the next decade, and by a further 2.3 million in the next 20 years (there being no census taken in 1941). In 1961 it stood at just over 46 million. There was a further bulge in the early 1960s, and in 1964, for example, there were 30 per cent more live births than there had been in 1955. The 1971 Census showed, moreover, that nearly 3 million British residents had been born outside the United Kingdom, including just over $1\frac{1}{4}$ million in Commonwealth countries. But the restriction of immigration from 1962, and the downward trend in the birth-rate which began in 1965, slowed the advance. By 1981 the population of England and Wales had struggled to 49 million, a mere half a per cent increase over the 1971 figure. By the 1970s and 1980s the birth-rate in England, in common with that of most Western European countries, had fallen below the replacement level. Unless other factors – reduction in infant mortality, increased longevity, immigration – occur to any significant extent, the replace-ment level of the population depends essentially upon the total fertility rate (TFR). This may be simply calculated as the number of live births recorded to each woman. Replacement naturally requires a total fertility rate of just over two live births per woman. In 1983 the TFR was below 1.8.

In the twentieth century, as in the nineteenth, the effects of popu-lation growth, and decline, upon educational provision were signifi-cantly compounded by emigration, immigration, internal migration and age distribution. Even during periods of slowed population growth some areas of the country experienced massive increases. For example, in 1911 Dagenham in Essex had a population of some 8,000. By 1931 that figure had mushroomed to 89,362. In the last 20 years population in many inner city areas and areas of high unemployment has tended to decline, whereas large increases have occurred in the Home Counties around London. New towns and housing estates, moreover, which originally attracted high proportions of younger couples and thus of children, may, 30 years on, become the habitat of the middle-aged and elderly. Both at the micro and the macro levels, population history is characterized by such wave effects. Even against the background of an overall decline in population it seems likely that the bulge of the early 1960s will be reflected in a bulge in the late 1980s and early 1990s. This factor has led to predictions that there may be half a million more children in primary schools in 1998 than there were in 1986 (Sanderson, 1987, p.17).

The rapid population increase of the nineteenth and early twentieth centuries contributed strongly to the problem of educational and school supply. The building of schools (and churches) was a major activity, and many of these constructions, for example the great three decker edifices of the school board period, have been in commission until the present day. Some indeed appear to be in better shape than the flat-roofed, system-built schools of the 1950s and 1960s.

In 1851 about a quarter of the inhabitants of England and Wales were under ten years old. A century later that fraction had declined to less than a sixth. Although in modern times there has as yet been no absolute decline in the overall population, there have been periods of significant decline in the numbers of the school population. For example the numbers of pupils in elementary schools in England and Wales rose from 5.2 million in 1920 to 5.6 million in 1930, but had declined to 5.1 million by 1938. Much greater falls have been recorded in recent years. Thus whereas in January 1979 there were 8,900,386 pupils in full-time attendance in schools, by January 1984 that figure had slumped to 7,848,752. Pupil numbers also affect the recruitment of teachers. Whereas the inter-war years saw a relatively constant number of elementary school teachers, with class sizes increasing in the 1920s and diminishing in the 1930s, in the early 1980s teacher numbers declined. In January 1979 there were 470.6 thousand full-time equivalent teachers employed in maintained nursery, primary and secondary schools in England and Wales, by January 1984 there were only 438.7 thousand.

SOCIAL CLASS

Social class has been an important factor in modern English history, and may be related here to the issues of population and education. In the nineteenth century, as child mortality decreased, it was the middle classes rather than the working classes who first adapted to such decrease by limiting the size of their families. In the twentieth century, whilst all social classes have adopted the smaller family size, there is some evidence from the period 1973 to 1983 that legitimate births in the professional and managerial classes actually increased, whilst the over-all birth rate and that of semi-skilled and unskilled workers declined (Halsey, 1986, p. 105). Whether such differences will continue, or whether, as in the nineteenth century, new trends in family size set by the middle classes will become the norm for the population as a whole, is not yet clear.

The relationship between social class and school provision is one of the most noted features of English education. In the nineteenth century public schools were essentially for the sons of the upper and middle classes, and were engaged in a status confirming and conferring exercise. Grammar schools, which in the first half of the nineteenth century had often provided some elementary schooling, divested themselves of this work, and of these pupils, as the century progressed. In the last 30 years of the century some of the grammar school endowments were used to provide secondary schooling for girls. The majority of children, however, attended elementary schools, some provided by private schoolteachers, some provided by the societies of the various Christian groups, and others, from 1870, supplied by the school boards. Children who attended such elementary schools did not normally expect to progress to the grammar schools and certainly not to the public schools. Indeed even in 1895, of every 1,000 children who attended an elementary school, only four or five proceeded to a grammar school.

Within these three broad bands of schooling, however, there were significant gradations. Eton remained the predominant public school

111

and was one of only nine 'great' schools examined by the Clarendon Commission in the 1860s. The Taunton Commission which reported in the same decade designated three levels of secondary schools. These would be graded according to the social background and aspirations of parents, and would cater for pupils wishing to stay at school until 18, 16 and 14 years respectively. In the 1880s Charles Booth even divided the elementary schools of the London School Board into six 'Classes', with Class VI schools attracting large numbers of pupils from the lower middle classes. Fleet Road Board School, Hampstead became famous as 'the Eton for a penny a week'. The success of its pupils in winning scholarships to secondary schools made it as popular and oversubscribed as those twentieth-century primary schools whose pupils regularly sailed through the eleven plus examination.

Booth and his researchers tended to use income as the means of measuring economic and social status. From 1911, however, the Registrar General has divided the population into social classes based on occupational groups. Class I was taken to include professional and similar occupations – doctors, lawyers, company directors. Class II comprised retailers, local authority officers, pharmacists, teachers. Class III were the clerical workers, sales staff and the skilled trades, Class IV the semi-skilled manual workers, Class V the unskilled labourers. Such classification poses several problems and there have been significant changes in perception since 1911. Thus whereas in 1911 more than 80 per cent were classified in occupational terms as foremen and manual workers, by 1979 only 54 per cent were so described. Professional groups on the other hand had increased from 4 per cent to 17 per cent over the same period (Sanderson, 1987, p. 114). Nevertheless such divisions, and the associated hierarchical assumptions which they convey, have been important both in English history and in English education.

Though a fivefold division is in itself very crude, and further sophistications of technique have been employed in recent years, overlaps, particularly between Classes II and III, have led some analysts to distinguish just three broad social groups – upper and middle classes, lower middle classes and the labouring classes. Goldthorpe (1980) described these groupings as 'service class', 'intermediate class', and 'working class'. Halsey, Heath and Ridge, on the other hand, in their influential study of 1980, whilst adopting the Goldthorpe classification and its terminology, proceeded to further subdivisions. The service class comprising 13.7 per cent was divided into two, the intermediate class of 31.4 per cent into three, and the working class also into three. This final class of 54.9 per cent included both skilled and unskilled manual industrial and agricultural workers, and smallholders. One of the major problems with all such classifications is that the social class of the family, and hence of the children, is considered to be determined by the status of the father, or of the so-called father substitute. Yet the paid employment of married women has increased from about 10 per cent at the beginning of the century to over 50 per cent today. Such classifications also take no or little account of women's unpaid employment in the home, of the increasing numbers of one parent families and of children born outside marriage, nor of the large numbers of unemployed – both male and female.

SOCIAL MOBILITY

In the nineteenth century the most able children in the country might, if born into poor circumstances, simply attend the nearest elementary school and commence work at an early age. In the twentieth century, however, the concept of an educational ladder whereby boys and girls from the lowest social groups might attain entry via secondary school to Oxford and Cambridge, and to positions of influence in society and the state, emerged. Scholarships to grammar school and to university were intended to increase social mobility. The grammar school became the agency whereby children from all social classes might mix together in the pursuit of truth and excellence. In the first half of the twentieth century progress was made towards the goal of increasing equal opportunities in education. Success in educational terms could be achieved by the intelligent, talented and hardworking, irrespective of their social class origins. This did not mean equal access to secondary schooling and the university, but it did represent an important change from the situation which existed in the later nineteenth century. In the 1930s 96 per cent of children with an IQ of 140+ from professional families attended grammar or private secondary schools, as opposed to 57 per cent of children from clerical, and 32 per cent of children from unskilled family backgrounds (Sanderson, 1987, p. 35).

Expectations aroused by the 1944 Act and the Second World War that such inequalities of access would be further diminished or even ultimately disappear were to be frustrated. Studies undertaken in the 1950s showed that working-class children were not only failing to gain the proportion of grammar school places consistent with their numbers in the population as a whole, but that even those who did reach grammar school performed less well there than those from lower middle- and middle-class homes. Floud, Halsey and Martin (1956) in their study of grammar schools in Middlesbrough and South-west

113

Hertfordshire revealed that in 1953 only 9 per cent of boys from the families of unskilled manual workers were being admitted to grammar schools as opposed to 60 per cent and more of sons of professional workers, and owners and managers of businesses. They concluded that, even in the post-war years as the scholarship ladder widened, its rungs were climbed not by increasing proportions of working-class children but by those from middle- and lower-middle-class homes. Their research showed that 'the probability that a working-class boy will get to a grammar school is not strikingly different from what it was before 1945, and there are still marked differences in the chances which boys of different social origins have of obtaining a place' (Silver, 1973, p. 163).

The combination of arguments and political processes which led to the widespread, though not universal, abandonment of selective secondary schooling, and its replacement by a comprehensive system, are dealt with in detail elsewhere in this book. During these debates it became apparent that performance in the eleven plus examination could be affected by various social factors. These included home environment, the child's age, sex, and position in the family, the size of family, family attitudes and expectations, and the cultural nature of the tests employed, particularly in respect of language. These and other factors not only applied at age eleven, but could also be significant throughout formal education. They helped to explain why, for example, on average, children from working-class homes left grammar schools earlier than, and failed to achieve as many qualifications as, children from professional and clerical backgrounds. Thus in his classic study of the relationship between the home and the school, published in 1964, Douglas showed the effects of a variety of domestic influences upon children's school performance. The Swann Report of 1985 demonstrated, moreover, that for many children from ethnic minority backgrounds these disadvantages were compounded by further factors, including the racist attitudes of some teachers and employers. Such analyses have led to the generation of strategies to compensate for perceived disadvantages, including the designation of educationally deprived areas. Special access courses have also been established to prepare mature students from ethnic minority groups to enter upon teacher training courses without the usual entrance qualifications. How the formal system may be made more accessible to previously under-represented groups remains extremely problematic. Halsey has concluded that 'comprehensive reform of the secondary schools has contributed heavily to the output of entrants to higher and further education but without changing the correlation between social origin and educational attainment'. Indeed, if anything, such correlation has strengthened, perhaps as a result of the 'neighbour-hood' effect, and whereas the professional and managerial class consti-tuted 18 per cent of the population in 1971, 'their children formed 51 per cent of university entrants in 1975 and 54 per cent in 1979' (Halsey, 1986, p.143).

Such evidence as to the relationship between social class and access to higher education leads on to two further questions. Even if the children of Social Classes I and II are maintaining or increasing their share of the educational cake, is there significant movement between social classes, and is such mobility associated with educational per-formance? Studies of the children of families surveyed by Rowntree and Lavers in York in 1950 have shown that, by the later 1970s, of the 465 born into low-income families, 224 were still in that category but that 155 had moved to the intermediate-income group whilst 86 had become comfortably off. Conversely, of 597 born comfortably off, 265 had remained in that group, whilst 174 had an intermediate income and 158 had fallen into the low-income bracket. Though there are con-siderable problems surrounding such analysis, not least those associated with the ages of the subjects and their places in the earnings cycle, it is interesting to note that in no instance were the majority of those in a particular group in the 1970s actually born into that group. Measured on a simple income scale as related to National Assistance in 1950, and Supplementary Benefits in 1975–78, very considerable social, or rather income, mobility had taken place. Other studies, including those of Glass, 1954, Goldthorpe *et al*, 1980, and Heath, 1981, have indicated both the relatively constant pattern of overall social mobility and the increasing rates of upward mobility. Although, using a three class division, it would appear that the majority of adults in England stay in the same social class as that into which they were born, a very sub-stantial minority, well over 40 per cent, move into another class.

Such mobility and its relationship to education has been well summarized by Halsey, and this account draws heavily upon his work (Halsey, 1986, pp.118–44). Data collected for the Oxford Social Mobility Project (Halsey, Heath and Ridge, 1980), showed that those who moved upwards in terms of social group exceeded the educational norms of their group of origin. Similarly those who declined had fewer educational qualifications than their group average. More interestingly those who move upwards have, on average, fewer educational qualifi-cations than those of stable members of the destination group, whilst those who move downwards have a higher educational profile than the stable members of that group, and thus also by definition a still higher one than those recruited to the same destination group from below. So an overall apparent constancy in terms of broad social groups and their access to, and success rates in respect of education, masks a considerable amount of intergenerational class mobility.

It is also important to put educational qualifications into perspective. Education is important in promoting social mobility, both upwards and downwards, but it is not the only factor. Nearly 90 per cent of male university graduates find their way into Classes I and II on the Registrar-General's scale. Nevertheless, even in Class I, non-graduates considerably outnumber graduates. On the other hand conclusions drawn from some of the research of the 1950s and 1960s have been too pessimistic. Recent studies, for example by Rutter *et al*, 1979, and Mortimore *et al*, 1988, emphasize the importance of good schools, and the extent to which such schools can, and do, overcome the negative effects of poverty, class, gender and race.

EMPLOYMENT

One of the most striking features of education in England in the twentieth century has been the early age at which children leave full-time education. In part this reflects the early starting age of full-time schooling, at age 5, as opposed to other countries where 6 or even 7 was, and is, the norm. There has also been a long tradition of child labour as being essential to the profitability of certain industries, for example textiles. Even during the 1920s and 1930s when mass unemployment stalked the land, reaching a figure of 2.9 million in 1933 for Great Britain as a whole, 14- and 15-year-olds were particularly sought after in the labour market. Their employers were not required to supply an insurance stamp, and low wages could be paid. For many families it was essential that their children left school at the earliest opportunity. The chances of many children who qualified for grammar school, and might thereby have escaped from the precariousness of working-class existence to the relative safety of a white-collar or professional occupation, were sacrificed to the more immediate goal of a pittance at 14. Thus in 1880, when compulsory schooling was introduced, the leaving age was fixed only at 10, to be raised to 11 in 1893, 12 in 1899, 14 in 1918, 15 in 1947 and 16 in 1972. Although these were minimum leaving ages and many pupils stayed longer at school, a problem occurred in the post-Second World War period. The sixth form of the English secondary school was traditionally a place where academic subjects were studied to Advanced level by those pupils who wished to proceed to university or to professional occupations. Even today whereas in

Japan or the USA some 80 per cent of pupils stay on in full-time schooling until 18, in England the figure is about 20 per cent. This situation reflects the failure to develop either a comprehensive secondary school system which caters for the educational and training needs of all its pupils, or separate technical and vocational institutions.

Comprehensive secondary schools, their buildings, their staffs and their curricula, still too often reflect the assumption of general education for all to 16 and specialist academic education for a minority to 18. They represent a fusion of the grammar school and secondary modern school traditions. The technical and vocational ethos of so much of German education, for example, which had exercised many English observers since the last decades of the nineteenth century, found little place in English secondary schooling. Junior technical schools and central schools were established prior to the First World War but they were few in number and considered to be inferior to the grammar schools. During the First World War, as during the Second, recognition of the superior quality of German technical education led to proposals for radical action, proposals which were never implemented. The Departmental Committee on Juvenile Education in Relation to Employment after the War, established in 1916, which reported in the following year (the Lewis Report) used the 1911 Census returns to calculate the proportions of young persons in education and work. Only 4 per cent of 15–16-year-olds, 2 per cent of 16–17-year-olds and 1 per cent of 17–18-year-olds were engaged in full-time courses. The figures for part-time study were 14 per cent, 13 per cent and 10 per cent respectively. The Report posed the question 'Can it be established that the educational purpose is to be the dominating one, without as well as within the school doors, during those formative years between 12 and 18?' The Fisher Act of 1918 was prepared to answer that question in the affirmative by raising the school-leaving age to 14 and by providing compulsory part-time continuation schooling for all young people aged 14–18 not engaged in full-time education. The Lewis Report had envisaged the provision of a general rather than a technical education but argued that continuation classes should 'from the very beginning have something of a vocational bias'.

The fate of the Fisher Act has been considered elsewhere in this book, but the Spens Report of 1938 also recognized the problem and, rejecting the solution of the multilateral or comprehensive school, turned again to the option of creating high status technical schools. It thus regretted the demise of the higher grade, organized science, and day technical schools of the last quarter of the nineteenth century, and called for the upgrading of a number of junior technical schools into technical high schools. Such schools, they advised, 'should be accorded in every respect equality of status with schools of the grammar school type'. Neither these proposals, nor the sections of the 1944 Act which provided for compulsory part-time education up to age 18 in county colleges, however, were implemented. Junior technical schools, which were catering for less than 1 per cent of the 11–17 age school population at the time of the Spens Report, declined in numbers still further after 1944. In consequence England found herself as ill-equipped, in terms of many types of vocational training and education, to face the peace, as she had been to face the war.

There is little doubt that England's serious relative economic decline over the last 40 years is not unconnected with the failure to provide skilled vocational training. The magnitude of that decline is difficult to appreciate, but in 1950 only Switzerland and the USA had higher living standards than the United Kingdom. In 1962 a White Paper on Industrial Training concluded that 'There is no doubt that shortages of skilled manpower have been an important factor in holding back the rate of economic expansion – not least in those parts of the country where such expansion would have done most to reduce a level of general unemployment higher than the average.' Evidence from the more advanced industrial economy of the USA indicated clearly that technological societies had more need for skilled employees, and less for the unskilled or semi-skilled. International comparisons from the 1960s and 1970s, however, showed that England still sent a far higher proportion of unqualified 16-year-olds on to the labour market than any of her major economic competitors. In consequence, as unemployment mushroomed in the 1980s to pass the 3 million mark, many young people went straight from school to the dole, with little prospect of ever finding a permanent job. In contrast West Germany, with her system of full-time vocational education and apprenticeships, had the lowest percentage of unemployed young people in the EEC.

The impact of unemployment upon those who in other countries might have been in full-time education was most keenly felt at the start of the 1980s. Between the first quarter of 1980 and the same period in 1981 unemployment rose from 6 per cent to 9.8 per cent. The proportion of the labour force under 18 registered as unemployed, however, rose from 11 per cent to 19.2 per cent (Ryder and Silver, 1985, p. 324). In 1983 the Conservative government launched a Technical and Vocational Initiative, under the auspices of the Manpower Services Commission. Its purpose was to enable schools to devise and run courses which would have direct application in the worlds of commerce and industry. Other MSC initiatives included a Training Opportunities

Scheme, a Youth Opportunities Scheme, and, from 1983, a Youth Training Scheme. The Youth Training Scheme was intended to prevent any young person from going straight on to the dole at 16 or 17, and thus at a stroke to eliminate juvenile unemployment. YTS is a work experience programme which utilizes the participation of more than 100,000 employers. It has been dismissed by some critics as basically a cheap labour scheme, and YTS participants are not included in EC figures for full-time training. From 1986 YTS was extended from a one year to a two year programme. The most recent proposals in the campaign to promote links between education and employment include the creation of 20 large city technology colleges. These are to cover the full secondary school age range and to provide a curriculum in which science, technology and commercial subjects will form a central core. Like the junior technical colleges of the earlier twentieth century, however, they are but a drop in the ocean. Many of the present government's educational initiatives in respect of vocational education seem not merely to be overlapping, but even contradictory. Thus under the Education Act of 1988 city technology colleges are to adhere to the substance of the new national curriculum, which though it includes mathematics and science as two of the three core subjects and technology as one of the seven foundation subjects, is essentially a resurrection of the grammar-school curriculum of the first decade of the twentieth century as set out in the Regulations of 1904.

CONCLUSION

Three points may be made in conclusion: in respect of social class, recent legislation, and population.

One of the most frequently-noted features of English society, and of its educational system in the twentieth century, has been its hierarchical nature. This has led to repeated expressions of concern about the wastage of talent, wastage both in individual and societal terms. Boys from the lower social classes, and girls from all groups in society, have not had access to prestigious public schools like Eton and Harrow, and have had only a token foothold in the universities of Oxford and Cambridge. Even in 1989 some half of the undergraduates at these universities were still recruited from fee-paying schools.

In 1926 in *Social Progress and Educational Waste*, Kenneth Lindsay described the much-vaunted educational ladder as being rather more like a greasy pole. He calculated that the ability of at least 40 per cent of the nation's children was being denied proper expression, as a result of their exclusion from secondary schools. In 1964 Douglas' final chapter to *The Home and the School* was entitled 'Wastage of Ability'. He concluded that 'The evidence set out in this book gives strong reasons for believing that much potential ability is wasted during the primary school years and misdirected at the point of secondary selection' (p. 119). Thus the pool of talent finally available at the end of secondary schooling was substantially less than it would have been had it been possible to draw on potential, rather than realised, ability.

A recent study of education in the period covered by Douglas' research has reached much the same conclusion. Whilst acknowledging the expansion of educational opportunity during that period, and the widespread concern to promote the egalitarian and democratic dimensions of education, Lowe has argued that 'Between 1945 and 1964 the English education system developed in ways which were to confirm the deep social cleavages which only became fully apparent during the 1980s' (Lowe, 1988, p. 202). This he attributes to two major factors. The first was the continuing tradition of hierarchy, so that in higher education, for example, the polytechnics would have less prestige (and funding) than the newer universities, which in turn were less prestigious than the old. The second was a suburbanization of society and the growth of home ownership, which created new types of structural divisions. Accordingly the secondary comprehensive schools would reflect different, but in some senses even more predictable and intractable, social class inequalities, than the former elementary/secondary or grammar/secondary modern divides, and in so doing would seem, to many observers, to have failed to fulfil the predictions of their promoters.

Though Lowe states that 'what no one foresaw was that the comprehensive schools might help to confirm the stratification of English society' (Lowe, 1988, p. 149), such an outcome was predicted by the *Black Paper* writers, by observers of the neighbourhood school effect in the United States, and foreshadowed by Michael Young in his brilliant satire which first appeared in 1958. *The Rise of the Meritocracy* was predicated upon the argument that social progress depended on the degree to which power could be matched with intelligence. Young, however, in pointing out the dangers attendant upon following that argument to its logical conclusion, showed that such a goal would require the earliest possible identification of intelligence and ability in all children, and a rejection of the ideal of common schools, common culture and a common curriculum.

The changes which the Education Act of 1988, with its clauses permitting schools to opt out of local authority control, and parents to send their children to schools of their choice, may produce in the relationship between education and social structure, initially at school, and subsequently at further and higher levels of education, cannot easily be predicted. This is partly because there is a deep contradiction underlying the Act, which on the one hand seeks to privatise education, and on the other, as for example in curriculum matters, to increase central government control. This contradiction was exemplified by the ballot which showed that 94 per cent of parents wished to retain ILEA. In this instance the clearly-expressed wish of the consumers was simply ignored. Much will depend upon the ways in which parents become organized, the causes which they espouse, for example for single sex or mixed schools, for multicultural or separate culture schools, and the extent to which a central government will be prepared to overrule, as in the case of the ILEA ballot, parental choices which run counter to its own philosophy.

Finally, however, one fundamental issue of supply and demand which is entirely predictable relates to the numbers of young people in the 1990s. In 1979 there were just over 4 million pupils in secondary schools in England and Wales. By 1988 that figure had declined to 3.3 million, with a further decline expected to 3 million by 1991. Even in the year 2000 it seems probable that there will be fewer pupils in secondary schools than there are today. Population changes of this type necessitate the making of fundamental choices about education. Declining pupil rolls may lead to further school closures and amalgamations, dismissals of teachers, curtailment of the curriculum. Similar problems are affecting higher education. The numbers of 18- and 19year-olds will fall by a third over the period between 1984 and 1996. Higher education will be in severe competition with employers to attract school leavers of ability. One response to this situation might be to cut places in higher education by a third, and to do so by closing some institutions altogether. This policy would be consistent with the reduction in financial support for higher education which has taken place under the present government. An alternative might be to engage in substantial retraining of those who are currently under- or unemployed, and, noting the low proportions of those in England who proceed to higher education in comparison with other industrialized countries (notably Canada, Japan and the USA) to use this opportunity to catch up.

FURTHER READING

T. Barker and M. Drake (eds.), *Population and Society in Britain 1850–1980*, 1982, provides a useful introduction to the demographic scene. Studies of English society which deal with education include D.C. Marsh, *The Changing Social Structure of England and Wales, 1871–1961*, 1965, A. Sampson, *The Changing Anatomy of Britain*, 1983, J. Ryder and H. Silver, *Modern English Society*, 1985 and A.H. Halsey, *Change in British Society*, 1986. M. Sanderson, *Educational Opportunity and Social Change in England*, 1987, is an excellent short account, whilst H. Silver (ed.), *Equal Opportunity in Education*, 1973, provides extracts from such seminal studies as R.H. Tawney, *Secondary Education for All*, 1922, K. Lindsay, *Social Progress and Educational Waste*, 1926, F. Clarke, *Education and Social Change*, 1940, J.E. Floud (ed.), A.H. Halsey and F.M. Martin, *Social Class and Educational Opportunity*, 1956, G.H. Bantock, *Education in an Industrial Society*, 1963, and J.W.B. Douglas, *The Home and the School*, 1964, studies which have themselves become part of the history of education. Last in this list, but first in promoting independent thought in this field, comes M. Young, *The Rise of the Meritocracy, 1870–2033*, 1958.

CHAPTER NINE

Education of Women and Girls

INTRODUCTION

Much has been written about the early promoters of women's education in the nineteenth century and their frequent battles to overcome prejudice and ill-informed opinion in their struggles to found schools and colleges and establish a foothold in key professions such as medicine. The turn of the present century has been seen as a watershed. The right of young women to pursue an academic education was largely accepted. All that remained to future generations was to build on this success. At this stage storms gathered. Women's suffrage became the central feminist issue and enveloped almost all the aspirations of the Edwardian women pioneers. In addition, the advent of a class-based party, Labour, which focused on class inequalities, presented further difficulties.

The struggle of the early pioneers to provide both intellectual fulfilment and access to coveted professions meant little to the majority of working mothers and daughters. From the 1960s, the role of education in the process began to be investigated. If, for instance, middle-class women had been able to share in a genuine academic education it was difficult to explain their conspicuous lack of success in securing a significant proportion of key positions in commerce, industry and the professions. Part of the explanation has turned to the schools, previously regarded more often as a place of constraint and control than of emancipation and liberation.

EDUCATION, SOCIETY AND THE MIDDLE-CLASS GIRL, 1900–1918

At the beginning of the new century education for girls, as for boys, took place in two systems: the elementary inhabited by the working-class child, and the emergent secondary system, the preserve of the more affluent middle class. From the attempts of the early pioneers such as Frances Buss in the 1860s had emerged, in 1872, the Girls' Public Day

School Trust (GPDST) which set the pattern for girls' secondary schools. They were large, divided into three departments, preparatory, junior and secondary, and recognized the need for regular inspection and staff educated at the universities. Other groups, notably the Anglican Church Company Schools, took up many features of their non-denominational rival. Certainly the need for highly educated teachers to staff these schools stimulated the expansion of women's colleges at the great university centres. A presence at Cambridge had first been established by the foundation of Girton and Newnham. In the later 1870s the Anglican Lady Margaret Hall and its non-denominational counterpart, Somerville College, were set up at Oxford, to be followed in the 1890s by the establishment of Westfield College and Royal Holloway on the fringes of London. Nor must it be forgotten that in the early civic colleges mushrooming in this period many of the full-time students, often reading for London external degrees, were women. It has been estimated that by 1911 one in five full-time students at universities were women. Girls' secondary schools were innovators in other ways, from their beginnings, promoting the training of teachers for these places. In 1877 a Headmistresses' Association was founded, a recognition of the growing importance of women in the world of education. The success of these headmistresses and principals of colleges often acted as a spur and model for younger women struggling to establish themselves.

Girls' secondary education was shaped by the experiences and the motivation of the pioneers. The schooling of the middle-class girl, as well as of her male counterpart, was closely related to their position in society. Educated girls were expected to settle down in marriage, to provide a secure well-ordered home and family and finally to manage an army of servants and workpeople with whom they came in contact. Thus the parents who paid the fees were seldom anxious for their daughters to become thoroughly emancipated. They desired their daughters to emerge into adulthood as marriageable products, and were well aware of the loudly-proclaimed opinions of some clergy and doctors that an extended intellectual education might damage the prospects of marriage and family. There was a sustained attempt in these schools not to offend. Frances Buss, for example, in the 1870s, extolled the virtues of non-residential schools which enabled close links to be maintained between mothers and daughters. Free time was set aside in the afternoons to enable the girls to go home early to absorb from their mothers the lessons of good household management. Dorothea Beale, in the 1880s, cast doubts on undue emphasis on the values of examinations, competition and a too heavy stress on academic work. Much attention was paid to the plight of unmarried daughters, who, without education and training, were likely to finish in marginal lowly positions like many of the 25,000 governesses recorded in the 1851 Census.

A more complex economy from the 1870s was extending employment opportunities. New careers in teaching, social work and the office shifted the boundaries between the private household domain and a public career. Nevertheless these did not differ markedly from earlier associated activities connected with the family, philanthropy and home visiting. It was a feature of the pioneers' tactics to secure the support of wealthy, influential male figures who presided over management committees and trust companies. Philip Magnus, the author of the celebratory volume of the GPDST, commented on this: 'But true and vital as this is, women alone could not have carried their cause, or would never have carried it so quickly to a successful issue, if they had not been able to rely, at their meetings and gatherings, on men of rank and eminence in the public eye' (Magnus, 1923, pp. 32–3). Once young women departed from their secondary schools and escaped for the first time from home and family they discovered that the women's colleges surrounded their charges with restrictions. In their rooms they were expected to recreate the trappings of home, and the college calendar was marked with social gatherings, entertainment and excursions to advertise the non-academic side of their life.

This did not mean that the key figures of early struggles for middle-class education, notably Emily Davies or Elizabeth Garrett, members of the first London School Board, battled for limited ends. They were feminists who recognized that their struggle was firmly related to the issue of equality of the sexes. On the whole they favoured a gradualist campaign and wherever possible co-operation with sympathetic males. Many of them owed their starts in life to progressive fathers. However they also worked alongside the more vocal elements in the feminist movement. The equal rights feminists, too, were eager supporters of equal educational opportunities together with equal pay and marriage rights, but they insisted that the vote and proper representation in Parliament was of utmost importance in the fight to secure real equality.

Throughout the Edwardian era, girls' schools and colleges remained under close scrutiny. Indeed there were new alarms. Eugenists and national efficiency advocates were dismayed by the falling birth rate, particularly among the most prosperous sections of the nation and the educated professional middle class. The activities of the Men and Women Club, established in the 1890s, with advanced views on marriage and family, and taken up by a few feminists, aroused anxieties in conventional circles. In a society increasingly beset by alarms about instability, aggression and individualism it was urged that the female needed to exert all the womanly values of patience and understanding to maintain social stability. Pressure was increasing to ensure that girls' secondary schools proclaimed these virtues rather than pursuing so-called male values. A range of arguments was put forward to support the significant upgrading of domestic subjects in the curriculum. The management of the household with its new appliances and fewer servants demanded more careful attention. If science was to be popularized in these schools domestic subjects related to practical problems in the home might well aid this process. During the Edwardian period a number of GPDST schools introduced domestic science and, in 1920, it was recognized for the School Certificate. Nevertheless the responses of headmistresses in dealing with this pressure differed widely. Some declined to introduce housecraft subjects, claiming that this teaching was more appropriate for the mother to give. They argued that the secondary curriculum was already extended to its limits. Others kept the subject in the margins, confining it to the low achievers, or delaying its introduction to the final weeks of a girl's schooling.

At the end of the Edwardian period the quality and quantity of education for many middle-class girls had improved markedly. The claims that girls, emotionally and physically, could not stand the pressure of an academic education had been largely rebutted. There was no doubt that the increased assurance with which the suffragettes put forward their claims after 1900 owed much to this sustained growth. This, in turn, aroused fears among those with strongly entrenched beliefs about gender differences and separate spheres which, they argued, held society together.

EDUCATION AND THE WORKING-CLASS GIRL, 1900–1918

For the majority of working-class girls, even in the more fortunate families, access to learning was difficult. Ruth Slater and Eva Shawson, in South London at the beginning of this century, came from families where education received respect. Nevertheless in their letters to each other they often expressed resentment at the narrowness of their lives. The former described some of the acute problems she faced: 'I think I may have told you how from my earliest years I have longed to study and learn.' Yet she had feelings of guilt: 'I want to read and study, and yet at the same time to be helpful at home, and spare Mother all the work I possibly can and between the two feelings I am often sorely vexed' (Thompson, 1987, p.61).

There were significant variations in the lives of working-class families, depending on income, occupation and even locality. Historians have long detected a labour aristocracy, situated either among the well-entrenched artisans or the newer foremen, supervisors or mechanics in the factories. Frequently they have been distinguished from the rest by their life style. They often married later than other workers, had smaller families and owned their houses at a distance from the workplace. A mark of their position in society was that their earnings were usually regular and sufficient to ensure that their wives devoted their entire time to household and family. They valued schooling and were prepared to make sacrifices to see that their children secured the maximum benefit from it. Sons were expected to stay longer at school, enter an apprenticeship and take courses at mechanics institutes and evening classes. Daughters were not ignored in this process. It was widely believed that successful schooling might ensure a better, more upwardly mobile marriage, and that in the period leading up to it respectable work in the expanding clerical, secretarial and retailing areas would be secured. Thus daughters of the labouring aristocracy were prominent in the top layer of elementary education where they were taught commerce, book-keeping and knowledge of a foreign language. Some would go on to join the ranks of the elementary schoolteachers themselves.

For the majority of working-class girls, as for their brothers, education was limited by family needs. Since the 1850s real wages had risen and most homes afforded more material comforts. Economic depression, sudden illnesses, unwanted pregnancies and the arrival of aged parents in the household still stretched family resources and brought destitution and the hated Poor Law nearer. A husband's wage on its own rarely kept the bulk of working-class families intact. In turn, the children from an early age participated in the family economy. Girls, in particular, found themselves running errands, cleaning and looking after younger siblings. Attendance officers complained that a household crisis would find the oldest girl being kept away from the classroom for long periods of time. The family economy and survival counted for everything and children were expected to leave school as quickly as possible. There was little chance of prolonged education to ensure better long-term prospects.

Social investigators were deeply concerned, from the 1850s onwards, at the prevalence of a group called, on occasions, the residue or the submerged class. Although often portrayed as a hidden canker silently eating at the heart of the nation this group was, in reality, highly visible in the urban centres where they roamed the streets as costermongers, hawkers or shoeblacks. They were regarded as potential criminals. Fears were expressed that they were a dangerous influence in working-class neighbourhoods and there were constant warnings that their numbers were growing. Advocates of national efficiency insisted that elementary school teachers should encourage them to become socially responsible.

All this anxiety had a decided effect on what was taught to girls. As most working-class girls were likely to take the most unskilled work, it was not deemed essential for them to receive the kind of vocational education seen as necessary to prepare their male counterparts. While boys received a groundwork in manual training, girls were being taught lessons related to their future roles as housewives or mothers. Facilities became increasingly available for dressmaking, laundry and cookery work, and the period at a day centre became a marked feature in the schooling of older girls. Here they were taken out of their schools and given a preparation for their future domestic role in specially equipped and staffed centres. Schemes abounded for these older girls to be taught about infant welfare, nutrition and family budgeting. It occasionally strayed into dangerous areas, as lessons on hygiene and personal health might touch on the very sensitive subject of sex education. What was vibrant in the Edwardian period was the concern about infant mortality, poor physique and urban squalor. Some like Sir George Newman, appointed as first Medical Officer at the Board of Education in 1907, argued that these problems stemmed mainly from maternal ignorance and heavy reliance on misguided traditional family and neighbourhood knowledge. In his view there must be a two-pronged approach. One line would be to set up infant welfare centres, which would provide some basic medical benefits such as safe milk, but which would see their prime task as teaching mothers 'proper' methods of childcare. The other course was to continue the process of protective legislation, partly on humanitarian grounds but also to 'free' women for their domestic duties. In 1891, it was made illegal for employers to employ women within four weeks of confinement.

The pressures mounted on the working-class girl. Many women elementary teachers had reservations about 'girls' subjects', especially where they were located in centres away from the school, and which, they believed, distracted the girls from school-life. Nor did the mothers have much time for the domestic training which they believed had little relevance to the real working-class economy. Deprivation and poor physique owed much more to low wages and bad housing than to maternal shortcomings. Working-class women were often clear about the knowledge that they needed to ensure that their families were provided with an adequate start, particularly on birth control. A correspondent to the Women's Co-operative Guild touched on this sensitive matter: 'There is one thing as to mechanical prevention of family. I know it is a delicate subject, but it is an urgent one as it is due to low paid wages and the unending struggle to live respectably' (Llewellyn Davies, 1984 (ed.), p.59). It was an issue that caused difficulties for governments which feared that knowledge of contraception might lead to sexual freedom and the abandonment of family life. In 1927 the Board of Education recommended the provision of sex education in schools, though it was estimated in 1939 that fewer than a third of secondary schools made any such provision. Where it was taught, it was done entirely by special lectures. The Labour party found the subject acutely difficult, the leadership searching for respectability, attempting to keep the issue under the surface, but with a vigorous feminist lobby pushing hard for knowledge of birth control to be made freely available.

A concerted campaign by state, local authorities and voluntary agencies in the early part of the century, directed at working-class mothers and daughters, presented difficulties to the feminist movement. Clinics, mother and baby classes, and infant welfare might ease working-class mothers' problems, and even highlight some of the acute difficulties of bringing up young children in poor social conditions. Women could hardly object to medical inspection and the supply of free meals for necessitous children, or even, in 1919, to the establishment of a sub-department in the reconstituted Ministry of Health to deal with maternal and infant welfare. Measures of this kind could nevertheless be associated with attempts to uphold the domestic sphere for women.

The impact of total war, as we have seen, did little to break down gender divisions permanently. The presence of women as bus drivers, munition workers and even 'dilutee' engineers was a temporary affair. In 1919 the government, supported strongly by most male trade unionists, made it illegal for employers to retain dilutees who had, in wartime, solved the shortage of skilled labour. Many women found themselves cast out. Most female labour, in any case, found itself in male-directed, low-level work. For their part, girls were engaged in the schools in efforts to aid a male-dominated war and they had been encouraged to take up ancillary tasks such as packing bandages or knitting scarves for the soldiers. Even the most highly publicized gain, in 1918, the franchise (albeit with significant omissions) and later, in

1919, the passage of a measure that ended restrictions on access to professions, owed much to pre-war campaigns. Much attention was paid to the allegedly new women of the 1920s, liberated, unchaperoned and driving fast cars in a reaction against wartime austerities; however, their influence was often exaggerated.

In 1918, then, the situation became less promising for most women. There were acute fears, in political circles, about a lost generation that made it imperative that future generations received the utmost care. This did not mean, in the retrenchment-minded 1920s, dramatic rises in social welfare or the introduction of child allowances. On the contrary it was seen as important that the mother, especially in the working-class localities, should be given more intensive training in childcare. Some of the pressure for the continuation school clauses in the Fisher Act of 1918 arose directly from these preoccupations. Life in the factory, to be accompanied by leisure in dancehalls and the street corner, were believed to encourage bad habits. Continuation schools appropriately staffed and equipped would, it was hoped, provide the necessary social training to ease a difficult transitional period. Wherever money was granted, as in 1920 and 1921, to maintain centres for training girls, priority was given to courses related to domestic service. It was hoped that this would ease the servant shortage and provide young women with an appropriate grounding for their future roles as wives and mothers.

EDUCATION, SOCIETY AND THE ROLE OF WOMEN, 1919–1939

The main feature of the inter-war period, casting its shadow over prospects for women, was unemployment and economic depression. By the 1920s the nation had begun to show signs of a divide between an ailing North and a much more prosperous South. In the northern industrial heartlands the traditional export industries struggled to maintain themselves against increasingly successful, more advantageously based, competitors. Textiles, at the heart of the Industrial Revolution, and an employer of large armies of women, suffered very badly in this period. In comparison, by the mid-1930s in the South and the Midlands a wide range of newer industries grew up related to the protected domestic market and growing consumerism. Here the assembly line was a prominent feature of the layout, and women were regarded as more suitable labour because they were supposed to resent less the drudgery. In addition, the absence of equal pay meant that newer industries found this source of supply attractive. In the 1930s, employment for women presented a mixed picture. Even in the depressed areas women maintained the family economy by resorting to traditional practices, taking in an extra lodger or finding outwork. It was noted by observers such as J.B. Priestley that, in many areas, they were frequently the only wage-earner and their traditional role as controller of the budget was thereby strengthened. It was hardly likely that working-class parents would be persuaded that extra years at school would promote more opportunities for their daughters.

For the middle-class woman the inter-war period presented few opportunities for new kinds of employment. Private employers, state and local government agencies were all reluctant to continue to employ women after they had married. It has been estimated that in the Edwardian era 25 per cent of the women teachers were married. After 1920 there was a significant tightening up of regulations and many local authorities, supported by the newly formed National Association of Schoolmasters, enforced marriage bar clauses. Anger arose over the unequal pay conditions in teaching embodied in the newly-formed Burnham Committee structure set up after the war. The National Union of Teachers declined to fight this with any vigour despite the strong endorsement in the 1919 referendum held by its members.

Cultural changes did little to make the position of women more assured. Illiteracy, almost always higher among women in the nineteenth century, now largely disappeared. As a result there was a marked growth of magazines aimed at different groups of women. The messages coming from most, apart from *Time and Tide*, were overwhelmingly traditional. Appearance, sociability and preparation for marriage were stressed in advice columns and articles. The home was placed firmly in the forefront of changes in style of living. Labour-saving devices were proclaimed as making housework less dreary. The model home that was displayed, with its fitted kitchen and bathroom, was drawn from the USA. For the majority of wives, still living in sub-standard housing with outdoor lavatories and no bathrooms, the prospect of these changes seemed distant. Nevertheless the decline of heavy export-led industries meant that the home market and the housewife became a target for the advertisers. Moreover, the advent of the radio and the gramophone and the expanding network of electricity made the housewife likely, by the 1930s, to seek her recreation in the home. In this way all these pressures strengthened the domestic role of women. •

The women's movement was ill-equipped to deal with these new challenges in the period after 1918. The culmination of the suffrage campaign left the activists struggling for an identity. Some resolutely continued to battle for equal rights in the workplace and the law and went on to press for equal pay, reform of the divorce laws and better training opportunities. Success was not totally lacking: the divorce laws were amended in 1937 to give women equal rights in guardianship of children. Other groups, such as Eleanor Rathbone and her supporters, chose to concentrate attention on campaigns to see that women, especially in working-class localities, received more help in their struggle to bring up their families, in the form of family allowances payable to mothers, maternity grants, better medical attention and the opening of nurseries. Male trade unionists eagerly espoused women's call for a social wage, seeing it as a weapon to push up their own wages. Younger feminists, notably Sylvia Pankhurst, Ellen Wilkinson and Leah Manning, were drawn into Labour politics. For them the struggle for women's equality joined up with the battle to destroy class inequality, and it became difficult to disentangle or even identify women's grievances.

Schooling, as always, reflected the state of society. There was by 1920 a well-established secondary system for girls, fee-paying or accessible by examination success. A smaller proportion of girls than boys stayed on for the full secondary course. Subject differentiation was quite marked. As late as 1923, the Board of Education's Consultative Committee had investigated the particular needs of girls in education and once again raised issues about differentiation, both in ability and requirements. The findings were inconclusive but warned secondary school headmistresses that they must continue to stress qualities such as 'ladylike behaviour'. In the new central schools, which provided a more vocational education, there were markedly different paths for the two sexes. Girls were to be trained to enter nursing, the office or the department store. In the new senior schools of the 1930s there were obvious differences in the curriculum to be provided. The issue of secondary education, which had been raised by R.H. Tawney in 1922, focused on class access, and probably directed attention away from the issues that affected girls and women specifically. There was still a long way to go for the most successful young women even at university level: the University of Cambridge, reflecting the strength of backwoodsmen MAs, resisted completely equal status until after 1945.

EDUCATION, SOCIETY AND THE ROLE OF WOMEN, 1939–1960

The debates about reconstruction and plans for improved welfare and education provision after the two World Wars had implications for the future role of women in society. The large numbers of women engaged in the war effort and movements of younger women away from their home localities aroused considerable concern. Misgivings were expressed by social survey teams that much of the younger female generation would be reluctant to return to domestic life, and in the post-war era would seek to pursue outside careers. In 1943, some of these anxieties culminated in the appointment of a Royal Commission on Population. As plans for a post-war world began to take shape much emphasis was placed on strategies to end unemployment and to ensure that the male breadwinner could look after his wife and family. For the sake of family, community and nation it was deemed important to ensure that the majority of married women spent their lives at home.

Thus much of the legislation emanating from the Beveridge Report of 1944 and the White Paper on Unemployment (1943) assumed that the married woman, dependent on her husband, would be entitled to support for herself and the children through him in time of family crisis. A range of reports on delinquency and deprivation stressed the importance of the mother as the provider of a secure childhood. Psychological findings, such as those of John Bowlby published in the late 1940s, supported the view that proper adult relationships would only emerge if the mother of small children totally absorbed herself in childcare. The 'pronatalism' of much of the thinking at this time made government planners hostile to those groups seeking universal provision of nursery schools for the very young. Indeed nursery education was seen as an exceptional remedy in case of dire necessity in the family. The 1944 Education Act did not make the provision of nursery education unambiguously statutory for local authorities, and in 1945 the Exchequer grant to local authorities was cut by half. There was here a very clear implication that young children should receive their first steps in social training from their mothers. Other indications of the determination of the Coalition government and its Labour successor to stress the domestic role of women emerged in the resistance to equal pay demands. Indeed when backbenchers added an equal pay clause to the passage of the Butler Bill the government, even in war-time, made the issue one of confidence. It was feared that the male wage-earners and women who stayed at home would greatly resent such a measure. This continued to be accepted by senior Labour politicians when they considered the Equal Pay Report in 1947.

Changes in education put forward by officials in the Ministry of Education realigned the position of women dramatically. The implication of the 1944 Act was that girls who displayed academic abilities were entitled to progress along the broad path of schooling to higher education in the company of their male counterparts. If increasing numbers of young women chose to do this it might well lead to alienation from home duties. During the post-war period, Ministry of Education pamphlets constantly warned academically able women that there would be no ready supply of domestics to undertake housework. The full blast of socialist egalitarianism was used to make them think domestically. They were reminded that household management and childcare were the concern of all women, even the most intellectually gifted. In 1947 there was an attempt through the creation of the National Institute of Houseworkers to upgrade the status of domestic work by certification and professional training.

In the newly-created modern school, in spite of Ellen Wilkinson's vigilance, the bulk of the schoolgirl population in their practical and project work were encouraged to direct themselves to home-based activities. The proposed county colleges mentioned in the 1944 Act, which aimed at easing the transition between adolescence and adulthood, would have offered a range of social training for these girls. They would have helped to 'set the tone' for relationships with the opposite sex.

The unfolding of development plans after the war raised many issues that touched on gender. First of all there was the issue of scarce grammar school places. Should they be allocated equally between the two sexes, or allocated to the top 25 per cent regardless of sex? Girls were acknowledged to be more capable academically at the age of 11, but local authorities introduced mechanisms to ensure that they did not receive the majority of places in grammar schools. Co-education received considerable attention and this was reflected in many of the development plan proposals sent to the Ministry. Official reaction was mixed. There was a welcome for the mingling of the sexes in the more family-based primary schools, and later in their careers in the further education colleges. However the view was expressed that there ought to be a period of separation whilst at the secondary stage of education.

After the war there was a marked change in attitude to the married woman teacher. To some extent this was the result of the chronic shortage of teachers, but the decision to scrap the marriage bar was not wholly related to this factor. In the new secondary schools with their growing numbers of academic girls, the spinster teacher was no longer regarded as an appropriate model for a youthful population. By a curious twist unmarried women became an object of concern, especially where they formed the majority of the staff, while the older married women were to be welcomed. The Ministry's commitment to the medium-sized school as the ideal unit owed much to the belief that it could replicate the home and family. Even the daily school dinner, attended by the majority of staff and pupils in austerity-ridden Britain, was considered important for its promotion of a family atmosphere.

Many of the post-war fears about marriage and family were soon to prove groundless. Perhaps the creation of the welfare state and the improved services to hard-pressed housewives made an impact. As the 1950s arrived, the Conservative government, faced with a bulging population, began putting limits to welfare provision. There were steady rises in the costs of school dinners, and a marked decrease in enthusiasm for universal benefits. Nevertheless, the 1950s was the decade of the family, as the post-war baby boom moved into childhood. In contrast to the 1920s the unemployment figures generally remained low. From the time of the publication of the 1947 Economic Survey, one of the preoccupations of successive governments was shortage of labour. Women found themselves courted, persuaded and cajoled both to be responsible mothers, and to return to the labour market for the sake of national productivity. Increasing numbers of women, married and single, were recruited for factories, offices and the burgeoning welfare departments. The division between the public and private sectors of education seemed to be more blurred.

The 1950s, lacking the heroism of the previous decade and the vibrant energy of the later 1960s, has been seen as a highly conventional, inward-looking period. Mothers in waged work might become the norm but this did not mean that women moved into the commanding positions in society. The image of the era was of the woman providing the 'extras' to improve the family income, which could include the purchase of the television set, the washing machine or, more ambitiously, the motor car. Women were expected to work not only for their own satisfaction but to secure a prosperous home. Underneath this conservatism there were signs of change. Debates were initiated on homosexual law reform in the late 1950s, and there were moves towards easier divorce. For many of the successful girls moving through the academic secondary school the experience of this education opened up new vistas. Grammar schools with their uniforms and restrictions angered the more rebellious schoolgirls, but could prove of great benefit. Liz Heron, in a recent 1950s collection, summed up this mood: 'The first step on the academic route was the eleven-plus ... a hurdle which a substantial number of working-class children did overcome, though many did not. For a number of us writing here, that first step made a lot of difference to the future' (Heron, 1985, p.7).

EDUCATION, SOCIETY AND WOMEN SINCE THE 1960S

The 1960s have been depicted as a decade that changed the life style of women. Changes in the law concerning divorce and abortion, the dramatic rise in educational opportunities particularly in relation to access to higher education, the development of more effective birth control methods and a Labour government with a most determined campaigner, Barbara Castle, at its heart, all have been seen to play a part. The forces of convention found themselves challenged. This picture is probably too stark, and for much of the population traditional assumptions about behaviour remained; indeed, they may have been reinforced by fears of breakdown in society. The network of women's protest groups which sprang up were never wholly in harmony with each other. Feminist groups were rightly suspicious of some of the notions of liberation, which often meant sexual exploitation in another guise. There was disagreement too about the nature of change required and the degree to which existing society could be altered. This became an issue in the women's movement and culminated in the meetings at Ruskin College in 1970 when a programme of demands was agreed upon.

Governments in the 1960s eagerly pursued modernization policies. This meant, as we have seen, not only searching out talent by locating the under-achievers but intervention in the territories of the discontented who might eventually threaten social cohesion. The Crowther Report, issued in 1959, uncovered the extent to which girls still needed to be catered for in the secondary schools. They tended to leave school earlier, take fewer external examinations particularly in the upper reaches of the school, and were in a decided minority in the prestigious science-based courses. Attempts were made, some with success, to ensure a longer education for girls. It was hoped that a more extensive recruitment into higher education would ease the acute teacher shortage and lack of welfare workers. The Report showed that, despite talk of changing attitudes, many of the older assumptions about the place of women in society remained fixed.

Changes in the law, especially in the 1970s, promoted equal pay, employment protection and job opportunities. The passing of legislation did not always amount to total victory, for enforcement proved very difficult and the authorities were anxious to avoid long legal confrontation with offenders. Although an Equal Opportunities Commission was set up in 1972, it was never given the powers to deal with many of the unfair practices that were brought before it. Government departments were often optimistic in their assessments. In 1972, in its evidence to the House of Lords Select Committee on the Anti-Discrimination Bill (No. 2), the DES gave a rosy picture of progress made. The line taken was that the momentum was being maintained by judicious prodding from the centre. 'The spectrum of girls' education is broadening albeit not as quickly as many would wish. The role of the DES is to give sympathetic encouragement to the demand for broadening opportunities for girls and do nothing to stop it' (Evidence, Select Committee on Anti-Discrimination, July 1972, p.25). Lady Summerskill, an experienced campaigner, sensed complacency. 'There is in this memorandum as a whole – perhaps I am misinterpreting its indications – that you feel that things are running happily in the right direction and there really is no need to fuss' (Summerskill, ibid, p.32). She then proceeded to challenge the figures indicating the striking rises in the percentage of girls taking such subjects as mathematics and chemistry in the external examinations. At a later stage of the proceedings Lady Summerskill touched on another issue. 'We are told everything in this particular world is well because the majority of teachers are women. But of course education has always been a women's job and what has been common since the days of governesses in the nineteenth century, is that it has been badly paid in relation to other professions' (Summerskill, ibid, p.32). For good measure she drew attention to the fact that 60 per cent of the teaching force was drawn from women but that only 40 per cent of headships were held by women. In face of these attacks the Department representatives found themselves in difficulties. They expressed the hope, which Lady Seer challenged, that the spread of co-education would not only provide major opportunities for girls to improve at science – because they would be in contact with more highly qualified male teachers – but would also lead to better relationships between the sexes.

A growing feminist movement was bound to turn its attention to deficiencies in education for women. Since the early nineteenth century generations of feminists had argued that education held the vital key to change in employment practices, pay and expectations. What many groups have done, since the 1960s, has been to monitor the practices in the classroom. There was a growing awareness of the way in which women had been held back by ideas propagated in the family, the locality and the churches. All these ideas were seen to be reinforced by the school experience. Children absorbed from textbooks, individual subjects and the attitudes of teachers, that men and women had very different roles to play in society. Attention was now directed at the expanding world of mixed education where males tended to occupy the policy-making posts while their female colleagues were given the pastoral, caring positions. There have been growing doubts about what so-called equality of education has achieved.

Many feminist groups, in the 1990s, can see how illusory progress towards equality has been. There is no doubt that the shift away from the welfare state – the curtailment of school meals, assistance for heating and clothing, and health care – has borne most heavily on women in the poorer sections of the community. In the harsh economic climate of the early 1980s, there were calls for a return to the old definition of women's role within the family, thus ensuring stability in society, and at the same time helping to ease the unemployment problem. Areas of education heavily used by women, notably adult and extra-mural education, through which many of the older generation were able to make up for lost opportunities, have been most savagely cut. All this is anathema to a radicalized feminist movement. One possible course of action is to line up with other forces to defend an educational service or the welfare state, which, whatever the short-comings, contained germs of progress. The alternative is to ignore or stand aside from the debate, arguing that these services have long been at best peripheral, and often, at worst, part of the controlling mechanism which itself needs to be challenged. For the more radical, the tactics for the present time remain rooted in self-education through local groups, and in self-help activities.

SUMMARY

Education for women in the present century is clearly present in terms of wider opportunities, but has remained a battleground. It has, as we have seen, been an arena in which the role of women in society has been strongly contested. For the male section of the population there was little doubt that education was regarded as a preparation for life as the breadwinner. Class might well decide, for most of the century, their destination, but the thrust was rarely in question. For the female section, career, domesticity and self-fulfilment have struggled for primacy. Responses have varied greatly. Many of the leading pioneers were promoters of assimilationism. Their starting point was that, because there were no discernible differences intellectually between men and women, what their students required was access to the same kind of education as their male counterparts. This explained their often deep suspicion of domestic studies for girls, which amounted to a differentiated curriculum. A second group, while retaining many of the older assimilationist attitudes about access to curriculum, has been more aware of the pressures on girls to conform to powerful traditional patterns. They have pressed for broad-based school policies to promote confidence, awareness and real equality, which require more appropriate teacher training, local authority in-service courses and 'space' within the schools to allow girls to work out their strategy for living.

Assimilationists have traditionally encouraged male support for their cause, believing that most reasonable men would accept its justness, and ultimately its benefits to society. Even the more sceptical second group believed that males in authority would eventually yield to their demands if sufficient pressure was brought to bear. A more radical approach, a product of the sombre 1970s, has argued that the predominant male structure will continue to exploit the present education system to maintain male domination. The dramatic rise in women's studies since the 1960s both in formal institutions and the more informal networks has been an attempt to challenge this source of power. Most academic disciplines are now showing the extent of this influence. Radical feminists have insisted that women must shift their demands from mere access to a male curriculum. What needs to be done is to accept that girls do have special needs, though not in the patriarchal sense, and that only a transformation of the whole educational system and its values will ultimately secure their rightful position in society. It would also, ultimately, mean a drastic change in the education of males.

FURTHER READING

There is now an extensive range of work on women's history in this century though we still await an overall study of the education of women and girls. Two excellent general studies are J. Lewis, *Women in England 1870–1950*, 1984, and her edited collection, J. Lewis, *Labour and Love*, 1986. F. Hunt (ed.), *Lessons for Life*, 1986, has a number of contributions on aspects of education. On the attempt to promote domesticity in the schools at the beginning of the century, see C. Dyhouse, *Girls Growing Up in Late Victorian and Edwardian England*, 1981. Two major works challenge the optimistic interpretation of the effect of total war on the role of women: G. Braybon, *Women Workers in the First World War*, 1981, and P. Summerfield, *Women Workers in the Second World War*, 1984. E. Roberts, *A Woman's Place*, 1984, details the struggles of working-class women, using an impressive array of oral evidence. D. Gittins, *Fair Sex: Family Size and Structure 1900–39*, 1982, is an important work on a significant aspect of a changing situation. For a stimulating work on many aspects of life for women after 1945 there is E. Wilson, *Only Halfway to Paradise*, 1980. D. Riley, *War in the Nursery*, 1983, details some of the pressures put on mothers in post-war Britain. L. Heron, *Truth, Dare or*

Promise: Girls Growing Up in the 1950s, 1985, offers insights into a neglected area. The position of various feminist groups on a range of issues is ably analysed in A. Coote and B. Campbell, *Sweet Freedom*, 1982.

CHAPTER TEN

Leisure, Broadcasting and Cinema

INTRODUCTION

In the nineteenth century liberal education and the provision of leisure were closely associated. Aristocrats and landed gentry were not expected to occupy their time in the daily tasks of earning a living. They were held to be responsible for the government of the nation, both at central and local level, and space was needed to pursue their role as ministers, lords lieutenant, magistrates or voluntary patrons of schools, hospitals and charities. Subjects were pursued at schools and at university without thought of specific occupations. A highbrow culture existed, desired by the wealthier middle classes as a mark of gentility, but remote from the everyday life of the mass of the population. Those who did not possess the attributes of this culture, particularly civilized conversation, classical allusions and oratorical skills were effectively excluded from power in the nation. This explains, for instance, the lack of success of a reformer like John Bright, so successful as a leader out of doors but a marginal figure in the House of Commons.

Amongst the middle classes a new element emerged after 1850, an intelligentsia, the product of university reform and of a prosperous metropolitan society. This group saw themselves as a Coleridgean clerisy, the arbiters of taste, the Platonic guardians of the best standards in society. They taught, tutored and, above all, wrote in the mass of periodicals which were a marked feature of the late Victorian period. The arch-apostle was Matthew Arnold, a vigorous critic of Philistinism, which he regarded as a dangerous aspect of society. He was highly critical of the entrepreneurial, largely Dissenting, section of the middle class. So concerned had they become with aspects of money-making that they ignored the higher purposes of life. Their homes, domestic refuges from the world outside, havens from the harsh competitive world, were often narrow and cramped. Some members of

141

the working classes enjoyed greater leisure as the century progressed. There was a general, if uneven, rise in wages, the introduction of half-day Saturday working, and an extended railway network which offered cheap excursions.

The second half of the nineteenth century was also characterized by the development of codified games and team sports, often segregated on social-class lines. Many of such activities were the product of public school athleticism, but political parties, aware of the need to capture an expanding electorate, also encouraged leisure occupations. None was better at this than the flamboyant editor of the socialist *Clarion*, Robert Blatchford, who promoted cycling clubs, choirs and rambler groups to preach the message. The more upper-class-dominated Primrose League engaged in much the same task for the Conservatives. Increasingly the state began to involve itself in the promotion of the nation's health. Municipal authorities embarked on schemes for recreation grounds, parks and the preservation of historical sites. Education Acts, from 1918, insisted on the provision in each local authority of facilities for sport. In the darkening 1930s the pressures grew. While there was no fascist-style youth militia, increased stress was placed on physical fitness and the spread of facilities for outdoor activities through such organizations as the Youth Hostels Association.

The legacy of the past century has weighed heavily on the present. Culture has remained highly stratified. A high culture, largely metropolitan, of opera house, quality press and theatre, supported by intellectuals, critics and the growing ranks of professional academics, has continued to exist. It has never been wholly conventional and, at times, has been at odds with the values of the rest of society. It is complemented by a distinctly working-class culture of popular newspapers, professional sports and mass entertainment. Between these two ranges there has been a lower-middle-class culture, sustained by middlebrow newspapers, popular fiction and weeklies, uncomfortable with some of the modernistic manifestations of high culture, but decidedly hostile to working-class vulgarity.

RADIO AND TELEVISION

From 1900 a range of amateur wireless societies came into existence to explore the new world of sound transmitted on the air-waves. Activity had been stopped at the beginning of the 1914 War because the military feared that it might interfere with the transmission of messages for their purpose. While Britain lagged behind, developments were moving apace in the USA, where, by 1920, a number of companies were transmitting programmes. In 1920 the powerful Marconi Company was experimenting with a radio programme which was restricted to the south-eastern region. Lord Northcliffe, the innovator of the popular press, had sensationally transmitted the voice of Melba at the Chelmsford Exhibition. In existence was a model of private enterprise which the Conservative-dominated Coalition might be expected to endorse.

Telephones and telegraphic services, however, were under the control of the Post Office, and radio could be seen as an extension of these services. Moreover the might of Marconi cast its shadow over the other companies producing radio sets. There were fears that in an openly competitive war Marconi would capture the entire market, and that unrestricted competition would lead to the air-waves being jammed. Underlying these concerns were more serious matters. In the Great War the enormous potentialities of propaganda, public relations and persuasion had come to light. Political figures surveyed a world witnessing mass democracy, Communist revolution and social uncertainty. The establishment of the British Broadcasting Company in 1922, financing its operation from a Post Office licensing fee and royalty on the sale of all marked receiving sets, reflected the uneasiness of the period. It was the most satisfactory device for preventing domination by a single company and for providing broadcasting without the government itself being responsible for the composition of programmes.

Under the scrutiny of the dour Calvinistic Scotsman, John Reith, the new company soon established itself among the powerful institutions of the nation. He looked at the press with disfavour, agreeing with politicians like Baldwin that it was free but totally irresponsible. Reith saw his company as a national institution, like the Church, the older universities and the Law, moulding the nation's life. His appointments reflected this outlook, and those entering the company felt themselves to be a secular priesthood, giving leadership in taste and culture.

He believed strongly that radio could benefit the education of the nation. Advisory Committees were soon in operation, covering areas such as Spoken English, Music for Education and Schools Broadcasting. In a few years the BBC became one of the largest employers of musicians, actors and writers. If the radio was to become a national institution Reith was determined that its status as a company should be transformed. It was vital that it should become a national corporation with a properly constituted, Crown-appointed governing body drawn from the highest circles, with a Director-General of wide authority.

This was finally achieved in 1926, and though the autocratic Reith was to clash with individual governors over ultimate responsibility for decisions, he never deviated from the position that there ought to be a governing body, representing not private interests, but the nation at large.

Early on, radio was seen to have direct educational impact. In 1924 a separate Education Department within the Company was set up with J.C. Stobart, a former HMI, as its Director of Education. In 1926 the Hadow Committee decided to set up an inquiry into the educational possibilities of broadcasting, and this produced a powerful endorsement of the use of radio in the classroom. Practical work followed quickly, notably the Kent experiment in 1927, jointly funded by the Carnegie Institute, the Board of Education and Kent County Council, which was prepared to allow the use of its classrooms for educational broadcasting. The results were generally favourable. It demonstrated that broadcasting might successfully provide news and information which the teachers themselves could not supply. Collaborative enterprises between teachers and broadcasters began to spring up. Nevertheless frustrations grew in the 1930s. Much depended upon the generosity of local authorities in being prepared to provide receiving sets in the classroom. The severe financial constraints of the period made this less than forthcoming. In 1934, the Central Council of School Broadcasting was established, and a number of subject committees were set up to link up with schools.

From the beginning there was criticism that Stobart was too school-directed. Many adult educationists seized on broadcasting as a key ally in their task. In the aftermath of war adult education was often regarded by reconstructionists as the cornerstone of their plans to build a new society. The British Institute of Adult Education in the early 1920s called on the BBC to transmit adult learning programmes. Listeners were to be encouraged to receive these talks in groups, partly because in the 1920s in many localities, only a minority possessed a receiving set. Such groups, it was hoped, would encourage a sense of community and enable individuals to extend newly acquired interests in a range of adult institutions. At their peak, in 1930, there were over a thousand listening groups, with leaders provided with background material. Two years later, the experiment was faltering. The leaders were often unaware of the techniques necessary to stimulate discussion, while those in the groups were often already attending adult education classes. Listening groups were wound up in 1934, but they have left legacies. First of all, they could be seen as some kind of model for the use of radio and television in the Open University. The immediate effect on the BBC planners was to make them view with hostility proposals for a separate educational channel which was likely to be a heavy burden. Finally there was a change of tactics. Attention was centred on home-based leisure pursuits such as gardening or musical appreciation which could easily be stimulated by short talks. Areas of history began to be treated in lighter ways than the dry academic lecture, scrapbooks relying on pieces of evidence taking their place.

By the late 1930s Reith had achieved many of his aims. Listening to the wireless was a national occupation almost everywhere. Nevertheless complaints began to surface about his autocratic behaviour, poor labour relations and lack of consultation. In 1937, believing that he was destined for higher national purposes, Reith stepped down, leaving behind a proud public service for his successors to defend.

Broadcasting came into its own in 1939. In these early stages of the War the government expected the closest collaboration between the broadcasters and the supervisory Ministry of Information. Departments of state wanted to shape programmes, and attempts were made to use the wavelengths for propaganda purposes. On the whole this was resisted by producers, and broadcasters took it upon themselves to become the representatives of the nation. Discussions and documentaries abounded, and the Brains Trust was only one of these new forms of programme. Attempts were made to extend the news, by additional items in Radio Newsreel and feature programmes that explained the background to war-time issues. The need for radio to entertain came to the forefront. As a result the muted Sunday schedule was gradually changed, and lighter shows and variety filled peak times. This development was accentuated in wartime, particularly with the setting up of the Forces network, designed to sustain morale with light diversions such as games and quiz shows. Listening facilities were provided for workers employed in long shifts in the factories, and they required background music. In spite of this shift of emphasis, and Churchill's impatience with distractions from winning the war, the BBC was in the forefront of the debates about the future of society in the post-war era.

The post-war period was to see important changes in the direction of broadcasting. The new Director-General, William Haley, who took up office in 1944, saw his task as being to build on the reputation achieved in recent years. The war had confirmed that listeners were clamouring for real choice and new patterns of programming. The answer was to establish three different stations, the Home, Light and Third. In 1949 the Beveridge Committee was set up to investigate the whole question of monopoly, prior to rechartering. It coincided with both the peak of radio listening, and the return of television. This medium had operated in a restricted fashion in the years 1936–39 but was confined to the Home Counties. During the war the service ceased to operate. In 1946 the service resumed as a single channel, a repetition of mixed programming. The appearance of the new medium raised issues of importance about the continuation of the monopoly. Charges were circulating that the BBC, still dominated by Reith's priestly cadre of professionals, was hostile to the development of television which they looked upon as a threat to literacy standards and good taste. Although the Beveridge Committee generally upheld the principle of a public monopoly there were danger signs. The membership debated the introduction of a commercial element through advertising, and Selwyn Lloyd, a prominent Conservative member, issued his own minority report attacking the Corporation for its top-heavy bureaucracy, its inability to keep up with technical progress and its negative attitude to popular taste. In the White Paper on Broadcasting of July 1951, the Labour government, not surprisingly, firmly upheld the public monopoly and rejected all forms of commercialism.

In the early 1950s powerful elements came together to press for an end to monopoly. Advertisers, sensing the growth of consumerism, were seeking new outlets. Many of the television producers, in particular Norman Collins, were convinced that the narrow outlook of the Corporation was holding them back. Finally, powerful elements within the Conservative party were clamouring for change. The Labour party generally upheld the Corporation's position, though within its ranks were some who deplored what they saw as a patronizing attitude to working-class audiences, and the domination of metropolitan interests. In 1952 the National Television Council was formed to fight commercialization, and the figures of Lords Halifax, Salisbury and Hailsham ensured a powerful Conservative presence that the government dared not ignore. They continually maintained that competing channels, financed by advertisements, would lead to the deterioration of standards and the introduction of American-style programming. As a counter to this very influential organization, the Popular Television Association emerged, headed by Lord Derby. It is difficult to estimate the extent of public feeling on the whole issue. Ultimately, within the Cabinet the forces of change triumphed, but so narrowly that unrestricted commercialism did not emerge. There had to be compromises.

Two points stand out in the Television Bill of 1954. Advertising was to be restricted to television. Radio was to remain in the hands of the Corporation. In one sense it was the last fling of the old order, for this medium was regarded as the more vital, which clearly, at the end of the decade, was not the case. In addition, a number of safeguards were set up to ensure that the new commercial channel was not allowed to submit to the wishes of the advertisers. Thus the Independent Broadcasting Authority (IBA) came into existence to monitor standards, to ensure that programmes covered a wide spectrum of tastes and that British features were prominent. Provision was made for educational television. All television companies had to carry at least nine hours a week in schools' programmes while schools were in session. They had to broadcast a further regular pattern of educational programmes for adults.

After early problems the new channel soon proved to be a serious threat to its rival. Within five years 70 per cent of the audience had been weaned from the BBC. By the 1960s even news, political programmes and documentaries had more personal touches, and were much less respectful in interviews of prominent figures. There were more regional programmes and the strengthening of local radio. As extra channels were allocated they fell first to the BBC and then to Independent Television. Both the second channels have provided much of the more serious content in the last decade.

CINEMA

Cinema, in contrast to literature, painting or music, has always struggled to be accepted as an art form. Its mode of production, assembling and distribution has been seen as an industrial or business process. While individuals can study literature as isolated texts, films almost always have been viewed in the mass. For much of the earlier part of the century, it looked likely, in its appeal, to supersede all other forms of leisure. Throughout this stage it was viewed by educationists and social commentators with grave concern. There were powerful reasons for the extent of criticism. First of all, those who commented unfavourably on the appeal of cinema were those least touched by its appeal, namely the products of the literary world dominated by the written word. Moreover, its origins were in the lower order of entertainment, the travelling booth, music hall and hired tent. It emerged at the same time as the spread of the popular press and professional sport. The tendency was to put the new forces together and condemn them as products of mass taste, mass education and impending mass democracy. Cinema, in its infancy, struggled against its lowly beginnings and, by 1914, new purpose-built places of entertainment, with socially edifying themes, came into existence. As the century progressed the screens became filled with American films, and an array of politicians, churchmen and moralists assailed this impending threat of American cultural dominance. The City had been slow to invest in a British film industry and later attempts to catch up never succeeded. Throughout its life the cinema appeared as the adjunct of the great producing chains.

There was always a minority group who saw the educational potential of the cinema. Their problem was that the cinema had been exploited by entrepreneurs, of limited outlook at best, and ignorant at worst. The Great War had been a period of experimentation in using film for training purposes, news and overt propaganda. In the 1920s film societies proliferated, intent on engendering a more critical awareness of what was being shown. The films, produced for a non-commercial audience, stressed themes of a political and social nature, and were often influenced by the Russian Revolution and its film-makers. Some of this activity, distrusted strongly by Tory governments, became absorbed in the documentary film movement, a broader attempt to show more 'realistic' films and associated with the names of John Grierson and Paul Rotha. Many who participated in this movement were the products of public schools and Oxbridge, and they saw the task of the élite in the twentieth century as being to instruct, and to make people more aware. John Grierson believed that the cinema could be the most effective instrument in citizenship, since it could show most strikingly how society worked. For him, it was important that the unpalatable poverty and distress should be highlighted, and he wanted the cinema to denounce, unsettle and make people angry. He was representative of the mood of the 1930s when the forces of democracy seemed to be fighting a desperate battle against those of authoritarianism and mass intolerance.

For the majority of the cinema-goers in the period 1920–50, the visit to the cinema became the 'treat' as they found themselves in increasingly well furnished picture houses. Attendance at the cinema was marked by certain characteristics. First of all, it was overwhelmingly local, spreading out to every suburb, and often within walking distance for the audience. Second, it became increasingly a family affair in which husband and wife went as a pair. It was often argued that this had been the most beneficial effect in that it strengthened patterns of marriage. High attendance masked significant differences in the composition of the audience. Boys usually began to attend at an earlier age than girls. By adolescence girls had become more interested in cinema-going. Children from secondary schools and post-Butler grammar schools tended to go less than those at elementary and post-war secondary modern schools. Age played its part in attendance figures, for the older portion of the population went less frequently. Finally, it was predominantly a working-class or lower-middle-class phenomenon.

The cinema industry was soon aware of these characteristics. From the Edwardian period there had been a distinct attempt to make the whole operation more respectable. In 1912, the industry placed itself under a voluntary code of censorship. The choice of subject for the new features became more family-oriented, with emphasis on costume drama and literary classics adapted for the screen. The prevalence of large working-class audiences was recognized and shaped the association of cinema with dream factories. The majority of the population was presented with a form of escape from the endless struggle of everyday life. Accompanying this was the creation of a star system of well-publicized, big names. Finally there was the continual search for innovation to ensure that the audience's attendance rate was maintained. Each new development, such as the introduction of sound or colour process made the industry more costly, so that by the end of the 1920s the production and distribution of films was controlled by two or three powerful circuits. In 1932, the passage of the Sunday Entertainment Act gave local authorities the right to license Sunday cinema, but directed that a percentage of the money must be subscribed to a Cinematograph Fund to develop a prestigious British Film Institute. Most cinemas tried to provide as much variety as possible, with films changing in mid-week, and attempts to create a distinct Sunday audience.

From the beginning concern was expressed about the quality of films seen by children. A number of enquiries dating from the time of the Great War were set up to examine the impact of cinema on children's behaviour. There were warnings about eyestrain, excessive restlessness and bad moral influence. The industry responded in three ways, moving first of all to exclude children from films that were deemed to be unsuitable for their viewing. More positive was the creation of special feature programmes specifically aimed at children in the mushrooming Saturday clubs. These were generally of poor quality. Finally, there was the development, particularly in the 1930s, of educational films. A number of investigations of the potentiality of film in the classroom had been launched in the 1920s. Certain subjects appear to lend themselves to the use of film, notably history, geography and science. Indeed the Historical Association was in the forefront of the promotion of film in the teaching of history. However, in the 1930s progress was very slow. Equipment was costly, and special classrooms for viewing were non-existent. Much of the early apparatus involved the acquisition of skills which most people did not possess. Doubts continued about effectiveness in the classroom.

By 1924, the British film industry was overwhelmed by the pressure of Hollywood, already well cushioned with its own internal market and able to build up massive profits by selling to the outside world. To help in this situation, in 1927, the Baldwin government passed the Cinematograph Act which required that a quota of British-made films must be screened, and that this quota would be increased over the years. In retaliation Hollywood threatened to withhold films totally from the British market. Trouble then arose over the definition of 'British'. Individual American companies bought themselves into the British industry and proceeded to produce poor quality fill-ins. In this way a move to boost a home industry rebounded as these so-called British films were associated with the shoddy and second-rate.

The 1930s saw world crisis with depression, mass unemployment and the threat of war. It was often through the eyes of the camera that audiences witnessed the Nuremberg rallies, the hunger marches and the destruction of cities in the Spanish Civil War. Newsreels distributed by a number of companies became a common feature of the 1930s programme. It was claimed by the companies that they presented a balanced view of the world around them and that all points of view were represented. Historians of the period have been less kind. They have pointed out the close relationship that existed between the companies and the senior politicians. The government approach to issues was usually accepted. The hunger marches were portrayed as a law and order affair. Even the growing threat from Germany was diluted by a tendency to highlight Britain and its Empire as an oasis of undisturbed peace remote from a troubled Europe. The implication was that the British had a certain style that kept them free from the twin dangers of communism and fascism.

The commercial cinema was in its heyday as a dream factory in the 1930s. Hollywood was in the forefront of lavish musicals, while British producers concentrated on costume drama, historical features and light comedy. The key producers, Alexander Korda and Michael Balcon, reflected a strong patriotism and concern for empire. Films, often located in India or Africa, displayed British character at its best, both concerned with the lot of subject peoples, but at the same time exercising authority almost by habit. Great institutions were portrayed as standing the test of time. Nothing demonstrated this better than the theme of education. Until the 1950s, as in the school story or novel, it was the world of public and preparatory school that was featured. Gowned masters, uniformed children, the dormitory and the games field were the background of films associated with schooling and adolescence. Similarly, with few exceptions, little attempt was made to show real conditions in industrial areas. The distributors insisted that these themes were not what a mass audience wanted to see. All this made the critical minority, struggling to come to terms with the new forces, more hostile.

At the beginning of the 1939 War all cinemas were ordered to close. It was argued that the coming of the bomber made them potential death traps. Within weeks, this order had been rescinded. Cinema-going provided entertainment, escape and diversion. As war continued the film industry took a new turn. Productions were aided and sponsored by government. In addition, film-makers, sensing the mood of intro-spection, began to raise issues about why the war was being fought, what it was to be British, and the need to end outmoded traditions. From 1942, films became more critical and satirical. They attacked muddle and incompetence in high places, and implied that things must change. There was even more awareness among politicians of the significance of huge cinema audiences. One sign was the creation of the Palache Committee, in 1944, to investigate the condition of the industry. Its recommendations reflected a strong fear of American cultural and political dominance in the post-war world, which pushed its members towards active government finance of the British industry. There was an acceptance that, in the war, a popular British style had emerged.

The aftermath of war saw film audiences at their peak. It was a period when the industry was built up on a large scale, particularly with the energy and resources of the Methodist flour miller, J. Arthur Rank. To many, Rank represented the growing responsibility and respectability of the film industry. He was concerned with moral issues, the creation of a flourishing children's cinema and the making of documentaries. Others saw him as a manipulator, hand in glove with American producers, whose goodwill he needed to circulate his British films in the rich USA market and to keep his own chain of cinemas well stocked. In a period when the trade balance became fraught with acute difficulties, the Labour government grew alarmed at the costs of American film imports. In the crisis of 1947 the government imposed an import tax on American films which led to threats from Washington of a counter embargo. Thus the Rank circuit found itself starved of films, while Rank, in turn, found difficulties in showing his films in America. By 1948 he was in trouble with his own investors, and the British govern-ment was compelled to repeal the tax. Harold Wilson, at the Board of Trade, continued to display a strong interest and, in 1948, set up the

National Film Corporation with a sum of £5 million which would enable established film-makers to top up their budgets for major production. In 1957 the Corporation was further strengthened by the Cinematograph Film Act which channelled a small proportion of box office receipts into the funds. It hardly helped the cause of innovation since it supported the well established.

From the 1950s cinema-going as the major form of outside leisure declined sharply. In 1954, 24.5 million people went to the cinema each year. By 1960 that audience had shrunk to 10 million and the decline continued into the 1970s. Cinemas were closed in many suburbs, to be replaced by newer forms of entertainment such as bingo halls or bowling alleys. Some fine 1930s buildings were transformed into supermarkets. Clearly the growth of television, the crisis in Hollywood and the rise in car ownership all played their parts. Admission charges rose sharply. The new classification, an attempt to come to terms with the treatment of adult issues, may have hastened the decline. It too often led to the swamping of the screens with poorly made, crudely sensational films.

Since the 1960s the cinema has fought back against competitors such as television and the more recent video-recorder, both of which rely heavily on the production of films. Cinemas have been made smaller and more intimate, and frequently have been broken up into smaller units to cope with the more diverse audience. There has been more flexibility in the release of new films which have often been given longer runs. Attitudes towards censorship changed, particularly after the demise of the Lord Chamberlain's control over the theatre. Under John Trevelyan and Stephen Murphy there was a more relaxed approach to what was considered fit for screening, particularly in films that were deemed to have artistic integrity. Opponents of censorship maintained that this was unsatisfactory, since the standards applied to this category were too personal and arbitrary. Attempts were made, in 1970, to invest more money in the National Film Finance Corporation, but the incoming Conservative government declined to implement the measure of its predecessor. The advice to the Corporation was to seek private enterprise finance, and this remained Conservative policy into the 1980s. The White Paper on Films, issued in 1984, argued that a British industry would survive if the public wished this to happen. Thus the industry lost its government funding and now is forced to rely on the forces of the market.

SUMMARY

Debates about leisure and its role have formed a backcloth to many of the debates about education in the present century. For the older cultural minority, the heirs of the intellectual aristocracy of the previous century, the creation of a mass civilization, essentially urban, was seen as a source of concern, even danger, to society's well-being. For these cultural conservatives the necessity has been to preserve some standards in such areas as broadcasting and the cinema, the two examples considered in this chapter. In the right hands the mass media could raise the horizons and the educational expectations of the population. Much of the Reithian philosophy of public service broadcasting upheld this view, and sought to reverse Gresham's Law of good being driven out by bad.

FURTHER READING

T. Bennett, C. Mercer, and J. Woollacott, *Popular Culture and Social Relations*, 1986; J. Curran, A. Smith, and P. Wingate, *Impacts and Influences*, 1987; J. Walton and J. Walvin (eds.), *Leisure in Britain*, 1983, and S.G. Jones, *Workers at Play: a Social and Economic History of Leisure 1918–39*, 1986, all look at particular aspects of mass entertainment and popular culture. L. Johnson, *The Cultural Critics*, 1979, examines the attitudes of literary intellectuals. On broadcasting and television there is A. Briggs, *The BBC: The First Fifty Years*, 1985; A. Boyle, *Only The Wind Will Listen. Reith of the BBC*, 1972; M. Pegg, *Broadcasting and Society, 1918–1939*, 1983; and B. Sendall, *Independent Television in Britain, Vol. 1*, 1982. Cinema and its influence has been investigated in J. Curran and V. Porter, *British Cinema History*, 1983; R. Low, *Films of Comment and Persuasion of the 1930s*, 1979, and *Documentary and Educational Films of the 1930s*, 1979. There are perceptive studies by J. Richards, *Visions of Yesterday*, 1973, and *The Age of the Dream Palace*, 1984.

PART THREE
Educational Institutions

CHAPTER ELEVEN

The Emergence of the Primary School

One of the problems of discussing aspects of primary school education in the present century is that of definition. Before the 1944 Education Act, schools were either elementary or secondary: the former catered for children between the ages of five and 14 attending, as will be shown, schools organized in a number of different ways and overlapping into what is now taken to be the secondary age group. This chapter therefore will be concerned only with the education of children up to the age of about 11, and leaving the older age group to be dealt with in Chapter 12.

It is difficult to distinguish any clear pattern of schooling for this age group at the beginning of the present century. By the 1890s, some school boards had begun to divide schools into infant departments, junior departments and senior departments. During that decade, too, mixed departments became more popular, replacing separate departments for boys and girls at each level. In the late 1890s and with the ending of 'payment by results', a number of boards were developing junior schools up to the ages of 11 or 12 which resembled modern primary schools in many respects.

A more identifiable encouragement came with the 1902 Education Act, which converted many higher grade schools to secondary schools, and with the establishment of officially recognized higher elementary schools in 1900. But although great strides were made in the provision of primary age schools in the following year, the Board of Education's statistics as late as 1918 kept the distinction only between 'infants' and 'older children', with infants taken to be those between three and nine years of age (Board of Education, 1931, p.18). What became three stages in primary education – nursery, infant and junior – will now be examined in turn.

NURSERY SCHOOLS

As early as the Cross Commission on Elementary Education, 1888, the need for providing for pre-school age children was recognized. Patric Cumin, the Secretary of the Education Department, was a witness and agreed that children between three and five were capable of going to school, though the Department would not be able to supply accommodation in all cases. Another witness, the Rev. T. W. Sharpe, a Chief Inspector, made a strong case for 'baby rooms', to be provided in poor neighbourhoods where mothers were obliged to go out to work. Such an arrangement would also free elder children from childminding, thus allowing them to attend school regularly (Cross Commission, 1888, p. 54).

One of the first tasks given to the newly-formed Women Inspectorate in 1905 was to make a survey of children under five in public elementary schools. Some thousands of children were examined by the five Women Inspectors. Cyril Jackson, the Chief Inspector for Elementary Schools, wrote in the Introduction to the Report that 'there is complete unanimity that the children between the ages of three and five get practically no intellectual advantage from school instruction' (Board of Education, 1905, p. i).

Witnesses before the Inter-Departmental Committee on Physical Deterioration had made a case for separate nurseries rather than schools for children between three and five, as had one of the Women Inspectors involved in the survey (Gordon, 1988, p. 202). The Board, however, issued a Code following the Women Inspectors' survey stating that LEAs might refuse admission to children in this age group. By 1908, more than half the LEAs had taken advantage of this provision and excluded such children. In 1900, 43.1 per cent of three- and four-year-olds attended school: by 1910 this had fallen to 22.7 per cent.

The Board was happy to leave any initiatives to private bodies and individuals, for example Margaret and Rachel McMillan, who founded a nursery school at Deptford in 1911. Their school was seen as a 'healing agency' which attended to the health as well as the educational needs of young children. Although the 1918 Education Act allowed LEAs for the first time to provide funds for nursery schools, only a few actually did so; much of the experimentation was carried on in middle-class private schools, like the Malting House School founded by Susan Isaacs in 1924.

The Hadow Consultative Committee Report on Infant and Nursery

Schools, published in 1933, drew on research into physiological and psychological development to support the call for nursery schools as an integral part of the national education system. These schools were still considered to be primarily for children from an 'unsuitable environment' (Board of Education, 1933, pp. 187–8). Much of the ground for a sympathetic view of such education had been laid by various pressure groups, notably the Nursery School Association, founded in 1923. Lobbying of LEAs, MPs and the Board of Education featured large in its activities (Blackstone, 1971, p. 4). The Labour party had pressed for this reform and a start had been made during their second term of office (1929–31) in encouraging LEAs to make some provision.

The fall in the birthrate during the economic recession of the 1930s and government cutbacks made for slow progress before the Second World War. There was a dramatic expansion of facilities during the war, when women were required for war work, with the provision of full-time nurseries and the admission of children from two years of age to existing infant schools. By 1944, there were over 200,000 under-fives attending one or other of these institutions.

Although the 1944 Education Act encouraged LEAs to continue to make provision, nursery education suffered badly. The Ministry of Health ceased to pay full grants to day nurseries in 1946, and the 1948 (Miscellaneous Provisions) Act fixed the statutory age of admission at the term after which a pupil reached his/her fifth birthday. During the 1950s and 1960s the Ministry of Education gave priority to the later rather than the earlier years of schooling following the raising of the school-leaving age. However, the Plowden Report, *Children and their Primary Schools* (1967), recommended a large increase in nursery education: the major manifestation of this new mood was the provision of 10,000 more places designated in Educational Priority Areas (EPA) in 1970 and 5,000 in the following year (Whitbread, 1972, p. 113).

Self-help, in the form of the Pre-School Playgroups Association, founded in 1961, filled some of the gap. Half-day sessions for children, conducted by a qualified supervisor with volunteer help from mothers, became popular, as were day nurseries for children 'with special needs', but provision was uneven and they were not nursery schools in the accepted sense. A National Campaign for Nursery Education was begun in 1965, and it received backing from parents and teachers' unions. The 1972 White Paper was one successful outcome and more resources were allocated to LEAs for this purpose. By the 1980s, 42 per cent of under-fives were receiving some form of nursery education.

INFANT SCHOOLS

Separate infant schools had been a feature of English education since the early nineteenth century. The distinction between the infant school and the main elementary school was emphasized by the Education Department in 1871, which, in giving guidance to school boards on planning and equipping schools, stipulated that separate accommodation was necessary for infants. Further official recognition of the needs of this younger group was demonstrated in a Circular to Inspectors issued in 1893 on the Instruction of Infants, which recommended Froebelian-based activities rather than formal lessons.

We have seen in the earlier part of this chapter that the 1905 Code, by discouraging LEAs from accommodating the under-fives in infant schools, delineated the age group in such schools as ranging from five to seven. Whilst agreeing with the 1893 Code on the need for encouraging 'mental and physical growth and the development of good habits' rather than standards of attainment in the 3Rs, little action was taken by the Board to further these aims. Much of the initiative lay elsewhere. The writings of progressives, such as John Dewey, were influential. An account of Edmond Holmes's visit to Rome in 1911 to study the teaching methods of Maria Montessori appeared in a Board of Education pamphlet the following year, though a guarded Prefatory Note by the Board pointed to the need for more experiments under varying conditions before the system was adopted (Board of Education, 1912, p. 3). Following the meeting of the Conference on New Ideals in Education in 1915, the virtues of the new and enlightened approaches to teaching the young attracted many distinguished educationists, including Cyril Burt, Beatrice Ensor, Edmond Holmes, Percy Nunn and Michael Sadler. However, experimentation between the two World Wars in state schools was limited. It was perhaps unfortunate that these ideals were not shared by such politicians as Lord Eustace Percy, President of the Board of Education, 1924–29. An opponent of Dewey and his followers, Percy, when confronted with the need to make economies in the education budget in October 1924, suggested that this could be achieved by totally excluding five- to six-year-olds from school (Simon, 1974b, p.93).

Nevertheless, the cumulative effect of the progressive movement can be seen in the Report of the Consultative Committee on Infant and Nursery Schools, issued in 1933. Chaired by Sir Henry Hadow, this Report followed two years after an investigation by the same body into the Primary School (see p.162 following). The earlier Report had already set the scene by recommending separate infant schools for children under seven. This view was endorsed by the 1933 Committee, though it stated that the primary stage of education was to be regarded as a continuous whole and that there should be no abrupt break in that education (Board of Education, 1933, pp.174–5). However, in many LEAs, infant schools continued to be situated some distance from the nearest junior department. Suitable accommodation was also urged. Given the need for activities in small groups and for physical activity, the Board's allowance of nine square feet per child was inadequate. The two-decker or three-decker school with a central hall, a legacy of the school board era, was particularly unsuitable. Pavilion type schools of single storeys, which had become popular in the 1920s, met some of these needs.

Research work undertaken by Susan Isaacs at the Department of Child Development, London Institute of Education, into the emotional, social and intellectual development of the young child exerted enormous influence on generations of teachers in their teaching methods from the 1930s. This work was carried on by her successor, Dorothy Gardner. During the Second World War, the experiences of evacuation were described and analysed by Anna Freud and Dorothy Burlingham. These pioneers advanced the notion of the importance of incorporating aspects of home experience into school life (Weber, 1971, p.166).

In the 1944 Education Act, the infant stage of education was not specifically mentioned, being subsumed under the heading of primary education. With the large building programme undertaken by the Ministry of Education after the war, economic considerations proved as important as the educational ones in the favouring of combined junior–infant schools. Whereas before the Second World War 70 per cent of infant schools were in separate buildings, the number had been reduced to 56 per cent by 1965.

Organizational considerations have been a prominent feature of post-war infant education. Continuity in the primary sector of education, as advocated by the 1933 Hadow Report, resulted in calls for combined nursery–infant schools. One example was the Evelyn Lowe School in South London, which catered for children from $3\frac{1}{2}$ to nine years: this consisted of a nursery, and family grouping of four- to six- and seven- to nine-year-olds. The Plowden Report recommended a slightly different arrangement of nursery groups from three to five and 'first schools', taking children at five and transferring at eight, in both instances in the September following their birthdays. When first schools were set up from the late 1960s, most LEAs opted for a five-to-eight age range, whilst others preferred a five-to-nine arrangement. With the shift in political and parental thinking since then, some of the more enlightened aspects of the infant school have been subject to attack. As the DES document *Education in Schools*, issued in 1977 as part of the 'Great Debate', stated: 'There are some skills for which primary schools have a central, and indeed over-riding, responsibility. Literacy and numeracy are the most important of these: no other curricular aims should deflect teachers from them' (DES, 1977, p.9). A survey of 80 first schools carried out by HMI in 1978–79 and published in a report *Education 5 to 9* (1982) concluded that whilst the older and more able children made too little progress in mathematics and language, overemphasis on basic skills limited the time available for extending the range of curricular activities.

JUNIOR SCHOOLS

In contrast to the infant school, the junior school was a comparatively late development. Although mixed junior schools or departments evolved about 1895, accepting pupils up to the age of 12, they were criticized on the ground that they saw neither the beginning nor the end of a child's school life.

Two separate administrative actions helped to determine the age group of junior school departments. As mentioned earlier, the 1905 Regulations strengthened the position of infant schools, whilst the development of secondary schools and central schools, offering practical courses for post-primary age pupils, accentuated the tendency in urban areas to make a break in school life about the age of 11. The other stimulus came from the Board of Education's 1905 Regulations for the Instruction and Training of Pupil Teachers, which required pupils intending to teach in elementary schools to receive a sound general education for three or four years in secondary schools. Scholarships awarded by LEAs for this purpose were normally in the 11-to-12 age range. A third development came in 1907 after the return of a Liberal government, when the so-called Free Place Regulations were inserted into the Secondary Regulations, whereby 25 per cent of scholars were admitted from elementary schools without payment of fees. These moves led elementary teachers to devote more time to the instruction of pupils under 11 years of age.

The 1918 Education Act introduced a compulsory leaving age of 14 and encouraged LEAs to reorganize the arrangements for the education of children below the age of 11. More directly, Circular 1350 of January 1925 pointed out that this age was 'the most suitable dividing line between what may be called "Junior" and "Senior" Education'. The organization favoured by the Board was, strangely, two separate and parallel departments of mixed infants and juniors. The *New Prospect in Education* three years later showed that the Board officials had had second thoughts and now supported a scheme of separate infant and junior departments where numbers warranted it (Birchenough, 1938, p.434).

The dividing age of 11 was adopted by the Consultative Committee on the Education of the Adolescent (1926) chaired by Sir Henry Hadow. The famous quotation, 'There is a tide which begins to rise in the veins of youth at the age of eleven or twelve. It is called by the name of adolescence', sets the tone of the Report. Briefly, it recommended that primary education should be regarded as ending at the age of 11+, when pupils should pass on to a secondary stage. The Report stated that the term 'elementary school' should be replaced by 'primary' and pupils above that age were to be transferred to a different school. Reorganization followed rapidly, though the percentage of pupils in 'senior departments' in fact represented only a modest part of the total in elementary schools (see table below).

REORGANIZATION OF ELEMENTARY SCHOOLS, 1927–30

	31 March 1927		31 March 1929		31 March 1930	
	Pupils	% of Total	Pupils	% of Total	Pupils	% of Total
Senior Departments	25,293	1.2	33,437	1.4	37,269	1.5
Boys, Girls and Mixed Departments	1,896,655	89.5	1,966,535	84.0	2,012,210	79.5
Junior Departments	150,923	7.1	277,330	12.0	416,405	16.5
Infant Departments	45,386	2.2	61,652	2.6	63,569	2.5
Totals	2,118,257	–	2,388,954	–	2,529,453	–

Source: Report of the Consultative Committee on the Primary School (1931), p.19.

This reorganization was not completed until well after the Second World War. If the Report on the Education of the Adolescent had dealt tangentially with the primary school, the Hadow Report on the Primary School (1931) fully examined the subject. The Consultative Committee's task was to make recommendations on the curriculum of children between seven and 11, but it commented on a number of other features. The enlightened views expressed in successive *Handbooks of Suggestions for Teachers* and the activities of the progressives had been absorbed into the Committee's thinking. It summed up its philosophy in the phrase: 'the curriculum is to be thought of in terms of activity and experience rather than of knowledge to be acquired and facts to be stored' (Board of Education, 1931, p.93). The ending by the Board of Education in 1926 of the regulation of the primary school curriculum was an encouragement for teachers. By 1937, the *Handbook of Suggestions* was promoting systematic courses based on children's natural interests (Board of Education, 1937, p.107). In contrast to this liberal approach, the *Primary School* Report included a memorandum by Cyril Burt (Appendix III), suggesting that a suitable classification of children should be made according to their abilities. The Report endorsed this view, recommending that by the age of ten, children should be organized in three groups (Board of Education, 1931, p.35). 'Streaming', into classes labelled A, B and C in the appropriate year group, was widely adopted. The growing popularity of the 'eleven plus' examination had at least two important consequences: the curriculum was narrowed to meet the needs of the examination and special 'scholarship classes' were formed for the abler pupils. Despite the official rhetoric there was little change during the next 20 years, with emphasis on numeracy and literacy still predominant and class sizes remained large (Galton, Simon and Croll, 1980, p.36).

Although the 1944 Education Act formally established the primary stage of education, progress was largely impeded by the predominance of the 'eleven plus' examination in the junior school. It is clear that the Ministry of Education played a passive role in promoting change in the primary school during the 1940s and 1950s. Structural problems, particularly in coping with the growing school population, occupied much of the energies of officials. Circular 30/45 regretted that it was not yet possible to prescribe a lower maximum than 40 for junior and infant classes, and underlined the considerable difficulty involved in achieving classes smaller in size until staffing and accommodation could be improved.

The initiative for change came mainly from LEAs and practitioners. One outstanding example was that of Hertfordshire LEA and its Director of Education, John Newsom. Newsom hoped to build schools which encouraged the use of progressive teaching methods. Rejecting the temporary HORSA huts which were then standard, Newsom made use of factory-made components which allowed for greater flexibility in building design. Other authorities followed Newsom's lead and a consortium of LEAs (CLASP) was formed in 1957 for bulk buying. The Ministry of Education disseminated new ideas in primary school design in its Building Bulletins from 1949 and through its Architects and Buildings Branch (Seaborne and Lowe, 1977, p.170). There were also LEAs which, through the active assistance of their advisers, promoted innovative teaching as in Oxfordshire, Bristol and London. This was often possible particularly in areas where the 'eleven plus' examination was being abolished and where streaming no longer existed. The open plan schools of the 1960s provided further opportunities for advance.

These enlightened views were encapsulated in the Plowden Report (1967). Its terms of reference, 'primary education in all its aspects and the transition to secondary education', were wide-ranging. Plowden found that the Hadow Reports had understated rather than over-estimated the differences between children. Streaming, it believed, was not the answer but, with emphasis on the child as an individual, teachers were to adapt their methods to individuals within a class, recognizing the different needs of, for example, gifted and slow-learning children (Plowden, 1967, i, p.460).

The Committee were concerned with the relationship between attainment and home conditions and recommended a policy of postive discrimination in the education system through designated Educational Priority Areas, with extra resources allocated to the schools. The idea of EPA action programmes was quickly taken up, with Crosland, the Secretary of State at the DES, taking a prominent part in its establishment (HMSO, 1972, p.vii).

Another of the major Plowden recommendations was a change in the age of transfer within primary schools and between primary schools and secondary schools. Experiments in the West Riding in 1963 for one of its Divisional Executives, Wakefield, led to the adoption of a three-tier system of 5 to 9 first schools, 9 to 13 middle schools and 13 to 18 upper schools. The Minister of Education, Sir Edward Boyle, was approached with a view to relaxing the statutory requirements. In 1964, an Education Act allowing the setting up of middle schools received parliamentary approval. Shortly afterwards, a Labour government was elected. Crosland, the new Secretary of State, in Circular 10/65 recommended to LEAs the middle school as one of the six forms of planning for comprehensive education. Plowden had concluded that there is 'no universally right age ... so various are human beings', but on balance favoured 12 as the age of transfer; children would have three years in an infant school, arriving at the middle schools at about eight years of age. By 1970, the DES had approved middle schools schemes in 49 LEAs, spanning different age ranges – eight to 12, nine to 13 and 10 to 13 (DES, 1970, p.viii). Some LEAs may have been influenced by Circular 13/66 which announced the Government's plans for raising the school-leaving age. The subsequent failure of the two major political parties either to support or oppose the concept of the middle school proved to be a handicap to its development (Blyth and Derricott, 1977, p. 180).

If the 1950s and 1960s signalled advances in primary education, there were setbacks in the decades following. Academic criticism of the 'Plowden philosophy' was voiced by Richard Peters and others in *Perspectives on Plowden* published in 1969; it was lacking in aims, overstressed personal autonomy and laid too little emphasis on standards. Disquiet was voiced from another quarter, the writers of the three *Black Papers* published between 1969 and 1975. The editors, C.B. Cox and Rhodes Boyson, claimed that the original *Black Paper* was 'the first serious attempt in Britain to provide a critique of the move to progressive education' (Cox and Dyson, 1975, p. 3). Plowden, to them, represented the height of progressive euphoria and the authors challenged the basis of the figures on reading standards quoted in the Report. The 'back to basics' debate coincided with the economic recession of the early 1970s, which led to cutbacks in educational expenditure as well as a fall in the number of pupils in primary schools.

Some of these concerns were expressed in the regional conferences following the Ruskin College speech of the Prime Minister, James Callaghan, in October 1976. The section on the primary schools curriculum in the consultative document *Education in Schools* (1977) mentioned the beneficial effects in recent years of much wider curriculum and the 'child-centred' approach. At the same time it was noted that in the hands of less experienced teachers, this approach had not been carefully organized and monitored; as a result, the basic subjects had suffered. 'The challenge now is to restore the rigour without damaging the real benefits of the child-centred developments' (DES, 1977, p. 8). The middle schools also raised problems, particularly those of continuity, resources and the range of curriculum offered.

The apparent dangers posed by this open approach to primary school methods were exposed to public scrutiny in a report published in 1976, following an inquiry by the Inner London Education Authority into affairs at the William Tyndale Junior School in North London. The disquiet concerned the teaching methods used by members of the staff who had radical convictions. The subsequent events involved the parents, local inspectors, managers and local politicians as well as the teachers. The Auld Report, commissioned by the Inner London Education Authority, highlighted the need for criteria by which to assess a school's efficiency (Gretton and Jackson, 1976, p. 124). One significant aspect of the case was that the DES refused to intervene in the dispute, turning down a request for HMI to give their judgements on the school.

However, the Inspectorate had been stimulated into action before the Great Debate had begun by starting a national survey of the primary curriculum in 1975. Comparatively little was known of practices, so assessments of children's work at seven, nine and 11 were made in a representative sample of 542 schools. The Report, *Primary Education in England* (1978), criticized teachers for often under-estimating children's abilities and noted the lack of specialist teachers who could draw up schemes of work and give guidance to their colleagues. A similar survey for the younger age range was carried out by HMI in 1978 and 1979. The report, *Education 5 to 9* (1982), was also critical, particularly stressing the need to update teachers' skills. It is, however, a significant index of the changing climate of primary schools that HMI observed that too much time was being devoted to the basic subjects. Doubts on the future of middle schools were expressed in a 1983 survey of these schools; given the falling rolls their cost was becoming increasingly hard to justify. Between 1980 and 1987, the number of middle schools fell from 1,396 to 1,213 (DES, *Statistics of Schools, January 1987*, 1988, p. 140).

Many of these views were incorporated in *Curriculum 5–16* (1985), an Inspectorate discussion document. A more positive approach was the publication of an HMI series *Curriculum Matters* from 1984. Here, the teaching and learning of subjects such as English, mathematics, music and home economics were discussed in a 5-to-16 framework and responses from schools encouraged e.g. *Mathematics from 5 to 16: The Responses to Curriculum Matters 3* (1987). This curriculum debate has drawn in many primary schools, many of whom have contributed positively to official thinking.

With the publication of Inspectors' reports on schools since January 1983, a clearer picture of the state of primary schools has emerged. By May 1984, 123 such reports had been published. No fewer than a half of these schools were housed in pre-1914 buildings and some were using rather old temporary classrooms. Teacher–pupil ratios ranged widely, from 1:14.2 to 1:27.2, with the majority falling in the band 1:20 to 1:25. All the schools had guidelines for languages and mathematics, but fewer planned other elements of the curriculum as systematically (DES, 1984, pp.4–6).

Ministerial initiatives in improving standards in education have, in some instances, been favourable to the primary school. In *Teaching Quality* (1983) the DES stated: 'It is important that the prospective expansion of opportunities for new primary schools should be widely recognised' (p.7). The lack of 'match' in primary education between the expertise of staff members and the curriculum was noted, as well as the need to promote science education and to redress the existing heavy weighting towards the humanities and aesthetic subjects (p.9). Subsequently, the DES encouraged institutions offering PGCE courses to establish or expand courses in the primary field.

A new element which has obvious implications for the primary school is the introduction of national testing with agreed attainment targets. Teacher assessment is a fundamental part of the system, which would include both seven- and 11-year-olds. The Task Group on Assessment and Testing, set up by the Secretary of State for Education, Kenneth Baker, in 1987, recommended the implementation of this programme as soon as possible. Of the ten levels, seven-year-olds would be expected to achieve levels one to three. Because of the ambitious nature of the programme, some modifications have since been effected.

SUMMARY

The concept of the primary school evolved slowly. For almost a century after the State first made provision for education, the term 'elementary' covered children of all ages other than those attending 'secondary' schools. The change to a more enlightened approach followed the ending of 'payment by results' in 1895, and was reflected in official publications such as the *Handbook of Suggestions for Teachers*. Progressive educators, who preached the gospel of child-centred education, included administrators and inspectors as well as academics.

The separation of children at the age of 11, advocated by the 1926 Hadow Committee, was an important step forward. For the next quarter of a century, schools were reorganized and an identifiable primary sector, with its own philosophy and curriculum, came into being.

Separate infant schools for children under seven had been established before the present century, though with the 1933 Hadow Committee's recommendation that the primary phase should be regarded as a continuous experience, schools were built with junior and infant departments on the same site.

Official enthusiasm for nursery provision was, with exceptions, lukewarm. Except for the periods of the two Great Wars, when women's work was encouraged, few LEAs took advantage of the permissive legislation to develop nursery education. Pressure groups made some impact but it was not until the Plowden Report (1967) demonstrated the immediate need that large-scale provision was made.

This Report also brought about the subsequent division of primary education into first and middle schools in many LEAs. The optimism expressed in Plowden on the state of primary education soon began to be questioned. Surveys by HMI of this age group found that children's abilities were not always recognized and noted the over-concentration on basic subjects. The middle school, created as a result of comprehensive reorganization from 1966, found favour with many authorities. But after a relatively short period of popularity, the number of middle schools has diminished nationally. However, the recognition by the DES in 1983 of the need to make special provision for the expanding primary schools, especially the need for more specialised expertise, is a welcome move.

FURTHER READING

For early schooling, see N. Whitbread, *The Evolution of the Nursery–Infant School 1800–1970*, 1972, and P. Lodge and T. Blackstone, *Education Policy and Educational Inequality*, 1982. See also the Hadow Report, *Report of the Consultative Committee on Infant and Nursery Schools*, 1933.

On the primary school as a whole, the following deal with many aspects of policy: J.W.B. Douglas, *The Home and School: a Study of Ability and Attainment in the Primary School*, 1964, A. Clegg (ed.), *The Changing Primary School: its Problems and Priorities*, 1972, and M. Clarkson (ed.), *Emerging Issues in Primary Education*, 1988. The Central Advisory Council's *Children and their Primary Schools* (Plowden Report), 1967, is an important document which generated much discussion, for example, R.S. Peters (ed.), *Perspectives on Plowden*, 1969, and a special issue of *Oxford Review of Education*, 'Plowden Twenty Years On', Vol. 13, No. 1, 1987. The *ILEA Report by Robin Auld, Q.C. on the William Tyndale Junior and Infant Schools*, 1976, throws light on decision-making in the primary sector.

For the middle school, see J. Burrows, *The Middle School*, 1978, and the HMI Survey, *Education 8 to 12 in Combined and Middle Schools*, 1985.

Official reports and surveys of primary schools are numerous. See, for example, *Primary Education*, 1959, *Primary Education in England*, 1978, and *Education 5 to 9: An Illustrative Survey*, 1982.

CHAPTER TWELVE

Secondary Education for All

TOWARDS A UNIFIED SYSTEM

A striking feature of those schools offering some sort of secondary education during the second half of the nineteenth century was their wide variety. The rise of the middle classes after the Napoleonic Wars led to a demand for secondary schools for a growing clientele. From the time of the Crimean War, the need for reforms in many spheres of public affairs and institutions was investigated by Royal Commissions. The Clarendon Commission (1861–64) examined the nine major public schools and the Taunton Commission (1864–68) the remainder of the endowed schools as well as proprietary and private schools. The Taunton Commission recommended the establishment of a national system of secondary education, working within an administrative framework and overseen by a central authority. This part of the Commissioners' recommendations was not implemented, but a start was made on categorizing schools into three grades, corresponding to the social class of children attending them. The first grade, with a leaving age of 18, prepared pupils for university and were mainly classical schools; the second grade, giving an education up to 16 for boys preparing for the professions, business and the armed forces, provided an appropriate curriculum; and the third grade, for sons of shopkeepers and superior artisans leaving at 14, offered a more practical curriculum. The Endowed Schools Commission (from 1874, the Charity Commission) was responsible for reviewing the endowments of the schools.

These categories were once again used by the Royal Commission on Secondary Education (Bryce) in 1894 which was asked to 'consider what are the best methods of establishing a well organized system of Secondary Education in England taking into account existing deficiencies'. By this time, there had been developments in the post-elementary sector which made the need for some action necessary. A number of first grade schools had become public schools and many

170

third grade schools were now elementary schools. School boards with ambitions for providing advanced work had instituted higher grade schools for pupils of 14 years or over. The Technical Instruction Act of 1889 allowed for locally-appointed committees of county boroughs to spend Excise money on technical and semi-technical subjects in the curriculum; they were also empowered to levy a 1d. rate if they wished to do so. The Science and Art Department also made grants to students attending any kind of institution, in a large list of subjects, except for Latin and Greek. One result of these new sources of revenue was that in a large number of towns Organized Science Schools, giving full-time instruction to boys and girls, sprang up; these were, except in name, secondary schools. To complicate the picture further, many of the older endowed schools made changes in their curriculum in order to qualify for recognition as Science Schools. Mention should also be made of pupil teachers' centres, which catered for the training of future teachers in elementary schools, and gave an education for the 14- to 18-year-olds. It is interesting to note that of the first four new secondary schools provided by the West Riding of Yorkshire following the 1902 Education Act, three were converted pupil teachers' centres.

The Bryce Commission strongly urged the establishment of 'a well-organized system of secondary education in England'. It recommended that as a first step, the three separate central agencies – the Education Department, the Science and Art Department and the Charity Commission – should be merged into a single department, headed by a Minister responsible to Parliament. Local authorities for secondary education in county councils and county boroughs were to be created with nominated membership. These bodies would be expected to supply, maintain and aid the necessary schools in their areas. The Board of Education Act 1899 went some way towards meeting the Bryce proposals, the most important of which was the creation of a central authority for education.

Morant, shortly to be the first Permanent Secretary of the Board of Education, was encouraged by Sir John Gorst, the Vice-President, to effect a clean break between the elementary and secondary sectors. This was achieved by challenging the right of school boards to support, through their rating, 'secondary' education in their higher grade schools. The London School Board was spending Science and Art Department grants on their higher grade schools. T.B. Cockerton, the District Auditor, withheld payments from these schools and in the courts, his action was upheld. The Cockerton Judgment of 1901 effectively spelt the end of these schools in their existing forms:

they now became absorbed into the secondary system or reverted to elementary schools.

EFFECTS OF THE 1902 ACT

Mention is made elsewhere in this volume of the role envisaged for the new secondary schools by Morant and other officials at the Board of Education. The creation of a specifically Secondary Branch at the Board enabled policy to be formulated or discussed at this level for the first time.

The 1902 Act empowered LEAs to 'take such steps as seem to them desirable', after consultation with the Board, to supply education other than elementary. The Board provided finance for schools, subject to regulations issued by them. Given the situation where the LEA, not the Board, was empowered to establish schools, the Board at first could do little but give advice. However, between 1902 and 1904, the Board made 'scientific instruction' the main criterion for granting support to secondary schools. It provided encouragement by awarding monies on the basis of a school's classification: Division A schools, which included the former higher grade and smaller grammar schools, with a predominantly scientific curriculum, and Division B, largely traditional grammar schools which qualified for grants only on the basis of their science courses. By 1903, 226 schools received grants in Division A and 160 in Division B schools (Kazamias, 1966, p. 132).

This emphasis on the scientific rather than on the humanistic aspects of the secondary school curriculum was criticized by inspectors and educators who preferred a wider liberal education (Banks, 1954, p. 38). The 1904 Regulations for Secondary Schools therefore represented a broad spectrum of consensus on the nature of the curriculum rather than Morant's personal vision. The balance was achieved by schools devoting $7\frac{1}{2}$ hours to science and mathematics and 8 hours to English, history, geography and a foreign language.

Although the term 'secondary education' had been used in the 1889 Technical Instruction Act and by the Bryce Commission, no attempt had been made to define it. The Board did not fill this gap, but instead described the secondary school in the 1904 Regulations as 'a Day or Boarding School which offers to each of its scholars, up to and beyond the age of 16, a general education, physical, mental and moral given through a complete graded course of instruction, of wider scope and more advanced degree than that given in Elementary Schools'. The careful wording of this definition displays Morant's view of the place of secondary education in an overall plan. As regulations for elementary education had been issued at the same time (see Chapter 2), the distinction between the two types of school was clear. The graded nature of the secondary school instruction indicates Morant's intention of providing for those hoping to go on to higher education. He shared with Michael Sadler, then Director of the Special Office of Inquiries at the Board, the belief that the new secondary school was intended mainly for the sons of middle-class parents. (In 1904–5, out of 575 schools on the Grants List, only 99 were girls' schools as compared with 292 boys' schools and 184 mixed schools.)

To avoid school boards overlapping into secondary education, Morant had issued a Minute in 1900 permitting higher elementary schools which would prepare children, by means of a four-year course, for occupations in which 'scientific methods have to be employed'. These schools were not popular with LEAs: by 1904, only 29 had been established. Anson, the Parliamentary Secretary to the Board of Education, admitted that the higher elementary school was a failure. A new Code in 1905 reduced the period of attendance at the school to three years and suggested a broader curriculum than in the 1900 Minute.

The status of the higher elementary school was the subject of disagreement between officials at the Board. To keep the newly-created Consultative Committee occupied, Morant referred the matter to them (Eaglesham, 1967, p.98). In its Report, the Committee justified the separation of elementary from secondary education, placing the higher elementary school firmly in the former category. It believed that grammar-school pupils previously attended a pre-paratory school, that pupils stayed on longer than at elementary schools and that the grammar school prepared pupils 'for the higher ranks and for the liberal professions'. Further, whereas parental support for secondary-school pupils could be assumed, 'in the case of the Higher Elementary School, the home conditions, at best, do little to favour the end of school education, and at worst are antagonistic' (Board of Education, 1906, p.8). A reduction in the length of the course at these schools was recommended, from four years to three, and the teaching of a limited number of subjects, and with a practical bias.

Criticism of the Consultative Committee's recommendations and the Board's policy was particularly strong from teachers' associations, especially the NUT. At the 1907 Annual Conference, the President, A.R. Pickles, stated that the clear discrimination against the higher elementary school was 'to fend off from the secondary schools proper all but a few of the workers'. LEAs remained cool towards adopting these schools, and by 1919, only 30 were in existence. Morant's unpopularity with the NUT on this issue possibly began the trail which led to his removal from the Board following the issue of the Holmes–Morant Circular four years later.

THE FREE PLACE REGULATIONS

Morant had envisaged the secondary school as the preserve of the middle classes; however, after 1905 the composition of its intake was to change. In that year, the Board's Regulations required boys and girls who intended to enter the teaching profession to receive a sound general education in a secondary school for three or four years. Many LEAs were already offering scholarships for elementary school pupils, often with preference given to intending pupil teachers. With the return to office of a Liberal government in 1906, there was pressure by the NUT, the Trades Union Congress and many MPs for the government to pay more attention to the educational needs of the working classes. The Secondary Regulations of 1907 went some way towards meeting these demands. In future, secondary schools were to provide up to 25 per cent free places to pupils from public elementary schools. The purpose of this Regulation, as a Board official noted, was 'to secure that the Board's grants are not paid to schools which are in a real sense exclusive class schools used chiefly by those who ought to pay for the education of their own children' (PRO 24/372, Memorandum, 1907).

The discretionary element, by which the Board could vary the 25 per cent requirement, was quickly taken up. In 1907–8, schools were allowed to admit as few as 12 per cent free-placers, though this was not to be repeated in subsequent years. Some secondary schools were reluctant to accept free places, for financial as well as social reasons: the 1907 Regulations had swept away the provision for awarding grants for science at double the rate received for others. Now all grants were assessed at a uniform rate of £5 for all pupils in the school. The Regulations placed the financial responsibility directly upon the school without regard to its ability to meet the cost. Apart from the problems connected with selection (dealt with in Chapter 11), schools had to revise their curricula to include more practical subjects as the nature of their intake changed. Unless they met these requirements, as well as accepting representatives from LEAs on their governing bodies, the schools would not be eligible to be placed on the Board's Grant List. Moreover, it was likely that free-placers would leave school early, thus disrupting the pattern of school life: this was largely avoided by LEAs exacting 'school life undertakings', binding pupils to stay for three years. After the First World War, undertakings to remain at school until the age of sixteen were almost universal.

The growing popularity of the secondary school can be seen from the following table:

	1904–5	1909–10	1914–15	1919–20
Boys	61,179	85,427	105,096	159,294
Girls	33,519	72,447	93,788	148,568
Total	94,698	157,874	198,884	307,862

Source: Board of Education Pamphlet No. 50, *Recent Development of Secondary Schools in England and Wales*, 1927.

WAR AND REFORM

The Board's main achievements in the field of education occurred in 1917. Attention to the development of sixth forms had been noted in a 1913 Circular concerning their curriculum; four years later, a Circular announced the encouragement of sixth forms by supplying additional money specifically for the expansion of 'Advanced Courses'. The other reform was the establishment of the Secondary School Examinations Council, and general principles to be followed for the new First Examination (the School Certificate) and the Second Examination (the Higher School Certificate), both of which were instituted in that year (see Chapter 20).

As the war progressed, attention turned to schemes of reform for the post-war world. In November and December 1916, three bodies put forward plans for secondary education. The Workers' Educational Association called for secondary schools, variable in type, with a curriculum which would match the needs of the pupils. The NUT also endorsed the need for 'different types' of secondary school. The third body, the Education Reform Council, consisting of Liberal educationists such as William Garnett, Gilbert Murray, Percy Nunn, Michael Sadler and A.N. Whitehead, took a narrower view, preferring transfer at the age of eleven, based on examination results, to either secondary grammar or higher elementary schools. None of these three schemes envisaged secondary education for all (Simon, 1974a, p. 349). In contrast to this, at a conference called by the Bradford Trades Council in October 1916, a programme of universal, free, compulsory secondary education for all was approved: in the following year, the Labour party adopted it as their official programme.

A revealing picture of the educational opportunities available at this time is to be found in the Report of a Departmental Committee on *Juvenile Education in relation to Employment after the War* (Lewis) published in 1917. Set up by Arthur Henderson, the President of the Board, it demonstrated the chaotic state of education for the post-primary age group. Only 13 per cent of pupils at day schools were likely to experience any form of full-time education after 14, and not more than 5 per cent would attend a secondary school. Between the age of 14 and 18, as few as 18.5 per cent were enrolled in day or evening schools. The Lewis Report's main recommendations were that the leaving age for elementary school pupils should be uniformly 14 and that there should be compulsory attendance for a number of hours per week or year for those between 14 and 18. Fisher, the President of the Board since 1916, advocated that LEAs should provide all types and grades of schools to meet the differing needs of pupils. He sponsored the 1918 Education Bill which facilitated these changes: the school-leaving age was raised to 14, but the hopes for the continuation school scheme were not realized.

The Board of Education now recognized the need for alternative forms of post-primary education which would not impinge on the existing secondary grammar schools. The 1918 Act gave responsibility to LEAs providing elementary education to

> secure adequate and suitable provision by means of central schools, central or special classes or otherwise ... courses of advanced instruction for the older and more intelligent children in attendance at such schools, including children who stay at such schools beyond the age of fourteen.

Central schools, offering a curriculum with an industrial or commercial bias or both, had been established by the London County Council in 1911 to replace the higher elementary schools. Each of the schools served a number of elementary schools, selecting abler children at the age of eleven. This early experiment in making the break at eleven anticipated the Hadow Report by 15 years (Gibbon and Bell, 1939, p. 205). Manchester followed in 1912 and this type of school was quickly adopted by LEAs. The movement, though remaining firmly within the elementary tradition, was a successful one. In London alone, by 1927, there were 71 central schools.

However, the schools did not enjoy the same popularity as the junior technical schools, which became near rivals to the secondary grammar school in many LEAs. Started in the first decade of the century, the junior technical schools, some of which had developed from trade schools, were recognized by the Board in 1913 as supplying courses for artisans and other industrial occupations or for domestic employment. These courses were normally planned for pupils leaving the elementary school at the age of 13 or 14. Such a late entry age meant that the course usually lasted for two years. Just before the First World War, the Association of Teachers in Technical Institutions protested to the Board that junior technical schools should be allowed to offer a curriculum which would equip their pupils to occupy higher positions in industry. The Board, for instance, forbade the teaching of a modern language except in exceptional circumstances.

Another contention was that the starting age at the schools was too late, especially as the grammar and central schools attracted pupils at 11. Although the restriction on modern language teaching was eventually removed, the Board throughout its existence refused to consider lowering the age of entry. The official view of the Board, supported by politicians, was that the secondary grammar school should develop technical education and, in any case, should be the source of supply for the middle and higher ranking posts in industry. However, the secondary schools for the most part continued to offer a liberal-humanities-based curriculum, and the prestige of the junior technical schools continued to rise up to the outbreak of the Second World War, being very popular with employers.

THE HADOW REPORT, 1926

The post-war economic recession, leading to the 'Geddes Axe' of 1922, spelt the end of compulsory day-continuation education. This high-lighted the division between pupils leaving elementary schools at 14 and those enjoying secondary education until 16. Disparities in opportunity were the central feature of the report *Secondary Education for All* produced by R.H. Tawney in 1922, which the Labour party immediately adopted as a policy statement. Tawney considered primary and secondary education as two stages of a continuous process, 'secondary education being the education of the adolescent and primary education being preparatory thereto'. All children, therefore, should be automatically transferred at the age of eleven plus 'to one type or another of secondary school and remain at the latter till sixteen' (Tawney, 1922, p. 7). This was a long-term goal, and left vague the kind of secondary education envisaged.

During the brief Labour administration of 1924, action towards implementing this policy was severely limited by financial constraints. Secondary school accommodation was expanded and LEAs were encouraged to increase the percentage of free places from 25 per cent to 40 per cent and to raise the leaving age to 15 within their own areas. But even before this, by May 1923, the Consultative Committee had persuaded the Conservative President of the Board, Edward Wood (later Lord Halifax), through persistent requests, to refer the whole subject to the Consultative Committee (Firmager, 1981, p.272).

Although the terms of reference excluded the secondary grammar school from the Committee's deliberations, the incoming Labour government which gave its approval for the investigation made no changes. Under its chairman, Sir Henry Hadow, the Committee was requested 'to consider and report upon the organization, objectives and curricula of courses of study suitable for children who will remain in full-time attendance at schools, other than Secondary Schools, up to the age of 15'.

The Hadow Report made wide-ranging recommendations. It endorsed the view that the separate systems of elementary and secondary schooling were no longer desirable and that there should be a continuous process of primary and secondary stages, divided at the age of eleven plus. The school-leaving age was to be raised to 15 within six years in order to allow all pupils at least four years of secondary education. The reorganization of schooling was to be on the following lines: the grammar schools would continue to take the ablest children; the secondary modern school would be developed from existing central schools and senior elementary departments, offering a more practical curriculum in the final two years; and junior technical schools, which were praised by the Committee, would continue to recruit pupils at 13 from the modern and grammar schools.

Lord Eustace Percy, the Conservative President of the Board, immediately upon receiving the Report sent a letter to Hadow dismissing the feasibility of raising the school-leaving age (Doherty, 1964, p. 120). The Hadow Committee's assumption of parity of esteem between grammar and modern schools was not shared by the Board of Education. It studiously avoided using the term 'secondary' in referring to the modern school in its pamphlet, *The New Prospect in Education*, issued by the Board in 1928. According to its authors, the objective of this school was

> to prepare children for a life of active labour and social co-operation ... it is not sufficient to provide 'advanced instruction' of a more or less literary type for a selected group of children who would otherwise be 'marking time'; it is also our task to meet the

needs of those children, whose outlook on life is more directly practical, or who wish to turn to some form of constructive work. (Board of Education, 1928, p. 9)

The modern school, too, remained within the purview of the Elementary Branch of the Board and was administered locally by Part III Authorities, i.e. those responsible for elementary education only. The faith placed by the Hadow Committee in psychological testing as a basis for classification stemmed from the fact that the Hadow Committee started its deliberations in May 1924, immediately after the completion of its Report on Psychological Tests of Educable Capacity (Board of Education, 1926, p. xvii). The so-called 'Hadow reorganization' of schools, into primary and post-primary aspects, had begun in 1925, but was now increased in pace. Between August 1926 and December 1927, senior departments catering for children over 11 increased from 598 to 652. During the year ending March 1928, 742 departments had been affected by reorganization. Progress was hampered through the existence of the dual system and the scattered nature of rural schools. The school-leaving age remained at 14 and the modern school did not develop along the lines suggested by Hadow. A member of the Committee remarked some 27 years later: 'We believed in a great variety of teaching developments on the secondary level. The undifferentiated modern school for all and sundry of a 75 per cent assemblage of our adolescent children was never within our range of conceptions when the Report was written' (Judges, 1954, p. 59).

An attempt was made by the 1936 Education Act to expedite the Hadow reorganization, and to raise the school-leaving age from September 1939. The latter provision was postponed because of the outbreak of the war. By this time, more than half the pupils over 11 were in reorganized schools (Evans, 1985, p. 94). One part of the secondary school system received a boost from 1926. The 1902 Act had established that schools observing certain standards could secure grants from central government. Circular 1381 of 1926 created a direct grant list for schools sponsored by voluntary bodies and grant-aided by LEAs: the 1944 Education Act was to stipulate that at least 25 per cent of these schools' places should be free.

SPENS TO THE 1944 EDUCATION ACT

The further reductions in educational spending following the Report by the Committee on National Expenditure (May Report) in 1931 had many consequences for the secondary school. One which affected its pupils was the scrapping of the free place system and the substitution of the special place system. Circular 1421 of 1932 introduced a means test for all entrants: open competition replaced the existing condition that candidates should have previously been in attendance at a public elementary school.

In 1933, the last task given to the Consultative Committee before its abolition was

> to consider and report upon the organization and interrelation of schools, other than those administered under the Elementary Code, which provide education for pupils beyond the age of 11+, regard being had in particular to the framework and content of the education of pupils who do not remain at school beyond the age of about 16.

The Consultative Committee on Secondary Education with special reference to Grammar Schools and Technical Schools, chaired by Will Spens, took five years in its deliberations. Its Report, published in 1938, stated at the outset that the Committee followed the Hadow philosophy of regarding secondary education as 'a single whole'. As it considered that all education after the age of 11 should be termed 'secondary', it recommended one code for all schools for children at this stage. The Spens Report advocated a new type of secondary school, the technical high school, which provided a broad liberal education, and which had equal status with the grammar school. Thus, there would be three kinds of secondary school – grammar, technical and modern – enjoying parity of esteem. Psychological evidence was relied upon once again to demonstrate that there were two types of pupils, those capable of thinking in abstract terms and those who were more adept at practical activities. However, the first two years of the curriculum (11–13) was to be common to the three kinds of schools.

The Spens Report can be criticized on the ground that whilst promoting a common code for the schools, it recommended a tripartite system of secondary education. In fact, as Joan Simon has shown, the Board had been outmanoeuvred by the strength of feeling of the Committee's members (Simon, J., 1977, p. 179). For example, the Hadow term 'modern schools', which had been avoided by the Board, was revived to designate a school of equal status with grammar and technical schools. The Spens Report also emphasized that the term 'practical' in the modern school should not be narrowly interpreted as vocational education. R. A. Butler, when drafting his Education Bill a few years later, accepted 'the need for a system of free secondary education for all as outlined in the Spens Report of 1938. This was imperative' (op. cit., p. 179).

Within three years of the publication of the Report, in October 1941, a Committee of the Secondary School Examinations Council was appointed by the Board of Education 'to consider suggested changes in the Secondary School curriculum and the question of School Examinations in relation thereto'. The findings of the Norwood Committee are discussed in Chapter 20. It is sufficient here to remark that the Committee did not confine its recommendations to curriculum and examinations, but made firm assertions, not supported by evidence, on the nature of secondary education. The tripartite division outlined in Spens was strongly advocated by Norwood in a Report less than a third the length of the former. Much of Norwood's own predilections can be detected in the drafting. As headmaster of Harrow (1926 to 1934), he had remarked, 'Incomplete as it is, elementary education has become a steadily civilizing agency. It has, I think, been the main influence which has prevented Bolshevism, Communism, and theories of revolt and destruction from obtaining any real hold upon the people of this country' (Norwood, 1929, p. 171). One aspect of the Report which has received little attention was the recommendation that the break at eleven plus should be replaced by a 'lower school' for the 11 to 13 age range where the curriculum should be roughly common. At the end of this period, pupils would be transferred to the appropriate secondary school. This arrangement accorded with Norwood's own experience of public schools (Armytage, 1978, pp. 13–14). No action was subsequently taken on this recommendation. A few days before the Norwood Report was published in 1943, the White Paper on Educational Reconstruction recommended the tripartite division of secondary education, much along the lines of Norwood.

FROM 1944 TO COMPREHENSIVIZATION

The 1944 Education Act stated that public education should be organized in three stages, primary, secondary and further. Although official policy favoured tripartitism, there was much debate during the next 20 years on alternative forms of organization of secondary education.

The Labour government which came into office in 1945 was faced with an increasing school population at a time when the school-leaving age was to be raised to 15, in 1947. Continuity with existing policy was accepted by the first two Ministers of Education, Ellen Wilkinson and George Tomlinson, in *The New Secondary Education* (1947) and, in spite of protests from Labour supporters, the period 1945–51 achieved little in moving towards a more unified system of secondary education. In 1963, one writer on the secondary modern school remarked: 'it is true that the work of the Modern school today is very different from that of the senior departments and the Higher Elementary schools of sixty years ago, but changes in theory and attitudes have been greater than changes in the distribution of subjects and the structure of the timetable' (Taylor, 1963, p. 83).

Support for the modern school was stated in the Crowther Report *15 to 18* (1959), which recommended that abler pupils should sit GCE O level subjects and that, in conjunction with the raising of the leaving age to 16, more challenging work should be presented to pupils. More startlingly, the 1963 Newsom Report on the average and less able in these schools found that 80 per cent of school buildings in which they were taught were defective. Sir Edward Boyle, the Minister of Education, considered the need for action important enough to bring the matter to the attention of the Cabinet (Kogan, 1971, p. 138). Throughout its existence, the modern school was at best a pale imitation of the grammar school and, in the eyes of parents, lacked its prestige.

The technical high school had been enthusiastically promoted by the Spens Committee and again endorsed by Norwood. But whereas Spens's *raison d'être* for these schools was to broaden the education given in grammar schools, Norwood regarded the technical high school as the pathway to universities for those with particular aptitudes in mathematics and science. Bitter rivalry displayed by grammar schools and the half-hearted adoption of technical schools by LEAs were only two of the reasons for their slow growth. The schools were often seen as second best for those who had failed at eleven plus to obtain a place in a grammar school. Even more importantly, the technical high school failed to find a distinctive personality in terms of curriculum and organization. By 1952 there were 291 secondary technical schools as compared with 1,189 grammar schools.

The secondary grammar school continued to attract pupils. With the abolition of fees after the 1944 Education Act, there was increased pressure on numbers at the entrance stage. The raising of the school-leaving age in 1947 generated demand for longer secondary courses: the proportion staying on until 17 increased by more than half between 1953 and 1960. The sixth forms were the entrance to the professions: of the 18-year-olds leaving grammar schools in 1965–66, 70 per cent of boys and 83 per cent of girls went on to some form of full-time further education (Edwards, 1970, p. 54). The Ministry of Education complained in its Annual Report as early as 1951: 'Local Education Authorities are subjected to strong pressures to admit children who are unsuited to a grammar school course to what may appear to parents in some cases to be the only true secondary school available' (p.11).

Sociological investigations during the 1950s and 1960s undermined confidence in selection procedures. The Early Leaving Report of the Central Advisory Council for Education (1954) found, on a 10 per cent sample of all grammar schools in England for 1946–47, that a disproportionately large percentage of places was allocated to children of professional and managerial parents. Professor P.E. Vernon, in a pamphlet, *Intelligence Testing. Its Use in Selection for Secondary Education* (1952), demonstrated that average rises in I.Q. of up to 14 points could be achieved by coaching. Another influential study, J.W.B. Douglas's *The Home and the School* (1964), illustrated the regional differences in the provision of grammar school places which ranged from over 30 per cent to less than 10 per cent. It was now accepted by both major political parties that the promise of equality of opportunity in secondary education, as implied by the 1944 Act, had not been fulfilled. The debate on the case for and against comprehensive education, which had its beginnings in the 1920s, was re-opened.

Even before the Hadow Report had been completed, there had been calls for a 'multi-bias' secondary school. The conference of the Association of Assistant Masters in January 1925 expressed the view that children over the age of 11 should be 'transferred to secondary schools containing departments of different types', a view endorsed publicly by the NUT three years later (Simon, B., 1974b, p.142). The failure of the two interim Labour governments to deal with this issue and the reduction in free places from 1932 made the realization of this plan unlikely. The view of the Conservative party was expressed in Parliament by the Parliamentary Secretary to the Board in the following year: 'to throw secondary education open to all and sundry would very likely be the reverse of an educational advance and might easily be an educational regression: we might easily turn the nation into something like an educational soup kitchen' (quoted in Parkinson, 1970, p.29).

The Spens Report had noted 'with some reluctance' that it could not advocate the adoption of multilateralism as a general policy (p.291), and the Norwood Report was only lukewarm on experiments in combining schools (p.19). Although multilateralism was officially adopted as Labour party policy in 1939, there was a division of opinion on its translation into practice. When the Board of Education began planning in 1940 for after the war, a Permanent Assistant Secretaries'

Committee was set up. W.C. Cleary, of the Elementary Branch, was the only member who regarded the common secondary school as one answer to the problem (Gosden, 1976, p.247).

Development plans were submitted by LEAs following the 1944 Education Act. After the war, the multilateral principle found less favour than that of the comprehensive; the former no longer formed part of Labour educational policy from 1948. Bilateral schools were set up in some LEAs, and multilateral and comprehensive schools in rural parts of Wales, and between 1946 and 1949 the London County Council established eight large secondary schools composed of former senior and central schools. However, the Labour government, during its terms in office from 1945 to 1951, was hesitant to push ahead with any radical departure from tripartitism. Only six Labour MPs voiced their support for comprehensive schools during this period (Fenwick, 1976, p.58). The 1945 Labour party election manifesto was silent on the issue and Ellen Wilkinson, the Minister of Education, was attracted to the notion of equality of opportunity associated with access to the grammar school (Vernon, 1985, p.219). One example of this ambivalence was the refusal in 1949 of George Tomlinson, Wilkinson's successor, to accept the Labour-controlled Middlesex Authority's plans for comprehensive schools.

During their 13 years in office between 1951 and 1964, the Conservatives carefully controlled the growth of comprehensives, limiting them to purpose-built schools, mainly in new housing estates or new towns. The London County Council and South-West Middlesex were the first two English LEAs to establish such comprehensive schools: in 1954, the first comprehensive school was opened at Kidbrooke in south-east London.

The defeat of Labour at the 1955 General Election resulted in its National Executive Committee reformulating the party's education policy. An important step forward was the acceptance by the Ministry of the 'Leicestershire Plan', which came into operation in 1959. Devised by Stewart Mason, the County's Director of Education, the Plan created high schools for pupils between 10 and 14 and upper schools, all but one of which were former grammar schools, for 14- to 18-year-olds. This scheme overcame the Ministry's insistence on comprehensive schools being able to accommodate at least 1,500 pupils.

A second event, influenced by growing parental disenchantment with selection at 11 and by the findings of the Central Advisory Council's Early Leaving Report, was the issue of the government's White Paper, *Secondary Education for All. A New Drive*, in 1958. Whilst it still supported the case for the continued existence of the grammar school, the White Paper acknowledged the need for comprehensives in rural and other areas, but hoped that there would be opportunities for pupils to maximize their abilities within separate schools also. The White Paper committed the government to a £300 million spending programme on secondary schools and the ending of all-age schools.

By the early 1960s, comprehensive education was not a matter of national major political debate. The Labour party changed electoral tactics, stressing the direct economic advantages of unsegregated education and giving less emphasis to the social justice argument (Parkinson, op. cit., p.88). LEAs were now taking the initiative in the matter, exchanging information and seeking guidance from authorities such as London, Coventry and Bristol which had established such schools (Benn and Simon, 1970, p.29).

When Sir Edward Boyle became Minister of Education in 1962, the comprehensive movement was gaining momentum. His officials estimated that, by 1963, 90 out of the 163 LEAs were working on or had completed schemes for reorganization. Boyle accepted the inevitability of the pressure for change; the bilateral system of the 1940s no longer made sense with the growing opportunities for higher education; educational theory which had supported selection had been heavily criticized; and an increasing number of parents of the professional classes were unwilling to accept secondary modern education for their children (Boyle, 1972, pp.32–3).

One of Boyle's last acts before relinquishing his post in 1964 was to introduce a bill to allow the setting up of middle schools. This measure facilitated the full introduction of comprehensivization by the Labour government when it came into office later that year. The subsequent development of comprehensive education will be dealt with in the following chapter.

SUMMARY

There was no cohesive system of secondary education until the present century. The need for such a system had been voiced in many quarters, the most powerful being the Bryce Commission of 1895. The architect of the system was Robert Morant, an administrator rather than a politician. Together with other officials at the new Board of Education, he was able to secure the separation of secondary and elementary education, providing each with their own distinctive sets of Regulations. Nevertheless, the Free Place Regulations (1907) ensured that the secondary schools did not become the exclusive province of the middle classes, containing up to a quarter of former elementary school pupils.

A distinctive feature of the secondary schools was the development of sixth forms, aimed at producing students for higher education. The Board encouraged schools to make such provision. At the same time, the Board discouraged any possible rivals: it acted firmly to prevent the popular junior technical schools from competing on equal terms with the grammar schools.

There was political disquiet within the Labour party about the lack of opportunities for the majority of elementary school pupils as compared with their secondary counterparts. Tawney's *Secondary Education for All* (1922) became the official policy of the Labour party. Four years later, the Hadow Report, which did not consider the grammar school in its remit, recommended universal secondary education, suggesting the establishment of modern schools, alongside existing grammar schools, for the majority of pupils.

Shortly before the war, the Spens Committee (1938) agreed with Hadow that secondary education should exist as a single whole. This view was not widely shared by either Ministers or Board officials. Indeed the Norwood Committee, reporting in 1943, firmly favoured a tripartite division of secondary education, a concept embodied in the new Education Act in the following year.

The post-war years saw a movement towards comprehensive education after various experiments had been either mooted or tried out. Both Labour and Conservative ministers were cautious in abandoning the modern school. It was only in the early 1960s that it was generally acknowledged that a secondary system based on social justice could not long be delayed.

FURTHER READING

One standard book for the earlier period in this field is still R.L. Archer, *Secondary Education in the Nineteenth Century*, 1921, reprinted Cass, 1966. For a broad general account of policy in the present century see O. Banks, *Parity and Prestige in English Secondary Education*, 1955. Highly recommended is A.M. Kazamias, *Politics, Society and Secondary Education in England*, 1966.

The moves leading to the differentiation of elementary from secondary education are set out in C. Birchenough, *History of Elementary Education in England and Wales*, 3rd edn., 1938. See also the Report of the Consultative Committee on *The Education of the Adolescent* (Hadow Report), 1926, and Board of Education, *Recent Development of Secondary Schools in England and Wales*, Educational Pamphlet No. 50, 1927. Widening opportunities for secondary education are discussed in *Secondary Education for All*, 1949, and R. Barker, *Education and Politics, 1900–1951: a Study of the Labour Party*, 1972.

Official publications following the 1944 Education Act include *The New Secondary Education*, Pamphlet No. 9, 1947, Central Advisory Council for Education, *Early Leaving*, 1954, and *15 to 18* (Crowther Report), 1959–60. Secondary schools other than grammar schools are discussed in R. Edwards, *The Secondary Technical School*, 1960, and W. Taylor, *The Secondary Modern School*, 1963.

For the background to comprehensive education, see I.G.K. Fenwick, *The Comprehensive School 1944–1970*, 1976. See also E. Boyle and A. Crosland, *The Politics of Education*, 1971.

CHAPTER THIRTEEN

The Development of Comprehensive Schools

REORGANIZATION AND ITS PROBLEMS, 1960–1975

Comprehensive education clearly reflected the changing mood of the nation which now appeared much more ready to experiment. A Conservative government, victorious at the polls for the third time in 1959, in the following year appeared to run out of luck. Economic failings, technical inefficiency, wastage of talent, and the smell of scandal threatened to undermine Conservative supremacy and were increasingly well exploited by the Labour opposition, especially after Harold Wilson's succession to the leadership in 1963. Plans for more universities, colleges of education and technical institutions were already about to be launched. The grammar school, catering for only a small proportion of the population, was now seen to be too élitist in character. Modern schools for their part did not meet the aspirations of the majority of parents for their children. Those already working in comprehensive schools pointed to the changes which had taken place in secondary education since the late 1940s. Margaret Miles, an early advocate of comprehensives, argued that comprehensive schooling was part of the urgent modernization process that was in the air, stating that Britain was 'possibly more united than any society has been before by its physical means of communication. But educationally and culturally it is divided because an educational system which was designed to serve a very different kind of society has lasted too long' (Miles, 1968, p. 16). Harold Wilson, as Prime Minister, was quick to seize on a widespread desire for new attitudes, new approaches, reconciliation and modernization. A product of the 1945 victory, he was keen to represent the wishes of broad sections of the middle classes by making Labour a progressive party of government.

Thus one explanation of the reorganization of secondary education in the 1960s has relied heavily on the acceptance of the political world to meet new forces and make adjustments. Progressive Conservatives and reformist Labour politicians were in general agreement that the tripartite system no longer satisfied the desire for social cohesion. The way forward was not always clear. For example, Tony Benn, a Labour minister from 1964, already enthusiastic about reorganization, reflected in his diary how little had been thought out by Bristol Labour group who had won control of the city and intended to push through with comprehensive schools. On a train journey to Bristol he met a newly elected and bewildered chairman of the Education Committee: 'He really didn't know what to say or do ... Happily I was able to tell him about the New Bristol Group broadsheet and he decided to drive straight from the station and collect a copy of it and read it before to-morrow's meeting' (Benn, 1987, 29 May 1963, p.28).

There was, however, a more convincing explanation of the changes. By 1963, in the industrial heartland local authorities won by Labour were already well advanced in their plans for implementing schemes for comprehensivization. Through a coalition of parents, local politicians, and grassroots opinion, the pressure from without could no longer be contained. In this sense a reluctant Conservative government and its tentative successor were carried along by this groundswell. All that officialdom could salvage in the long-drawn-out consultations in the early 1960s was to avoid too radical changes in the best practices of the grammar schools.

This explanation has come under severe attack from the forces of the New Right which gathered strength in the 1980s. According to this group, policy-makers, both Conservative and Labour, yielded ground to a highly vocal number of progressive educationists, socialist activists and social engineering sociologists who seized on defects in the tri-partite system to impose on the public an egalitarian system of educa-tion. Groups ranging from the Campaign for the Advancement of State Education, to *Forum*, a journal started in 1958 and devoted to the promotion of comprehensive education, have been singled out for attack. It has been argued that in various localities determined individuals and groups seized control of vital positions to force through reorganization, often with little or no popular support. Thus one researcher, concluding his survey of the rise of the comprehensive school, stated: 'What is fascinating – given the claims made that comprehensive reorganisation was a popular movement and demo-cratically supported – is how few people even within the dominant political party were involved' (Shaw, 1983, p.60). The charge has been made that educational arguments were ignored as the new kinds of schools were introduced to push forward the impetus to social change.

The impetus towards comprehensive education has often been

associated with the figure of Tony Crosland (1965–67). It ought to be noted that he was not the first of Wilson's ministers of education. Michael Stewart, certainly an advocate of change, was the minister for a very short period (1964–65). The more ardent reformers were suspicious of Crosland's reliability. Tony Benn recorded his misgivings. 'I'm sorry that Michael has moved from a more important to a less important job and particularly that he has given up education where he was an anchor man who knew what he wanted' (Benn, 1987, 22 January 1965, p.208). There were doubts about the decision to move forward by means of issuing circulars rather than by legislation. Maurice Kogan's interviews with his former political superior revealed some of Crosland's considerations: 'My decision to go for "request" was strongly influenced by my meetings with the AEC (Association of Education Committees) and my judgement of the general mood of the local authority world' (Kogan, 1971, p.189). Thus the famed Circular 10/65 allowed the local authorities much latitude in implementing secondary reorganization, and great scope for delay, as its wording indicated:

> The Government are aware that the complete elimination of selection and separatism in secondary education will take time to achieve. They do not seek to impose destructive or precipitate change on existing schools; they recognise that the evolution of separate schools into a comprehensive system must be a constructive process requiring careful planning by LEAs in consultation with all those concerned. (DES, Circular 10/65, July 1965, p.16)

Clearly the preference in the options laid out was for all-through 11–18 schools with strong sixth forms. The geographical location of schools in the locality determined the extent to which reorganization was possible. The government's approach allowed for three possible outcomes. First of all, it was likely that the range and variety of reorganization would be even more extensive than the existing system. Second, for those local authorities that were unhappy about comprehensive education, consultation and negotiation with interested parties allowed for the process to be slowed down, even halted. Finally, from 1965 the Department was involved in fighting long court battles over timing, ratification and consultation.

Changes in local authority control in the May 1968 elections and the prospect of a Conservative government pledged to revise Circular 10/65 encouraged opposition: centres of resistance were able to use the support of threatened grammar schools and their old pupils' associations. The chairman of the Ealing Joint Parents' Committee revealed that in their battle they 'were very fortunate in having had the benefit of the advice of headmasters, headmistresses and teachers in the Ealing Secondary Schools throughout the whole period that the Reorganisation of Secondary Education has been under review in the Borough' (Rubens, 1970, p.81). The decision to allow the local authorities to determine their pace threw the battle over re-organization into the centre of local politics, and in many areas after 1965 it was one of the main issues that divided the parties in the town halls. Circular 10/65 settled doubts within the Labour party that the comprehensive school movement was now secure. There was also a significant shift within the teachers' unions. The National Union of Teachers which had ploughed an unsteady furrow on the issue rapidly moved, after 1965, to support.

There were also changes in the attitudes of unions making up the Joint Four grouping which had hitherto pursued a hostile line. An interim report from the Incorporated Association of Assistant Masters argued, 'It is not an attack on the comprehensive schools, it is not a balance sheet or a judge's summing up. It is not any part of the debate about the kind of society we need' (IAAM, 1967, p.2). The report did discuss the uneasiness in many areas about early selection and its inadequacies. Behind Circular 10/65 was the weapon of financial sanctions, for in the following year Circular 10/66 laid down that funds could be made available for comprehensive schools only when major building projects were under consideration by the central Department. In its annual report for 1966 the DES recorded the pattern of develop-ment: 'The growth in the education service was not in numbers alone. At all levels a sustained effort was going forward to reorganise the system in the direction of wider opportunity – whatever the back-ground, degree of attainment, or pattern of ability of the individual pupil or student' (DES Report, 1966, pp.9–10). By 1970, aware of the declining influence of Sir Edward Boyle within the Conservative parliamentary party, Edward Short, then Labour Secretary of State for Education, moved to a tougher line. In presenting the ill-fated Educa-tion Bill which could compel local authorities to take note of compre-hensive reorganization, though not compelling them to implement it, the Minister's motion, introduced in the Commons early in 1970, reflected the degree of progress already made, the effects of selection and the evolution of the system:

> That this House, conscious of the need to raise educational standards at all levels, and regretting that the realisation of this

objective is impeded by the separation of children into different types of secondary schools, note with approval the effort of local authorities to reorganise secondary education on comprehensive lines which will preserve all that is valuable in grammar school education for those children who now receive it and make it available to more children. (Hansard, Vol. 795, Col. 1463, 12 February 1970)

Delays and inadequate whipping with Labour members absent from vital votes ended the opportunity of the Bill being passed before Labour's defeat at the polls.

Labour left office in 1970 having laid the foundation for comprehensive reorganization. It was likely, given the emphasis of the Crowther and Newsom Reports, that there would have been a substantial shift away from tripartitism whatever government had been in power since 1964. This did not mean that the senior ministers could shake off their own assumptions and background easily. Richard Crossman, with children of his own of secondary school age, revealed some of the dilemmas of the highly educated, articulate group in his party. He exchanged experiences with other Labour colleagues like Wayland Young, who warned him: 'They had sent their children to primary and comprehensive schools in London but now they're sick of it because the children don't do well' (Crossman, Vol. 3, 18 May 1968, p. 68). The only model of proper secondary schooling even for Labour politicians was the grammar school with its emphasis on examination success, academic performance and competition. Comprehensive schools were defined by negative qualities, namely the absence of early selection and separation of children from each other. They had been launched with an absence of research or national planning, in marked contrast to similar reorganizations in Sweden. In educational circles, particularly the university departments and colleges of education, there was general approval of a move that was seen as a shift away from selectivity and failure, and of a further step on the road to schooling that paid much greater attention to the needs of the individual child. Much slower, however, was a recognition that the change implied new approaches to methodology, curriculum and pastoral organization. Part of the problem was that the college lecturers were themselves deeply immersed in reorganization of their own institutions and coping with teacher shortages.

The 1960s saw the growth of a passionate belief that if the right kind of structure was decided upon, inevitably the right pattern of changes would emerge. It was not only in schooling, but also in health and local government that this principle was applied. Finally it was clear by the end of the Wilson government in June 1970 that some of the pre-conditions for a successful launch had not been met. Comprehensive reorganization fought for resources at a time when similar demands were being made by higher and further education, and schools were short of teachers. The heated debates about the timing of the raising of the school-leaving age, proposed for 1971, caused further pressures. On more than one occasion education ministers were near to despair over inadequacy of funding, and Edward Short, a former headmaster, almost threatened resignation. His colleagues were only lukewarm in their support, though the Prime Minister was anxious to keep one of his more secure supporters. As economic recession loomed, most ministers wanted the Education Minister to single out his clear priorities. If comprehensive reorganization was the Minister's most urgent need, it was agreed, then most resources must be generally made available in this area. 'Everyone was sympathetic ... We said, "Ted, you must have some priorities. If you want to save your compre-hensive education, which we are all deeply committed to in the party, you must say that is what you want"' (Crossman, 1982, Vol. 3, 18 November 1968, p.262). At a later stage, in the closing years of the 1970s, supporters of the comprehensive school expressed their disappointment with the Wilson government's inadequacies. Just as Attlee's government had failed to build on the enthusiasm for the common school engendered by the war, the next Labour government had hampered progress by inadequate resourcing and planning.

Speculation was rife over the direction of Conservative policy in 1970. Within a month the new Minister, Margaret Thatcher, swept aside Circular 10/65 and brought in Circular 10/70 which proclaimed a policy of co-existence. She supported the view that the best of the older, well-established grammar schools could co-exist in a locality alongside the new comprehensive schools. Parents would then be able to judge between the two kinds of schooling for their children. The Minister did act to prevent the closure of a number of well-established schools, but the most significant feature of this administration was that few local authorities were prepared to contemplate a return to tripartitism, and the pace of reorganization quickened. Some of this impetus could be accounted for by the success of Labour at the local elections in 1971. It was clear, too, that the principle of selection, which was at the heart of the older system, was unpopular with most parents. With a groundswell of public opinion in favour of change, it was likely that there would be limited survival for grammar schools in strongly Conservative areas, and perhaps greater attention to how comprehensive schools would

eventually be shaped. However, the trend towards comprehensivization at the expense of the grammar and modern schools in the decade
between 1965 and 1975 was an impressive one, as the table below
indicates.

SCHOOLS AND PUPILS

	1965	*1970*	*1975*
Modern			
Schools or depts.	3,498	2,566	1,177
Pupils	1,470,840	1,178,815	677,997
Grammar			
Schools or depts.	1,180	975	547
Pupils	659,959	568,513	333,119
Comprehensive			
Schools or depts.	221	1,016	2,398
Pupils	210,932	839,317	2,262,136

Source: DES Statistics of Education 1979, *Schools*, Vol. 1 (1981), HMSO.

As the comprehensive schools began to become a familiar part of the
educational landscape a range of issues came to the forefront which
continued to be debated throughout the next decades. The most
immediate was that of selection within the new schools and the extent to
which this should be applied. Should there be open access to all courses
and at all stages of life in the school? The features of the external
examination system at 16 often mirrored much of the early tripartite
system. The GCE Ordinary Level Examination was supposed to be
taken by 20–25 per cent of the school population, the proportion
originally ascribed to grammar school education. For about 40–45 per
cent of the population, the Certificate of Secondary Education (CSE)
had been set up in 1965, and the remainder of the intake were entered
for locally set and validated examinations or no examinations at all. In
reality pressures built up in the schools to enter as many pupils as
possible for the prestigious GCE Ordinary Level which was recognized
by parents, employers, and the pupils themselves as the only proper
leaving certificate at 16. The debate was also sharpened about the
ethics of streaming or banding according to academic ability in these
schools. Those who wished for a more co-operative enterprise urged a
commitment to mixed ability teaching. More practically, in some cases
schools moved in this direction simply as a management strategy to
spread the more difficult pupils among a range of classes.

In the early 1970s comprehensive school advocates in their search for a new identity began to argue for the concept of the community school. It was widely accepted that, particularly in the large cities, the features of a neighbourhood, such as the narrow streets, the cornershop, the chapel or the public house no longer remained to bring people together. In addition people travelled long distances to their work-places. In the past schools had not fulfilled many community services; indeed the grammar or direct grant schools, serving a wide catchment area and detaching sections of the working class from family and friends, often created dislocation. What was needed was a school which would serve the whole of the community and, in turn, the children would take their part in caring for the old, the sick and the less fortunate. Thus a whole range of activities was to be encouraged within such schools to promote these ends, though this was often restricted to the less academic sections of the school population. Nevertheless building up the community school presented difficulties. First of all there were sizeable elements that could not be included because of single sex schooling or special schools. There were difficulties in defining neighbourhoods surrounding a school. In many large con-urbations, zoning by class or ethnic grouping had already taken place. One of the substantial claims of early comprehensive advocates was that this form of education would lead to social mixing. Local authorities struggled with two distinct ideas, the balanced school created for a broad catchment area, and the neighbourhood community school. The first involved issues of parental choice, of some children travelling long distances and perhaps, in the end, the experience reinforcing rather than weakening existing practices. This was the opinion expressed by Julienne Ford in her book, *Social Change and the Comprehensive School*, published in 1969, which questioned whether much social mixing was taking place in these new schools. On the other hand, in areas which were already predominantly of one class, a neighbourhood school would tend to reinforce the *status quo*.

Finally there was much debate about the common experience within the classrooms, and this inevitably turned attention to the curriculum. David Hargreaves, in *The Challenge of the Comprehensive School*, published in 1982, sketched the tensions that soon sprang up between the former grammar school teachers who were in charge of large subject departments in comprehensive schools and anxious to retain their position, and those responsible for wider pastoral groupings. Arguments were often put by egalitarians that in their early years all pupils needed to be given the same mix of subjects. There were fears that to cut off children prematurely from the academic disciplines might restrict their future prospects. There was hostility by this group to the provision of too many alternative routes that might easily lead to differences in esteem. Others saw the justification of comprehensive education in the range of choice that was to be given to all the pupils.

COMPREHENSIVE EDUCATION UNDER ATTACK, 1975–1985

The return of a Labour government, albeit with a wafer-thin majority, gave the impetus for the further promotion of comprehensive education. The direct grant schools were offered a place in the comprehensive system or suffered a withdrawal of government funds. Many of the Catholic direct grant schools opted for comprehensive education. The 1976 Act empowered local authorities to submit plans for comprehensive reorganization which could be implemented within five years. Attempts continued to be made to force laggard authorities to comply. At the same time, however, there was a marked loss of confidence in what the schools were supposed to be achieving. Supporters of the comprehensive schools argue strongly that, in the 1970s, a crisis in the schools was being manufactured by the Conservative party. Examination successes, evidence of satisfied parents and better relationships between staff and pupils were played down. On the other hand every scrap of evidence that revealed a school with disruptive pupils, high truancy rates or inadequate teaching was exposed to the glare of publicity.

Three points need to be made. Throughout the previous hundred years of compulsory education the schools housing the majority of the pupils, whether board, all-age elementary or secondary modern, had suffered the same kinds of attacks. Moreover as the 1970s moved to a more crisis-ridden atmosphere, unemployment, the running down of industry and social disruption gathered pace. It was unlikely that the schools in the areas most deeply affected would remain untouched. Politicians of all parties, already reeling under public criticism, were searching for scapegoats. In this decade, there was a growing disenchantment with experts who were blamed for high rise flats, urban motorways, and comprehensive schooling. Equality of opportunity came to be translated in a way that argued strongly for the ablest of the population, from whatever their social class, to receive a suitable education alongside their peers at an early age. The comprehensive school, as a leveller, deprived the able child of opportunity. Moreover if all the children were directed to a neighbourhood school, it made nonsense of parental choice.

This attack might have made less impact if the Labour government had not appeared to shift ground. It might well be that the Ruskin speech of James Callaghan in 1976 was a clever ruse by a master politician to defuse criticisms by turning the tables. However, airing the view that it was time for these schools to mend their ways sapped confidence. Moreover the emphasis on social justice, the liberation of individuals and broadening horizons began to be lost. Instead the schools were now placed under pressure to produce a workforce better equipped to take its place in the world of industry. The implication was that for too long schools had allowed themselves to be turned into centres of experiment and innovation which had taken them away from the world of work. Even while continuing to espouse the comprehensive schools, Labour ministers did little to counter the critics. While rejecting calls for a major enquiry on the grounds that 'this would be to pull up the plant just when it is beginning to put out roots', Shirley Williams, Secretary of State for Education, 1976–79, made it clear that the excitement and the innovation of the early years was now at an end. What was now needed was a period of consolidation. This came as the critics of the Right were gathering, but also at a time when some of the strongest comprehensive advocates were voicing misgivings that the reorganization was only half-completed. There was a further complication. The later 1970s and 1980s were a period when the issue of falling rolls loomed on the educational scene. Local authorities and headteachers noted the diminishing number of children entering the secondary schools. They also faced the prospect of amalgamation, closure, and the decimation of sixth forms. In January 1981, the number of pupils attending comprehensive schools was 3,168,337. By 1988, the total had dropped to 2,631,618 (DES Statistics of Education, *Schools*, Vol. 1, 1989).

The period from 1979 was, in one sense, a continuation of the 1970s. Margaret Thatcher, now Prime Minister, immediately repealed the 1976 Education Act. It was quite evident, in this respect, that policy changed according to politicians' wishes with little reference to permanent officials or other involved agencies. Although there were some attempts to restore selective schooling in certain areas, these have met with limited success. Nevertheless the government has been far more interventionist in determining what the comprehensives should do. This has included a clear recognition that the schools of the majority of the population ought to be more aware of vocational training as well as experiencing a liberal education. In this respect there has been a powerful impetus to restructure the curriculum, particularly for many sections of the school-age population in the age range of 14 to 19, with the introduction of the Technical and Vocational Education Initiative in 1983. In addition an element of creaming and differentiation has been introduced in the recently established city technical colleges. Finally the government has moved towards the imposition of standards largely through national testing, in which pupils' performance in relation to attainment targets will be assessed and reported on at the ages of 7, 11, 14 and 16.

Many of these initiatives have reopened debates about the nature and desirability of comprehensive education. Sympathisers have sought to redefine what a comprehensive school should set out to achieve and what needs to be done to make schools more fully comprehensive. There have been a range of studies, such as Steven Ball's *Beachside Comprehensive* (1981), that have looked at individual schools as they wrestled with curriculum development, whole-school policies and staff–parent relationships, whilst a number of educationists have been pressing to regroup the forces of support to ensure that the virtues of comprehensive education are made known.

CONCLUSION

It has never been easy to define what the comprehensive experience would mean. Those who have often been associated with processes of modernization have seen it as allowing more opportunities to be made available to an ever widening section of the population. Success or failure would be judged by examination successes and the securing of access to a range of occupations hitherto closed to many groups in society. Others, inclined towards egalitarianism, have argued that the schools must become an important instrument for breaking down social and class barriers which exist in society. What matters to this group is evidence of sweeping changes in curriculum, relationships at school, and new teaching approaches. Divisions of this kind have not always made it easy to withstand the criticisms of the Right.

FURTHER READING

On the history of the comprehensive school there is D. Rubinstein and B. Simon, *The Evolution of the Comprehensive School*, 1973. B. Shaw, *Comprehensive Schooling: the Impossible Dream?* 1983, is much less sympathetic. A more recent reappraisal is A. Weeks, *Comprehensive Schools. Past, Present and Future*, 1986. The views of the Labour party are dealt with in M. Parkinson, *The Labour Party and the Organisation of Secondary Education, 1918–1965*, 1970. There is much information on the teachers' unions in I.G.K. Fenwick, *The Comprehensive School 1944–1970*, 1976. A. Griffiths, *Secondary School Reorganization in England and Wales*, 1971, was a pioneering study of local reorganization. On this there is the more recent P.H. James, *The Reorganization of Secondary Education*, 1980. For an early study of change at the local level, see R. Batley, O. O'Brien, and H. Parris, *Going Comprehensive: Educational Policy Making in two County Boroughs*, 1970.

CHAPTER FOURTEEN

Public Schools

INTRODUCTION

The characteristics of public schools have never been easily defined. Connections between these schools and the older universities, the liberal professions, and, above all, the political and social establishment have been stressed. Those who were educated at public schools left with the qualities of a gentleman, attributes that other gentlemen were expected to recognize. However, the number of schools capable of providing this education, and even the mixture of the terms 'public schooling' and 'independent education', indicate the possibility of confusion. The clientele, too, varied greatly. Eton and Harrow were marked out almost exclusively for the aristocratic landed orders, while others, particularly some of the later nineteenth-century foundations, were providing the sons of the commercial and entrepreneurial classes with the manners of a gentleman. Definition, it appeared, came from within: an acceptance, a recognition, an instinct of others who had received a training which could be labelled 'public school'. Confidence in these schools had grown, it was argued, because they had created a broader, more cohesive and united governing class, bringing together the older and newer forms of wealth in British society.

In time this wider establishment was able to supply not only a growing collectivist state at home with an array of higher civil servants, but also an expanded Empire and colonies with a devoted selfless administration. Preparation for such work was undertaken in this public-school world. The majority of the schools were residential, situated in rural areas, and therefore able to create a sense of shared community away from the distractions of home and the surrounding locality. Here the boys – and despite the foundation in the nineteenth century of such prestigious girls' schools as Cheltenham Ladies' College, Roedean and Wycombe Abbey the emphasis was essentially on boys – were moulded and trained. From the 1850s boys had been immersed in the life of the schools where, surrounded by equals within this closed community, they would develop interests, life-long friendships, and qualities which would sustain them throughout adult life. Public schools therefore had a national function. Local boys, regional accents and cultural diversity were to be excluded. At the top of the school, under the surveillance of powerful housemasters, older boys developed the skills of leadership and the habit of authority. The younger boys, who needed thorough preparation for this kind of life, found themselves excluded and confined to a preparatory sector, which trained, sifted, and sometimes excluded unsatisfactory elements.

In comparison with other forms of schooling the public schools, even in the present century, have been distinguished by the age of the school community and its emphasis on the top end of schooling. The fact that for long periods the teaching of Classics held such a powerful sway, even into the 1920s and 1930s, was scarcely surprising since its remoteness from everyday experience ensured that the boys could be directed to a proper role for gentlemen away from the world of profit and gain. Scholarship never lost its appeal to a world so closely tied to the older universities, but the qualities represented by the playing field often threatened to overwhelm even this highly-regarded attribute. Team games therefore meant more than the using up of adolescent energy, and became seen as the agencies by which boys learned to co-operate, sweep away individual selfishness, and develop moral and physical courage of the highest order. These were the attitudes deemed necessary, particularly for the small band of administrators and soldiers who tirelessly supervised the life of vast tracts of the colonial empire.

If a group identity was to sustain the public schools in the new century it was generally held to be located within the Headmasters' Conference, first established in 1869. It was no easy matter to set up a body to deliberate on matters common to them all. At that time, as in the future, alarm generated action. A reforming Liberal government, elected in 1868, might well institute the full recommendations of the Taunton Commission, endangering the carefully built up reputation of some of the major schools. Those schools, identified as 'public' by the separate Clarendon Commission which reported in 1864, particularly the most prestigious, were in no hurry to be invited, and Eton did not join the Conference until 1879. Nevertheless the Headmasters' Conference had close contacts through pupils' families, Old Boys' networks, Church and governing bodies with the most powerful politicians and senior civil servants, including those at the Board of Education. It was a national body drawing members from all parts of the United Kingdom. Significantly, too, though the religious atmosphere in the schools was predominantly Anglican, ranging from Tractarian or

Evangelical to lukewarm acquiescence, Roman Catholic, Dissenting and even Quaker schools could be included in its membership. Thus the public schools never split apart on religious differences, and could always call on the support of groups in the major denominations of the country if troubles were looming.

In the Edwardian public school there was a period of confidence. In 1900 almost all significant male groups in society received their education at these places. It was now difficult to be considered suitable for a place at Oxford or Cambridge without residence at one of the public schools. A scan of government benches, ranks of civil servants and bishops revealed the same picture. Nevertheless Edwardian England presented the opening shots of a long battle. In the aftermath of the setbacks encountered during the Boer War voices were raised about national efficiency, a more modern leadership and the competence of the nation to survive. It was not long before the public-school élite began to be weighed against the allegedly more vigorous leaders of more modern nations.

There were anxieties, too, in the public schools about the new secondary system. Less exclusive, cheap, locally-based, perhaps more academic, and after 1907 with a free-place scheme more meritocratic schools, they presented a threat to those at the edge of the public-school network. Increasingly, too, the secondary school was seen as the proper institution for the early development of the potential teacher. As a result, although the similarities remained, there was a divide between the two sets of schools which continued through most of the century.

In 1914 war found the public schools outwardly confident but not without their critics from inside their own world, and a growing array of opponents in the expanding political world. In common with other sections of the community the younger masters and senior boys entered that conflict with enthusiasm. They seemed almost prepared, for since the turn of the century a prominent feature of many of these schools had been the drilling, military manoeuvres and annual camps. Within months, prefects had been transformed into subalterns. Life at the Western Front in the early months was portrayed as an extension of school life with regimental loyalty replacing that of house and schools, and younger officers embracing the routine battalion duties almost as if they were promoting the efficient running of the school. While headmasters and chaplains continued to list with pride the heavy sacrifices made by many of these young officers, others began to reflect on their doubts. The writer, William Plomer, who left Rugby early, disclosed that the war heightened his misgivings about the kind of education to which he was being subjected (Greene, 1984, pp.111–26). Generations were split by the war experience. At Repton younger teachers such as Victor Gollancz and Donald Somervill attempted to devise new courses stressing reconstruction and internationalism. Their activities displeased the headmaster, and Gollancz disappeared from the staff. A period at the trenches made many of the younger teachers returning to the classroom less tolerant of older, stuffier colleagues.

THE STORM CLOUDS GATHER, 1918–1944

For the majority of public-school headmasters the task, as war ended, was to return to normality. Recruitment of new staff and the refurbishment of equipment and buildings were only part of this process. They needed, above all, to ride the storm of criticism and dissension. By the early 1920s many of the signs appeared to be hopeful. Indeed numbers of pupils applying for places at the public schools rose to their highest level. The attacks from within the confines of these institutions began to diminish. Perhaps the growth of a network of new progressive schools such as Leonard Elmhirst's at Dartington Hall in 1926, with child-centred, informal atmospheres, aided this. Although they might well present a challenge to the older schools by drawing away groups which hitherto had been within, they also absorbed and diverted potential, divisive critics. Several new schools came into existence, very much in the older mould but more aware of the criticisms accumulating in the war period. Redlands (1920) and Bryanston (1928) were notable examples, but the most striking development took place at Stowe (1923) where the headmaster, J.F. Roxborough, a product and admirer of a public-school education, nevertheless strove to create a more relaxed, artistic education in its confines.

Some of the older traditional public schools, too, began to relax many of the cultural rituals and distinctive uniforms, as at Charterhouse. In a growing recognition that the post-war world might present a more dangerous hostility, an attempt was made, in 1919, through discussions at the Board of Education, to find bursaries for a few boys from the elementary sector to go to certain public schools. It failed to generate much interest among the majority of headmasters or senior civil servants. Generally the public schools settled down, in the 1920s, to a period of growth and expansion of facilities. This was in stark contrast to the difficulties being encountered in the maintained sector in the period of acute post-war retrenchment.

Nevertheless the political threat grew. Deep divisions within the Liberal party brought the possibility of a future Labour government much nearer. The possession of a certain kind of education was increasingly seen as a part of the class division in British society. This was to be the most notable feature in the political criticism, but it was accompanied by other themes. An attack was made on the wealth of schools, the charge being made that by the erosion of traditional local rights by self-seeking headmasters, 'the birthright of the poor' had been stolen. This appealed strongly to the trade-union wing and there were calls at TUC Congresses, as in 1922, for Commissions of Inquiry, 'to go into the details of legacies and bequests being absorbed by the creation of increased numbers of scholarships and bursaries at the leading schools' (TUC *Annual Conference Report*, 1922). There was a strong feeling that these well-run, serious schools shielded many private schools with dubious reputations. In 1930 the minority Labour government proposed a Commission of Inquiry to investigate the state of independent schooling, and suggested vigorous checks on health and working conditions. Although the proposal was not implemented, it was a weapon that never entirely vanished from Labour's armoury.

The major difficulties of the 1930s did not come, however, from a hostile political climate. The gentry and the liberal professions, much associated with rural society and the land, were affected by the fall in prices of agricultural products. A declining birth-rate, always most clearly marked in the wealthier landed section, already hit by heavy war losses, did nothing to ease these problems. In the heady days of the 1920s, money had been spent on extensions and rebuilding. By the early 1930s it was no longer certain that returns would be forthcoming on such investments. Pressures, too, mounted from the maintained sector in the inter-war years. The Burnham Committee had laid down uniform salaries and conditions of work which, together with pensions, ensured a career structure that even the most financially hard-pressed public school had to emulate. Faced with the hard economic reality of straitened finances there were a number of alternatives which might be followed.

Fees could be increased very sharply which might drive away the traditional recruits. Rationalization, a modish word in the 1930s, was another possibility, as weaker schools either closed or were amalgamated with stronger units. Finally, some reforming headmasters edged towards a third and recurring solution, the widening of the appeal of the schools to take in a broader section of the population. This, however, carried perhaps the most dire perils, since it not only threatened many of the traditional strengths, but opened up the issue of the relationship between the independent public-school sector and the whole maintained system. In the feverish atmosphere of the 1930s, particularly with the growing external threats, several of the younger public-school headmasters were determined to face this challenge and began to explore previously-discarded proposals about wider access. The tide of opinion seemed to be moving towards cohesion, and rejection or indifference might turn it irrevocably against the public schools. Harold Macmillan's influential *Middle Way*, published in 1938, expressed concern about the total educational separation of the classes: 'It would do nothing but good to the children of every class if the early years of life were spent in the same school. Even when some children went to higher education and others directly into manual or clerical employment the early association would not be forgotten' (Macmillan, 1938, pp. 64–5).

The opening years of the 1939–45 War did nothing to lessen the growing gulf between the two sectors of education. While the Board of Education worked hard to shift sections of the maintained school population from threatened areas, public schools were often too remote to be in this situation or were left to make their own arrangements. In 1943 the submission of the TUC to the Fleming Committee, which reported in 1944, summed up the case against the retention of these schools in their present form in a post-war era:

> The argument is often heard that the public school is necessary to produce our leaders. While it is true that our governors and administrators largely come from the public schools, the cause of this effect is obvious. Because of economic and social privilege the public schools have an altogether unfair choice when the selection of such people is being made. (TUC, *Annual Conference Report*, 1943)

Generally the public-school lobby realized that their position had become more precarious. At the height of the war conferences did take place at local level between secondary and public-school heads which, in looking at common problems, discussed the possibility of closer links. This might well have been the spur for the initiative of the Headmasters' Conference and the Governing Bodies Association in requesting the Board of Education to set up an inquiry to investigate ways in which public schools could become more closely associated with wider educational reconstruction. In stemming the tide of criticism in wartime they could rely on allies. Not only was the coalition maintained by a heavy Conservative majority, but the senior officials at the Board were unlikely to be indifferent to their fate. Indeed in their own proposals put forward in *The Green Book* in 1941, the Board had chosen to avoid the public-school issue altogether when surveying educational reconstruction. There was also clear indication that although the criticisms were stronger than ever, opponents did not present a united front on the kind of changes they wished to see being introduced. R.H. Tawney, whose sharp attacks on public schools had been deeply influential, welcomed the establishment of the Fleming Committee, and argued that these schools, already threatened by a falling birth-rate, competition from the maintained sector and spiralling war taxation, would co-operate readily in any proposals that would allow all sections of the population to benefit from them.

However the ultimate reason why public schools escaped frontal assault at this period was that the nation's attention, including the coalition of Labour and progressive opinion, was directed increasingly to the reorganization of the education of the majority, particularly in respect of a free secondary stage. This involved long, tortuous negotiations with Churches, local authorities and teachers. Against this background the argument that a review of independent schooling could receive proper attention only after the passage and implementation of a major Education Bill was widely accepted.

Whatever the motives for establishing the Fleming Committee, its subsequent report has been generally dismissed, because of its failure to recommend any substantial changes in the relationship between the maintained sector and the public schools. Although critics were allowed to state their case, the membership drew attention to the strengths of these schools which they believed ought not to be swept away. They were particularly well-disposed to the residential value of many of the institutions: 'We place first a training in community life which enables the boys and girls to work in and for a society composed of very different types, to sacrifice their personal wishes to the general good, to find their place in the community and to be ready, if called upon, to take responsibility' (HMSO, 1944, p.47).

One of the recommendations of the Committee was that pupils from the state sector could proceed to public schools, which were accepted by the Board of Education as efficient, if they were prepared to offer such pupils up to 25 per cent of their places. Bursaries would be provided to pay for these pupils. There were divisions within the Committee and also among the headmasters on this proposal. In particular there was concern not only about the numbers, which might upset the 'tone' of the schools, but also about the criteria for selection. Suitability for boarding education might mean, for instance, the absorption of pupils from disturbed households. In fighting a rearguard action public-school headmasters could count on lack of enthusiasm among the Board's senior advisers and the indifference of most outside critics who saw the move, at best, as a feeble concession to a new wartime spirit and, at worst, as a means to prop up an ailing, financially embarrassed set of schools.

SURVIVAL AND REGROUPING, 1945–1980

The recommendations of the Fleming Report became the responsibility of a new Minister, Ellen Wilkinson, one of the more radical members of the new Labour government. This might well have alarmed the public schools, but as we have seen, her energy was devoted to rebuilding the shattered maintained sector and implementing the Butler Act. At times she toyed with the possibility of wider residential provision as part of secondary education, but it never became a priority. Part of the problem for Labour politicians was that they discovered that, for all their previous assaults on public schools, no effective policy for their replacement had been devised. Consequently the strategy of attrition was widely accepted. Ellen Wilkinson declared: 'therefore my own view is to make the schools provided by the State so good that it will seem quite absurd to send children to these schools' (Labour Party *Annual Conference Report*, June 1946). One of the consequences of free secondary education, open to all people, would be the erosion of independent schooling. There was a sustained belief that in a new socialist Britain, even among classes that had always supported these schools, there had been a substantial shift of opinion. Improved access to universities, better sixth forms and wider opportunities in maintained secondary schools were believed to make public schools less relevant.

It was only in the final years of the Labour government that this strategy was challenged. The establishment of a confident maintained system at the secondary stage took much longer to secure than the reforming Labour government had anticipated. Parents, administrators and educationists became increasingly concerned about selection procedures, the nature of secondary schooling and the shortcomings of modern schools. In contrast many of the public schools, with their continuity and settled pattern, looked far from unattractive. Those in the Labour Party, such as Richard Crossman and Peggy Jay, who drew attention to the failure of the policy of attrition, now argued that the attributes of public schooling, particularly its concern for leadership skills, should be put to the use of a more democratic society. Most Labour leaders, however, were content to leave matters alone. Few, as the General Election drew near, wanted to generate controversy on this issue.

Conservative victories in 1951, 1955 and 1959 eased considerably the anxieties of the public schools. In the reaction against overall socialist uniformity even the more sceptical R.A. Butler endorsed their value as an important barrier against state monopoly. Moreover, just as Socialists anticipated their decline, as the post-war middle-class generation grew away from the need for independent schooling, many Conservatives began to anticipate growth, as socially ambitious parents decided to send their children to these schools. Growing affluence enabled the clientele to be widened, and to become less socially exclusive and élitist.

Attacks on the public schools continued from the Labour side. Tony Crosland's *Future of Socialism*, published in 1956, was a most significant and influential work. In it he portrayed a nation still largely stratified and conditioned by older class attitudes, while external competitors appeared to be forging ahead. For him equality, modernization and national survival seemed bound together, and the continuation of private education not only affected the nation's inability to move forward, but ultimately might become a cause of decline. In a debate in the House of Commons on the public schools in 1961 he characterized the public schools as follows:

> The emphasis on character and manner rather than brains; on the all-rounder and the amateur rather than the professional; on the classics rather than science; on the insular rather than the international, and on the orthodox and traditional rather than the new, are precisely wrong from the point of view of our national needs in the 1960s. (*Hansard*, Vol 642, Col. 829, 18 June 1961)

The return of a Labour government in 1964 increased the pressures upon the public schools. Crosland's arrival at the Department of Education, talk of government modernization and the preaching of technological revolution, all cast their shadows. Yet the Public Schools Commission, established in 1965 and headed by the far from radical John Newsom, was given relatively limited terms of reference. There was clear evidence that the new Minister failed to generate much interest among his colleagues. It was considered more important at this time to secure a modernization of the maintained sector, particularly the implementation of comprehensive education.

The Public Schools Commission produced little that was new. Sociology, now fashionable, loomed large in many of the findings. The Report of 1968 showed that public-school masters and pupils were recruited from a very restricted social group. In consequence, from the later 1960s, more attention was paid to the use of marketing techniques, public relations and publicity. The appointment, in 1972, of the Independent Schools Information Service (ISIS) was a product of this new awareness of the value of marketing. In 1974 the Independent Schools Joint Council was created, a recognition that the older techniques of quiet, sustained pressure needed to be supplemented by more vigorous campaigning. Public schools, too, began to exploit the debate about wastage of talent, the leading schools increasingly stressing their determination to uphold strong academic standards. As the 1960s came to an end, pupils from public schools not only became more visible in localities through community service projects, but also presented in their life at these schools a more relaxed, informal atmosphere. One of the most striking examples was the introduction of girls into some boys' public schools, either within sixth forms or throughout the age range.

The Second Report of the Public Schools Commission, chaired by David Donnison, appeared in 1970 and was to have important consequences for future developments in the independent sector. Donnison's Report, though not unanimous, presented the direct grant schools with a stark choice between independence and selection on the one hand, and integration and open access on the other. It was pointed out that for a government which, in 1970, had shown its determination to enforce non-selection by law if necessary on obstinate local authorities, to continue to fund fee-paying, highly selective schools was no longer tenable. Before this could be taken up, Labour was defeated at the polls and a new Minister, Margaret Thatcher, highly sympathetic to the schools, and by inclination disposed to widen the list, was in office. However, the return of a Labour government in 1974 signified a dramatic change in the future of the direct grant list. Although some schools, notably the Roman Catholic, decided to accept comprehensive education, the majority decided for independence and selection. This decision gave the public schools a broader image, academic prestige, and more extensive connections with the work of science, technology and modern subjects. The term 'independent', implying vigour, enterprise and initiative, began to be used more extensively than the older 'public school' nomenclature.

In 1973, shortly before Labour's return to office, Roy Hattersley had made it very clear that his party's objective in creating a public-school policy was no longer reform, integration or collaboration, all of which implied some kind of continuation of their present identity. He laid down a programme for action, starting with the phasing out of direct grant lists, the dismantling of local authority schemes for independent school provision and ending with investigations into both charity status and conditions in these schools. In this way it was anticipated that only the strongest would survive the onslaught. However, after 1976, there was little real attempt to take steps to weaken their position. In particular senior diplomats and service personnel not only continued to send their children to these schools, but continued to receive financial assistance from government sources. In that year, the Callaghan speech at Ruskin College did little to build up the confidence of the maintained sector. Labour leaders now seemed content with symbolic gestures including the publicized withdrawal of their own children from independent schools.

Since the mid-1970s the fortunes of independent schooling had become closely associated with those of the Conservative party. Those Conservatives who in the past had been disturbed by division, and were inclined towards reform or integration, lost influence. In their place figures such as Rhodes Boyson now stressed the strengths of independent schooling for individuals and the nation. Dependence on market forces, in the past half-concealed, was now praised for its efficiency and careful tuning to consumer needs. Poor teaching, ill-considered curriculum changes and dangerous progressive thinking would receive short shrift from parents who were required to pay high fees for their children's education. In 1980 an Education Act established assisted places in independent schools. The 1988 Education Act with its provision for opted-out schools and local school management may further blur the lines between the independent and maintained sectors.

CONCLUSION

Throughout the twentieth century, in spite of the reports of commissions and committees, and the policies of Labour politicians, both in opposition and in government, public and other fee-paying schools have continued to occupy a central position in English education and society.

In the early 1990s, although only some seven per cent of children attend such schools they supply half of the undergraduate students at Oxford and Cambridge. In 1979 Margaret Thatcher's Cabinet contained seven Old Etonians. In 1983 former pupils of Eton occupied the posts of Governor of the Bank of England, Chief of the Defence Staff, editor of *The Times* and head of the home civil service and of the foreign service (Sampson, 1983, p.144). The Conservative Cabinet of 1990 had 22 members. Of their 56 children all but eight attended or had attended fee-paying schools (*Sunday Times*, 18 February 1990).

FURTHER READING

J.R. Honey, *Tom Brown's Universe*, 1977 and J.A. Mangan, *Athleticism in the Victorian and Edwardian Public School*, 1981 deal with the early part of the century. On the period 1914–45 there is C. Heward, *Making a Man of Him*, 1988; N. Annan, *J.F. Roxborough of Stowe*, 1965; A. Hearnden, *Red Robert: a Life of Robert Birley*, 1984, and P. Parker, *The Old Lie: the Great War and the Public School Ethos*, 1987. On the period from 1945: see J.C. Dancy, *The Public Schools and the Future*, 1963; J. Rae, *The Public School Revolution. Britain's Independent Schools 1964–79*, 1981; C. Griggs, *Private Education in Britain*, 1985; D. Johnson, *Private Schools and State Schools*, 1987, and B. Salter and T. Tapper, *Power and Policy in Education*, 1985.

CHAPTER FIFTEEN

Adult Education

FOUNDATIONS

Adult education is not easily defined. It is not simply the education of adults, i.e. those aged over 18 or 21; full-time university or polytechnic students, for example, are not usually considered as being engaged in adult education. Nor is it just the part-time education of adults, or the non-vocational, or voluntary educational activity of adults, although these elements have been important in adult education as traditionally conceived in this country. As defined at the Unesco World Conference in Tokyo in 1972 adult education means:

> A process whereby persons who no longer attend school on a regular or full time basis, undertake sequential and organized activities with the conscious intention of bringing about changes in information, knowledge, understanding or skills, appreciation and attitudes: or for the purpose of identifying or solving personal problems. (quoted in Legge, 1982, pp.4–5)

Such a general description, whilst suitably all-embracing, must be complemented by a definition based upon actual activities which in an historical sense have been considered to constitute traditional adult education in England.

At the start of the twentieth century that tradition was based upon a variety of nineteenth-century foundations. These included the mechanics' institutes pioneered originally by George Birkbeck in Glasgow. Birkbeck also became president of the London Mechanics' Institute established in 1823. By 1826 there were more than 100 institutes, and some 700 by 1851. These varied greatly in size and purpose from large urban institutes with substantial buildings and a range of courses, to small village meetings held infrequently in the local hall or public house. Their subjects of study ranged from science and technology, Birkbeck's original purpose, to history, literature, phrenology, music, and even to basic entertainments. Their clientele were probably drawn mainly from the skilled working and lower-

212

middle classes. The first half of the nineteenth century also saw the formation of literary and philosophical societies, as for example those set up at Liverpool in 1812 and Leeds in 1820, and of nationwide specialist scientific societies – the Geological Society of 1807 and the Chemical Society of 1841.

The 1830s and 1840s produced a number of political and reform movements which set particular store by adult education – the Chartists and the Anti-Corn Law League, the Owenites and the Co-operative movement. Many adults also attended Sunday schools and evening weekday schools. The Methodists, for example, placed particular emphasis upon the education of adults through such schools and through the weekly class meeting.

Other dimensions of adult education to develop in the first half of the nineteenth century included the production of cheap, instructive pamphlets and magazines, as exemplified by the work of the Society for the Diffusion of Useful Knowledge, and the production of a relatively cheap and unfettered press. Although many societies, institutes and churches had libraries, the Public Libraries Act of 1850 made it possible for local authorities to raise money from the rates for this purpose.

The second half of the nineteenth century saw the founding of new types of adult education, and the continuation or adaptation of those already in existence. The 1851 Census recorded some 1,545 evening schools for adults in England and Wales with 39,783 students. Such schools were particularly numerous in Lancashire and the West Riding of Yorkshire. Nearly one third of the students were women. The schools were often remedial in nature, with reading and writing as the most common subjects of study, followed by geography, grammar and history (Kelly, 1970, pp. 155–6). The Quakers were particularly involved in adult schools as part of their missionary work, and by the end of the century 29,000 students were in Quaker adult achools (Kelly, 1970, p. 204). Other religious organizations which contributed to adult education included the Young Men's Christian Association, founded in 1844, and the Young Women's Christian Association which dates from 1877. These were complemented by temperance groups, co-operative and friendly societies and trade unions, many of which provided libraries, reading rooms, lectures and classes.

The most important single foundation, however, was the London Working Men's College, opened in 1854 to all males over the age of 16 who were competent in the 3Rs. This was the product of an influential group of Christian Socialists headed by J.F.D. Maurice who became the first principal, and which included J.M.F. Ludlow, Thomas Hughes and Charles Kingsley, all of whom also taught at the College. A separate Working Women's College was established in 1864. The London Working Men's College, though beset in its early years by many difficulties, made a significant contribution to the concept of adult education. In providing liberal education of the highest quality it went beyond the work of the mechanics' institutes. Indeed by the end of the nineteenth century the mechanics' institutes were being supplanted by, or incorporated into, other institutions, notably the technical colleges and polytechnics. In 1879 the first technical college was established by the City and Guilds Institute at Finsbury in London. Three years later Quintin Hogg opened the first of the new polytechnics, also in London, in Regent Street.

For centuries working men, and women of all social classes, had been excluded from university education in England. The second half of the nineteenth century saw the extension of university education with the foundation of new colleges and universities in such cities as Birmingham, Bristol, Leeds, Liverpool, Manchester and Newcastle. It also witnessed an heroic attempt by the older universities to reach out into the community. The pioneer of this movement was James Stuart of Trinity College, Cambridge, who gave the first course of lectures in 1867 in Leeds, Liverpool, Manchester and Sheffield. The universities of Oxford and London were also to the fore, together with the new federal Victoria University, which comprised Manchester, Liverpool and Leeds, and by 1893–94 there were some 60,000 students attending University Extension courses (Kelly, 1970, p.223). The Extension movement contributed to the founding of new university colleges – as at Exeter, Nottingham and Reading. Its day classes were mainly attended by women, and its evening sessions attracted mixed audiences of professionals and artisans, with pupil teachers and elementary school teachers particularly prominent. From 1893 summer schools were held at Cambridge and Oxford so that some of those who had attended lectures in their own localities could, for a brief period, pursue their search for enlightenment and truth within the hallowed courts and cloisters themselves.

Members of the universities also established settlements to promote missionary and education work in the poorer districts of major cities. Toynbee Hall opened in the East End of London in 1885 with Samuel Barnett as Warden, and a wide range of adult educational activities from remedial classes to Extension courses. There were concerts and art exhibitions, and a permanent home was provided for the latter in the Whitechapel Art Gallery, opened in 1901.

Thus by the start of the twentieth century the concept of adult education in England had been fashioned largely by a series of unrelated initiatives and events. It was essentially part-time. It was not the result of direct legislative intervention. Nevertheless the provision of compulsory schooling from 1880 had meant that elementary instruction for adults would increasingly be regarded as a remedial activity. Education of a vocational kind was being supplied in technical colleges and polytechnics. Liberal or non-vocational education, however, as provided in the London Working Men's College or in the University Extension movement, came to epitomize a particularly prestigious form of adult education. Such courses, which were freely chosen by students for the purpose of self-fulfilment and access to the highest form of culture, served little or no utilitarian purpose in terms of employment or personal reward of a financial kind. For the first half of the twentieth century, at least, adult education in England would reflect a hierarchy of values similar to, and indeed acquired in large part from, the traditional world of higher education.

WORKERS' EDUCATIONAL ASSOCIATION

The Workers' Educational Association, founded in 1903, was the most distinctive and influential adult educational organization of the first half of the twentieth century. Its declared purpose was, and is, 'to stimulate and to satisfy the demands of adults, in particular members of workers' movements, for education, by the promotion of courses and other facilities ...' (Russell Report, 1973, p.37). Albert Mansbridge, its founder, was born in Gloucester in 1876 but educated in London, leaving school at 14. From 1896 he worked as a clerk in the Co-operative Wholesale Society's warehouse at Whitechapel. An Anglican lay preacher, a teacher in Sunday and evening schools, an attender at Extension lectures and at Toynbee Hall, Mansbridge personified many of the strands of later nineteenth-century adult education. In 1903 he wrote a series of articles for the *University Extension Journal* which called upon trade unionists, co-operative supporters and others not to be satisfied merely with political and economic activity but to 'lift themselves up through higher knowledge to higher works and higher places' (quoted in Harrison, 1961, p.263).

The first four branches were founded at Reading, Derby, Rochdale and Ilford in 1904–05, and in this latter year the name WEA was adopted in place of the original 'Association to Promote the Higher Education of Working Men'. Mansbridge's supporters included influential Anglicans, Charles Gore and William Temple, and university tutors, particularly those who were already committed to the Extension movement. J.A.R. Marriott, the Oxford Extension Secretary, and other academics, however, were happier with the approach 'What Oxford can do for Workpeople' rather than with the theme of 'What Workpeople want Oxford to do'. These differences of emphasis emerged at a conference of university and WEA representatives held at Oxford in August 1907, a conference which led to the establishment of a joint committee of seven WEA nominees and seven dons. Their report, published in 1908 as *Oxford and Working-Class Education*, recommended the establishment of joint WEA–university committees and tutorial classes. By 1914 all universities and university colleges in England and Wales, bar Exeter and Southampton, were helping to organize tutorial classes. Of 142 classes comprising more than 3,000 students, 30 were connected with London, 18 with Oxford and 17 with Manchester.

Tutorial classes, indeed, had originated from a conference held at London University in 1906, and had begun with a ten-week course in Civics at a WEA branch in Battersea in 1907. Longer courses, however, began in January 1908 under the tutorship of R.H. Tawney. At Longton in Staffordshire and Rochdale in Lancashire, students embarked on a three-year tutorial course in economic history. Weekly meetings, on Friday evenings at Longton and Saturday afternoons at Rochdale, and the writing of fortnightly essays, marked a significant change from the mass lecture approach associated with the Extension movement. The classes were relatively small, typically some 12 to 30 men and women, united in social and intellectual purpose, with a tutor as guide as well as mentor. Attendance at 24 two-hour sessions over three years both required considerable commitment, and built up a strong sense of corporate identity. Although some students found the going hard and failed to complete their essays, the work of the best was at times favourably compared with that of first-class candidates from the universities themselves. Unlike the Extension movement the WEA flourished during the First World War, not least because of the increased numbers of women students. In 1918–19 the WEA had 219 branches, 153 tutorial classes, 404 other classes and 12,438 students, some 40 per cent of whom were women. Although social sciences, including economics, economic history and government, remained the principal fare of tutorial classes, other courses in such subjects as literature, music, French and folk dancing marked a dilution of the original social and political purposes and a metamorphosis into a general adult educational movement.

RUSKIN COLLEGE AND THE NATIONAL COUNCIL OF LABOUR COLLEGES

Problems faced by the WEA in curriculum matters were brought into sharper relief in the early history of Ruskin College. Ruskin Hall, established at Oxford in 1899 by two visiting American students, Charles Beard and Walter Vrooman, was to be a residential college where members of the working classes could study 'those subjects which are essential for working-class leadership, and which are not a direct avenue to anything beyond' (quoted in Kelly, 1970, p.244). Ruskin College (as it became in 1907) therefore was not intended to provide an educational ladder whereby individuals might escape from the working class, nor to encourage workers to accept their lot by simply enriching their lives through literary, artistic and social pursuits. Its early years, however, were plagued with management and financial problems, until the establishment in 1909 of a new governing council composed of representatives from the Trades Union Congress, the General Federation of Trade Unions, the Co-operative Union and other working-class organizations which pledged financial support. In new buildings from 1913, Ruskin, with some 30 students per year, many of them on two-year courses, survived, but was too small to be of great significance, and was not destined to be followed by residential colleges for working people at other universities.

One reason for this failure to multiply was a crisis over the ethos and curriculum of the college, which began in 1907 upon the complaint of a group of students who saw the whole enterprise as becoming too bourgeois and accommodating. In 1909 the dismissed principal, Dennis Hird, and a group of present and former students, established a rival body in the shape of the Central Labour College. This new institution, which was firmly committed to socialist education, also received trade union support, and in 1916 was taken over by the National Union of Railwaymen and the South Wales Miners' Federation. Though the Central Labour College itself closed in 1929 when the miners felt obliged to withdraw their financial support, a Marxist-based analysis of the need for truly independent working-class education had been established. The Plebs' League, founded in 1908 with a monthly journal, *The Plebs*, and classes organized throughout the country in labour colleges, which from 1921 were incorporated into a National Council of Labour Colleges, promoted class-conscious education. The idea that independent adult education could take place in university or state-supported institutions was rejected. The Plebs'

League advised members of the working classes that the coming of socialism would indeed depend upon the diffusion of education, but education which was essentially propaganda:

> What kind of propaganda? Propaganda based upon the ideas of the ruling class, taught in the Universities which express its class outlook upon society; or propaganda based upon the point of view of the working class, and designed to equip the workers for their struggle against capitalism and capitalist ideology? (quoted in Harrison, 1961, p.295)

In 1922–23 the NCLC ran 529 classes with 11,933 students, together with further correspondence courses and other lectures and activities. Political, economic and social education (or propaganda) for the overthrow of capitalism was the essential aim. Thus in the inter-war years the WEA frequently found itself occupying an uncomfortable middle ground – regarded by the universities as being too committed to the working class, and by the Plebs' League and the NCLC as being too committed to the universities. Conflict between the NCLC and the WEA was exemplified by two publications of 1924. In *Working-Class Education* J.F.C. Horrabin argued for working-class education for working-class purposes under working-class control. Basil Yeaxlee's *Spiritual Values in Education* on the other hand, written from a WEA standpoint, condemned the NCLC as divisive and provocative.

THE 1919 REPORT

In 1917 a Committee on Adult Education was appointed by the Ministry of Reconstruction. Its chairman was A.L. Smith, Master of Balliol College, Oxford, and long-standing friend of the WEA. University and WEA members, who included Mansbridge and Tawney, were in the majority but the Central Labour College, Co-operative movement, adult achools, YMCA, trade unions, LEAs, employers and the NUT were also represented. The Committee's Final Report of 1919 was an expression of optimism and idealism for the brave new world of peace. It has been described as 'a work on the grand scale, a history, survey and philosophy of adult education. It is certainly the most notable and useful monument in our adult education literature' (Waller, 1956, p.22). In his prefatory letter to the Report, addressed to the Prime Minister, Lloyd George, Smith declared:

that the necessary conclusion is that adult education must not be regarded as a luxury for a few exceptional persons here and there, nor as a thing which concerns only a short span of early manhood, but that adult education is a permanent national necessity, an inseparable aspect of citizenship, and therefore shall be both universal and lifelong. (Waller, 1956, p.55).

The Report therefore proposed that provision should be made for all types of adult education needs. All universities should play a full part in this work by establishing extra-mural departments with academic heads. Local Education Authorities should provide institutes with a wide range of activities. The Board of Education should give generous financial assistance, and joint committees of local authorities, universities and voluntary bodies should be established. The first university extra-mural department was established at Nottingham in 1920, and by 1939 only Leeds, Reading and Sheffield had failed to implement the Committee's recommendations in this respect. In 1923, moreover, Nottingham appointed the first professor of adult education, Robert Peers. These initiatives breathed new life into university interest in the field of adult education, and Peers indeed pioneered a comprehensive adult education programme for the East Midlands region. At the same time the work of the WEA was diversifying in terms of the nature, length and subject matter of its courses.

Unlike the school boards whose powers were limited to elementary education, the LEAs created under the 1902 Act were able to assist and provide adult education. The 1919 Report thought it 'imperative that Local Education Authorities should take a large and important place in the development of adult education' (Waller, 1956, p.152). It recommended that LEAs should submit plans to the Central Department for adult education provision in their areas, inaugurate Adult Education Joint Committees, establish evening institutes, promote students' societies, support the proposed local colleges, provide assistance to university, WEA and other agencies in their courses and classes, and give scholarships to adults to enable them to attend summer schools and other residential educational opportunities.

The best known local authority institutes were those of the London County Council, of which the largest was the City Literary Institute, established in separate premises in 1928. This provided courses in a wide range of subjects, from English literature to musical appreciation and dancing, and fostered a strong community sense with clubs, societies and various extra-curricular activities. The first of the LCC's literary institutes for cultural subjects was founded in 1919, the first of its men's institutes for practical and recreational activities in 1920, whilst its women's institutes which included practical, recreational and humane studies dated from 1913. By 1937–38 the LCC had 40 women's institutes with 44,000 students, 13 men's institutes with 17,000 students, 12 literary institutes with 14,000 students and a number of other general evening adult institutes (Kelly, 1970, pp.289–90).

Rural education received particular emphasis in the 1919 Report. Many parts of the country still exhibited medieval characteristics. Feudalism prevailed in social relations, and in scattered, isolated human settlements men and women eked out lives of unremitting drudgery and poverty. The Report drew attention to the need to develop 'new social traditions and a new culture' (Waller, 1956, p.156). It recommended the establishment of village institutes, with central government providing 90 per cent of the capital costs, and with adult educational work placed upon a permanent basis. Resident organizers, tutors and lecturers would be required, residential continuation schools should be established, whilst larger villages and market towns should regularly supply weekend conferences, exhibitions and classes. Substantial grants from central and local authorities would be needed.

In the inter-war years many multi-purpose village halls were built, with financial assistance from national and local governmental authorities, including the National and Local Councils of Social Service, from the Carnegie Trust, and from local benefactors. Similar provision was made on many new housing estates in the shape of community centres. One of the most comprehensive and ambitious of rural schemes took shape in Cambridgeshire where village colleges were established along the lines proposed by Henry Morris. These included not only a village hall, but a library, tutorial rooms, recreational facilities, and shared use of other facilities with the incorporated primary and secondary school. Village colleges would, Morris hoped, provide both a community centre and an educational resource from the cradle to the grave. Only four, however, were opened in Cambridgeshire before the country was plunged into another world war.

The optimism and vision of the 1919 Report may be contrasted with the bleakness and uncertainties of the next 20 years – in respect of economic disasters, unemployment and a rapidly deteriorating international situation. Some specific recommendations, notably the establishment of university extra-mural departments, were implemented, albeit in a more restricted way than the Committee had envisaged. There was a greater coordination of services, and the British (later the National) Institute of Adult Education was established in

1920 to bring together the various adult educational interests in conferences and committees. Impetus was also given to the work of existing providers of adult education.

NEW DIRECTIONS

Two major features of the inter-war years, the setting up of extramural departments and the increasing involvement of LEAs in adult education, have already been noted. The work of the WEA, YMCA, YWCA, the Working Men's and Women's Colleges and other long-term providers of adult education continued. In 1920 the YWCA sponsored its first residential college for working women which in 1926 was established as Hillcroft at Surbiton in Surrey. In 1924 the London Working Men's College reasserted its independence from the LCC. In 1927 Coleg Harlech was opened as a residential college for Wales, with financial support provided by the Board of Education, LEAs and trade unions. Courses lasting a year, and a month, were provided for students recruited from a variety of adult education classes. In 1927 its first summer school was attended by 116 students, 34 of whom were women.

New directions in the inter-war period can be grouped under two headings: the foundation of new organizations for the adult education of women, and the increasing influence of the media – particularly cinema and the radio.

The first Women's Institute was established in Anglesey in 1915, the movement having originated in Canada in 1897. By 1927 there were some 4,000 institutes with a quarter of a million members. It was essentially a rurally-located enterprise, begun under the auspices of the British Agricultural Organization Society, and operating from 1917 with the backing of the Board of Agriculture. Open to 'countrywomen of all ages, interests, politics and creeds', its purpose was 'to bring countrywomen together to learn things which will be of help in their homes; to improve conditions in the village; to consider the needs of country people throughout the land and to develop a spirit of friendliness, co-operation and initiative, and to promote international understanding' (quoted in Legge, 1982, p. 138). The Women's Institutes did not seek to challenge the existing economic and social hierarchies of rural life, but they did provide opportunites for women to escape, however briefly, from the home, to accept complete responsibility for organizing meetings and the movement as a whole, and to acquire and perform a variety of craft, artistic and other skills. Lady Denman who chaired the W.I. from its early years until 1946 was a vital influence upon the organization and spirit of the movement. Her contribution

221

was honoured in the naming of Denman College, the residential college established in 1948 by the National Federation of Women's Institutes at Abingdon near Oxford.

In urban areas the Women's Institutes were to be complemented by the Townswomen's Guilds, although these originated from a quite different source. In 1928 women having finally obtained the vote on the same terms as men, the National Union of Societies for Equal Citizenship decided to turn its attention to educational activity. Its purpose was 'to encourage the education of women to enable them as citizens to make their best contribution towards the common good' (quoted in Legge, 1982, p. 139). The first guild was founded at Haywards Heath in Sussex in 1929, and by 1933 the reconstituted National Union of Townswomen's Guilds boasted over 150 guilds, a number which by 1939 had grown to 544. Like the institutes the guilds were linked through regional federations to a national body. Whereas the Women's Institutes naturally took the county as the basic local unit, Townswomen's Guilds were federated in groups of not more than 30 at the local level.

The Public Libraries Act of 1919 was the most important piece of legislation in this area since Ewart's Act of 1850. Library provision was extended to rural areas by clauses which empowered county councils to provide public libraries. These libraries were administered by county education committees, and in some instances special provisions were made for books for adult education classes. The overall quality of the service was improved by the removal of the restriction of library expenditure to a maximum of a penny rate, and by financial aid from the Carnegie Trust. Even outlying rural areas were served with the introduction of library vans.

Book borrowers and purchasers benefited from the proliferation of popular cheap editions both of classical and modern works, by such publishers as Dent, Collins and Nelson. The writings of George Bernard Shaw and H.G. Wells were particularly influential in adult education, and were further popularized when in 1935 Allen Lane launched the Penguin series of sixpenny paperbacks. Lane's concern for the adult education market was shown by his recruitment of W.E. Williams, the secretary of the British Institute of Adult Education, as an advisory editor for the Pelican series.

The mass circulation newspapers of the inter-war years, the *Daily Mirror, Daily Express* and *Daily Herald*, on the other hand, were widely viewed as an antidote rather than as an adjunct to adult education. Much the same feelings were entertained about another organ of mass media – the cinema. In the 1920s and 1930s the silver screen became the most popular entertainment form, and adversely affected attendances at many music halls, theatres and possibly adult education institutions. By the 1930s talking pictures had replaced the silent films and consigned many of their leading stars to instant oblivion. But the cinema opened up and enriched lives in a unique and remarkable, if often tangential, way. The world and its peoples, its history and geography, on occasion its literature and beliefs, even though at times cynically distorted to suit the requirements of commercial film-makers, were brought into the nation's cinemas and thereby into the national consciousness. At its peak in the 1940s the cinema had some 5,000 outlets in Britain with a weekly audience in excess of 20 million. Though in the 1930s there was a significant production of documentary and educational films, use of these by adult education classes was hampered by traditional attitudes and lack of appropriate equipment.

Broadcasting was the other new media phenomenon of the inter-war period. The British Broadcasting Company was set up in 1922 under the direction of a stern and devout Scotsman, John Reith. By 1927 when it was reconstituted as a public body, the British Broadcasting Corporation, there were over two million licensed receivers, and by 1938 over three quarters of the nation's 12 million households had a radio set. Attempts to organize specific adult education programmes by arranging for radio listening and discussion groups, however, were not very successful. Indeed the most successful adult education programme, the Brains Trust, emerged by chance from a modest series of six programmes begun in 1941. Radio's general contribution to adult education, however, was immense. News bulletins, political speeches, talks, plays, discussions, music, brought a whole range of new experiences and understandings into people's homes.

FURTHER EDUCATION

The overlap between adult and further education necessitates some separate, albeit brief, treatment here of the main features of the further education scene. This is a vast and varied area which, prior to 1944, was more often referred to as technical education.

Student numbers in this sector grew steadily in the first 40 years of the century, from about 750,000 in 1909 to 1,300,000 in 1938. Full-time students constituted a very small proportion of these totals, 4,000 in 1909 and 42,000 in 1938 (Argles, 1956, p.69).

Under the 1944 Act, however, LEAs were required to make provision for further education, which was then broadly construed as the full- and part-time education, and the leisure occupation, of the post-school population. County colleges were intended to be key institutions in such provision.

Student numbers rapidly increased, so that the 1,600,000 students of 1946–47 had become more than four million by 1975. Though the county colleges were never established, by 1956, the year of the White Paper on Technical Education, there were 22 regional colleges, 731 area and local colleges, and 9119 evening institutes (Cantor and Roberts, 1969, p.5). The White Paper recommendations led to the transmutation of ten of the regional colleges, firstly into colleges of advanced technology (CATs), and then into universities. Other regional, area, and local colleges continued under a variety of names: colleges of technology, technical colleges, colleges of further education, colleges and schools of art.

In the later 1960s the creation of 30 polytechnics led to a further development of advanced work within the further education sector. By the early 1980s the polytechnics had nearly 300,000 full-, part-time, sandwich and short-course students, and provided a wide range of advanced courses at postgraduate, graduate and sub-degree levels.

Non-advanced further education has been particularly concerned with the transition from school to work, especially as a result of the decline in traditional apprenticeship schemes. The Haslegrave Report of 1969 led to the establishment of a new Technician Education Council in 1973, and a Business Education Council in 1974, Councils which in 1983 were merged into a Business and Technician Education Council. By this date BTEC oversaw courses and awards for more than half a million students in some 500 colleges.

Other recent initiatives, prompted by large-scale juvenile unemployment, have emanated from the Manpower Services Commission, set up in 1974. The Youth Opportunities Scheme, instituted in 1978, was designed to provide training for jobless school-leavers, both in employment and in college situations. By 1981–82 more than half a million young people were on the scheme. In 1983 YOP was replaced by the Youth Training Scheme which was intended to provide places for every unemployed school-leaver.

THE 1944 ACT

The relationship between war and educational activity is an important one and during the Second World War, in spite of obvious problems of dislocation, adult education entered a new phase. Compulsory education, indeed, was introduced into the Army in 1941 with weekly sessions devoted to citizenship and current affairs. Other initiatives included the widespread use of correspondence courses for those denied access to civilian adult education facilities, and schemes to combat basic illiteracy amongst those in uniform. The 1944 Act, however, promised to be the major step in adult education during the war period and for a generation to come. For the first time LEAs were required, rather than empowered, to ensure that adequate and sufficient provision was made throughout their areas for 'all forms of primary, secondary and further education'. The LEAs thus became the major partners in adult education and by 1980 provided over 85 per cent of courses. Local authorities also came to control most of the 50 or so short-term residential colleges for adults. At present there are additionally eight long-term residential colleges (six in England and one apiece in Wales and Scotland) which provide full-time one- or two-year courses. Some indication of the LEA contribution is shown by the following figures taken from the official DES handbook *The Educational System of England and Wales* for 1985. Figures are for England and Wales, except for those of Open University students which are for Great Britain as a whole. The majority of students in non-university maintained further education establishments, however, would not normally be classed as adult education students.

STUDENT NUMBERS, 1982–1984

Students in non-university maintained further education, November 1983:

men 1,036,876 women 1,029,226 total 2,066,102

Students in adult education and youth centres, November 1983:

men 548,915 women 1,185,493 total 1,734,408

Students in adult education provided by responsible bodies, academic year, 1982–83:

Universities	men	72,780	women	104,452	total	177,232
WEA	men	50,380	women	77,358	total	127,738

Open University, undergraduate students, 1984:

men 36,586 women 30,177 total 66,763

Source: DES, *The Educational System of England and Wales*, 1985, pp.98–9.

Yet in spite of the 1944 Act and the great interest in adult education which was apparent in the immediate post-war period, once again, as after the 1918 Act and the 1919 Report, a period of disappointment and disillusionment was to ensue. The county colleges, the essential base for a new approach to continuing education embodied in the 1944 Act, were never established. Adult evening institutes were invariably located in existing primary and secondary schools. Whilst this reflected an understandable wish to make the fullest possible use of educational buildings it too often meant that adult education staff and students had no places, facilities or resources which they could genuinely call their own. After a healthy rise in the post-war period, the year 1950 saw a downturn in numbers of adult education students and courses which affected both LEA and voluntary provision, and continued in many instances throughout the decade.

This decline may be attributed in part to economic and financial problems which were particularly severe in the period 1949–51, and to the general attitude and particular response of central government. For although after 1944 the Ministry of Education continued to give direct financial assistance to the extra-mural departments, WEA and other 'responsible bodies', even by the mid-1960s the central grant was still less than three quarters of a million pounds per annum, less indeed than the cost of a single mile of motorway. The Russell Committee was appointed in 1969 to assess the need for, and to review the provision of, non-vocational adult education in England and Wales 'and to make recommendations with a view to obtaining the most effective and economical deployment of available resources'. Its Report, completed in 1972 and published in the following year, however, took the central government to task for its failures in the field. It tellingly observed that 'In a negative sense the recent history of adult education makes clear how important is the lead from central government', and demanded 'a clear commitment from the central government to the place of adult education as an essential element in the national system of education' (Russell Report, 1973, paras. 155, 160). The Committee concluded that successive ministers had failed to fulfil their statutory duty under the 1944 Act of promoting adult education in England and Wales. Such failure had affected the commitment of LEAs, some of whom by the later 1960s were contemplating the suspension of their own adult educational provision and the withdrawal of financial aid from voluntary bodies. This, the Committee observed, was not surprising given the neglect of adult education by the central authority and the fact that circulars and memoranda which emanated from the Department of Education and Science seemed to be principally concerned with the raising of students' fees. The very terms of reference of the Russell Committee indeed reflected the concern for economy and cost-cutting.

The Report, however, proposed a revision of Sections 41 and 42 of the 1944 Act to ensure that adult education received a due share of resources and attention.

OPEN UNIVERSITY

The economic crises which affected the United Kingdom with monotonous regularity from the later 1940s onwards bore heavily upon adult education, which proved to be inadequately protected under the terms and implementation, or lack of implementation, of the 1944 Act.

At the same time, however, it must be acknowledged that overall there was a gradual rise in the standard of living and increased leisure time, and the promotion by central government of a most important new means of adult education – the Open University. Increased affluence was reflected in wider ownership of homes and property, of household appliances and gadgets, of tape recorders and record players, of television sets, and of cars. Increasing mobility meant improved access to a range of places of interest both in this country and abroad. The most influential new medium, however, was that of television, which ensured that entertainment, and education, were supplied to the living rooms of the great majority of homes throughout the country.

The Open University drew upon traditional methods of adult education and combined these with radio and television programmes. Reference has already been made to the use of summer schools in university centres, which became a compulsory feature of Open University foundation courses. Particular use was also made of correspondence learning, a system developed in the later nineteenth century by such institutions as Wolsey Hall to prepare adult students for a variety of professional examinations and for those of the external degrees of the University of London. Indeed a Council for the Accreditation of Correspondence Colleges was instituted in 1969, the year in which the Open University was established by Royal Charter.

The idea of the Open University, originally referred to as the University of the Air, was born in the early 1960s and nurtured by Jennie Lee during the Labour government of Harold Wilson. Study packages, assignments, tutorials, counselling, residential courses and broadcasting constituted the major elements of tuition. There were no formal entry requirements, except for higher degree work, and students' progress was measured by continuous assessment, with the completion of six credits for a pass degree and eight for honours. Only two full credit courses could be taken in one year. The Open

University, whose first students began in 1971, soon became the largest university in England and Wales with some 70,000 students. Its head-quarters were located at Milton Keynes, and 13 regional offices and some 300 local study centres were established throughout the United Kingdom. Non-degree courses were also provided. The achievements of the Open University have been considerable. Tens of thousands of adult students, many of whom had no chance of entering university by the traditional route, have achieved degrees, degrees which are recognized as equivalent in standard to those of other universities and of the CNAA. Open University course materials and methods, indeed, have been at the forefront of pedagogical advance. Similar university institutions and teaching packages have been introduced in countries around the globe. Moreover, although it has been objected that few Open University students are themselves manual workers, neverthe-less the proportion of students whose parents were in the manual workers' category, over 50 per cent in 1971 for example, has been much higher than for those in other universities in the United Kingdom.

One further product of the Open University was the Venables Report of 1976, the final report of the University's Committee on Continuing Education. This took a broad view of continuing education and, by adding to the pressure of the Russell Report, resulted in the establishment of national advisory councils for adult education. The Advisory Council for Adult and Continuing Education in England and Wales was set up in 1977 to promote co-operation and policy-making between the various organizations in the field.

CONCLUSION

Adult education is as difficult to encompass within the span of a short chapter as it is to define. In the 1980s in official parlance it became 'adult and continuing education' which included:

> provision for cultural pursuits, physical activities and crafts, acquiring general education (e.g. literacy/basic numeracy) and communication and coping skills; social, community and politi-cal education; education for disadvantaged groups and those with special needs; consumer education; health education; pro-fessional development and updating for these in employment. (DES, *The Educational System of England and Wales*, 1985, p.85)

This definition reflects, in part, the present central government's intervention in the adult educational field for the purpose of promoting vocational skills. Thus in 1980 the Adult Literacy Unit was replaced by an Adult Literacy and Basic Skills Unit with broader terms of reference to encourage communication skills across the board. In 1984 a programme was launched to encourage the provision of educational facilities for unemployed adults, whilst the professional, industrial and commercial updating programme (PICKUP) was designed to improve the skills of those in employment.

Yet however adult education has been or is being defined there seems little doubt that, barring some major economic or social catastrophe, it will become a, possibly the, key educational issue of the future. The nineteenth century saw the provision of elementary schooling for all, the twentieth century the attainment of universal secondary schooling. As work declines and life expectancy increases the development of genuine, though not compulsory, universal continuing or adult education, becomes not merely a possibility but a necessity.

FURTHER READING

T. Kelly, *A History of Adult Education in Great Britain*, 1970, with seven chapters on the twentieth century, is the standard work and may be supplemented by J.F.C. Harrison, *Learning and Living, 1790–1960*, 1961. R.D. Waller (ed.), *A Design for Democracy*, 1956, contains an edited version of the 1919 Report, whilst the Russell Report is published as Department of Education and Science, *Adult Education: a Plan for Development*, 1973. P. Jarvis (ed.), *Twentieth-Century Thinkers in Adult Education*, 1987, includes studies of such pioneers as Mansbridge, Yeaxlee and Tawney. D. Legg, *The Education of Adults in Britain*, 1982, and D.B. Rees, *Preparation for Crisis: Adult Education 1945–80*, 1982, cover the post-Second World War period. Finally W. Perry, *Open University*, 1976, is a personal account by its first vice-chancellor, whilst W.A. Devereux, *Adult Education in Inner London 1870–1980*, 1982, provides a detailed survey of a service which is currently under threat.

The most useful general work on further education is L. Cantor and I. Roberts, *Further Education in England and Wales*, 1969. S. Cotgrove, *Technical Education and Social Change*, 1958 and M. Argles, *South Kensington to Robbins*, 1964, are wide-ranging accounts which encompass technical, adult, further and higher education. P. Ainley, *From School to YTS. Education and Training in England and Wales, 1944–1987*, 1988, provides a highly critical survey of government attempts to promote vocational education.

CHAPTER SIXTEEN

Higher Education

THE RISE OF THE SYSTEM, 1900–1939

In the years 1900–14 a number of universities were created in a period of expansion which was only exceeded in the mid-1960s. Thus an identifiable university interest was created, one which would merit, and at times forcefully seek, government attention. Some of these institutions were the result of a reorganization, even a restructuring of older establishments. In 1900 the University of London was reconstituted, in future drawing its strength equally from internal students and designated schools, and from external students who were taking its examinations throughout the United Kingdom and the Empire. Thus the university became a regional centre serving the south-eastern hinterland, while also maintaining its wider metropolitan role as the examining body for the entire Empire. In 1903–04 the federated Victoria University, hailed at its birth in the 1880s as the protecting shield for emerging northern colleges, split into constituent parts, spurred on by the concern of Liverpool and Leeds at Manchester's domination of the federation.

This development encouraged other cities to demand that their local needs and positions should be recognized. In 1900 Joseph Chamberlain gained for Josiah Mason College a charter which transformed it into Birmingham University, which he hoped would be a focal point for that city's industrial prowess. Two other major cities, Sheffield in 1905 and Bristol in 1909, also secured university status. In addition it must not be forgotten that universities represented more than local or regional pride. Scotland still regarded its universities as part of a national heritage that defined part of its differences from the rest of the United Kingdom. The creation of a federated University of Wales, expanded in 1920 to take in University College, Swansea, was a belated mark of recognition of the growth of Welsh cultural nationalism. At this time, too, a network of university colleges had been established in Ireland, an indication that the twin forces of Catholicism and

Presbyterianism were determined to assert themselves against the traditional Anglicanism of Trinity College, Dublin.

A comparison of the two significant periods of expansion, those which saw the rise of the predominantly redbrick Edwardian universities, and of the plateglass universities of the 1960s, reveals significant differences. First of all, the redbrick universities emerged from a conglomeration of older establishments ranging from mechanics' institutes to lyceums and people's colleges. Buildings, students, teachers and a tradition of learning were already in existence. They had developed from local interests and commitments, and during much of the present century continued to draw on the surrounding communities for financial support, resources and most of their students. New universities of the 1960s embodied a different ethos. Many were on campus sites, in specially created environments, and there was a determined intention to draw their teachers and students from the widest possible national constituency.

The Edwardian universities' success in receiving their charters encouraged a range of colleges situated in smaller regional centres, notably Leicester, Nottingham, Southampton, Exeter and Reading, to press their case for university status. Although charters were given very sparingly in the period up to 1950, Exeter struggling long and hard into the late 1950s to obtain its university charter, all of these smaller regional centres ultimately achieved their end. Doubts were expressed as to whether these colleges were adequately based or could generate the kind of environment needed for a university. There was also a concern that a multiplication of degree-awarding bodies would lead to a debasement of existing degrees. However, throughout the early part of the century the door was left open. In the 1960s new universities were created with the clear intention of providing a complete system, a message that was reinforced by the launching of a binary sector in 1965.

Expansion in the Edwardian period depended on private initiative, the energy and determination of a figure like Joseph Chamberlain in Birmingham or of a family like the Wills in Bristol. Frequently the new enterprises owed much to the concern about the industrial needs of localities, a growing recognition that traditional methods of training needed to give way to more specific scientific education and research in the increasingly complex and competitive economy. Nevertheless, none of the redbrick institutions was created to satisfy the requirements of local industry alone. They were catering for a whole range of needs within their communities. Professional groups, often medical practitioners and lawyers, were at the forefront of campaigns for charters, aware of the importance of degree-awarding institutions for their particular professions' status. From the beginning, too, teachers used their facilities to secure degrees to enable them to teach in the growing secondary sector.

Much of the impetus came from the university extension movement of the later nineteenth century, with Oxford, Cambridge and London to the fore, which had reflected, sometimes with missionary zeal, a concern to widen cultural horizons in all parts of the country. The external London degree, recognized for its high standard, gave the opportunity for the more leisured, affluent and eager to pursue full-time degree courses. Some women were determined, at this time, to pursue vigorously the quest for higher education and were often a powerful element in its progress. Indeed, as the Edwardian institutions matured and developed, their staff become more highly specialized, and their particular schools became widely known throughout the country. Liverpool, for instance, was able in a relatively short period to secure recognition as a prestigious centre for the study of tropical medicine and architecture. As the universities became established there was a shift from part-time or evening students, often the majority in the earlier institutions, to full-time students pursuing degree-awarding courses. The presence of this group was seen as a mark of university status.

The spirit of activity which characterized the redbrick universities in the Edwardian period was less evident within the universities of Oxford and Cambridge which, in the public mind, were often the image of what a university should be. Each year the public keenly supported the sporting contests between these older universities, the Boat Race, for instance, generating fierce partisanship among sections of the population with no ties whatever with either place. Politicians eagerly graced debates at the two Unions. College Fellows found themselves invited to a network of clubs, societies and country houses, all of which were centres of the social calendar. In some ways this represented a remarkable change of attitude from the earlier part of the previous century, when Oxford and Cambridge had been denounced for their deplorable teaching, narrow studies and religious exclusivity. By 1900 many of the criticisms had been met, but in a way that fitted in with the traditions of the older universities.

Science and modern studies now featured as degree courses, although Classics at Oxford still remained the cornerstone of a liberal education and was at the heart of much undergraduate study. Fellowships, too, had been reformed. Perhaps the greatest success had been the integration of alternative cultural networks, particularly after the religious tests had been abolished in 1871. Thus old-established

Dissenting families, who had often, earlier in the century, pursued a policy of opposition, were now drawn towards the older universities. Attempts were made by the Roman Catholic hierarchy to keep its aristocracy and gentry away from the charm of the older universities, but by the 1890s they had conceded and allowed their absorption into university life. Change, however, was never wholly welcome, and collegiate authorities were not slow to act as a brake. Science at Oxford, as Professor Frederick Lindemann discovered in the 1930s, was not popular or well esteemed. The attempt in 1919 to remove the restrictions on women at Cambridge, who could not receive degrees, was defeated by the vote of backwoodsmen graduates, a position that remained unchanged until 1948.

The older universities have continued to exert a powerful influence on higher education in this century. There is no doubt that in the public mind higher education was associated principally with Oxford and Cambridge, where the richest and most influential sent their children. As a result, higher education was seen, first and foremost, as a finishing school for people of wealth and standing which had little contact with the rest of the education system. The life of the undergraduate, revolving very much around college activities and societies, with its emphasis on fellowship, community and association, all of which encouraged lifelong social contact, strengthened the view that residence was a prerequisite for a university course. In the early years of the twentieth century many tutors, because they were so deeply engaged in collegiate life, had little time for independent research and the production of new knowledge, a marked feature of many Western European universities. As many of the students who came were already prosperous, their teachers were little inclined to provide a training for particular professions. The tutors were influential in presenting a view of education which emphasized that diligent study in the older disciplines produced better men with alert minds who would be able eventually to fulfil their proper calling within a governing élite. Higher education has struggled hard to move away from this early influence. Blueprints for mass higher education or poly-universities have not met with enthusiasm in governing circles. In essence all that has appeared to change during the century has been the vision of the directing class. After 1945, for instance, there was much talk of institutions of higher education becoming centres of training for the growing group of scientific and administrative experts who were to promote the welfare state.

In 1900, therefore, higher education was seen as élite education and placed very firmly in the category of 'self-help'; families who wanted such education for their offspring ought to pay for its benefits, and therefore the provision of large public funds from the state was out of the question. Nevertheless, even in the mid-nineteenth century, the state had not remained entirely aloof from funding, providing, on occasions, money to fend off crisis as in the case of London University, or as a pump-primer to stimulate local benevolence. As the nineteenth century drew to a close the mood in political circles was shifting. The Devonshire Commission of 1872, among others, had drawn attention to the kind of work undertaken by German universities where the training of specialists was seen as the proper function of a place of higher learning. A number of influential British students, notably James Bryce, T.H. Green and R.L. Nettleship, all of whom had spent time in Germany, returned to add their voice to those who saw the growing importance of universities to the future needs of the state. Increasingly adjustments were being made, and from the late 1880s there were funding developments that anticipated future changes. From 1889 an incipient University Grants Committee was established which collected evidence, inspected and paid grants. Several government departments, notably those of Education and Agriculture, became involved in the disposal of parliamentary grants. On the whole emerging university institutions voiced few concerns, for funding from a distant paymaster, the state, might offset the increasingly resisted intrusion of local dignitaries who were seen to exert too much lay control. Robert Morant wished all funding to come through the Board of Education, not the Treasury, but this was not welcomed since this department was seen by academics as overfond of codes, regulations and detailed inspection. The separation from the Board of Education strengthened the uniqueness of the universities, and appeared to divorce them from all other education developments. Yet total separation was out of the question, for universities through their entrance and subsequent requirements deeply influenced the kind of education provided for young people in the upper secondary age range.

The importance of the expanding university sector was finally recognized in the shattering experience of the Great War. Like the public schools, universities, in the early years, lost large numbers of teachers and students who joined the armed forces. As the conflict dragged on, however, evidence mounted that the war effort was severely hampered by deficiencies in scientific research and expertise. A number of key areas such as the chemical and the dyeing industries, and even munitions, were in crisis by 1915, largely because of their pre-war reliance on foreign, often German, skills in these areas. The formation in 1915 of the Department of Scientific and Industrial Research which was placed under the Lord President of the Council's jurisdiction, was hailed as a significant breakthrough. Its function was to encourage scientific inquiry, award research fellowships and co-ordinate government and university research. Much depended on the energies of the minister. Lord Balfour, who enjoyed the company of scientists, was one who did give the matter extensive attention. What was abundantly clear was that the amount of funding to be distributed by the DSIR was so limited that it was not likely to have a decisive impact on university policy or life.

The creation of a University Grants Committee (UGC) in 1919 has also been seen as the belated recognition by politicians of the national need for universities and the production of highly skilled people. In fact it was set up primarily to deal with a range of immediate problems. Student numbers had fallen in the war and, with them, the fees that they paid. Buildings and equipment had been neglected or even requisitioned. Finally, with the end of war universities found themselves with a bulge in numbers as the demobilized servicemen returned to complete their studies. Throughout the inter-war period the amount of money allocated to the various universities was quite small. The staff of the UGC which gathered to distribute its resources was both small and makeshift. Nevertheless it survived, and its very smallness, its closeness to university circles and the position of the chairman, increasingly gave it acceptance and support. Another important group established at the same time was the Committee of Vice-Chancellors and Principals (CVCP), which met at intervals to discuss joint collective interests. It remained an informal body without formal charter or constitution. A third important development was the institution of the state scholarship system, although initially there were only 200 per year, and in the harsh financial climate of the Geddes Axe no state scholarships were awarded at all. Sir Charles Trevelyan restored them during the minority Labour government of 1924, and by the late 1930s the number of state scholarships awarded had increased to 400.

During the 1920s and 1930s, full-time higher education was largely restricted to the wealthier classes. Although Royal Commissions for Oxford and Cambridge reported in 1922, their findings did little to alter life at these institutions. This does not mean that the ambitious, determined working-class boy or girl was excluded entirely. There was a scholarship ladder, often provided by the local authority. In this respect access depended on good fortune, the condition of the local economy and perhaps the political complexion of the local authority. Frequently, too, the grants did not meet the full costs. Scholarship students, particularly at the most prestigious places, might find the life uncomfortable and stressful. As for the redbrick universities and the aspiring university colleges, both staff and students often found they faced considerable problems. Small departments meant heavy lecturing loads, little individual tuition and, for the academics, little time to pursue their own special interests. Nevertheless intellectual life at the universities continued, and there were important developments in such areas as science, economics and history. It was not, however, a period of confidence and growth, and for some of the redbrick universities and university colleges mere survival proved difficult. Only Reading, in 1926, advanced to full university status.

HIGHER EDUCATION COMES OF AGE, 1939–1963

The transition from peace to war was carried through more smoothly in 1939 than in 1914. Efforts were made to allow student scientists, engineers and doctors to complete some of their training. Arts students fared less well and as a result the balance at university changed. Some universities, notably London, found themselves dispersed. Leading university academics, particularly scientists, were brought into administrative and policy-making posts. Churchill appointed his old ally, Frederick Lindemann, to be his Chief Scientific Officer, and created him Lord Cherwell. The Home Secretary, Herbert Morrison, was another senior politician who relied heavily, in civil defence matters, on scientists.

By the middle of the war, in the various discussions on educational reconstruction, university lecturers were prominent speakers, and the future of university education itself became an issue. Pressure groups such as the WEA argued that access to higher education in the inter-war years had been shamefully limited, that many who were capable of real benefits to their lives from this kind of education had been deprived, and that expansion was necessary for social justice and the future of the country. In their own submissions the Committee of Vice-Chancellors and Principals, the National Union of Students (formed in 1922) and the Association of Scientific Workers all agreed not only that expansion was necessary, but also that the government must provide the necessary funding for its growth. As the war drew to a close government reports added to the calls for expansion. The Barlow Report, issued in 1946, pronounced that the universities were the key to scientific growth, and argued for a doubling of the production of scientists over a ten-year period. The McNair Report on teacher training of 1944 and the Percy Report on higher technological education of 1945 also had important implications for higher education. In 1946 the Ministry of Education tried to wrest the universities from Treasury supervision, but this was thwarted. As a result the universities continued to stand apart from the rest of education. The UGC was reconstituted in 1947, and its membership enlarged, with a range of subject sub-committees set up to promote the supply, for instance, of scientists, managers, administrators and teachers, the army of high-skilled specialists, the technical élite of the welfare state. In this sense the universities signalled that they were aware that the more ample funding from the state had some price on it. However, with figures like Hugh Dalton at the Treasury, prepared for instance to set a five-year period for their grants, they not only had considerable freedom, but an assured financial future.

By the 1950s external pressures were being felt by the universities. As the outcome of the tripartite system began to raise questions, the issue of equality of opportunity came to the forefront. A grammar-school education followed by a career at university and the award of a degree was taking the place of birth and position as the gateway to many secure, prestigious occupations in the post-war world. It was there-fore not surprising that not only the grammar schools, but also the universities came under scrutiny. What had been sufficient for the majority of the population in the 1930s, or even the late 1940s, was no longer satisfactory in the more affluent 1950s. There were also concerns about Britain's economic performance. The opinion was frequently expressed that not enough young people were being attracted to the fields of applied science, engineering and technology, and that too many of the most talented of them were drawn into academic study. Part of this was attributed to the fact that most applied courses were confined to part-time study in low-level technical colleges. For ministers such as Lord Cherwell and Lord Woolton the need was seen as one for new institutions, more generously funded, adequately staffed and highly resourced. Above all they insisted that technology, for instance, should be removed from the existing universities and directed towards a centralized university-type institu-tion devoted to this area of study. Lord Woolton put the case very strongly:

> It is this disregard of the application of science and scientific method that we have to overcome and it is my belief that we should establish for industry a school of university standing equivalent in its prestige to the schools of medicine for doctors or the staff college for the services. I do not believe that we shall get

the support and understanding of the employers and managers in industry for anything less than a separate and national institution which establishes a course of training of university standing around a degree in technology. (Woolton to R.A. Butler, PRO UGC 7/867, 16 April 1952)

Lord Cherwell, too, was opposed to the extended provision of technological education through the existing universities. Instead he pressed for an independent committee, detached from the UGC, to initiate change as rapidly as possible. 'The great thing, I am sure, is that the committee should be told to propose the way or ways of building up technological universities and not to say whether they are required or not' (Cherwell to Woolton, PRO, UGC 7/867, 9 December 1951). R.A. Butler was not prepared to yield to the clamour of his colleagues. He was anxious about the costs of their proposals, the possibility of angering university opinion and a too abrupt break with existing practices. He therefore proposed to expand Imperial College and the Manchester College of Technology which were already in the framework of university institutions. It was left to David Eccles as Minister of Education from 1954 to push for further growth in this area. He returned to themes contained in the 1945 Percy Report, notably the upgrading of regional technical colleges which would teach courses for a new degree-type examination, the Diploma of Technology. Colleges of Advanced Technology were to dispense with low level part-time courses and replace them with full-time or sandwich courses. Once started these colleges raised many problems, especially the issue of their relationship with the rest of the higher education system. In particular, there was the question of whether, and at what stage, some of them would shed local authority supervision, receive university charters and come within the orbit of the UGC.

As the 1950s closed there were signs that the Conservative government had committed itself to growth in higher education. Research work at the universities was expanded by an increase in DSIR studentships, no longer means-tested, and a state studentship scheme for research in the arts. As a result there was an explosion of graduate courses. The Anderson Committee tidied up the complicated arrangements for supporting students in higher education and created a uniform system of grant awards, almost totally funded by the state, but still means-tested. Finally it was becoming increasingly evident that the government was sympathetic to the creation of new universities. The Robbins Committee on Higher Education, set up in 1961, was in no sense the springboard for expansion. That fight was already won, and its task was to present the figures.

YEARS OF EXPANSION AND CONTRACTION, 1963–1980

It has been argued that demography alone could explain the government's conversion to growth, and Robbins acknowledged that the advancing cohorts of the post-war baby boom, now reaching their late teens, were an important consideration. Brian Simon (1985) has suggested a further factor, the build-up of pressure from below as a rising standard of living fuelled expectations that a Conservative government found too politically inexpedient to hold in check. From the Education Ministry convinced expansionists such as David Eccles and Edward Boyle continuously urged the case for growth. There were fears, expressed in the 1959 Crowther Report and later in 1963 in the Newsom Report, that the pressure on university places was severely damaging the secondary school curriculum and holding back vital innovations. Both politicians shared a 'One Nation' philosophy and therefore were anxious to promote access which they believed would generate social mobility and destroy class-based politics.

Efforts had been directed since the early 1950s to the build-up of sixth form courses in the grammar schools, in a determined attempt to prevent pupils from leaving early. In this way therefore the Ministry was responsible for the pressure of numbers. Government had become convinced that the prerequisite for a sustained boost to a sluggish economy was the extensive upgrading of education throughout the workforce. Newer industries would need a different type of manager, technologist or supervisor whose training could no longer be passed on at the workplace. Close attention was paid to Britain's strongest economic rivals in Europe, and the Robbins Report confirmed that they were mobilizing a highly educated workforce to keep themselves in the front of the economic race.

The main task which confronted the members of the Robbins Committee was to calculate the size of the demand into the 1980s. On the whole they were cautious in their estimates, but were agreed that all those who were qualified for places in higher education ought to be given the opportunity to take them up. Fears that large numbers would destroy standards, raise the number of drop-outs and ultimately erode the essential characteristics of higher education were dismissed. Robbins, in every sense the author of the Report, believed that these dangers would be averted if the greater proportion of higher education and its expansion was firmly located in the universities. He himself had little knowledge of other forms of higher education, and in the recommendations he rejected the option of new types of higher edu-

cation institutions. His proposals centred upon the expansion of existing universities, upgraded colleges of advanced technology, new
universities and, most controversially, colleges of education given
more academic freedom, associated with universities, and taken out
of local authority control. In later conferences, notably the 1965
Gulbenkian Conference, he expressed deep disappointment that his
proposals for the former training colleges had not been taken up, but
reserved his most withering criticism for the proposed binary system:

> I just can't understand what has happened. Here you have a
> Labour government which is attempting, for good or bad, to
> introduce the comprehensive principle into the schools, which I
> think is the right thing to try to do provided that it is done
> with good sense and prudence. At the same time they are
> deepening the existence of lines of division in higher education
> and actually announcing as a matter of policy, which has never
> been announced before, that these divisions are to be permanent.
> They are making the system more hierarchical than ever before.
> (Robbins, 1965, pp.6–7)

The incoming Labour government, in 1964, was certain to advance
expansion in higher education. It had campaigned strongly during the
election campaign on the need to modernize the economy. It was
anticipated that Richard Crossman, whose concerns had ranged over
higher education and science provision while a member of the Shadow
Cabinet, would be the Minister who pushed through the expansion.
Much of his thinking was directed at breaking down barriers in higher
education. As a constituency member representing Coventry, situated
near an aspiring university, and containing a powerful college of
technology and a teaching training institution of standing, he was
attracted to proposals to amalgamate and combine. He made it clear
that if he had been placed in charge of higher education his policy would
have been markedly different from the one later adopted. 'When I was
Shadow Science Minister I became more and more convinced that one
of the biggest jobs for the next Labour Secretary of State for Education
was to break down the rigid division between higher and further
education' (Crossman, 1975, Vol. 1, 15 September 1965, p.326).

For Richard Crossman, a politician critical of the influence of the
senior advisers, the adoption of the binary system in 1965 owed much to
pressure behind the scenes. In conversations with Maurice Kogan,
Tony Crosland, the Minister responsible, expressed regret for the
haste with which he had launched the policy, and particularly for the
Woolwich speech of 1965 which, on reflection, he thought had been

unnecessarily aggressive and anti-university. His wife and biographer hinted at the difficulties of the period: 'Tony had to struggle for the intellectual cohesion with which he defended the binary policy to democratise higher education; he succeeded in altering the terms of the debate: the Robbins attitudes lost their dominance' (Crosland, 1982, p.159). Speculation has continued as to the major influence at work. The senior advisers at the Department of Education, notably Sir Toby Weaver, have been singled out for attention. They saw the adoption of the binary policy as a *de facto* recognition that a binary system already existed, and that its control mechanisms, in comparison with those of the universities, were too valuable to be allowed to slip away. The Minister, too, was anxious to promote the cause of high-level, more vocationally-oriented courses, as an alternative to the pattern of academic university study followed by professional training.

Whoever was responsible for the policy, its outcome has been of major significance to higher education. The designation of 30 poly-technics in 1966, all of which were to remain under local authority control, ended once and for all the scramble for university recognition by aspiring bodies. Higher education ceased to be equated with uni-versity education which alone had the right, by charter, to award degrees. The universities in the mid-1960s not only seemed to accept this position, but eagerly co-operated in the work of the Council for National Academic Awards (CNAA) which sprang up in the next decade to approve degree-level courses at polytechnics. Indeed there were significant groups in the university sector who welcomed this development. The 30 polytechnics, less expensively endowed and less prestigious, would serve as a filter, allowing universities to continue to draw in the abler academic students, to maintain their style of teaching and research, and to claim that they were the centres of excellence in higher education. The polytechnics, far from rivalling universities, were widely regarded as subordinate institutions.

The explosion of higher education was a significant feature of the 1960s, and there were hopes that the impetus of this fresh start would encourage experimentation in new kinds of courses and examinations. Sussex, with its broader areas of study, and à la carte approach and course-based assessment, led the way. If there were a model, however, it was Oxford and Cambridge rather than the old redbrick universities of the urban civic tradition. Most of the new universities were situated on campus sites, on the outskirts of such cities as Canterbury, Norwich and York. Communal living was the central feature of student life, and many became almost detached from the world around them. The academic profession also experienced a boom. Departments saw them-

241

selves expanding, sub-dividing and perhaps re-grouping. A whole array of teachers, researchers, technicians and support workers were recruited at a great pace to keep up with growth. The results of such rapid expansion were to be felt into the 1990s. First of all, many academic staff recruited in the 1960s were young and hence likely to remain in the profession for the next 30 years. This would have serious consequences if expansion were halted. Second, any prospect of a community of scholars working together in a common enterprise faded in the pace of change, the competition for resources, and the speed of recruitment. Finally, at this time, few defence mechanisms were built up against the day when such expansion would come to an end.

Changes in higher education also resulted in a change of management. The Treasury could no longer continue to act as paymaster, manager and supervisor of a greatly enlarged sector. Its size increased the desire of the Ministry of Education to take over an area now considered to be a vital part of the nation's investment. There was little doubt that, if the previous arrangements were to be changed, the universities would have preferred to see the creation of a Minister of Higher Education to promote their case in the Cabinet. There had been some attempt in the later years of the Conservative government to move to this position, but the eventual solution, a Department of Education and Science, with a junior Minister for Higher Education, reflected the need for a unitary approach. As a result the universities, represented by a Minister with a wide responsibility for a range of educational services, would no doubt find it harder to ensure that their particular interests predominated. In addition the Department contained officials who regarded universities as over-protected and over-resourced in comparison with other demands.

As the 1960s drew to a close the binary system became more firmly established and recognized. Since higher education was seen to be crucial to the drive for economic supremacy, it was scarcely surprising that the hand of government grew ever more obtrusive. Some of the claims made for the relevance of polytechnics were eventually to have their impact on the universities. If polytechnic courses were more relevant, more socially aware and more adapted to local needs the implication was that university courses were none of these things. In fact the differences were never that sharp. Universities did provide courses related to society's needs while many polytechnics, aware of their somewhat shabby image in the public eye, rushed to cater for full-time students with university-style courses. As a result locally based, so-called low-level work was pushed to the margins. Moreover in spite of the repeated claims that industry and employers needed a better-educated, increasingly graduate range of managers, there was little evidence that they knew how to use these new employees when they arrived. The result was that large numbers of graduates continued to be attracted to a range of occupations away from the world of industry and commerce. All of this raised doubts about the more optimistic forecasts which had generated growth in the early 1960s.

By the end of the decade a visible student estate had come into existence in many areas of the country. It had its own work pattern, lifestyle and yearly cycle of holidays. Success in the newly-created university clearing system took the place of the rapidly dying eleven-plus selection. Families and neighbourhoods were often divided and categorized by the proportion of their children receiving higher education. The student body certainly began to see itself as a separate interest. First of all, large numbers of newcomers were drawn together in a fresh experience, and often in localities away from their previous backgrounds. Academic staff, recently recruited and taken up with rapid planning decisions, now had less time for the face to face contacts of earlier years. Some of the discontent that erupted after 1968 clearly resulted from insensitive handling of grievances in a changing environment. Other factors also created uneasiness in the student body. Disappointment grew in a Labour government which, by 1967, appeared to be more interested in survival and power than in carrying through fundamental reforms. World-wide issues such as Vietnam, black civil rights and South African apartheid brought the student populations of the USA and Western Europe into close alliance. They were able, too, to exploit new tactics, the sit-ins and occupations, which other protest groups had initiated. Claims were made by ministers that dedicated revolutionary figures had taken control and were using student protests to mount an onslaught on the system of government. There was more than a hint of generational struggle as the student body issued its protests against what they saw as the evils of their parents' often complacent consumer society.

In comparison with France or some American campuses the eruptions in this country were more limited, and most students continued their studies, obtained degrees and departed to find employment. Generally, by a mixture of reform, the concession of representation on policy-making bodies and, on occasions, tough disciplinary measures, the universities and polytechnics came to live with this student estate. In the early 1950s the student was often portrayed as a heroic figure prepared to forgo immediate gains for higher goals. By 1970, in the public mind, students often seemed to be delayed adolescents, spoilt by grants, and perhaps even potential and ungrateful troublemakers.

Professor Gareth Williams, in his address at the 400th anniversary commemoration of the foundation of the University of Edinburgh, in 1983, reflected that 'the 1970s was a bad decade for British higher education. It undoubtedly went down in political esteem' (Williams, 1983, p.236). Yet this was the decade when more students than ever were in universities, polytechnics or transformed colleges of higher education. However it was also a period when new building projects and new accommodation were diminishing. The spectre of excess capacity and over-staffed institutions was frequently raised. Demand was difficult to evaluate. Governments themselves, through wider discretionary grants for instance, could encourage groups often excluded for a range of reasons, to come forward to take up empty places. On the other hand, through tighter regulations and changes in policy, government could quicken the pace of contraction. As the 1970s wore on, higher education, like health services and transport, became subject to the harshness of continued restraint and budget-trimming exercises in attempts to limit public expenditure.

This cast a shadow over those in higher education who had become accustomed to expansion, accelerated promotion and new courses. There was a growth of uneasiness, and confidence was eroded. Elements had existed, particularly in higher education, which had always been doubtful about the need for more access to those institutions. From this quarter the impression was fostered that the period of expansion had led to a real decline in scholarship, standards and commitment. Demands were heard for more formal examinations, a return to academic rigour, and the promotion of disciplines that appeared to encourage sustained study. In some ways elements on the Right and Left in politics were in agreement that higher education had failed to address itself to the crisis which society was experiencing in the late 1970s. Critics on the Left, who might be expected to be defenders, turned their attention to limited access and restraint of opportunity, which had been a feature of the university world in particular. In turn the universities' desire for an already highly-sifted student intake damaged the prospects for the implementation of full-scale comprehensive education since successful schools needed to concentrate their attention too exclusively on the more academic pupils. For their part, Conservatives attributed some of the failures of the economy to lack of enterprise, an anti-business ethic and a collectivist approach, all of which they saw as being nurtured in higher education.

HIGHER EDUCATION IN CRISIS: THE 1980s

Ultimately it was a Conservative government, since 1979, which turned uneasiness from this quarter into hard, practical policies. The weapons forged to change direction were those of cost effectiveness, accountability, tighter auditing, and where necessary, more central direction. Underlying this campaign was the belief that universities had escaped careful scrutiny in the past, and that the application of market forces and better management techniques would yield vast savings. Universities were given the choice of retaining their autonomy by drawing less funds from the state, or of facing the consequences that the state which provided most of their funds had the right to make increasing demands on them.

Efforts to trim budgets and come to terms with government demands often led to acute internal tension. University staff, for instance, were very angry with the hitherto highly esteemed UGC which, to meet government pressure, had instituted a policy of discrimination according to excellence between institutes and departments. As a result its prestigious figures were now often seen more as collaborators than colleagues. Government intervention on occasions was very intrusive. Early retirement schemes were initiated to reduce the size of some departments, and new blood lectureships were introduced, almost wholly in the fields of information technology, applied science and business studies. Limited numbers of overseas students were welcomed from well-disposed, pro-Western countries. Attempts have been mounting to ensure that the bulk of research work in higher education accords most directly with government's needs. Critics have regarded the whole process as a carefully worked strategy, although there were indications that the outcomes of policies were not always what government had anticipated. In 1980–81 the cuts in quotas for university students did not lead to overall contraction in numbers since the polytechnic sector often took up those qualified students who were excluded from the universities. As a result the government, in 1981, was forced to institute the National Advisory Body (NAB) for Local Authority Higher Education, a belated measure to control numbers in the public sector sphere.

CONCLUSION

In the 1990s two potentially contradictory developments can be noted. The first is a move towards greater coherence. Local authorities have been forced to give up their major stake in higher education. Some of the more highly prized privileges of the universities, including academic tenure, are being whittled away. The result may be a unifying of higher education, in which funding, resources and conditions of service may be similar. Common problems could end many of the divisions that have dogged higher education in this century. On the other hand, as all institutions are drawn into the struggle for competitive tendering or accolades of excellence, bitter rivalry and more stratification may prevail.

FURTHER READING

R. Lowe, 'Structural Change in English Higher Education 1870–1920' in D. Muller, F. Ringer, B. Simon (eds.), *The Rise of the Modern Educational System*, 1987 offers a good starting point. A book that raises many issues is P. Scott, *The Crisis of the University*, 1984; more specialized is M. Sanderson, *The Universities and British Industry, 1850–1970*, 1972. For the early relationship between government and universities, see C.H. Shinn, *Paying the Piper 1919–46*, 1986. On the later period much information is provided in J. Carswell, *Government and the Universities in Britain. Programme and Performance 1960–80*, 1985. On the often neglected local authority sector there is P.R. Sharp, *The Creation of the Local Authority Sector of Higher Education*, 1987. The rise of the student body is contained in E. Ashby and M. Anderson, *The Rise of the Student Estate in Britain*, 1970. Individual institutions are covered in N. Harte, *The University of London 1836–1986*, 1986; T.E. Howarth, *Cambridge Between Two Wars*, 1978, and T. Kelly, *For Advancement of Learning; the University of Liverpool 1881–1981*, 1981.

PART FOUR

Teachers and Teaching

CHAPTER SEVENTEEN

The Training of Teachers

The history of the training or education of teachers from the last decade of the nineteenth century to the present time demonstrates the importance of central government in policy-making in the field of education. Three phases can be discerned: the secularization and diversification of teacher training, 1890–1944; expansion and the achievement of graduate status, 1944–72; contraction and increasing government intervention, 1972 to the present. Each of these phases will now be discussed.

SECULARIZATION AND DIVERSIFICATION, 1890–1944

From its beginnings, the training of teachers was sponsored by religious bodies. It was aimed at producing elementary school teachers whose training took place entirely within residential colleges. A flavour of the regime is captured in the reminiscences of one former student:

> Training college life in the early seventies was one round of chapel, lectures and study ... We had military drill time weekly ... (every student was an enrolled Volunteer), and alike for success at the target and in smartness on parade and at review, as well as for the healthy *Esprit de corps*, the authorities had reason for congratulation ... The library was curious enough to be negligible. The books were mainly cyclopaedias, old before Waterloo; pretractarian theological works; ancient law reports; and about a dozen volumes of general interest. No educational treatise encumbered the shelves. (HMSO, 1912–13, pp. 60–1)

Changes in the education system, developments on the Continent and the aspirations of the teaching profession itself were conducive to bringing about a closer investigation into the nature and purpose of the colleges. The implementation of the 1870 Education Act provided an impetus. The school population doubled between 1870 and 1876 and the number of certificated teachers trebled in the decade 1870–80. Even so, the schools could not have coped without the employment of pupil teachers and 'assistant' teachers, that is, ex-pupil teachers who had not become qualified. There was thus growing concern arising from the fact that uncertificated teachers now outnumbered those who were certificated (Dent, 1977, p.26). Admiration for the German system of education especially attracted many visitors from Britain. Their elementary schools were efficiently run and managed entirely without pupil teachers. The training departments, with their long history of pedagogy as a subject of study and espousing the principles expounded by Herbart, were equally admired (Armytage, 1969, pp.67–8).

There was also an increasing demand from teachers for a more unified profession by breaking down the division between the secondary and the elementary school teachers. Despite the recommendations put forward by the Taunton Commission in 1868, the bulk of secondary school teachers remained largely untainted by any form of training. Some of the newer civic universities, such as Nottingham, held evening classes in science teaching and school management from 1885 and, two years earlier, London University began to offer a Diploma in Education, a postgraduate qualification for practising teachers. A pioneering attempt was made by Cambridge University to establish a Teachers' Training Syndicate in 1879; after a promising start it quickly ran into difficulties of recruitment. However, progress was made by such women as Maria Grey and Frances Buss in London to supply training for secondary school mistresses (HMSO, 1912, p.4).

A Conference on Secondary Education held at Oxford in 1893 discussed the need for training of teachers as a prerequisite to entrance to the profession, a recommendation taken up by a Royal Commission on Secondary Education (Bryce) in 1895. The National Union of Teachers from its beginnings had pressed for university education for elementary school teachers. At the Union's 1881 Conference, the Chairman argued that 'a university training would doubtless tend greatly to the social elevation of the teaching profession ... and tend to a higher and more expansive culture than that obtained at the training college' (Langer, 1882, p.xxxvii).

Progress was achieved in meeting this goal as a result of the deliberations of the Cross Commission on Elementary Education (1886–88). Whilst taking evidence, the Commission had encountered opposition to the possible involvement of universities in teacher training from two interest groups: those representing the denominational colleges, and school boards, such as Birmingham, which hoped to set up their own colleges. The Final Report of the Commission unanimously recommended that local university colleges should be involved, on a limited scale, in a scheme of day training for teachers for elementary schools. The decision to base courses in universities rather than within school boards was made primarily on the grounds of cheapness (Tuck, 1973, p. 75). In 1890, six of these day training colleges – at Birmingham, Cardiff, King's College, London, Manchester, Nottingham and New-castle – were opened.

This new institution, the day training college, represented a break with past teacher training. Students could live at home or in approved lodgings, and consisted of a mixture of pupil teachers, two-year-course students, those taking a three-year undergraduate course and graduates following a one-year course. Cambridge, which formed a day training college in 1891, and Oxford which followed in 1892, differed from others in that their students were expected to read for university degrees (Searby, 1982, p. 15).

The success of the day training college was due to two main factors. First, with the recognition of education as a university discipline, the appointment of distinguished professors was possible. Up to this time, the only chairs created had been in Scotland, those of S.S. Laurie at Edinburgh and J.M.D. Meiklejohn at St. Andrews, both in 1876. Although Joseph Payne was made Professor at the College of Preceptors the year before, this initiative was not followed up by English universities for another 20 years. The day training college led to such appointments as Foster Watson at Aberystwyth, J.W. Adamson at King's College, London and J.J. Findlay at Manchester. The second factor was the possibilities now offered for student teachers, of widely differing backgrounds and qualifications, to receive their training together and for some to achieve graduate status. By 1902, there were 19 of these colleges including the largest, established that year, the London Day Training College (later the London University Institute of Education).

MORANT AT THE HELM

When Robert Morant became Permanent Secretary at the new Board of Education in 1903, he was determined to review the existing provision for teacher training. An investigation conducted by the Board in that year disclosed some disturbing facts. Although the day training college provided teaching of university level, only 15 per cent (130 out of 830) of the students passed the degree examination in 1903. The resources of the colleges were being deployed over an unnecessarily wide range of abilities. It was also discovered that university courses were being pursued by students who had no real aptitude for them. It is clear from Morant's later moves that he intended to strengthen the demarcation between the two types of colleges, with the day training colleges providing many graduates, some of whom would teach in secondary schools, and the residential training colleges catering almost entirely for the elementary schools.

No further day training colleges were funded during Morant's time. LEAs were allowed from 1904 to set up their own municipal training colleges. Undenominational in character, they had no connection with universities and university colleges. In the following year, regulations were tightened up to ensure that 'only those students whose general knowledge is wide and sure enough and whose health is strong enough, shall prepare for university degrees'. Protests from training colleges, backed up by statistics showing that students were able to study concurrently for a degree and a teaching qualification, were ignored. Instead, more stringent requirements for entry to a degree course were introduced from 1910.

These moves were in great contrast to Morant's attitude towards the university day training departments. In 1908, the Regulations for the Training of Teachers in Secondary Schools stipulated that separate secondary departments should be provided in institutions for graduates only: they would study a single curriculum subject and undertake 60 days' teaching practice. Morant himself wrote the Prefatory Memorandum, setting out his views on what makes a good teacher (HMSO, 1908, p.iv). Another major move forward was the introduction of the four-year course in 1911; the first three years would be taken up with studying for a degree and the final year with professional studies. The Board recognized university training departments, as they were now called, as suitable places for holding these courses. Training colleges were allowed to offer the four-year course only from 1920. It should be noted, however, that the great majority of students were still training for the elementary sector by the outbreak of the First World War. In 1914, there was only one secondary school student in training to every eleven elementary.

All students entering a four-year course were required to sign the 'Pledge', which was an undertaking to make teaching a career. As the McNair Report later pointed out, this system placed a moral strain on candidates and attracted a number of young people who were unsuited to teaching but who wished to benefit from a university education. It was not until 1951 that the 'Pledge' was abolished.

INTER-WAR DEVELOPMENTS

Reforms in education such as those envisaged in the 1918 Education Act, and the establishment of the Burnham Committee, which created a national salary machinery for teachers in the following year, had implications for teacher training. In 1923, a Departmental Committee under the chairmanship of Viscount Burnham was set up to review the existing arrangements for training teachers for public elementary schools and to recommend changes where necessary. The Board of Education omitted the training of secondary-school teachers from the Committee's remit.

One of the issues confronting the Committee was the desirable length of training courses for intending teachers. The majority of members favoured the continuation of the two-year course. A minority, headed by a senior official of the Board, E.K. Chambers, preferred a one-year course followed by either a degree or a Higher School Certificate. It was only following strong protests that the matter was referred to the newly-created Joint Examining Boards which were set up after the Committee had reported. This attempt by the Board to reduce the length of training was thus defeated (Browne, 1979, pp. 15–16).

The Joint Examining Boards were an important step forward in many ways. Formed in 1925, they represented a diminution of central control in teacher training. Twelve regional groups, with representation from the training colleges, LEAs and the universities, were empowered to set standards of courses and conduct examinations. HMI, who had until then played a major part in conducting the certificate examinations, now attended meetings of the Boards in an advisory capacity. 1928 was the last year in which the Board of Education examined the students, though they were still responsible for probationary teachers and thus full certification (Mitchell and Beaulavon, 1936, p. 40). In a few instances, such as the Reading Board, the associated colleges were able to end their isolation and share fully in exchanging information and views with the university department (Ogren, 1953, p. 81). For the most part, however, there was little contact within the groups, partly for geographical reasons, partly through lack of enthusiasm by the universities and colleges involved.

Teacher training has long been subject to strict governmental policy in the determination of student numbers and this has often caused great difficulties. In 1929 the Labour government announced the raising of the school-leaving age from 14 to 15 from April 1931 and the Board of

Education urged colleges to increase their numbers. The colleges responded by accepting almost 12 per cent more students in 1928 with a corresponding increase in the following years. In 1931, a Committee on National Expenditure, appointed to secure savings, reduced the level of teacher employment. The Board of Education suggested that colleges should attempt to discourage potential students, but it was in most cases too late. In 1932, the colleges' intake was restricted to the level of their 1928 entry (Dent, 1977, p. 104).

The Board was equally, if not more, firm with university training departments. A 10 per cent cut in student intake was enforced and a policy was adopted of reducing the number of four-year course students in favour of one-year postgraduate students. Numbers had been swollen by the comparatively large number of private, i.e. self-financed, students who were entering the departments. For example, in the academic session 1933–4, King's College, London admitted 92 private students for a postgraduate year. The Board declared that only 56 of these should be granted qualified status, with the onerous task of selection being left to the department (PRO ED 81/8 February 1933).

Expansion of university training departments was discouraged by the Board. After the founding of the London Day Training College in 1902, only four more departments were instituted in the next half century, those at Swansea (1921), Durham (1922), Leicester (1929) and Hull (1930). It is also clear from the Public Record Office files that the Board actively discouraged any experiments which involved bringing university training departments and training colleges together. The resignation in 1932 of both the head of the university training department and the principal of the training college at Leeds led to the two institutions suggesting the appointment of a single joint head to oversee teacher training. The Board rejected this request. A similar attempt in 1935 to integrate Durham University training department and the neighbouring Bede College was also firmly turned down (Gordon, 1986, p. 89).

EXPANSION AND ACHIEVEMENT OF ALL-GRADUATE PROFESSION, 1944–1972

During the Second World War, the shape of the education system in peacetime was discussed and planned. It was apparent in the early stages of devising the Education Act of 1944 that the envisaged raising of the school-leaving age would make demands on the supply of teachers. R.A. Butler, then President of the Board, appointed a Committee in 1942 headed by Sir Arnold McNair 'to investigate the present sources of supply and the methods of recruitment and training of teacher and youth leaders and to report what principles should guide the Board in these matters in the future'. The members of the Committee included Sir Fred Clarke, Director of the London Institute of Education, and Sir Frederick Mander, General Secretary of the National Union of Teachers. The evidence to the Committee showed that the existing training colleges were the poor relatives of the university training departments and should be brought into closer association with the latter if higher status was to be achieved.

This became a major recommendation of the Committee, though on the method by which this could be achieved members of the Committee were divided. Two alternative proposals were put forward. Scheme A would entail the creation of Schools of Education by universities, consisting of a federation of approved training institutions in a given area. Scheme B envisaged an enlargement of the then existing Joint Boards, with additional representation from teachers, parents, directors of education and others.

The Ministry of Education (which replaced the Board in 1944) realized that universities would not favour either solution because it might lead to interference by the Ministry (Niblett, 1975, p.112). The McNair Report had recommended that professional courses for graduates should be open to inspection by HMI in the same way as training colleges had always been. G.B. Jeffery, the Director of the London Institute of Education, speaking on behalf of other university departments, called such a proposition 'dynamite'. He wrote to the Ministry, 'If ever it was my sad lot to tell the University that its work was not an acceptable guarantee of academic quality unless it was supported by the verdict of HMI, the days of co-operation between the University and the Ministry would be numbered' (G.B. Jeffery to J. Rhodes, 18 April 1951, ULIE Archives). A compromise formula had been agreed to in 1947 whereby HMI would not have the right to inspect lectures or tutorials, but if invited to do so, would not report on the work of the individual (Lawton and Gordon, 1987, p.81). However, as the letter of Dr Jeffery demonstrated, ambiguities still remained as to the role of HMI in the sphere of teacher training in the universities. Better co-operation was achieved following a meeting between representatives of the Conference of Heads of University Departments of Education and of the Teachers' Branch of the Ministry of Education. A three-page memorandum of understanding, signed by Professors A.V. Judges and J.W. Tibble, was issued in 1960, embodying the procedures agreed upon by the two sides.

A modified form of Scheme A was eventually adopted. Four Area

Training Organizations (ATO), which established Institutes of Education, were formed in 1947 at Bristol, Birmingham, Nottingham and Southampton. These were followed by 10 more in 1948; by 1951 there were 16. They provided a stronger buffer between the Ministry and the training colleges, being largely university-based. The Institutes of Education offered research facilities for college staffs and teaching for students, co-ordinated college courses and recommended students to the Ministry for qualified status. Many ATOs appointed new professors and lecturers to carry out these enlarged functions.

The three-year training course recommended by McNair was not implemented, but one concession was that the 'Pledge' (see p.252) was abolished. The desirability of a Central Teaching Council, another McNair recommendation, was rejected by the Ministry. Instead, a National Advisory Council on the Training and Supply of Teachers (NACTST) was set up in 1949, consisting of 15 members from teachers' employers, 14 from teachers' unions and other members from a range of constituencies. Its task, to advise the Ministry on the training, recruitment and distribution of teachers, became in time a supporting body for policies emanating from the Ministry. The then Permanent Secretary, Sir Herbert Andrew, could claim in 1970 that the Ministry 'wrote all the stuff' for the NACTST and provided 'a great deal of the thought and all the statistical work' (quoted Hicks, 1974, p.258). Disbanded in 1965, the Advisory Committee was revived in 1973 under the modified title of the Advisory Committee for the Supply and Training of Teachers (ACSTT); it ceased to operate after the 1979 General Election. A third Committee, the Advisory Committee on the Supply and Education of Teachers (ACSET), was set up in 1980; this too ceased to function after 1984.

With the massive rise in the birth rate after the war – from 579,000 in 1941 to 881,000 in 1947 – the Ministry sought different ways of meeting the demand for teachers. An Emergency Training Scheme, begun in 1943, was devised under which intensive one-year courses of 48 weeks, followed by two years' part-time study, were mounted. The candidates were older than the usual students, normally being between 21 and 35, and were selected on a range of criteria. By the time the Scheme ended in 1951 some 54,000 students had attended the Emergency Training Colleges.

This initiative did little to solve the overall problems of teacher supply. In 1948, the Minister, George Tomlinson, announced the provision of 12,000 new places in colleges. Matters were made worse by a second bulge in the birth rate after a levelling off in the mid-1950s: from 700,000 in 1956 to 876,000 in 1964. It was envisaged that by the

1980s 100,000 teacher training places would be needed. The Ministry of Education suggested ways in which colleges might respond to these difficulties, such as the four-term year and 'Box and Cox' arrangements, with students working in college whilst others were on teaching practice. More serious was the issue of a Ministry's Balance of Training Letter in October 1960, which instructed colleges to produce 85 per cent primary teachers and only 15 per cent secondary teachers. The colleges naturally saw this move as working against their aspirations to be recognized as fully-fledged institutions of higher education. On the other hand, an important advance was made in 1960 with the introduction of a three-year course. This long overdue reform, recommended by McNair, had come about mainly through pressure from the Association of Teachers in Colleges and Departments of Education (ATCDE), which had been established in 1943 (Browne, 1979, p.43). There was general support from teachers' unions and HMI; the latter issued a constructive document in 1957 entitled *The Training of Teachers. Suggestions for a Three Year College Course.* The feasibility of a three-year course stemmed from the fact that there was a temporary decline in the school population and it was believed that without such an initiative there would be teacher unemployment in the 1960s. This forecast proved, as so often is the case with the planning of teacher supply, to be a false one.

A further chance of enhancement occurred with the recommendations of the Robbins Committee on Higher Education which reported in 1963. It recommended, to quote from the Report, 'a radical change' in the status of colleges. The Institutes of Education and university departments of education should become University Schools of Education which granted degrees to colleges. Training colleges would be renamed Colleges of Education and eventually pass from local authority control to full absorption into the higher education system. The colleges would also have independent governing bodies. The Report recommended a Ministry of Arts and Science which would fund the University Grants Committee and take away from the Ministry of Education the close control of the teacher-training system.

Opposition to these proposals came from local authority associations and the Minister of Education, Sir Edward Boyle; within the Ministry, the Teacher Supply Branch opposed it but the Teacher Training Branch supported it. In November 1964, the Robbins Report's recommendations were rejected on the grounds that the Department's and local authorities' expertise would be lost if the colleges were transferred to university control. The Robbins' suggestion for a new Ministry of Arts and Science was also turned down (Gosden, 1984,

p. 34). As a consolation, a review of the internal government of colleges was undertaken. A study group, headed by T.R. Weaver, Deputy Secretary at the DES, published a report in 1966, *The Government of Colleges of Education*, which recommended that each college should have an academic board, responsible for academic work, selection of students and other college business. The board was also given the task of electing members of the teaching staff other than the Principal to serve on the governing body.

The long awaited move to a graduate teaching profession was recommended by Robbins through the institution of a Bachelor of Education (B.Ed.) degree. Five universities – Keele, Leeds, Reading, Sheffield and Sussex – were offering B.Ed. courses by 1965: by 1974, 23 universities were involved and some 20,177 students had graduated. There were differences in the patterns of the course, depending on the universities which sponsored them. For example, some universities awarded honours degrees after further study, others awarded a pass degree only. Selection of students for the degree took place in some instances after the first year of the course, in others at the end of the third year. Nevertheless, the introduction of the B.Ed. had conferred many advantages on the colleges, particularly the opportunity for staffs to teach at degree level. For teachers, it heralded the arrival of an all-graduate profession. In 1947, 16 per cent of the teaching force were graduates, by 1982, 39 per cent.

The attention of colleges of education during the years 1965 to 1970 was occupied with coping with an expanded teacher-training programme and teaching the B.Ed. degree. There were important developments in teacher education in this period. In 1967 five regional technical colleges began to offer teacher-training courses, with the approval of the Secretary of State. Validation for courses was to be in the hands of the Council for National Academic Awards (CNAA). This action was strongly resisted by associations representing university departments and colleges (Robinson, 1973, p. 126). Nevertheless, it was obvious that the binary line in teacher-training had been breached and would have longer-term consequences. Criticism of teacher training had come from the Plowden Committee on Primary Schools in 1967 which had recommended a full enquiry into the system. A Select Committee on Education, appointed two years later to investigate student unrest in higher education, turned its attention to teacher education; in 1970, the Area Training Organizations were asked to review their procedures.

CONTRACTION AND INCREASING GOVERNMENT
INTERVENTION 1970 ONWARDS

The Labour government, which had initiated these investigations, fell from office in 1970. In the new Conservative government, with Margaret Thatcher as Secretary of State for Education (1970–4), further changes were undertaken. Late in 1970, a Committee of Inquiry into Teacher Education and Training, presided over by Lord James, the Vice-Chancellor of York University, was established. The Committee was requested to examine the content and organization of teacher education courses; whether a larger proportion of intending teachers should be educated alongside those entering other professions; and the role of colleges of education, polytechnics and other further education institutions and universities in teacher education.

The details of suggested reforms of teacher education, particularly that the professional training should be divided into three 'cycles', do not concern us here. One of the major recommendations was that much wider use should be made of the CNAA as a validator of awards, especially the new two-year Diploma in Higher Education. This, coupled with strong criticisms of the ATO system, led to other types of institutions becoming more involved in teacher education (Lynch, 1979, p.33). The White Paper, *Education: a Framework for Expansion*, issued in October 1972 went much further than the James' proposals. Colleges were to be placed within the non-university sector of further education (fe). A number of different patterns were possible: merging with polytechnics or other fe institutions; diversifying courses beyond those of teacher education and forming what became later Institutes of Higher Education; or merging with universities. The existing monotechnic college was not encouraged. ATOs were to be disbanded and replaced by Regional Committees.

If in the 1960s DES policy was seemingly based on expediency, the 1970s presented firmer ground for action, regardless of the political colour of the government in office. The steep drop in the birth rate in the decade 1965–75 greatly lessened the demand for teachers. In 1973, the DES announced a fall in teacher-training places from 114,000 to 60–70,000. At the same time, the severe economic recession which began during this period, stemming mainly from the oil crisis, made cutbacks essential. By the end of 1975, the future of more than three-quarters of the 157 colleges and the seven polytechnic departments had been settled (Taylor, 1984, p.25). As H.C. Dent has remarked, 'On 1 August 1975 new regulations of further education became operative which officially ended the "McNair" era for teacher training' (Dent, 1977, p.155).

It may be argued that the 1965 Woolwich speech of Tony Crosland, when Secretary of State for Education, supporting the binary policy in higher education, spelt the beginning of the end for the aspirations of colleges of education to become an integral part of the higher education system. On the other hand, the evidence seems to indicate that the political will was lacking during the 1970s to produce a coherent plan for teacher training.

A second round of cuts, involving the closure of colleges and departments, was announced in 1977 as the birth rate continued to fall. Of the 40,000 initial training places, 35,000 were allocated that year to polytechnics and colleges and 5,000 to universities. A third round of cuts followed in 1980, and new elements were now beginning to be apparent. The lack of popularity of the B.Ed. degree led to the questioning of its future. In 1981, the National Advisory Body for Local Authority Higher Education (NAB) was formed: the creation of its Teacher Education Group effectively ended the association of colleges with their former validating universities (Bruce, 1985, p.169). With an upturn in the birth rate in the late 1970s, colleges were directed to prepare more of their students for primary rather than secondary schools.

One feature of the 1980s has been the greater attention paid by DES to the professional preparation of students. A survey *PGCE in the Public Sector* (1980) and the pamphlet *The Content of Initial Training* (1983) demonstrated this interest. In 1978, the DES had proposed minimum English and mathematics standards for entrants to teaching. The White Paper *Teaching Quality* (1983) stressed the need for careful selection of candidates: it also declared that those involved in teacher education should have recent and relevant experience in schools. These points had been recommended by ACSET shortly before it was disbanded.

Tighter central control of teacher education has been manifest since 1984. A DES Circular 3/84 *Initial Teacher Training Approval of Courses* announced the establishment of the Council for the Accreditation of Teacher Education (CATE) from 1984. The Council was to approve all college courses of initial training before accreditation was granted by the Secretary of State. Before CATE would consider an application, the institution was to be visited by HMI who passed on a copy of their report to the Council. One interesting result of this policy is that for the first time since the 1947 agreement (see p.255 above), university departments have been open to visits (but not inspection) by HMI.

University departments of education (UDE), although hard hit in funding from the University Grants Committee, suffered less during the period of contraction than the colleges. From 1982, the government clearly favoured the PGCE route into teaching: UDEs were able to respond therefore more rapidly to the changing situation than colleges offering three-year B.Ed. courses. Between 1967 and 1989, virtually all teachers in State schools have been required initially to possess formal teaching qualifications: this requirement has changed with the introduction of the licensed and articled teachers' schemes. There have also been alternative sources of student supply, particularly at higher degree level, more involvement in INSET work and more concentration on attracting research funding. However, all institutions concerned with teacher training were affected by governmental changes from 1986 in the allocation of monies for inservice training. The 'pool' from which LEAs could recoup 75 per cent of the cost of paying for replacement of a teacher on secondment was no longer available.

The 1988 Education Act is evidence of the move towards the further blurring of the binary line. The removal of polytechnics from LEA control from 1 April 1989, the abolition of NAB and the establishment of a Polytechnics and Colleges Funding Council is one indication. Similarly, the setting up of the Universities Funding Council in place of the UGC is possibly designed as a move to remove the independence of universities in allocating their income. The effects of these recent Government moves on teacher education in the future remain to be seen.

SUMMARY

Teacher training in England was sponsored by religious and voluntary bodies until the last decade of the nineteenth century. Three factors combined to change this situation. The establishment of day training colleges attached to universities as recommended by the Cross Commission (1888); the growth of board schools after 1870 created a demand for teachers which could not be satisfied by the existing colleges; and recognition of the need for training teachers for secondary schools. The setting up of the first day training colleges in 1890 was a response to these needs.

The establishment of a national system of secondary education following the 1902 Act highlighted the need for trained graduates for these schools. In 1908, the Board introduced regulations encouraging day training colleges in particular to undertake this task. Four years earlier, municipal training colleges had been instituted offering two-year courses for intending teachers. During the inter-war period, the Board ensured that training colleges and university training departments were kept apart, forbidding attempts to unify the two systems. The McNair Report (1944) led to the setting up of Area Training Organizations which went some way towards making co-operation easier.

It can be seen that the new Ministry of Education's post-war policy towards teacher training lacked any long-term planning. The demographic explosion was dealt with by means of a number of makeshift expediencies. Tight control, however, was kept on target numbers and the balance of training.

The Robbins Report (1963) suggested that training colleges should become part of the higher education system, but the Ministry bowed to pressure from LEAs to maintain the *status quo*. Some benefits, however, did accrue, particularly the three-year course for colleges and the introduction of the B.Ed. degree, which helped to raise the status of these institutions.

From the early 1970s onwards, the DES has taken a more interventionist approach to both colleges and university departments of education. A large-scale programme of contraction of colleges and amalgamation with other institutions has taken place: monotechnics have virtually disappeared. All institutions offering initial teacher training received visits by HMI in order to gain accreditation by the Secretary of State. Of equal importance have been the changes in funding following the delegation of inservice education to LEAs. Finally, it is now clear that alternative routes into teaching which were promoted by the DES in the late 1980s will have long-term consequences for teacher training.

FURTHER READING

The nineteenth-century history is well covered in R.W. Rich, *The Training of Teachers in England and Wales During the Nineteenth Century*, 1933, reprinted 1972. For the first two decades of the present century, see L.G.E. Jones, *The Training of Teachers in England and Wales. A Critical Survey*, 1924.

University participation in the training of teachers is explored in D.W. Humphreys, *The Relationship between the Training Colleges and the Universities before McNair*, 1965, W.R. Niblett et al., *The University Connection*, 1975, and P. Gordon, 'Teaching As a Graduate Profession, 1890–1970', in *The Professional Teacher*, 1986.

The McNair Report, *Teachers and Youth Leaders*, 1944, is an important document. See also the DES *Report of the Study Group on the Government of Colleges of Education* (Weaver Report), 1966. The Committee of Inquiry,

Teacher Education and Training (James Report), 1972, stated the case for reform.

Subsequent events are recorded in J.D. Browne, *Teachers of Teachers. A History of the Association of Teachers in Colleges and Departments of Education*, 1979, and P.H.J.H. Gosden, *The Education System Since 1944*, 1983.

Two interesting collections of papers are D. Lomax (ed.), *The Education of Teachers in Britain*, 1973, and R.J. Alexander, M. Craft and J. Lynch (eds.), *Change in Teacher Education*, 1984.

Of the many recent official DES publications on teacher education, perhaps the most influential were *The New Teacher in School*, 1982, *Teaching Quality*, 1983, and *Better Schools*, 1985.

CHAPTER EIGHTEEN

The Teaching Profession

This chapter is divided into five sections. The first outlines the issues surrounding such terminology as 'profession', the second traces the origins and history of the major teachers' organizations. These are followed by sections on pay and conditions, a teachers' council, and autonomy and accountability. Finally some brief conclusions are drawn.

'PROFESSION'

'Association', 'union' and 'profession' are words frequently employed in any discussion of teachers and of teachers' organizations. They indicate different histories, concepts and philosophies and yet are often employed interchangeably. Historically speaking the term 'association' has been more applicable to a 'white collar/blouse' or clerical occupation, 'union' to manual employment. Similarly the terms 'schoolmaster' and 'schoolmistress' were used particularly of teachers in secondary grammar schools, and especially of graduate teachers in such schools, while the term 'teacher' was more commonly applied in respect of those working in elementary, primary and secondary modern schools. The very names Assistant Mistresses' Association and Association of Head Masters, for example, as opposed to the National Union of Teachers and National Union of Head Teachers, exemplified and perpetuated those divisions. The recently-formed National Association of Schoolmasters/Union of Women Teachers, however, indicated the greater contemporary complementary, or interchangeable, use of such terms.

A profession originally meant a vocation or calling, as when one professed the faith upon entry to a religious order. The further qualification 'learned' profession was used in English history to apply to those learned in the Latin language, particularly in such fields as divinity, medicine and law. Thus Anglican clergy, physicians and barristers were counted as members of the learned or liberal professions, professions which were suitable for, and indeed restricted to, gentlemen, and which were largely supplied from graduates and others who had attended Oxford and Cambridge. In the nineteenth century headmasters of the leading public schools and masters of the largest and wealthiest colleges of the two ancient English universities would also have enjoyed remuneration and status accorded to members of a leading profession.

Much ink has been spilled in producing lists of attributes or characteristics of a profession. Such a list might comprise, in addition to the original ideal of vocation: a non-manual occupation concerned with a defined area of knowledge; specialized training; qualifications for entry and practice; a code of ethics to govern the relationship between its members and the public; a controlling body composed of members of the profession which oversees knowledge, training, certification and the ethical code.

In many respects teachers do not approximate to such a model. The area of knowledge is less well defined and less arcane than those, for example, of law and medicine, or even of engineering and accountancy. Training for teaching has only recently become a universal requirement, and teacher training for most of the nineteenth century was a low-status activity concerned with preparation for posts in elementary schools. Even in the twentieth century many teachers in public, grammar and private schools have become teachers on the strength of their degrees alone, a situation which still exists in higher education. There is no separate code of ethics or conduct, no private law above, or separate from, the normal legal requirements. Above all, teachers in England have no controlling body of their own, equivalent to the General Medical Council or the Law Society. Thus their training, certification, remuneration, and conditions of service lie almost entirely outside the teachers' control.

The history of teachers in the twentieth century has frequently been written in terms of an unremitting struggle to become a true profession, and thus to secure for all teachers status and remuneration commensurate with that accorded to such groups as doctors and lawyers. There is no doubt that considerable progress has been made towards achieving some of the professional attributes outlined above. Thus the establishment of university departments of education from the 1890s, and the proliferation of professorships in education in the twentieth century, has helped to develop the concept of a defined area of knowledge. Entry to school teaching was restricted to graduates, all of whom, by means of concurrent or consecutive courses, have to be trained and certificated in the actual skills of teaching. All-graduate entry also encompassed a lengthening of the training period, from the two-year certificate courses of the first half of the twentieth century to the four-year B.Ed. courses of the 1970s and 1980s. The ending of the elementary/higher divide from 1944, and the introduction of comprehensive secondary schooling, also helped to lessen the divisions between teachers based upon divisions in school status. These developments, however, have not yet produced a united body for teachers, but simply distributed membership more evenly across the different organizations. Thus the most significant movement in the years 1985–87 was of primary school teachers leaving the NUT to join AMMA, a movement probably occasioned in a period of industrial action in schools by the former's 'union' as opposed to the latter's 'professional' image and policies.

Distinctions between the concepts of profession and union and the perception of teachers as a group steadily moving towards professional status have been questioned from several sides. Teacher organizations, whilst claiming the status of a profession, have become affiliated to the TUC. The very concept of profession is denounced by those who approve of the principle of public accountability. Client-related professions are widely seen as conspiracies against the public interest – groups seeking to establish and operate monopoly situations to preserve their own wealth and status. Teachers themselves have found their own freedoms or opportunities to exercise professional judgement seriously curtailed by recent legislation, in respect of such matters as their own appraisal and hours of work, and central control over curricula and pupil assessment. Thus while it has been argued that a good deal of the much vaunted autonomy of teachers in English schools has been illusory, given, for example, the control of curriculum and examinations by examination boards, there is little doubt that the 1980s witnessed the reassertion of specific and visible controls over teachers, comparable to those employed in the nineteenth century. Teacher numbers fell dramatically from 470,600 in England and Wales in 1979 to 438,700 in 1984 and the decline has continued. Teachers have neither become 'workers', shedding their professional aspirations and challenging the ideals and practices of social control and cultural reproduction, nor have they been sufficiently united, as the teachers' dispute of 1984–86 indicated, to exert significant influence within the educational system as it currently stands.

TEACHERS' ORGANIZATIONS

At the start of the twentieth century teachers' associations and unions reflected the wide differences which existed in the school system of the day. In 1889 the National Union of Elementary Teachers, originally established in September 1870 in the immediate wake of the Elementary Education Act of that year, dropped the word 'Elementary' from its title in pursuit of the goal of providing a single national union for all school teachers, but in vain. The College of Preceptors, founded in 1846 and accorded a royal charter in 1849, represented many teachers in private schools. The Endowed Schools Act of 1869, which facilitated the establishment of girls' grammar schools, had led to the foundation of the Association of Headmistresses in 1874 and the Association of Assistant Mistresses in 1885. These were followed by the Association of Headmasters in 1890 and the Assistant Masters in 1892. From 1919 these associations worked through a joint committee, and were referred to as 'the Joint Four'. Even the head teachers in elementary schools could not be contained within the NUT, and in 1897 a National Association of Head Teachers was established. The Endowed Schools Act of 1869 had also prompted the formation of a much smaller and more esoteric, but nevertheless powerful, group, the Headmasters' Conference. Promoted by Edward Thring, headmaster of Uppingham, who objected to being classified with 800 endowed schools rather than with the nine 'great' public boys' schools, after a modest start it soon came to represent the heads of some 200 public and leading grammar schools.

In the first two decades of the twentieth century there were two major secessions from the NUT. The first reflected the disappointment of many women teachers at their position within a union in which they seemed to occupy a subordinate role. Not until 1911 did a woman become president, and the NUT's membership would not endorse equal pay and status for women, or the franchise. In consequence, in 1909 the National Union of Women Teachers was formed to pursue these goals, and although the NUT adopted an equal pay policy in 1919, the NUWT remained a separate organization until, with the achievement of equal pay, it was disbanded in 1960.

The NUT's adoption of an equal pay policy caused concern amongst some of its male members, and at the Margate conference of 1920 a group of male teachers formed the National Association of Schoolmasters, which broke away from the parent union in 1922. NAS members were reacting against female majorities and policies, much as the NUWT had reacted against male dominance in the pre-war period. They felt that the issue of equal pay had been decided whilst many men were absent at war or awaiting demobilization, and that their pay and status would now be reduced. The NAS sought to recruit qualified male heads and assistant teachers in all types of school. Policies included male teachers for boys over the age of seven, and male heads for mixed schools. Neither the NAS nor the NUWT allowed its members to continue as members of the NUT.

These secessions however were compensated for, to some extent, by incorporations. Thus in 1919 the NUT at its Cheltenham conference not only adopted an equal pay policy but also decided to admit uncertificated teachers to its ranks. More than 10,000 joined the NUT within the next year, and in consequence the National Association of Non-Collegiate Certificated Teachers was dissolved in 1921. In the next year, however, the London Teachers' Association, a body founded in 1903 which like its predecessor the Metropolitan Board Teachers' Association of 1872 had hitherto retained a separate existence, and which had suffered from secessions to the NAS, agreed joint membership with the NUT. Other overlapping memberships included the Teachers' Labour League of 1922, which in 1927 was reconstituted into the National Association of Labour Teachers, and, in the aftermath of war, the National Association of Ex-Service Teachers and the National Association of Retired Teachers.

Other early twentieth-century associations whose histories lie largely outside the confines of this chapter include the Association of Teachers in Technical Institutions, which grew from a meeting in October 1904 of some 200 London technical teachers. The Association of University Teachers, formed in 1919, arose from a lengthy campaign to secure adequate salaries for non-professorial staff, those who did not enjoy the rewards and status of senior members of the universities, from whom they were separated by a wide gulf. A survey in 1918 of 330 lecturers in universities and university colleges showed an average salary of only £206 per annum (Perkin, 1969, p. 39).

Further foundations, defections and amalgamations occurred throughout the twentieth century, both at school and other levels. The rapid expansion, and subsequent decline, in teacher-training institutions in the 1960s and 1970s, led to the amalgamation of the ATTI and the Association of Teachers in Departments and Colleges of Education to form the National Association of Teachers in Further and Higher Education. The most significant changes in the school sphere since the Second World War have been the secession and rapid growth of the Professional Association of Teachers, formed in 1970 and dedicated to a no-strike policy, and the reformulation of the NAS as the NAS/UWT. The Assistant Masters and Mistresses have united together into AMMA, and the Headmasters and Headmistresses into the Secondary Heads Association.

Throughout the twentieth century the NUT has been by far the largest of the teachers' organizations, and indeed for most of the period its numbers have eclipsed the combined membership of all other associations. This situation continued well into the post-Second World War period.

MEMBERSHIP OF THE MAIN TEACHERS' ORGANIZATIONS, 1961

NUT	NAS	Assistant Masters	Assistant Mistresses
237,964	31,344	26,000	17,233

Source: Gosden, 1972, pp.6–17.

By the end of the 1960s NUT membership had reached nearly 300,000 but by the 1980s it was suffering severe losses, even amongst primary teachers, and in 1985 lost its overall majority on the Teachers' Panel of the Burnham Committee. At the time of writing, in the aftermath of industrial action in schools, 1984–86, it would appear that membership of teacher organizations is less dependent upon types of school than formerly, and more upon attitudes to strikes and other issues related to concepts of professional behaviour. Retired, overlapping and student memberships, coupled with changes in the total numbers of teachers, make direct comparisons difficult, but the following figures from 1982 and 1986 indicate a shift towards the more 'moderate' or 'professional' organizations. They also confirm that the NUT has lost its overall majority amongst school teachers.

'INSERVICE MEMBERSHIP', 1982

NUT	262,800
NAS/UWT	119,500
AMMA	89,100
PAT	22,600

Source: TES, 24 Sept. 1982.

'UNION MEMBERS PAYING SUBSCRIPTIONS', 1986

NUT	201,444
NAS/UWT	101,590
AMMA	113,751
PAT	41,536

Source: TES, 3 July 1987.

PAY AND CONDITIONS

In 1900 whilst headmasters and housemasters of public and leading grammar schools might be quite comfortably off, assistant masters (and mistresses) in secondary schools were poorly paid, their annual salaries averaging only some £100. Salaries in such schools varied according to the size both of the school and of the endowment. Similarly salaries in elementary schools ranged widely. A trained certificated male assistant teacher employed by a large urban school board might be paid £120 a year, twice as much as the headmistress of a rural voluntary school (Gosden, 1972, pp.21–3). Salaries paid to women teachers and headteachers would, on average, be some two-thirds to three-quarters of those paid to their male counterparts, and in 1900 some 60 per cent of certificated teachers, 80 per cent of 'assistant' or unqualified teachers and 80 per cent of pupil teachers were female (Tropp, 1957, pp.117–18).

The two most important developments in the first half of the twentieth century in respect of teachers' pay and conditions were the creation of a new administrative structure under the 1902 Act, and the establishment of the Burnham Committees from 1919. The new local authorities appointed under the 1902 Act were required to pay the salaries not only of teachers in council schools but also of those in voluntary elementary schools in their area. There was no national scale, however, and considerable differences existed between the various authorities. Thus in 1913–14 the average annual salary of a certificated teacher in a London elementary school was some £161 for a man and £119 for a woman. By contrast the average in county authorities was only £104 for a man and £83 for a woman (Gosden, 1972, p.28). In 1906 the London County Council introduced a general salary scale for assistant teachers in its secondary schools of £150–£300 for men and £120–£220 for women, a practice followed by other local authorities, though at a less generous rate. In January 1911 the average salaries in grant-aided secondary schools were £168 for men and £123 for women. The average salary for a headmaster was £438 and for a headmistress, £332 (Gosden, 1972, p.32).

Inflation in the second decade of the twentieth century bit deeply into the earnings of teachers, as into those of other workers. At the same time male teachers were in particularly short supply, and there was some concern lest a disgruntled teaching force should encourage the growth of revolutionary ideas, so evident in other parts of Europe from 1917. Both elementary and secondary school teachers now sought national salary scales, and the strength of feeling was shown by militant teacher action, both during and after the First World War, against miserly authorities. In 1917 H.A.L. Fisher, President of the Board of Education, appointed two departmental committees to inquire into salaries – one for elementary schools, and the other for secondary and technical schools and training colleges. Neither report, however, unequivocally recommended national salary scales. The Teachers' Superannuation Act of 1918 established a generous, non-contributory pension scheme, which covered both qualified and unqualified teachers, but not those who had already retired. This measure, however, failed to deflect the teachers' anger over salaries, and unofficial strikes mushroomed in 1918 and 1919. In July 1919 the Association of Education Committees at its Annual General Meeting declared its support for a system of national salary scales. In September of the same year Fisher established a Standing Joint Committee on a Provisional Minimum Scale of Salaries for Teachers in Public Elementary Schools, composed of 22 representatives of the NUT and 22 from the local authority side. In May 1920 a similar committee was established to determine salaries in secondary schools, with 26 representatives apiece from local authorities and teachers' organizations. Lord Burnham was appointed chairman of both committees, and also of a third concerned with salaries in technical institutions.

National salary scales, however, were not agreed for elementary teachers. Instead four standard scales were produced. Scale I was for teachers in rural areas, Scales II and III for smaller and larger urban areas, and Scale IV for London. Thus a college-trained, certificated male assistant teacher in a rural area would have a maximum annual salary of £325, with £260 for a female, whilst London teachers on Scale IV would have a maximum of £425 for men and £340 for women. Such standards, which reflected regional differences in costs of living and in previous salary structures, continued until 1944. Secondary-school teachers, however, were paid on a national salary scale, although with slightly higher rates in London. Graduate masters would be paid on a scale of £250 to £500 per annum, and mistresses from £225 to £400 per annum (Gosden, 1972, pp.46–8).

In the inter-war years a fall in the cost of living and widespread economic problems meant that teachers were engaged in protecting these scales established in 1920, rather than in advancing them. Thus the NUT and the secondary school associations, while reluctantly accepting a 5 per cent voluntary cut in salaries for the year 1923–4, still had to fight hard to prevent local authorities from abandoning the Burnham agreements and imposing further cuts. From 1925, moreover, teachers were required to contribute 5 per cent of their salaries to the superannuation fund. Salaries 1925–31 were set by Lord Burnham's personal arbitration at some 1 per cent below those of 1920, but in 1931, following the report of the May Committee, teachers' salaries were reduced by 10 per cent. This cut lasted until 1934, the reduction for 1934–35 was halved to 5 per cent, and from 1935 salaries were restored to the 1925 level. In 1936 the Standard Scale I was abolished.

In 1944 the government rejected the principle of equal pay for men and women teachers, although on 28 March the House of Commons had narrowly approved an amendment to that end. The three existing Burnham Committees were reduced to two, of which the main committee would cover teachers in all types of primary and secondary schools. This had 26 representatives from the local authority side and 26 from the teachers, of whom 16 were NUT, six from the Joint Four, and four from the ATTI. In 1961 the NAS secured two places and the NAHT one.

From 1944 there was one basic scale of £300 to £525 for men, and another from £270 to £420 for women. By 1950 these had been increased to £375 to £630 for men, and £338 to £504 for women. There were additions for graduates and for good honours degrees, and from 1956 a further range of head of department and graded posts (which carried extra allowances) was established. In 1965 head-teacher allowances were replaced by separate head-teacher scales. The principle of equal pay for men and women teachers was approved in 1955, and by 1961 equality had been achieved.

Relationships between the teachers' organizations both on and off the Burnham Committee were not always harmonious. The NUT was principally interested in a good basic scale for all teachers, whilst the Joint Four, though not opposed to this aim, also sought to secure extra payments which they argued were necessary to recruit and retain good honours graduates for the grammar schools. The NAS with two members from 1961 and three from 1966, under the energetic leadership of Terry Casey, sought to protect the interests of the male career teacher. From 1965 the Secretary of State was directly represented on the Burnham Committees, and provision was made both for arbitration and for backdating of awards. Details of negotiations, government pay policies, strikes, arbitration and the other dimensions surrounding salaries in the period from the 1960s to the early 1980s, with the peak of the Houghton award of 1974–75, can be followed in such works as Gosden, 1972, and Roy, 1983. In 1986–87 the Conservative government abolished the Burnham Committee, deprived teachers of their pay-bargaining rights, and imposed a basic scale of £7,599 to £13,299 with five incentive allowances ranging from £501 to £4,200. In addition, although teachers are employed by local authorities, a revolutionary (or reactionary) contract of employment has been imposed from the centre which defines exactly what teachers must do. Teachers must be available for 1,265 hours over 195 days performing such duties as may reasonably be assigned by the head, and also work such further hours as are necessary to enable them to 'discharge effectively their professional duties'.

A TEACHERS' COUNCIL

From its foundation in 1846 the College of Preceptors fulfilled some of the functions of a teachers' council. The General Medical Council was established by statute in 1858 but attempts to secure similar legislation for teachers met with little success. Bills were introduced in 1879, 1881, and two in 1890, but to no avail. In 1902, however, a Teachers' Registration Council was established as required by the Board of Education Act, 1899. There were to be 12 members, six nominated by the President of the Board of Education, and one each by the College of Preceptors, the Teachers' Guild, the NUT, the Headmasters' Conference, the Incorporated Association of Headmasters and the Association of Headmistresses. One alphabetical list of teachers' names was to be drawn up, as the 1899 Act required, but they were to be entered in two columns, column A for certificated elementary teachers and column B for teachers in secondary and independent schools. Those in column A were to be placed on the register *en bloc*, those in column B were to make individual applications. The NUT objected both to the separate columns on the register, and to the composition of the Council. By the end of 1905 whilst 10,459 teachers were registered in column B (as opposed to some 80,000 automatically entered in column A), only 230 of these had both a degree and training. In 1906 the new Liberal government closed the register, to the relief of the NUT, and to the dismay of the College of Preceptors and the secondary school associations.

In 1912 a new Teachers' Registration Council was established, as in 1902 by Order in Council. This was designed to overcome some of the previous objections and difficulties. There was an enlarged Council of 44, with 11 representatives each from the elementary, secondary and university spheres, and an independent chairman. There was to be one register and all registrations were to be voluntary. By 1922 more than 73,000 names had been placed on the register, but by 1929 when the whole enterprise was dignified by the title Royal Society of Teachers, numbers had only reached 78,000. The RST, however, had no power to control entry to the profession nor to oversee its training. Compulsory registration for those wishing to teach was not introduced, and in 1949 the whole enterprise came to an ignominious end.

In the 1950s and 1960s the teachers' organizations urged upon successive Ministers of Education the need for a General Teaching Council which would control the qualifications, entry and disciplinary matters of the profession. Naturally governments were not keen to hand such powers over to teachers but in 1969 Edward Short, Secretary of State for Education in a Labour government and himself a former head teacher, set up an official working party to consider the question. This decision was prompted partly by the establishment of a General Teaching Council for Scotland in 1965. The Weaver Report of 1970, however, recommended the setting up of two bodies, one a General Teachers' Council, the other an advisory body on the supply and training of teachers, but with the Secretary of State retaining powers to reject their recommendations. Nothing came of these proposals, and though in the 1980s Mark Carlisle indicated his support for an independent Teachers' Council, his successors as Secretary of State, Sir Keith Joseph and Kenneth Baker followed a different policy. Infuriated by what they saw as 'unprofessional' conduct by some teachers during the industrial action of 1984–86, in 1987 the Conservative government imposed central control of an unprecedented kind upon teachers.

AUTONOMY AND ACCOUNTABILITY

The system of payment by results introduced in 1862, whereby a considerable proportion of the income of an elementary school depended upon the performance of pupils in annual examinations, was a highly visible form of teacher accountability. The prospects and careers of teachers, indeed their immediate incomes, were directly linked to the performance of their pupils as assessed by Her Majesty's Inspectors. That system, however, was abandoned in the 1890s, and a further indication of the relaxation of central control, not only over standards, but also over curriculum and teaching methods, came with the Board of Education's Handbook of *Suggestions for the Consideration of Teachers and others concerned with the Work of Public Elementary Schools* (1905). Its prefatory memorandum (p. 5) declared that:

The only uniformity of practice that the Board of Education

desire to see in the teaching in Public Elementary Schools is that each teacher shall think for himself, and work out for himself such methods of teaching as may use his powers to the best advantage and be best suited to the particular needs and conditions of the school ...

Elementary schoolteachers, moreover, played a significant part in calling both the President of the Board of Education and the Permanent Secretary to account over the infamous Holmes–Morant Circular of 1910. This secret memorandum, which was concerned principally with the status and duties of local education authority inspectors, also contained the statement that 'elementary teachers are as a rule uncultured and imperfectly educated' (quoted in Tropp, 1957, p.271). The NUT were to the fore in a campaign which forced the removal in 1911 both of Walter Runciman and of Robert Morant. E.G.A. Holmes, the Chief Inspector, who accepted complete responsibility for the circular, had retired in 1910.

During the inter-war period teachers' independent or professional autonomy in matters of curriculum and teaching method continued. Of course severe restraints existed, and would continue to exist, in terms of examinations, resources and expectations, but the 1944 Act made no curricular impositions upon schools apart from those connected with religious instruction and corporate worship. The constitution of the Schools Council, established in 1964, declared that 'each school should have the fullest possible measure of responsibility for its own work, with its own curriculum and teaching methods based on the need of its own pupils and evolved by its own staff' (Lawn and Grace, 1987, p.150).

The abolition of the eleven plus examination, and the introduction of comprehensive schools and the Certificate of Secondary Education, were further steps along the road to teacher autonomy. The swinging sixties, however, were to be followed by the more sober seventies. To what extent Britain's economic problems could be attributed to failures in education and specifically to the failures of teachers, and to teacher militancy in the years 1968–74, is not easily determined. In October 1976, however, James Callaghan's speech at Ruskin College, Oxford, gave warning that accountability in education would become an issue across the political spectrum. The setting up of the Manpower Services Commission in 1974, the proposals for greater parental involvement in the running of schools contained in the Taylor Report of 1977, and the Green Paper of the same year, *Education in Schools* (Cmnd. 6869) which drew attention to the 'growing recognition of the need for schools to demonstrate their accountability to the society which they serve' (p.16) indicated the change in direction.

Thus in the last ten years teacher autonomy has been replaced by accountability and increased local and central government control. In 1983–84 the teacher-controlled Schools Council was abolished and replaced by the School Curriculum Development Committee and the Secondary Examinations Council. In 1987 a DES consultation document, *The National Curriculum 5–16*, announced proposals for a single curriculum for state schools composed of core and foundation subjects, and for national testing at ages seven, 11, 14 and 16, proposals swiftly implemented by the Education Act of 1988. Initial teacher training, even in university departments, was made subject to government inspection, and a Council for the Accreditation of Teacher Education was established. In-service training was brought under central control by a series of specific grants. A spate of legislation, 1986–88, encompassed teacher appraisal, the abolition of teachers' pay-bargaining machinery, and the imposition of actual hours and duties.

Yet although overall this package of measures has replaced autonomy with accountability there have been some increases in head-teacher autonomy, particularly in respect of local authority control. The reconstitution of governing bodies under the Education (No. 2) Act 1986, and the granting of budgetary control to governors and head teachers, are steps in this direction. The Act of 1988, which allows schools to opt out of local authority control and to be funded directly by central government, will further increase this process.

SUMMARY

The status of the majority of teachers in English history has seldom been high, a consequence, perhaps, of the hierarchical nature of English society and, in rural areas particularly, of the superior social and intellectual position of the Anglican priest. Divisions between teachers have been many, and have themselves reflected divisions of social class, gender, types of school, and the professional or union approach. Such disunity has prevented teachers from joining together in a single professional body which might, as central government power over education declined during the twentieth century, have assumed responsibility for entry to, qualifications for, and conduct within, teaching.

The consequences of such divisions and disunity have been particularly apparent since 1981 with the rapid increase in central government control over education. At the time of writing, in 1990, it seems that such an increase in control and power has been, and will be, at the expense of the ideal of an independent teaching profession – respected, responsible, self-regulating and united. Three examples may be given of this trend.

First, the Teachers' Pay and Conditions Act of 1987 with its statutory imposition of contracts and pay settlements indicated that teachers were to be treated neither as professionals nor as trade unionists but simply as irresponsible children whose prime aim appeared to be the disruption of schools.

Second, in 1988 Kenneth Baker rebutted overtures made by Alec Ross of the Universities' Council for the Education of Teachers, who was spearheading a new attempt to establish a General Teaching Council.

Finally, the introduction of untrained and unqualified staff into classrooms from September 1989, trained there on the job by teachers themselves, with the subsequent according after two years of a 'licensed' teacher status, represents a fundamental retreat from the concept of an all-graduate, all-trained profession. Even on an issue such as this, however, the teachers' organizations are fundamentally divided. At their Easter conferences in 1989, whilst AMMA advised its members not to act as mentors and trainers for the new entrants, the NAS/UWT welcomed such persons not only into teaching but also into membership of their own organization.

FURTHER READING

P. Gordon (ed.), *Is Teaching a Profession?*, 1985, provides a useful introduction to the issues of definition. P. Gosden, *The Evolution of a Profession*, 1972, charts the actual contributions of teachers' organizations to the development of school-teaching as a professional occupation. J.V. Chapman, *Professional Roots. The College of Preceptors in British Society*, 1985, is a study of the oldest of these organizations, whilst A. Tropp, *The School Teachers*, 1957, and R. Manzer, *Teachers and Politics*, 1970, are concerned with the largest, the National Union of Teachers. M. Lawn and G. Grace (eds.), *Teachers: the Culture and Politics of Work*, 1987, includes useful articles on the relationship between teachers and the state, on the National Union of Women Teachers, and on teachers' action, 1984–86, whilst R. Seifert, *Teacher Militancy*, 1987, surveys the history of teachers' strikes throughout the twentieth century. For a sociological perspective see G. Grace, *Teachers, Ideology and Control*, 1978, and J. Ozga and M. Lawn, *Teachers, Professionalism and Class*, 1981.

CHAPTER NINETEEN

The School Curriculum

Any attempt to explain changes in the curriculum has to take into account a large number of factors. Particularly important is the impact of examinations and this will be dealt with in Chapter 20. Others include political and philosophical considerations, the activities of professional associations and national 'needs'. The emphasis in this chapter will be mainly on central government policy but these other contributory factors should be borne in mind.

THE RE-ORDERING OF THE CURRICULUM, 1895–1911

For the 30 years from 1862, there had been a tight grip on the elementary school curriculum by the Education Department. In that year, Robert Lowe, Vice-President of the Committee of Council on Education, had introduced the Revised Code, better known as 'payment by results', whereby teachers' salaries were dependent on their pupils achieving a high standard of passes in the 3Rs, with plain needlework as an extra for girls. Although there was a progressive relaxation of the system under successive Codes as the century progressed, nevertheless there generally remained an emphasis on 'paying' subjects at the expense of a broader curriculum (Gordon and Lawton, 1978, p. 18).

The 1895 Code abolished the annual examination for older scholars, and teachers were allowed to become more adventurous. But as one Inspector, Edmond Holmes, later observed, 'The grooves into which thirty years of Code despotism had driven the teacher had become too deep for him ... What happened in many schools was that the teaching remained as mechanical and routine-ridden as ever' (Holmes, 1922, p. 727).

Secondary schools, under a variety of titles, offered a much less uniform curriculum. The public and endowed schools tended to emphasize the classics and humanities, though grants from the Science and Art Department to encourage scientific subjects attracted more schools to this area towards the end of the century. Perhaps the greatest beneficiary of these grants was the London Technical Education Board, set up in 1892 by the London County Council to promote technical education. The aim of its chairman, Sidney Webb, was to broaden the interpretation of this term so that it was synonymous with secondary education. After an interview with A.H.D. Acland, Gladstone's zealous Vice-President of the Committee of Council, in 1892, the Technical Board was able to add a long list of subjects to its existing ones. As Webb observed, 'We can now lawfully teach anything under the sun except ancient Greek and theology'.

MORANT AND CURRICULUM REFORM

There were other blurrings of the elementary–secondary lines, particularly by the higher grade schools, which were operated almost entirely by school boards, and with a curriculum often rivalling in breadth that of secondary schools. The legality of boards using their rating powers was in doubt. Morant, secretary to the Vice-President, Gorst, was largely responsible for drafting the Higher Elementary Schools Minute of 1900. The Minute effectively curbed the scope of higher grade schools; they were to be renamed higher elementary schools, non-fee-paying, with a leaving age of 15 and a curriculum geared to future manual work. Morant also took advantage of the Cockerton case (1900–1), which established that it was illegal for school boards to give secondary education in evening schools, by bringing in legislation in 1901 which curbed school boards' powers in this field (Eaglesham, 1956, p.224). The separation of elementary and secondary school curricula was now much clearer.

Morant was active in planning the 1902 Education Act and, as Permanent Secretary of the new Board of Education, readily found like-minded colleagues, eager to promote curricula which were appropriate to the different types of schools. Morant encouraged one inspector, James Headlam, a former Professor of Greek and Ancient History at Queen's College, London, to produce a Report on the Teaching of Literary Subjects in Some Secondary Schools, published by the Board in 1902. In it, Headlam commented on the disappearance of Greek from many schools and the diminution in the teaching of Latin; English subjects, too, were poorly taught. Headlam's views were shared by the Assistant Secretary, Secondary Branch, J.W. Mackail. Himself a classical scholar, he strongly advocated compulsory Latin in every secondary school. The only way that this ideal could be achieved, in his view, was to lay down a central standard curriculum.

Morant enshrined the spirit of these sentiments in the 1904 Regulations for Secondary Schools, though it is clear that the Treasury played an important part in planning the Regulations (Lowe, 1984, p.45). The secondary school course was to be a balanced one, with instruction in English language and literature, at least one language other than English, geography, history, mathematics, science and drawing, and in girls' schools, housewifery. When two languages other than English were taken and Latin was not one of them, the Board required a satisfactory reason for its omission. Time allocation for subjects was stipulated: not less than $4\frac{1}{2}$ hours a week was allotted to English, geography and history, not less than $3\frac{1}{2}$ hours where one language was taken and 6 hours for two, and $7\frac{1}{2}$ hours for mathematics and science.

A softening of this highly academic view of the curriculum is seen in the Board's 1907 Regulations. With the introduction of the free place system in the same year which opened the grammar school to many more elementary school pupils, curriculum provisions were relaxed. The minimum time prescribed for English language and literature, geography, history, science and one foreign language was withdrawn and more practical subjects were allowed. Physical education and manual work were now essential components of the curriculum. Still more scope was given to schools in 1908 to vary the curriculum whilst retaining the main features of a broad liberal education. By 1909, two-thirds of boys' grammar schools had some provision for handicraft, and domestic subjects were taught in almost all the girls' schools.

If the 1904 Secondary Regulations were somewhat *dirigiste* in character, those for elementary schools issued in the same year provided a refreshing contrast. The liberal tone of its Preface has led one educational historian (Eaglesham, 1967, p.162) to suggest that it was penned by Mackail rather than by Morant. It began:

> The purpose of the Public Elementary School is to form and strengthen the character and to develop the intelligence of the children entrusted to it, and to make the best use of the school years available, in assisting both girls and boys, according to their different needs, to fit themselves, practically as well as intellectually, for the work of life.

The curriculum, unlike that stipulated in the Secondary Regulations, was not prescribed in any detail but more general aims were expressed. Pupils were to become acquainted with the facts and laws of nature; they should be familiar with the literature and history of Britain; they should be introduced to hand and eye training; and they should be trained in appropriate physical exercises in order to develop better health.

One striking difference between the 1904 Elementary Code and previous ones was that the set of Instructions to Inspectors, together with Appendices of Specimen Schemes of Instructions which accompanied each Code, were dropped. Further, the Preface mentioned that the Board would 'issue shortly a companion volume to the Code containing various suggestions for the consideration of those who come into contact with the scholars in elementary schools, and are concerned with the educational as distinct from the administrative aspects of school life'.

This change of attitude followed the transfer of responsibility for the maintenance and control of elementary schools to the newly-created local education authorities. In 1905, the Board issued the volume *Suggestions for the Consideration of Teachers* (from 1927, renamed the *Handbook of Suggestions for Teachers*). Although the authors of *Suggestions* are anonymous, it is now known that most of the contributors were HMIs but that outside experts, distinguished educationists with specialist expertise, were responsible for some of the chapters (Gordon, 1985, p.43). The ten chapters devoted to subjects represented practical and enlightened approaches to the curriculum. Differences in children's abilities were recognized and the treatment of those below normal standard was discussed. Successive *Handbooks* issued up to 1944 were enlightened documents designed to encourage teachers to reflect on their practices.

NEW PHILOSOPHIES, AND THE EFFECTS OF WAR, 1911–1925

The impetus to open up new avenues of teaching was provided by the appearance in 1911 of Edmond Holmes's book *What is and What Might Be*. Holmes advocated a progressive attitude to the education of children, particularly at the primary stage. His admiration of Montessori was shared by many others and experiments in teaching methods were widely adopted; for example, the Play Way method was developed by Caldwell Cook at the Perse School, Cambridge, shortly before the First World War, and by 1920 Helen Parkhurst had promoted the Dalton Plan in the United States, which became popular in England. 'Broadly speaking,' she wrote, 'the old type of school may be said to stand for *culture*, while the modern type of school stands for *experience*. The Dalton Laboratory Plan is primarily a way whereby both these aims can be reconciled and achieved' (Parkhurst, 1922, p.15). More importantly, London inspectors such as C.W. Kimmins and P.B. Ballard disseminated her teaching in the schools (Selleck, 1972, p.108).

A further incentive to broaden the range of curriculum activities followed the raising of the school-leaving age to 14 as stipulated by the 1918 Education Act. There is much evidence to show the growth of the elementary school curriculum up to 1925 in a number of areas (Bramwell, 1961, p.x).

Rather different in character was the development of junior technical schools and central schools, particularly in London (1911) and Manchester (1913). The Board of Education did little to encourage secondary schools specifically offering a quasi-vocational curriculum designed to meet the needs of pupils entering industry at 16. In 1913, the Board introduced legislation which awarded grants to technical schools 'more commensurate to their importance'. The schools were only for those who had left elementary schools at 13 or 14; parents of entrants had to give an undertaking that their child would take up an occupation for which the school gave a preparation. At one stage, the Board forbade the teaching of a foreign language and regarded the schools as a continuation of the elementary tradition. Nevertheless, their popularity steadily grew, and by 1926 there was a variety of types of schools beside junior technical – junior commercial, nautical training, junior housewifery and trade schools, each offering their own curricula (Edwards, 1960, p.18).

In the same year, the Board issued another Circular dealing with the sixth-form curriculum. Overt specialization was to be avoided. It suggested that pupils should follow a course in a group of subjects, either in classics or in mathematics and science or in modern languages, literature and history: in both groupings, time was to be made for complementary subjects. The alliance of mathematics and science and of language, literature and history were later considered as radical innovations by the Board (Board of Education, 1927, p.20).

The curriculum of secondary schools came under scrutiny during the First World War after calls for a re-examination of the state of the whole education system. In July 1916, a memorial, signed by leading industrialists and educationists such as Sir Philip Magnus and Michael Sadler, was presented to the Prime Minister, Asquith, calling for a Royal Commission on the subject. Selby-Bigge, the Permanent Secretary to the Board, opposed such a body as it would act independently of the Board and thus weaken its control. He therefore canvassed an alternative scheme. A Reconstruction Committee, consisting of Asquith and seven Cabinet colleagues, had been created some five months previously to examine the organization of aspects of British post-war reconstruction. Selby-Bigge suggested that sub-committees which would investigate educational topics should be sub-committees of the Reconstruction Committee. The committees were to be appointed departmentally and were to be housed in and staffed by the Board of Education (Jenkins, 1973, p.47). When Lloyd George succeeded Asquith as Prime Minister in December 1916 this change hardly affected the Board's position. The terms of reference and membership of the committees were mainly settled by Selby-Bigge, and the Board's comments on the Reports were slow to appear.

There were four committees, on the position of Natural Science, Modern Languages, Classics and English; each produced an impressive document. The Science Committee recommended the inclusion of the subject in all general courses up to the age of 16; the Modern Languages Committee pointed to the need for a wider study of industry and commerce; the Classics Committee, whilst agreeing with their Modern Languages colleagues that French should be the first language, called for Classics teaching in elementary as well as secondary schools, with more emphasis on historical and archaeological backgrounds to the texts; and the English Committee advanced the subject's centrality in the curriculum, advocating the doctrine that 'every teacher is a teacher of English', a sentiment echoed by the Bullock Report in 1975.

The Board summarized the findings of the four Committees in Circular 1294 entitled *Curricula of Secondary Schools in England*. It concluded that as the curriculum was becoming so overcrowded, more specialization would be necessary. Nevertheless, the Board stipulated the minimum number of 45-minute periods in a 35-period week that should be allocated to subjects. The two languages would occupy nine periods, science six, mathematics six, history, geography, manual work and physical education two each and scripture and music one each (HMSO, 1922, p.2).

One topic touched on by the Circular was that of girls' curricula. The Board acknowledged that the recommendations of the Committees applied equally to boys and girls except that the Science Committee was prepared to accept a lower minimum for girls. Referring to the model curriculum quoted above, the Board stated that more time might be spent in drawing and music in girls' schools than in boys' schools, with domestic subjects replacing manual work. Difficulties arose from the fact that girls' school hours tended to be substantially shorter than boys'; the achievement of a minimum, balanced curriculum was, in the Board's view, 'an almost insoluble problem'.

The Circular was issued with some knowledge of the evidence which had been collected by the Consultative Committee of the Board on Differentiation of Curriculum for Boys and Girls in Secondary Schools. Its Report, issued in 1923, stated that the curriculum for girls was modelled too much on boys, was too competitive and was not sufficiently developed aesthetically. It recommended that girls should be encouraged to pursue 'boys' subjects', such as manual instruction, if aptitude was shown and that there should be a greater assimilation of teaching methods for boys and girls. One interesting recommendation was that research should be undertaken by psychologists and teachers in secondary schools with a view to collecting data on the intellectual and emotional differences between the sexes and their bearing on education. Investigation was also suggested into the achievements of groups of boys and girls in various subjects of the curriculum at successive stages of school life (HMSO, 1923, p.139).

The Board took little interest in following up these suggestions. Some 56 years later, the DES undertook a similar survey and concluded that 'it may be that society can justify the striking differences that exist between the subjects studied by boys and girls in secondary schools, but it is more likely that a society that needs to develop to the full the talents and skills of all its people will find the discrepancies disturbing' (HMSO, 1979, p.24).

STAGES OF SCHOOLING AND THE CURRICULUM, 1926–1944

One consequence of the Labour party's policy of secondary education for all which was adopted in 1922 was a national debate on its feasibility. The Consultative Committee approached the Board of Education in March 1923 in order to explore the possibility of the Committee carrying out such a study. In an interview in November with the Permanent Secretary of the Board, Selby-Bigge, a deputation from the Committee was told that 'an inquiry of this kind would be useful in dispelling the Socialist and Labour war-cry of "Secondary Education For All" and it was important to dispel the notion if possible before the Labour Party came into power' (quoted in Barker, 1972, p.50).

The Committee, under its chairman, Sir Henry Hadow, was given its remit in February 1924. It would report on the organization, objective and curriculum of courses for pupils in other than secondary schools up to the age of 15. The wider implications of the Committee's recommendations for the organization of education were discussed in Chapter 11. For the curriculum, the important recommendation was that a new type of post-primary institution, the modern school, should be established, with courses simpler and more limited in scope than grammar schools. As the Report, published in 1926 under the title *The Education of the Adolescent*, stated:

> A humane or liberal education is not one given through books alone, but one which brings children into contact with the larger interests of mankind. It should be the aim of schools ... to provide such an education by means of a curriculum containing large opportunities for practical work, and closely related to living interests. (HMSO, 1926, Chapter III, para. 3)

During the first year of the Hadow Committee's deliberations, the first Labour government was elected to power. It was short-lived (January–November 1924), and by the time the Report was issued, a Conservative Prime Minister, Baldwin, was in office with Lord Eustace Percy as President of the Board. It has been claimed (White, 1975, p.28) that the Conservatives in 1926 removed all parliamentary controls governing the elementary school curriculum in anticipation of a future Labour government. This move might also have had the effect of playing down the differences between the curricula of secondary modern schools and those of grammar schools. Nevertheless, the importance of the 1926 Hadow Report lies in its recognition of the differing needs of children at primary and secondary stages, particularly in the area of curriculum, which it considered 'should be thought of in terms of activity and experience rather than of knowledge to be acquired and facts to be stored'.

This progressive attitude to the curriculum also permeated the proposals of the Spens Committee on Secondary Education with special reference to Grammar Schools and Technical High Schools, published in 1938. It drew attention to the existing situation where pupils had to adjust to the curriculum rather than the curriculum servicing the needs and abilities of the pupils. The Report rejected the notion of the multilateral or comprehensive school, preferring the development of the technical school alongside the grammar and the modern. Parity of esteem was to be ensured between the schools. A common core of subjects was suggested for the 11 to 13 age group but with later differentiation through options. More emphasis on vocational subjects, based on pupils' interests, was urged in the upper ranges of schools.

In 1941, R.A. Butler, as President of the Board of Education, set up a Committee to report on Curriculum and Examinations in Secondary Schools, chaired by Cyril Norwood. This move raised a protest from Spens who 'expressed great alarm' at the new Committee's deliberations, stating that 'it would be "no less than a scandal" were it to replough the whole ground of curriculum' (quoted in Simon, J., 1977, p. 184). The Norwood Report, published in 1943, followed the thinking of Spens but pursued a much harder line. It justified the tripartite system of secondary education by postulating, on flimsy evidence, three kinds of children with abilities which should be catered for in different types of secondary schools. The curriculum would be academic for the grammar-school pupils, scientific and technical for the technical-school pupils and largely practical for the modern-school pupils.

COPING WITH CHANGE, 1944–1964

Butler accepted the Norwood Committee's findings as a basis for organizing secondary education after the war. The 1944 Education Act was silent on the curriculum except that religious instruction was made compulsory in all schools. The Secondary Regulations were discontinued from 1945, thus ending central control of the curriculum. In LEAs where the tripartite system was developed, the curricula of the different schools followed the Norwood guidelines. The Labour Education Minister, Ellen Wilkinson, authorized the publication of *The Nation's Schools* in 1945: the pamphlet advocated a tripartite approach to secondary education. Two years later, her successor, George Tomlinson, offered no resistance to the publication of a further pamphlet prepared under Ellen Wilkinson entitled *The New Secondary Education*, which still assumed a tripartite system with a range of differentiated curricula. A clear indication of this thinking is shown in the chapter on modern school education:

> The aim of the modern school is to provide a good all-round secondary education, not focused primarily on the traditional subjects of the school curriculum, but developing out of the interests of the children. (HMSO, 1947, p. 29)

During the following years, the Ministry was occupied with ways of dealing with the post-war demographic explosion as well as policies relating to curriculum. The raising of the school-leaving age to 15 in 1947 also occupied the minds of administrators and teachers. An important Report of the Central Advisory Council for Education entitled *15 to 18* (the Crowther Report), published in 1959, dealt with the changing social and industrial needs of society and the education of pupils in the age group 15 to 18. The Report stated that most children in this age group were not being sufficiently educated (HMSO, 1959, p. 3). Besides discussing the nature of the sixth-form curriculum, the

Report made suggestions for extending pupils' education beyond school age and strongly recommended raising the leaving age to 16.

This key recommendation of the Crowther Report was not adopted by the Minister of Education, David Eccles, who preferred a voluntary staying on by pupils. It was the Report of the Central Advisory Council on the education of pupils between the ages of 13 and 16 of average or less than average ability (Newsom), published in 1963, which caused the Minister to reconsider school-leaving policy (Kogan and Packwood, 1974, p.66). The Report challenged the traditional notion of the school day, preferring an extended day which included normally 'extra-curricular activities' within its ambit. No fewer than three chapters were devoted to the curriculum. Great stress was laid on providing links between school and adult life. One of the longest chapters in the Report (Chapter 19), entitled 'The Humanities', suggested ways in which new and valuable experiences could be provided for older pupils through presenting subjects such as English and social studies in such a way as to advance the capacity for thought, judgment, enjoyment and curiosity. The effect of this philosophy on the activities of the Schools Council, which was shortly to be established, is obvious.

END OF CURRICULUM CONSENSUS, 1964 ONWARDS

The coming to power of the Labour government in 1964 marked the end of political consensus on many aspects of education, not least in the area of curriculum. With the acceleration in comprehensive-school education after 1966 and the gradual disappearance of the grammar school, the main political parties began to interest themselves not only in the organization of schooling but also in its content. But even before this, in March 1962, David Eccles had set up a Curriculum Study Group, consisting of administrators, HMI and outside experts. Eccles envisaged the Group entering, in his own words, 'the secret garden of the curriculum' by means of 'a commando type unit' (Kogan, 1978, p.63). Its task would have been to foresee changes before they became apparent and to identify, analyse and publish accounts of curriculum development in order to inform schools.

The setting up of the Group caused great alarm amongst teachers who feared that a centrally controlled curriculum might result. To alleviate such fears, a DES Working Party on Schools' Curriculum and Examinations, chaired by Sir John Lockwood, was set up and reported in 1964. It recommended the establishment of a Schools Council for the Curriculum and Examinations, financed jointly by the DES and LEAs, to give advice on curriculum and examinations. Teachers were to be in the majority on all the important committees of the Council.

After the setting up of the Council in October 1964, much valuable research and development work was carried out in many areas of the curriculum. Major programmes were initiated including preparation for the raising of the school-leaving age, English sixth-form curricula and examinations, and a separate programme for Wales, as well as projects such as mathematics and science, modern languages and the humanities (HMSO, 1965, p.2). A major criticism which was made of the Council was its identification with teachers' unions and teacher politics. The built-in majority of teachers on the Council's committees was seen by its critics as a means of unduly influencing decision-making. Nevertheless, in 1981, after a review of the Schools Council, Nancy Trenaman, Principal of St. Anne's College, Oxford, in a Report concluded that 'the Schools Council should continue with its present functions'. DES officials in giving evidence to Mrs Trenaman had displayed their dislike of the Schools Council; politically, too, it was unpopular (Mann, 1985, pp.188–90). In April 1982, the Secretary of State, Sir Keith Joseph, announced the Council's closure in March 1984. In its place, two separate bodies were established, the School Curriculum Development Committee (SCDC) and the Secondary Examinations Council (SEC); the membership of both bodies was by nomination of the Secretary of State.

Apart from the Schools Council, the subject of curriculum became a matter for wider debate in the 1960s and 1970s. Much of it was stimulated by the three *Black Papers* issued in 1969 and 1970, with contributions from well-known Conservatives such as Rhodes Boyson and Angus Maude. One of the targets was the progressive aspects of the curriculum which were, it stated, partly responsible for the alleged decline in standards in the 3Rs. The DES set up an Assessment of Performance Unit (APU) in 1974 to monitor and assess the achievement of children at school on a national basis. Testing was subsequently carried out in subjects such as English, mathematics, science and modern languages.

In 1975, the DES was asked to produce for the Labour Prime Minister, James Callaghan, comments on various aspects of public concern on education, including the teaching of the 3Rs in primary schools and curriculum for secondary schools. The Department's critical comments (see Lawton, 1980, pp.37–8) embodied in the secret Yellow Book of 1976 indicated the strong line taken by the DES. The 'Great Debate', which followed Callaghan's Ruskin College speech in October 1976, officially opened the national debate on education.

Regional conferences were convened to discuss four issues, one of which was the curriculum 5–16. A Green Paper was subsequently produced entitled *Education: A Consultative Document* (1977). On curriculum, the publication made some significant comments. The notion of a 'core' or 'protected part' of the curriculum was suggested; LEAs were to carry out a review of curriculum arrangements in their areas in consultation with teachers. Circular 14/77 issued by the DES shortly afterwards requested detailed information on the state of the curriculum in order to build up a national picture. The LEAs' replies were summarized in a DES publication, *Local Authority Arrangements for the School Curriculum* (1979). One question which was posed, 'What curricular elements do the authority regard as essential?', received the following replies:

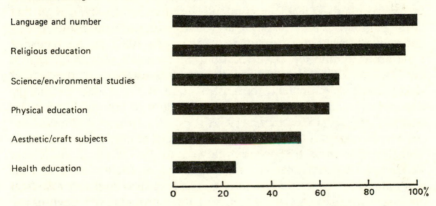

Of the authorities which listed essential primary school subjects, proportion mentioning:

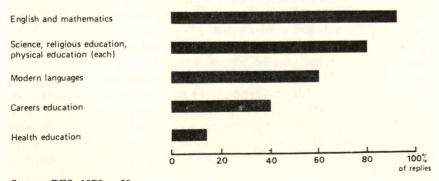

Of the authorities which listed essential secondary school subjects, proportion mentioning:

Source: DES, 1979, p.53.

289

Further evidence of DES initiatives in moving towards a tighter control of the curriculum emerges during the 1980s. HMI had become engaged in curriculum discussion before the Ruskin College speech and were thus in a good position to move foward soon afterwards. Their document *Curriculum 11–16* (1977) set out the case for a common curriculum, based on eight 'areas of experience', the linguistic, ethical, mathematical, physical, scientific, aesthetic and creative, social and political and spiritual. In contrast, the Secretary of State issued a brief document *A Framework for the School Curriculum* (1980), setting out a compulsory curriculum in terms of percentage of the total time which each subject should be allocated.

A clear picture of the tensions existing between DES and HMI can be gained by comparing the HMI response to the DES initiative, *A View of the Curriculum*, which was issued shortly afterwards in 1981. It reiterated the more liberal view expounded in their 1977 document, a far cry from the DES's instrumental approach. However, a further DES pamphlet, *The School Curriculum* (1981), appearing shortly before the *View of the Curriculum*, was strongly attacked by a House of Commons Committee on Education, Science and Arts as being 'a confused document, lacking in intellectual distinction and practicality alike. Many have doubted the DES's competence in this area of the curriculum, and this document ... will do nothing to dispel these doubts' (House of Commons, 1982, i, p.xxv). However, the pressure exerted by the DES on LEAs concerning curriculum policy continued. Circulars 6/81 and 6/83 were followed by the White Paper, *Better Schools*, in March 1985. As part of the government's aims to raise standards and to secure the best possible return from the resources invested in education, the document indicated that the government would take a lead in promoting national agreement about the purposes and the content of the curriculum. The 1986 Education Act required every LEA to provide a curriculum policy, stating their provisions for a balanced and relevant curriculum.

Meanwhile, there were governmental initiatives directed at introducing a larger vocational element in the curriculum. The Technical and Vocational Education Initiative (TVEI), begun in 1983, established courses for 14–18-year-olds for the study of crafts, design and construction. Interestingly, the funds were provided, not by the DES, but by the Department of Industry, as was the Youth Training Scheme for otherwise unemployed 16-year-olds. The city technical colleges, begun in 1988, offer a curriculum with a strong science and technology bias, including work experience.

In the 1987 Conservative party election manifesto, it was announced that there would be a national core curriculum for schools in the event of a Conservative victory. Following their return to government in June 1987, a consultation document, *The National Curriculum 5–16*, was issued in July setting out the need for such a curriculum and its composition. Like the 1980 DES *Framework For a National Curriculum*, the allocation of curriculum time was expressed in percentages. Between 30–40 per cent of curriculum time for years 4 and 5 at the secondary stage was to be devoted to the three core subjects, English, maths and science. Other foundation subjects were: technology, a modern foreign language, history, geography, art, music and physical education. During the passage of the 1988 Education Act, religious education was added, though unlike the others, it has no centrally determined curriculum. No criteria were stated for the inclusion or exclusion of 'subjects'. The consultation document suggests that foundation subjects take up 80–90 per cent of the curriculum 'in schools where there is good practice'.

When the Education Bill was published in November 1987, the Secretary of State, Kenneth Baker, conceded that the time devoted to foundation subjects was excessive and that it should be reduced to 70 per cent. Nevertheless, the over-prescriptive nature of the curriculum, especially when taken with other proposals for attainment targets and centrally imposed assessment procedures, has raised new issues about the future of determining curriculum policy in schools. As one leading educational journal commented on the publication of the 1987 Bill,

> What is being introduced is not a national curriculum but a Nationalized Curriculum. From now on, every political party will have to have its 'policy' for curriculum. Its manifesto will have to tell the world what is to be added or (less likely) taken away. Enter civics, or peace studies or racist awareness training – or Latin. The Nationalized Curriculum will, in short order, be the politicized curriculum. (*TES*, 27 November 1987, p.2)

The new National Curriculum Council must attempt to avoid this pitfall.

One of the outcomes of a national curriculum policy might be a greater concentration on pedagogy, that is, the establishment of general principles of teaching, based on what children have in common, in order to develop increasingly complex skills and abilities or mental operations. This approach to constructing the curriculum, as suggested by Brian Simon (1981, p. 142), differs from the child-centred teaching so long in vogue, and may throw new light on the nature of educational practice in schools.

SUMMARY

The ending of 'payment by results' in 1895 released schools from teaching a prescribed curriculum. Although the Education Department had been issuing more enlightened Codes for some years previously, official advice on the curriculum was not available until ten years later.

Morant wanted the elementary schools to offer a broad curriculum which developed character. The Regulations for Secondary Schools, issued in 1904, were in marked contrast to those for elementary schools. An academic curriculum which included Latin was stipulated, together with time allocations for each subject. Although several new types of school appeared during the first third of the present century, the Board took firm action to prevent the blurring of the curriculum between the elementary and secondary sectors. Aspects of the curriculum, such as that for girls and for sixth forms, were investigated but the curriculum as a whole was largely a traditional one. Nevertheless, the influence of progressive educationists made itself felt in the recommendations of the 1926 Hadow Report and by teachers imbued with the spirit of the new approaches.

Two important Committees, Spens (1938) and Norwood (1943), recommended changes. The former preferred a common curriculum in the 11–13 secondary schools to facilitate transfer; Norwood, on the other hand, recommended separate curricula for the three types of abilities catered for at the secondary stage. The Norwood principle was translated into the tripartite system after the 1944 Education Act.

Official interest in the curriculum was rekindled in 1962 when the Ministry set up the Curriculum Study Group in an attempt to initiate change. Opposition from teachers' unions and LEAs led to the establishment of the Schools Council which was responsible for producing development projects in many aspects of the curriculum. The take-up rate by teachers of these projects was, on the whole, disappointing.

From the mid-1970s, the school curriculum became a leading priority of successive Secretaries of State. There was little disagreement between the political parties on a recommendation contained in the 1977 Green Paper, *Education in Schools: A Consultative Document*, that there should be a review of the design and management of the school curriculum. Both HMI and DES produced discussion papers, the latter taking a harder line.

A more interventionist policy was adopted by the DES on curriculum from the late 1970s. Circulars to LEAs indicated the Department's determination to play a larger part in the determination of the curriculum. Ministerial advocacy of vocationalism has also been reflected in recent curriculum initiatives tied to financial incentives. Unlike the 1944 Education Act, which failed to mention the curriculum, the 1988 Act has, as one of its main features, the establishment of a national curriculum.

FURTHER READING

A detailed account of the elementary school curriculum from 1833 to 1910 is to be found in the *Report of the Board of Education 1910–11*, 1912, pp.2–41. R.D. Bramwell, *Elementary School Work 1900–1925*, 1961, deals with each subject in the school curriculum. For a general history see P. Gordon and D. Lawton, *Curriculum Change in the Nineteenth and Twentieth Centuries*, 1978.

From 1905, the Board of Education issued *Suggestions for the Consideration of Teachers and Others*, renamed, from 1927, *Handbook of Suggestions for Teachers*. Attitudes towards the curriculum by the Board can thus be discerned for the first 40 years of this century. For secondary schools, the Board issued Circulars, e.g. *Curricula of Secondary Schools*, 1913 and 1922. The Prime Minister's Reports, on Natural Science, 1918, on Modern Languages, 1918, on English, 1921 and on Classics, 1921, are under-used sources.

Most of the Reports of Consultative Committees and Central Advisory Councils include sections on curriculum, e.g. Hadow, 1926 and Spens, 1938 of the former, and Newsom, 1963 and Plowden, 1967 of the latter.

I. Goodson, *School Subjects and Curriculum Change*, 1983, and D. Lawton, *The Politics of the School Curriculum*, 1980, deal with the interplay between curriculum and the decision-makers: this point is also graphically illustrated in the demise of the Schools Council, for which see M. Plaskow (ed.), *Life and Death of the Schools Council*, 1985.

Since the 'Great Debate' of 1976, HMI have produced many statements on the curriculum, e.g. *Curriculum 11–16*, 1977, and *A View of the Curriculum*, 1980. Those issued by the DES give a clear indication of ministerial intent, e.g. *Local Authority Arrangements for the School Curriculum*, 1979, *A Framework for the School Curriculum*, 1980, and *The National Curriculum 5–16*, 1987.

CHAPTER TWENTY

School Examinations

There was a striking change in the attitude of central government at the turn of the present century towards the examination systems in elementary and secondary schools. In the former type, the Revised Code of 1862 had ensured that each child was examined annually in the 3Rs with the addition of plain needlework for girls. As the nineteenth century progressed, a more liberal attitude prevailed with a wider choice of subjects being made available for examining. The ending of payment by results in 1895 relieved elementary schools, at least temporarily, of the need to prepare pupils for examinations.

Before the present century, no government had imposed examinations on secondary schools. This had been attempted by the Endowed Schools Bill of 1868, which included provision for an Educational Council, consisting of six representatives of the Universities of Oxford, Cambridge and London and six Crown nominees. The endowed schools would have been examined in any subject nominated by the Council's inspectors, the cost to be paid by the school. Strong opposition by leading public-school headmasters led to the dropping of this part of the bill.

However, the initiative to institute suitable examinations for secondary schools came from universities. In 1858, both Oxford and Cambridge offered 'Local' examinations for schools wishing to enter candidates and granted certificates to successful candidates. A rather different examination was established by London University in 1862. The Matriculation examination, unlike those of the Oxford and Cambridge 'Locals', bore no relation to the course of study which students had undertaken: a narrower range of subjects was laid down by the University and candidates were not confined to the schools. Nevertheless, it became popular as a leaving examination for secondary schools. In 1874, the Oxford and Cambridge School Examinations Board was established specifically for sixth-formers who were aiming at university entrance.

The changes in British society, especially the replacement of patronage by competition for the civil service, Army and entry to the professions further stimulated the demand for examinations. Within schools, there was a proliferation of examinations. Pupils could, by the end of the century, be earning grants from Science and Art Department examinations, from County Councils for proficiency in technical work as well as preparing for 'Local' examinations. Uniquely in Europe, public examinations in England remained in private hands (Roach, 1971, p.256). Action was needed.

Another stimulus for change by the 1890s came from the growing number of elementary-school pupils who were entering the secondary schools. It may be useful to consider this aspect first.

A. ELEMENTARY SCHOOLS

Beginning of Free Place Examinations, 1907–1918

A big step forward in bridging the gap between the elementary and secondary schools came with the 1890 Local Taxation Act which made available sums of money ('whisky money') for technical subjects. An amending act of 1891 expressly allowed the newly-created County Councils to establish scholarships at schools approved by them. Technical Instruction Committees were formed to administer the scholarships. Selection procedures varied; some Committees produced their own examinations whilst others commissioned the Oxford and Cambridge 'Locals' boards to devise them.

The Fabian Society's wish to see a 'broad ladder' of education between the elementary and secondary schools came near to realization with the establishment of the London Technical Education Board in 1892. Headmasters of London's endowed schools had devised examinations for elementary-school pupils in 1890: six years later, there were 6,675 candidates for these examinations. Nationally, in the years 1895 to 1906, the number of scholarships provided by local authorities increased from about 2,500 places to over 23,500.

One of the early decisions taken by the new Board of Education in 1905 was to increase the number of scholarships, following the Regulations of that year which required boys and girls intending to become teachers to attend a secondary school for three or four years. Shortly afterwards, a Liberal ministry, headed by Campbell-Bannerman, was returned to office. In January 1907, the Secondary School Regulations stipulated that in future 25 per cent of secondary school places would be open to public elementary-school pupils who had been in attendance for two years. Education in secondary schools was to be open to children of all classes 'as near as possible upon equal terms'.

However, when discussing the matter with a deputation from the Incorporated Association of Headmasters, McKenna, the President of the Board, admitted that there would be 'certain difficulties' about the qualifying examination. It would be competitive only amongst scholars from public elementary schools. Further, 'it was not in the least his intention that the standard of the secondary school should be lowered in order to admit a different type of intelligence' (PRO ED 24/373, 13 June 1907). Alongside the free-place scheme were the scholarships offered by local authorities and schools with trust schemes. Uniformity of treatment of pupils varied therefore from authority to authority. Up to the First World War, the increase in the number of free-place pupils was low.

	No. of free-place pupils	*% of total admissions*
1908–09	42,200	31.2
1914–15	65,799	33.1

Methods of selection ranged widely. The most popular was the written test. Some authorities, particularly Kent, Northumberland and the West Riding of Yorkshire, included an oral examination to obtain a better all-round picture of the pupils. The use of school records was also recommended by the Board of Education (Board of Education, 1913, p.20). Headteachers of secondary schools set and marked examinations in some areas, and in Nottingham two elementary schools were reserved for children intending to proceed to secondary schools (Gordon, 1980, p.199), and special classes in elementary schools were formed in order to prepare for the relevant examinations. No standard age for entry was stipulated, Circular 569 of 1907 merely recommending that candidates 'as a rule' should be under 12.

Retrenchment and Psychological Testing, 1918–1945

The heady idealism of most governments during wartime when addressing post-war reconstruction was apparent in the Education Act of 1918, which was the product of a coalition ministry. Fisher, the President, was anxious to extend the benefits of free secondary education, a principle voiced by the Labour party. He ordered a Departmental Committee in 1919 to review LEA provision and admission procedures.

Section 4(4) of the 1918 Act had stated that free secondary education should be for those who were 'capable of profiting' by such a course.

The Committee recommended that the normal age of admission should be between 11 and 12 and that, in the first instance, the total of free places should be raised from 25 to 40 per cent. The post-war economic slump and political changes had their effect on this fairly modest scheme. The Interim Report of the notorious Geddes Committee in 1921 recommended a limitation to the existing 25 per cent of free places. During the brief Labour Government of 1924, C.P. Trevelyan produced plans to alleviate the situation in the form of a special grant to LEAs who provided free places in excess of 25 per cent.

Successive Conservative Presidents of the Board of Education, particularly Trevelyan's successor, Lord Eustace Percy, followed a harder line. Circular 1350 of 1925, entitled 'Free Place Grant', announced the ending of the special grants. The Hadow Report *The Education of the Adolescent* (1926) recommended the age of eleven plus as a suitable point for pupils to transfer to secondary schools. The alternatives to the secondary 'grammar' schools (see Chapter 12) which came into being in the post-Hadow era undoubtedly drew off many potential candidates for free places.

Following the economic slump at the end of the decade, savings in education were once more sought. Circular 1421 of 1932 changed the name from 'free place' to 'special place' examination; previous attendance at an elementary school was no longer necessary and open competition was encouraged. Objections to this move came from teachers' organizations, politicians and leading public figures and, although amendments to the Circular were later to be announced, the new conditions militated against working-class pupils' chances of success. The Spens Report on Secondary Education (1938) started from the assumption that there was already sufficient secondary provision and did not argue against selection at 14. One writer summed up the situation as follows:

> The Special Place Examination has become a national institution. It winnows elementary school children into three distinct classes: the best of all (rarely more than 5 per cent) go to secondary schools; the second best (roughly about 15 per cent) go to some such institution as a central school, or a technical school, the remaining 80 per cent stay on at the senior elementary school ... It is difficult, therefore, to over-estimate the importance of the Special Place Examination. Every year, the fate of about a half a million children hangs upon its results. In sheer magnitude it dwarfs every other public examination in the Kingdom. (Ballard, 1936, p. 111)

The nature of the 'eleven plus' examination, as it came to be commonly called, consisted of written (attainment) tests, usually in English and Arithmetic. This was supplemented by an intelligence test. Such tests, developed from the earlier work of Binet, were devised by psychologists in England such as Cyril Burt and Godfrey Thomson. Group tests became popular from the 1920s. Thomson, whose tests were adopted by the first LEA, Northumberland, to use them as part of the selection procedure, saw them as an instrument of social justice; the results, depending less on schooling and home background than did attainment tests, would, he believed, give more opportunities to working-class children (Wiseman, 1961, p.98). The whole-hearted adoption of these tests by LEAs in the early 1920s contrasted with the more cautious approach recommended in official pronouncements such as the Board's pamphlet *Examinations for Scholarships and Free Places in Secondary Schools* (1927).

The confident correspondence of ability, selection procedures and types of secondary schools was seriously questioned in 1938 by two researchers, Gray and Moshinsky, who discovered that between 43 and 72 per cent of central school pupils possessed superior ability to their counterparts in grammar schools (Gray and Moshinsky, 1938, p.147).

The 1944 Education Act achieved universal secondary education, though without the ending of selection. Confidence in the reliability of standardized tests of intelligence was further undermined by socio-logical studies such as those of Floud, Halsey and Martin in Middlesbrough and South-West Hertfordshire, published as *Social Class and Educational Opportunity* in 1956: this showed that selection methods affected the social distribution of opportunity. Psychologists, like P.E. Vernon and those undertaking work for the National Foundation for Educational Research, revealed many unsatisfactory aspects of the use of intelligence tests for selection purposes. Sir Edward Boyle, then Conservative Parliamentary Secretary to the Minister of Education, agreed with Opposition MPs in 1957 that 'the present system of selection causes a great deal of anxiety in many quarters, and it would be both foolish and wrong simply to remain content with it' (*Hansard*, Vol. 568, Col. 759, April 1957).

With the rise of comprehensive education after the war, the problems of selection took a different form. Where grammar schools still existed, selection tests continued; however, many LEAs still retained some aspects of intelligence testing as part of the battery of tests given to pupils transferring from primary to secondary schools.

Revival of central government interest in testing performance of pupils was seen in the establishment of the Assessment of Performance

Unit (APU) by the DES in 1974. This monitoring of national standards in a range of subjects was carried out by norm-referenced tests, but the earlier fears, that the APU's work would affect teaching and learning, have proved unfounded. More serious are the arrangements for testing all pupils at the ages of seven, 11, 14 and 16, as laid down by the 1988 Education Act. Attainment targets, the achievement of which will be seen through a combination of assessment and testing, have been devised in order 'to raise the level of performance of children of all abilities in all subjects'. This quotation from the Secretary of State, Kenneth Baker, during the passage of the bill was followed by an assurance that such tests were not a 'backdoor route to selection' but were aimed at helping children to reach their full potential.

B. SECONDARY SCHOOLS

Central Direction, 1900–1917

A need for rethinking the philosophy of the secondary school, urged by the Bryce Commission in 1895, was taken up by the Board of Education a few years later. One witness before the Consultative Committee on Examinations, in 1911, W.N. Bruce, Principal Assistant Secretary, Secondary Schools Branch, outlined recent changes which affected the examination question.

There had been a remarkable increase in the number of schools and pupils since 1903 when the new LEAs came into being; grants to secondary schools had increased in the following six years from £250,000 to nearly £750,000; the curriculum was much wider; methods of instruction had changed. The existing examination system, as represented by the 'Locals', was no longer adequate to test the educational efficiency or standards at which schools should aim.

Bruce stated that 'a new influence from the outside' was to be acknowledged, the Board of Education itself. Shortly after the Secondary Branch of the Board came into existence in 1903, a Secondary Inspectorate, charged with the task of inspecting schools at regular intervals, was formed and had a powerful effect. The Board's other weapon was the preparation and issue of Circulars which clearly set out the Board's attitudes to a range of issues affecting the secondary school. Like other witnesses from the Board and HMI, Bruce was concerned at the relation between inspection and examination, especially the difficulty of co-ordinating an inspecting body and an examining body which were quite independent of one another (HMSO, 1911, p.437).

The Board was slow to respond to the Consultative Committee's recommendations, its decisions being embodied in Circular 849 issued in 1914. Consultation with the universities had taken place and broad general agreement had been reached. Following the recommendations of the Committee, the Board suggested that the many examinations offered by universities and the professions should be replaced by a single examination in two parts, the first to be taken at about 16 years of age and a second, for sixth-formers, at 18 years. It was hoped that universities would accept the first, a General School Certificate, under certain conditions, as exemption from their own matriculation examination.

The Board's proposals envisaged a broad general education for intelligent secondary-school pupils between the ages of 12 and 16. It was to be a grouped system with candidates being examined in an English subject, a foreign language and a science or mathematics. To gain a Certificate, candidates had to be successful in each of the groups. Evidence of the Board's view of secondary education was demonstrated by its attitude towards practical subjects. A fourth group, consisting of subjects such as housecraft, manual work, music and drawing, was deemed not 'capable of being tested by a written examination'. Unless a candidate had been successful in the three main groups, success in the fourth group was not endorsed on the Certificate.

Much dissatisfaction was voiced at the Board's lack of recognition of Group IV subjects. The widening basis of entry to secondary schools since 1907 and the changing nature of the curriculum in secondary schools were not reflected in the compulsory elements of the Certificate. The National Union of Teachers complained that the Circular assumed that a strictly academic examination was appropriate 'regardless of the fact that by far the greater proportion of the scholars do not, and never will, proceed to the University' (quoted in O. Banks, 1955, p. 86). In the face of such criticisms, the Board allowed, by Circular 1002 in 1917, examining boards to experiment in bringing practical subjects within the scope of the examination. In 1918, the Northern Universities Joint Matriculation Board was allowed to count one Group IV subject towards a Certificate.

Co-ordination and Co-operation, 1917–1943

H. A. L. Fisher, in introducing the Education Estimates in the Commons in April 1917, stated: 'There are no less than one hundred separate examinations for which boys in a secondary school may, at one time or another, desire to prepare.' Shortly afterwards, in May, Circular 996 announced the creation of a Secondary School

Examinations Council (SSEC) from August 1917. The Board of Education would now act as a co-ordinating authority for examinations with the help of representatives from universities, LEAs and the Teachers' Registration Council. The SSEC would approve the different examining bodies, monitor and maintain standards and promote conferences for those concerned with the examinations. An attractive feature of the Circular was that the Board undertook to pay the fees of schools on the grant list for pupils undertaking an approved examination (Roach, 1979, p.51). A further Circular laid down that only two examinations, the School Certificate, to be taken at about 16, and Higher School Certificate, for sixth-formers, would be recognized by the Board. Subsequently, seven examining bodies were approved.

The setting up of the SSEC did not allay the fears of LEAs and teachers' associations that the Board was making a bid for the central control of examinations. For one thing, the SSEC was merely an advisory body: the Board of Education had, theoretically at least, the power to withhold approval of the Certificate examinations of an examining board. Financially, too, the Board was in a very strong position to influence events.

Many of these fears were without foundation. The SSEC was composed in the first instance of 21 members, 10 of whom were from examining bodies, six from the Teachers' Registration Council and four from LEAs. Compromises between the SSEC and examining bodies were worked out where opinions differed, and the President of the Board of Education never used his powers against an examining board (Petch, 1953, p.76). Nevertheless, it can be argued that the full-scale investigations of various examinations by the SSEC of the examining bodies, with the approval of the President, precluded this necessity. The President nominated small subject panels, consisting of HMI, university teachers and school teachers, to scrutinize each of the examining bodies in all aspects of their work (Brereton, 1944, p.96). Between the wars, the School Certificate was investigated in 1918, 1924 and 1931 and the Higher School Certificate in 1920, 1926 and 1937. The two examinations were monitored simultaneously. The popularity of the examinations can be seen from the entry figures during this period.

	School Certificate	*Higher School Certificate*
1918	14,108	550
1938	77,010	13,201

Central Control, 1943–1964

In the years before the Second World War, doubts were being expressed about the nature and suitability of the two examinations. The traditionalism of the syllabus and the lack of innovation were striking: for example, only four subjects were added to the list offered by one of the examining bodies, the Joint Matriculation Board, between 1918 and 1950, namely, geometrical and machine drawing, agricultural science, mechanical engineering and general science. An enquiry by C.W. Valentine, Professor of Education, Birmingham University, published under the title *The Reliability of Examinations* in 1932, demonstrated the variation in standards of marking, the varying difficulty of different papers and the effect of coaching (Valentine, 1932, pp. 162–3).

The Board of Education had also been aware for some years of the unsatisfactory relationship between the School Certificate examinations and Matriculation. The latter, originally designed for those proceeding to university, had become, in the eyes of prospective employers, a more desirable qualification. In the face of some opposition, the Board introduced regulations, to take effect from 1938, which removed from the School Certificate the burden of its use for university entrance qualification. Instead, the School Certificate and satisfactory performance at least a year later in the Higher School Certificate examination was substituted.

In the same year, the Spens Committee's Report asserted that 'the attempt to combine the two different objects [of selecting students for the university, and testing the schoolwork of the remainder] in one examination has been disastrous' (HMSO, 1938, p. 258). Limited by its terms of reference to 16-year-olds, the Committee made some pertinent comments on the School Certificate examination. Too many subjects were being studied and it suggested that candidates should be required to pass in only five subjects. The grouping system was considered too rigid: for example, candidates should be allowed to offer a foreign language or science and not necessarily both.

It was as a result of such criticisms that the 'investigators' of the SSEC, who carried out scrutinies of the examining boards (see p. 301 earlier) suggested to the Council in their 1937 Report that a committee should be established by the SSEC 'to initiate a long-term policy involving fundamental changes in school examinations'. In 1941, the chairman of SSEC, Sir Cyril Norwood, nominated members of the SSEC for a Committee on Curriculum and Examinations in Secondary

Schools 'to consider suggested changes in the secondary school curriculum and the question of school examinations in relation thereto'. Norwood himself acted as its chairman.

The Norwood Report, published in 1943, following on from Spens, recommended a radical shake-up of the examination system. It envisaged the replacement of external by internal examinations controlled by teachers; with the need to provide for the technical and modern schools, as well as grammar schools, this would be a more appropriate mode of examining. Until this change was achieved, the Report continued, the School Certificate examination should be without restrictions as to the minimum number of subjects and the 'group' requirement would be abolished. The Higher School Certificate was to be replaced by an external leaving certificate at eighteen plus. Returning to the notion advanced by the 1911 Consultative Committee of the relationship between examination and inspection (Norwood had been a member of this committee), the Norwood Report recommended an enlarged Inspectorate to accompany the new system.

Petch (1953, p.165) bitterly calls the circumstances in which the Norwood Report was published 'official chicanery'. Although the SSEC had initiated the Committee, Norwood bypassed it, reporting directly to R.A. Butler, then President of the Board of Education, in June 1943. In November, the SSEC was summoned for a two-day meeting on the Report. Norwood informed the members that they were assembled to receive the Report and not to discuss it. When it appeared that members would voice their disapproval, the meeting was dismissed after two hours.

Ellen Wilkinson, Minister of Education in the Attlee government, 1945–47, confirmed her acceptance of the Norwood proposals. The 1944 Education Act had changed the Minister's position from one of co-ordinator of secondary school examinations to that of directing policy in relation to them. By Circular 113 of June 1946, Wilkinson adopted this role, reconstituting the SSEC: one consequence was that the examining boards no longer had representation. Now there were six Ministry officials who acted as assessors and both secretaries were HMI (Montgomery, 1965, p.71). In 1947, the first Report of the new Council was issued, approving the Norwood proposals for examination reform.

The new General Certificate of Education (GCE) was established at three levels: the Ordinary (O) level for pupils of 16, the Advanced (A) level for pupils of 18, and Scholarship (S) level for those wishing to compete for university awards. Students staying on for A levels were not required to first take O level papers. As recommended by

Norwood, they were 'subject' not 'grouped' examinations, without restriction on choice.

Banks (1955, p.206) has written, 'It is impossible, in considering the various official pronouncements since 1947 to avoid the conclusion that the Minister was using the new examination as part of the general policy to raise the standards of secondary grammar education.' In the first examination taken in 1951, the standard of a pass was fixed between pass and credit levels in the School Certificate; in the following year this was raised to the old credit level. The Ministry made clear in a Circular issued in 1952 that it was 'not an examination primarily designed for school leavers as such'. Many educationists considered the Ministry's attitude to be too rigid. The majority of pupils still left school at 16 and the former School Certificate had been seen as a leaving certificate, with examinations in a range of subjects approximately reflecting the secondary school curriculum. Now, it was felt that the majority of pupils were being sacrificed for those who would be staying on until 18. Employers, too, were familiar with the School Certificate and would not appreciate the higher standards accorded to the grades of the new O level examination. Teachers were unhappy with the prospect of an internal examination in the future and were pleased that the GCE was to be an external examination in the first instance, as the School Certificate had been. (In fact, it remained largely an external examination throughout its existence.) The age restriction proved troublesome: on the one hand, very able pupils were unable to enter for the examination before the age of 16 whilst on the other, secondary modern schools, where the school-leaving age was still 15, were handicapped. In the face of these criticisms, in 1952 the SSEC recommended the abolition of the age restriction, and the Ministry relaxed some of the more rigorous requirements two years later.

In 1955, the Ministry, in its Circular 289, indicated its lack of enthusiasm for the establishment of any new examinations. Secondary modern schools, where there was now a substantial growth in GCE, found a useful avenue for examination candidates through the creation of a new GCE board. All eight existing boards were of university origin. A ninth board, the Associated Examining Board, sponsored by the City and Guilds of London Institute, the Royal Society of Arts and the London Chamber of Commerce and catering for technical and commercial as well as academic interests, came into being in 1955. Whereas in 1954 there were 5,500 pupils entered for GCE subjects, by 1958 it had risen to 16,787 (Montgomery, 1978, pp.47–8).

Even so, this growth did little to satisfy the parents and teachers of the majority of modern school pupils for whom the GCE was an unrealistic target. Whilst Norwood had encouraged the use of internal school examinations, the SSEC went further and recommended that these should be used for the 15-year-old modern school leaver. Although such local examinations organized by teachers had been in operation for some years, it was not until the 1950s that they became more common. A good example was the Harrow School Leaving Certificate, which began in 1954. Based on their last year's work at school, pupils were examined by papers set and marked within the schools and externally moderated. The Council responsible for the Certificate included representatives of industry, LEA, HMI and teachers.

Government reluctance to provide a national examination below GCE level continued. Urged by the SSEC to review the question of external examinations below GCE by referring to it in an *ad hoc* committee in 1957, the Education Minister, Hailsham, placed the matter with the Central Advisory Council. This was a tactical move by the Ministry in its campaign against external examinations in modern schools. The Council members, headed by Geoffrey Crowther, were nominated by the Minister and were, in the absence of interest groups amongst its membership, free from persuasive pressure. A new Minister, Geoffrey Lloyd, in 1958 agreed to allow the SSEC to form a sub-committee to investigate the matter. The chairman, Robert Beloe, invited an observer from the Crowther Committee to its own meetings and the Central Advisory Council conducted no enquiries of its own (Fisher, 1982, p.54). The Beloe Report, published in 1960, recommended an examination based on a two-year course for 16-year-olds in the next 20 per cent of the ability range below those attempting GCE O level. This group would take four or more subjects, with a further 20 per cent entering for fewer. Two aspects were emphasized: the examination, the Certificate of Secondary Education (CSE), was not to be modelled on the GCE but should be specially designed to meet the needs of the pupils, and the examinations were to be largely in the hands of teachers. David Eccles, the Conservative Minister of Education at the time, addressing a Party Conference, admitted that he did not favour such an examination on the grounds of its effect on children. It is interesting to note that the Beloe Report favoured regional bodies to administer the CSE to allow for full teacher participation rather than leave the examination in the hands of LEAs who might wish to play a larger part in determining the curriculum. In December 1962, Sir Edward Boyle, then Minister, approved the new examination. The co-existence from 1965 of GCE and CSE raised the problem of the relationship between the two examinations. With the spread of comprehensive education, teachers were faced with the decision of entering pupils for one or other of the examinations. The CSE results were expressed in five 'grades' plus an ungraded category. Increasing pressure, mainly from teachers, led to a demand for CSE Grade 1 to be made the equivalent to pass at GCE O level in order to meet the requirements of professional bodies and universities. The acceptance of this principle demonstrated that, in the eyes of many, the CSE was seen as an inferior examination which divided pupils within comprehensive schools as clearly as had been the case between grammar and modern schools.

Partnership to Central Intervention, 1964 onwards

With the setting up of the Schools Council for Curriculum and Examinations in 1964, the SSEC was disbanded. Now, the Schools Council was responsible for advising the Secretary of State on aspects of examination policy. It soon began to commission research and development work in the area of public examinations and was the official co-ordinating body for the GCE and CSE boards. It has been shown (Lawton, 1980, pp. 100–3) that the Schools Council was vulnerable to attacks from both the political right, who regarded any change in examinations as subversive, and the left, who wished to abolish 16 plus examinations as well as introduce major reforms at sixth form level. Proposals made in 1969 for a two-tier A level examination, Q (Qualifying) and F (Further), foundered because of outside opposition. A further recommendation for a 20-point grading system for A level, proposed in 1970, was rejected by the new Secretary of State for Education, Margaret Thatcher.

Stimulated by the prospect of the raising of the leaving age to 16 in 1972–3, progress was made on the reform of examinations at 16 plus. Trials carried out by the Schools Council in 1973 with CSE and GSE boards demonstrated that a common system of examinations rather than a single common examination for this age group was feasible. Although the Labour Secretary of State, Shirley Williams, accepted in 1976 the recommendation that GCE O level and CSE should be replaced by a common system, she yielded to pressure that the matter should be further considered. A steering group was set up, consisting of DES officials and HMI and chaired by Sir James Waddell. Its report, *Secondary School Examinations. A Single System at 16 Plus*, published in October 1978, largely confirmed the Schools Council's findings. Attention was drawn to the development of examining techniques and experience gained from CSE and the substantial body of expertise available from the boards and teachers. But, it pointed out, 'On the other hand, we also have a two-part examination system whose parts are not related to any natural division of pupils by ability or aspiration and a multiplicity of syllabuses and certificates issued by 22 independent boards which are a source of confusion to many people not least the employers' (DES, 1978, p.3). Evidence for the need for reform was provided by a breakdown of entries for the two examinations (see table below). Some attempts were also being made to bridge the separateness by the offering of joint 16+ examinations.

SUMMARY OF STATISTICS OF ENTRIES FOR GCE O-LEVEL, CSE AND
JOINT EXAMINATIONS SUMMER 1976
(extracted from *Statistics of Education 1976* Volume 2)

Subject	Total GCE O-Level Entries (including joint examinations)	Total CSE Entries (all Modes) (including joint examinations)	Total Entries Joint 16+ Examinations
English Language	452,179	} 471,525	28,077
English Literature	248,485		5,178
Mathematics	270,297	377,731	16,101
Physics	137,929	98,276	6,927
Chemistry	112,221	63,427	4,374
Biology	209,559	153,583	6,666
History	149,242	144,486	5,731
Geography	188,765	166,332	6,814
French	152,459	115,999	7,386
German	44,246	20,790	1,299
Latin	} 32,035	} 4,203	} 1,814
Latin and Classical Studies			
Commerce	29,472	39,828	2,275
Sociology and other Social Studies	42,398	109,888	602
Religious Studies	63,717	47,536	563
Craft, Design, Technology	20,534	58,482	892
Technical Drawing	49,858	83,266	3,175
Home Economics	5,030	102,474	2,324
Needlecraft	21,385	38,825	698
Art	112,422	148,820	12,120
Music	18,034	13,304	243

The Steering Committee recommended one examining system for pupils completing five years of secondary education with all certificates issued in single form. The examinations would be administered by a smaller number of examining authorities, five in all, which were regional consortia of the former GCE/CSE boards. The General Certificate of Secondary Education (GCSE) would provide an assessment of performance, on a single subject basis, for the range of candidates covered by existing examinations, i.e. 60 per cent of the secondary school population, on a seven-point scale corresponding to O level and CSE grades. Syllabuses were to be governed by national criteria with differentiated papers or questions in all subjects to accommodate the differing abilities of candidates. Grade-related criteria were to be used. The starting date for the new examinations, it was hoped, would be 1983, with the first candidates sitting two years later. One important feature was the greater participation of teachers in the examining process.

The reform of A level examinations presented many more difficulties. Following the rejection of the Q and F proposals, a joint working party of the Standing Committee for University Entrance and Schools Council was established. In 1973, it proposed that there should be a five-subject curriculum at two levels. Two subjects would be taken at the N (Normal) or higher level, and three at the F (Further) or lower level. All would be taken after two years in the sixth form. These proposals were debated throughout the country at meetings. In July 1979, Mark Carlisle, the Conservative Secretary of State, pronounced against any changes in A levels. His Labour predecessor, Shirley Williams, had also been reluctant to support reform.

Some progress was made with the announcement in March 1985, in the Government's White Paper *Better Schools* (Cmnd. 9496), that some broadening of the A-level examined curriculum could be achieved by A/S levels. These would involve half the time occupied by A levels and could be seen as complementary to or contrasting with them. A/S levels were first examined in September 1988.

A Government-appointed committee under Professor Gordon Higginson reported in June 1988 on ways in which A levels might be reformed. It recommended that five rather than three subjects should be the norm, leaner but tougher syllabuses and a range of new A/S levels which would 'service' main choice subjects, such as mathematics for humanities students and modern languages for scientists. The Higginson proposals were widely welcomed, but were rejected by Kenneth Baker, the Secretary of State. Senior officials at the DES stated that the Government found that the proposals would lead to reduced standards (*Times Educational Supplement*, 10 June 1988).

Also at the post-16 level is the Certificate of Pre-Vocational Education (CPVE), a one-year full-time course for a wide variety of abilities and administered by the Business and Technical Education Council, operating since 1986. Somewhat different in character is the Record of Achievement to be provided for all pupils leaving school. Prepared within the framework of a national policy, Records of Achievement can take account of both curricular and extra-curricular activities and will be used both by future employers and for admission to higher education.

Since the demise of the Schools Council and its replacement by two bodies, the Secondary Examinations Council (SEC), and the School Curriculum Development Committee (SCDC), the centralist tendency in both fields has increased dramatically. Sir Keith Joseph, in a speech at Sheffield in January 1984, announced plans to establish the goal of bringing 80–90 per cent of all pupils to the level now attained in individual subjects by pupils of average ability. The SEC was empowered to scrutinize individual GCSE syllabuses to ensure that they met the relevant national criteria. Courses began two years later, in 1986. It has been criticized by teachers for the hurriedness of its introduction, and by researchers (Macintosh, 1985, p. 7) for maintaining a single subject structure which fails to reflect present-day requirements. The five GCSE groups in England and Wales also maintain, to a certain extent, their previous autonomy.

Only six years after the SEC and SCDC were set up, they were superseded by the National Curriculum Council (NCC) and the Schools Examinations and Assessment Council (SEAC). The latter, under the terms of the Education Reform Act, 1988, has a wider remit, including the approval of public examination syllabuses. SEAC also monitors the Task Group on Assessment and Testing, which has drawn up graded schemes for assessing pupils nationally from the age of seven in a number of curriculum areas; this development may have a serious impact on public examinations in the future.

The concern expressed by the 1911 Consultative Committee on the question of inspection and examination has recently been revived by the requirement of the 1980 Education Act for schools to publish their examination results. Since 1983, reports by HMI on individual schools have been made public and attempts are being made by inspectors to evaluate schools' performance in a broader context (Gray and Hannon, 1986, p. 23).

A multiplicity of examinations once more exists, with their different principles of assessment and different target groups and their lack of flexibility in credit transfer. To what extent locally-based systems of validation can conform with national standards remains an open question. Centralization of the examination system has by no means solved the difficult relationship between curriculum and examinations.

SUMMARY

Unlike many other developments in English education, the examination system is largely a product of the secondary sector. It is a remarkable fact that, apart from the period of the Revised Code in the nineteenth century, examinations for elementary-school-leavers were never imposed. However, with the operation of Free Place Regulations from 1907, an increasing number of elementary school pupils sat the 'eleven plus' examination for entry to the new municipal grammar schools.

The demand for university-set examinations by secondary schools led to the Oxford and Cambridge 'Local' examinations from 1858. As the number of secondary schools grew during the late nineteenth and twentieth centuries, other examination boards came into being. The multiplicity of examinations available was noted by the 1911 Consultative Committee, which in turn recommended their replacement by a nationally-based School Certificate Examination. This was to be at two levels. The Board of Education bestowed its tardy approval on the plan some six years later.

With the setting up of the Secondary School Examinations Council in 1917 to oversee the new examination, the Board kept a vigilant watch on its progress through the civil servants and HMI who were members of the Council. Criticisms were made of the examination by the Spens and Norwood Committees. In 1951, the General Certificate of Education, a single-subject examination, replaced the School Certificate Examination. The Ministry's Circulars demonstrated that the new examination was designed for grammar-school pupils, being taken normally at the age of 16. Secondary modern schools were at first excluded. Much pressure was required to persuade the Ministry of the need for an examination suitable for this group. The Beloe Report (1960) paved the way for the Certificate of Secondary Education.

The existence of the two examinations raised anomalies in schools, especially with the spread of comprehensive education. The Schools Council, which had superseded the Secondary School Examinations Council, put forward plans for the reform of examinations, and recommended a common system. Although this was accepted in principle in 1976 by the Secretary of State, Shirley Williams, the first courses did not begin for a further ten years. Meanwhile, the introduction of national examinations offered by various agencies for the 16 to 18 range has once more complicated the picture.

FURTHER READING

Two of the most detailed accounts of the origins of the examination system are R.J. Montgomery, *Examinations*, 1965, and J.R. Roach, *Public Examinations in England 1850–1900*, 1971. An early twentieth-century view can be seen in the Report of the Consultative Committee on Examinations in Secondary Schools, 1911.

The relationship between examining boards and the Board/Ministry of Education during the School Certificate era is described in J.L. Brereton, *The Case For Examinations*, 1944, and J.A. Petch, *Fifty Years of Examining*, 1953. For events leading to the General Certificate of Education examination, see P. Fisher, *External Examinations in Secondary Schools in England and Wales 1944–1964* (1982). A key publication here is the Report of the Committee of the Secondary School Examinations Council, *Curriculum and Examinations in Secondary Schools* (Norwood Report), 1943.

Entry examinations to secondary schools, known as the 'eleven plus', and governmental policies are dealt with in K. Lindsay, *Social Progress and Educational Waste*, 1926, P. Gordon, *Selection For Secondary Education*, 1980, and G. Sutherland, *Ability, Merit and Measurement, Mental Testing and English Education, 1880–1940*, 1984.

Reforms in examinations are demonstrated in the Report of the Secondary School Examinations Council on *Examinations other than GCE* (Beloe Report), 1960, and the Report of the DES Working Party on *Schools' Curricula and Examinations* (Lockwood Report), 1964. Moves towards a common system of examining are considered in the DES Report, *School Examinations*, 1978. See also the Evidence and Reports of the Education, Science and Arts Committee of the House of Commons, *The Secondary School Curriculum and Examinations*, 1982, and DES, *Examinations at 16-plus: a statement of policy*, 1982.

Conclusion

Conclusion: The 1988 Act

There are few overall conclusions in history, and the attempt to draw any in respect of contemporary or near contemporary history is doomed to failure. Nevertheless the Education Reform Act of 1988 marks a watershed in educational policy in England, and represents, in itself, both a conclusion and a new beginning. Its implementation, even were it to be significantly modified, will determine the shape of educational policy until the end of the century and beyond. Indeed, on two accounts, it will probably prove to be the most significant single piece of educational legislation in the country's history.

The first relates to its breadth. Virtually no part of the education service has been left untouched, from the infant school child preparing by means of the national curriculum for a first national assessment at age seven, to the university teacher deprived of tenure for taking a promotion.

The second main feature is that the Act marks a reversal of many of the main directions of twentieth-century educational policy. For example, at a stroke, the powers of the LEAs have been seriously curtailed, and the largest of them, the Inner London Education Authority, simply abolished. Polytechnics and larger colleges have been removed from local authority control, whilst schools have been given the opportunity to opt out and to seek grant-maintained status.

At first sight the legislation appears to be consistent with the market-oriented and privatization philosophies which have characterized the policies of Margaret Thatcher's governments since her advent to power in 1979. Parents will have more freedom to exercise choice; individual schools, through their governing bodies and head teachers, will have more responsibilities for their finances and staffing. Some 94 per cent of parents, however, voted for the continuation of ILEA, rather than for its demise. The crucial issue of what shall be taught in schools, moreover, having been taken away from the producers – the teachers – has not been given to the consumers – the pupils, parents and employers – but has been placed firmly in the hands of central government in the shape of the Secretary of State.

This concluding chapter will be divided into three parts: the background, provisions, and implementation of the 1988 Act.

BACKGROUND

In 1984, some 40 years on from the Butler Act, several tributes were paid to the quality of that legislation, and to its enduring qualities. Two commentators, however (Aldrich and Leighton, 1985), employing historical and legal perspectives, argued rather that the 1944 Act was seriously outdated, and that many current educational problems stemmed both from its omissions, and from a failure of implementation. Attention was called to four particular areas of concern: role of central government, definition of the powers of the various groups engaged in education and the relationship between them, curriculum, and educational provision for the 16 to 19 age range. They concluded that a major new act was long overdue and that an immediate consultation process should be begun to secure this end.

By 1987 the Conservative government had arrived at the same conclusion, though by a different route. Public concern about education had been growing since the early 1970s. Such concern was of a bipartisan nature, and in 1976 it was a Labour Prime Minister, James Callaghan, whose 'common-sense' criticisms, in a speech at Ruskin College began, or significantly developed, the debate. Many of Callaghan's complaints – that schools were not preparing pupils adequately for the world of work, that the most able brains went into academic life or the civil service rather than into commerce and industry, that technology was neglected in the curricula of schools and colleges – had been voiced for a hundred years and more. But his doubts about progressive methods of teaching, his expression of a personal preference for a basic curriculum with universal standards, and his perception that education had swung from being over-concerned, as in the days of his youth, with producing docile factory fodder, to being over-concerned with self-expression and education for its own sake, indicated public concern that the educational priorities of the 1960s had become a liability. In the 1970s the United Kingdom's severe relative economic decline was bound to lead to a serious questioning of whether the country was getting value for money for the £6 billion spent annually on education. The perceived self-indulgence of the educational world, a self-indulgence characterized in the popular mind by such images as scruffy teachers, the William Tyndale affair, truanting pupils, rioting students, and the destructive pervasiveness of the new subject of sociology, was to be subjected to the doctrine of public accountability. Though Callaghan was careful to distance himself from what he referred to as *'Black Paper* prejudices', his question as to 'the proper way of monitoring the use of resources in order to maintain a proper national standard of performance' was exactly the same question as that which Keith Joseph and Kenneth Baker were to address, with much greater vigour, in the 1980s.

Nevertheless, in spite of Sir Keith Joseph's commitment to radical educational reform based upon competition and market forces, and in spite of his desire to implement a system of educational vouchers, his lengthy tenure of office as Secretary of State, from 1981 to 1986, was a disappointment to many Conservatives, a period characterized by piecemeal changes and the further disruption of schools by teachers. His successor, however, proceeded with all speed. Though a full-blown voucher system was not included, the Baker Bill, unlike the legislation of 1986 and 1987, was by any standards a massive measure, and one which was introduced with a minimum of time allowed for consultation and response.

PROVISIONS

The Education Reform Act of 1988 comprises 238 sections and 13 schedules. The first 25 sections are concerned with the national curriculum and national assessment. All maintained schools must provide for pupils during the compulsory years, 5 to 16, a balanced curriculum which includes three core subjects – English, mathematics and science – and a further seven foundation subjects – history, geography, technology, music, art, physical education and, in secondary schools, a modern foreign language. Religious education and religious worship are also required, and in Welsh schools the Welsh language is included as a core or foundation subject. Children are also to be tested in subjects of the national curriculum at ages seven, 11, 14 and 16. The national curriculum and national testing will apply in full to grant-maintained schools, but not to city technology colleges, nor to independent schools. Under Section 14 of the Act two National Curriculum Councils, one for England and one for Wales, and a School Examinations and Assessment Council are to be appointed by the Secretary of State who, though he must publish their reports, is not required to follow their advice. Though the principle of a national or core curriculum has received wide support, these particular proposals have been attacked from several sides. Conservatives, including Keith Joseph himself, have seen them as too restrictive, as placing too much power in the hands of the Secretary of State, and as outdated, both in terms of their expression simply in subject form, and in the very list of subjects itself, which mirrors that of the Secondary School Regulations of 1904.

Sections 26 to 32 deal with the admission of pupils to schools. Each school is designated as having a standard number of places, a calculation which takes the 1979 entry number as a base line. The principle of open enrolment gives parents the freedom to choose schools, and requires schools to admit pupils up to their maximum capacity. Thus, if in a given area there are 600 school places available for a particular age group, spread evenly across three schools, but only 400 pupils, unfettered parental choice may result in one school filling all 200 places, another 180, and the third merely 20.

Sections 33 to 51 cover the two areas of 'Finance and Staff'. They provide for a system whereby LEAs must prepare schemes, to be approved by the Secretary of State, to distribute funds on a weighted per capita basis to all secondary schools, and to primary schools with 200 or more pupils. School governing bodies will then be responsible for controlling these funds, and for appointing and dismissing staff.

Sections 52 to 104 are devoted to the issue of grant-maintained schools. The revolutionary nature of such a proposal is indicated by the more than 50 sections which had to be included to secure this end. All secondary schools, and primary schools with 300 pupils or more, may, if they so wish, choose to opt out of local authority control, and, if the Secretary of State approves, become grant-maintained, with direct financing from central government. Central government, however, will recoup from the local authority the money which it would have spent on the school had it not opted out. Parents may ballot on whether to opt out. If half of those eligible to vote do so, then a simple majority will decide the issue. If fewer than half of those eligible vote, then a second ballot must be held within 14 days. On this occasion the result will be binding, whatever the turnout. Whether the number of schools choosing to opt out will be a trickle or become a flood, is not at present clear.

Miscellaneous provisions under this first part of the Act, Sections 105–19, include such issues as the establishment of city technology colleges and city colleges for the technology of the arts, and charges in maintained schools.

Part two is concerned with higher and further education. Section 120 removes from local authorities the previous requirement to make provision for higher education. Subsequent sections provide for the establishment of higher education corporations, and of two new funding bodies, one for universities, the other for polytechnics and colleges. New arrangements for the finance and government of locally-funded further and higher education are also specified.

Sections 162 to 196 declared that the ILEA was to cease on 1 April

1990, and made provision for the transfer of its responsibilities to the 12 London boroughs and to the City of London.

The remaining Sections, 197–238, entitled 'Miscellaneous and General' cover such topics as the establishment of an Education Assets Board, the abolition of academic tenure and the outlawing of bogus degrees.

IMPLEMENTATION

One of the most significant features of twentieth-century educational legislation has been the gap between statute and practice. For example the continuation schools of the 1918 Act soon withered and died, whilst the county colleges of 1944 never even saw the light of day. Given the size and scope of the 1988 Act, its reversal of many previous policies, and the lack of consultation which preceded it, implementation will not be easy. For example, if the national curriculum is to be delivered, and if mathematics and science are to be the first secondary school subjects to be assessed at age 14, then the issue of providing sufficient qualified teachers in these subjects must be urgently addressed. The cost of recruiting such teachers, and teachers of other shortage subjects such as modern languages and technology, and of equipping all schools adequately to teach science and technology, added to the costs which will be incurred by the actual testing itself, will amount to a considerable sum.

It has been argued that such expenditure can be supplied by making savings in other areas, and that local school management will reduce overheads and administrative costs and enable more money and resources to be concentrated upon classroom teaching. There is, indeed, much spare capacity within the school system. For example, between 1974 and 1986 the number of primary school children in Kent fell by 35,000, nearly a quarter of the total, so that by 1988 Kent's schools had nearly 50,000 spare places, places which cost the LEA more than £7 million a year. Nevertheless this figure represented less than 2 per cent of the education budget, and whilst open enrolment may, in the short term, make it easier to close unpopular schools, there is no guarantee either than open enrolment will make for a more efficient overall use of education resources, or that grant-maintained schools will be cheaper to run than existing schools. Certainly the unit cost per pupil in a city technology college is likely to be higher than that of a pupil in a maintained school. If sufficient resources are not forthcoming, if schools are forced to make do with unqualified teachers, as in the nineteenth century, if rapidly declining pupil numbers in a school, as a result of open enrolment, produce a collapse of staffing and curriculum, forcing pupils from different age ranges into the same classroom, there to be supervised by an untrained apprentice, then the quality of education will simply, and demonstrably, deteriorate.

Two broader issues of implementation should also be noticed. Concentration of power into the hands of the Secretary of State will result in a large increase of work for the central administration, an increase which will necessarily transfer more power into the hands of central bureaucracy. It seems improbable that at present the Department of Education and Science has the necessary staffing and resources to fulfil the duties which will devolve upon it under the Act. Further expenditure will be necessary here.

Concentration of so much power into the hands of the Secretary of State will also permit rapid and fundamental changes of educational policy. For example, a different government, even a different Secretary of State in the present government, might have a very different view about such matters as grant-maintained schools, or the national curriculum. Margaret Thatcher and Kenneth Baker differed widely as to the number of grant-maintained schools which they envisaged. Keith Joseph, both before and during the passage of the bill, opposed the central imposition of a single curriculum upon all schools. Thus, on ideological grounds, one Secretary of State might make the terms for opting out so attractive that all schools would wish to leave local authority control. Another could, within a very short space of time, close them all down. Powers over the curriculum are even more firmly placed in the hands of the Secretary of State. The present government has decreed that a very traditional curriculum should be studied. Future political, social or economic changes may result in rapid and fundamental changes in what children are required to learn in the schools of England and Wales.

In conclusion, therefore, implementation of the 1988 Act, coupled with new developments, especially in the fields of further and higher education, will constitute the policy agenda for the final decade of the twentieth century.

FURTHER READING

R. Aldrich and P. Leighton, *Education: Time for a New Act?*, 1985, provides an historical and legal analysis of the case for major legislation. J. Haviland (ed.), *Take Care, Mr. Baker!*, 1988, is an invaluable digest of the thousands of responses to the various consultation papers, whilst D. Lawton and C. Chitty (eds.), *The National Curriculum*, 1988, and B. Simon, *Bending the Rules*, 1988, provide stern critiques of the proposed legislation. For an excellent summary and guide to the Act itself see S. Maclure, *Education Re-formed*, 1988. On implementation see M. Leonard, *The 1988 Education Act. A Tactical Guide for Schools*, 1988, which provides advice from an author who believes that the Act is both misconceived and flawed, on how to secure the highest possible standards of education under the new legislation.

Appendix

1899   *Board of Education* established. Consultative Committee to advise Board on matters referred to it.

1902   *Balfour Education Act*: creation of Local Education Authorities (LEAs) following abolition of school boards; voluntary (Church) schools given rate aid.

1904   *Report of Interdepartmental Committee on Physical Deterioration:* drew attention to the health and well-being of school children.

1907   *Free Place Regulations* allowed free places for up to 25 per cent of secondary school population.

        School Medical Service established by Board of Education.

1911   *Report of Consultative Committee on Examinations in Secondary Schools:* recommended system of public examinations at 16.

1917   *Secondary School Examinations Council* set up: beginning of School Certificate Examination.

1918   *Fisher Education Act:* proposed raising the school-leaving age to 15; part-time schooling from 14 years of age eventually up to 18; 50 per cent of approved LEA expenditure to be met by government.

1919   *University Grants Committee* established.

        Burnham Committee instituted national pay scales for elementary teachers.

        Report of Committee on Adult Education (Smith): recommended establishment of university extra-mural departments.

1921   *Report of Committee on National Expenditure (Geddes):* led to a reduction of £6½ million in the education estimates for 1922.

1922   *British Broadcasting Company* established.

1926   *Report of Consultative Committee on the Education of the Adolescent (Hadow):* recommended the separation of primary and secondary education at the age of 11. 'Modern' as well as grammar schools to be established.

1931   *Report of the Consultative Committee on the Primary School (Hadow):* curriculum was to be thought of in terms of activity rather than facts to be acquired.

Report of Committee on National Expenditure (May): led to further cuts in educational expenditure including a 10 per cent reduction in teachers' salaries.

1933   *Report of Consultative Committee on Infant and Nursery Schools (Hadow):* recommended separate infants schools and national provision of nursery school education.

1936   *Education Act:* school-leaving age to be raised to 15 in September 1939, but postponed by outbreak of war.

1938   *Report of the Consultative Committee on Grammar and Technical High Schools (Spens):* recommended a tripartite system of education according to ability; rejection of multilateral solution. Endorsement of junior technical schools.

1943   *White Paper on Educational Reconstruction* published.
Report of the Secondary School Examinations Council on Curriculum and Examinations in Secondary Schools (Norwood): supported the notion of a tripartite division of secondary education into grammar, technical and modern schools.

Ending of *School Certificate* recommended.

1944   *Butler Education Act:* creation of a Ministry of Education with Central Advisory Councils for England and Wales; end of feepaying in maintained schools; public education to be organized in successive stages – primary, secondary and further; compulsory education to be raised eventually to 16; county colleges to be established to continue education for school-leavers to the age of 18.

Report of Committee on Public Schools and the General Education System (Fleming): examined possible links between public schools and the state system.

Report of Committee to consider the Supply, Recruitment and Training of Teachers and Youth Leaders (McNair): recommended raising teachers' status and three years' training.

1945   *Ministry of Education* replaced Board of Education.

Report of Special Committee on Higher Technological Education (Percy): recommended upgrading of selected technical colleges to colleges of advanced technology.

1946   *Report of Barlow Committee on Scientific Manpower:* ten year programme to double the number of scientists at the universities.

1947   *School-leaving age* raised to 15.

1951   Introduction of the *General Certificate of Education* (GCE) at Ordinary and Advanced Levels.

1954   *Television Act:* establishment of an ITV network through the sale of advertising time.

1955   *National Council of Technological Awards* set up.

1956   *White Paper on Technical Education:* creation of colleges of advanced technology. Regional Colleges to cater for day release students.

1958   *White Paper, Secondary Education for All; A New Drive:* provision of secondary school buildings to complete re-organization; support for GCE examinations in modern as well as grammar schools.

1959   *Report of Central Advisory Council. 15 to 18 (Crowther):* a 20-year programme to ensure that by 1980 half the pupils in full-time education stayed on until 18.

1960   *Report of Departmental Committee on the Youth Service in England and Wales (Albermarle):* recommended expansion of work in Youth Service.

Report of Committee on Secondary School Examinations (Beloe): recommended Certificate of Secondary Education (CSE).

1961   *Commonwealth Immigration Act.*

1962   *Curriculum Study Group* set up within Ministry of Education.

1963   *Report of Central Advisory Council. Half our Future (Newsom):* considered the education of children of average ability between 13 and 16.

Report of the Committee on Higher Education (Robbins): recommended expansion of higher education by the creation of new universities; colleges of advanced technology to be designated as universities.

1964   Ministry of Education became the *Department of Education and Science* (DES).

Schools Council for Curriculum and Examinations established.

1965   *Race Relations Bill:* creation of Race Relations Board.

Circular 10/65; LEAs required to propose schemes for comprehensive reorganization on lines laid down by the DES.

1966   *White Paper on Polytechnics and other Colleges:* led to designation of 30 polytechnics.

1967   *Report of the Central Advisory Council. Children and their Primary Schools (Plowden):* expansion of nursery schooling recommended; introduction of concept of educational priority areas; importance of the relationship between school and home.

1968   *First Report of the Public Schools Commission (Newsom)* on boarding education.

1969   First *Black Paper* published.

Report of Committee on Technician Courses and Examinations (Haslegrave): recommended establishment of Technician Education Council (TEC) and Business Education Council (BEC).

1970   *Second Report of Public Schools Commission (Donnison)* on direct grant grammar schools.

Conservative government cancelled *Circular 10/65*. Replaced it with *Circular 10/70*: LEAs to decide the future organization of secondary education in their area.

1972   *School-leaving age* raised to 16.

Report of Committee of Enquiry into Teacher Education and Training (James): recommended reorganization of teacher training into three cycles.

White Paper. A Framework for Expansion: colleges of education to move away from being monotechnic institutions.

1974   *Manpower Services Commission* (MSC) established with responsibilities for training and employment.

1975   *Sex Discrimination Act:* Equal Opportunities Commission set up.

Direct Grant List for secondary schools ended.

1976   *Education Act:* to compel reluctant LEAs to introduce comprehensive education.

Commission for Racial Equality established with powers of investigation and enforcement of laws against racial discrimination.

Callaghan's speech at Ruskin College, Oxford, inaugurated

the education debate.

1977   *Green Paper, Education in Schools. A Consultative Document,* published.

1978   *Special Education Needs. Report of Committee of Enquiry into Education of Handicapped Children and Young People (Warnock):* handicapped children to be integrated into ordinary classrooms.

1979   *Education Act:* repeal of 1976 Act by Conservatives.

1980   *Education Act:* introduced assisted places at independent schools.

1981   *Education Act:* special educational needs, identification and provision.

1982   Ending of *Schools Council for Curriculum and Examinations* announced.

1983   *Secondary Examinations Council* and *School Curriculum Development Committee* formed to replace Schools Council.

HMI Reports on institutions published.

Technical and Vocational Education Initiative (TVEI) introduced specialized technical and vocational education for the 14–18 age range.

Youth Training Scheme (YTS) replaced the earlier Youth Opportunities Programme and provided a year's foundation training for all otherwise unoccupied 16- or 17-year-old school leavers.

1984   *Education (Grants and Awards) Act:* enabled the Secretary of State to support specific educational initiatives with grants.

1986   *Education (No. 2) Act:* dealt with composition and power of governing bodies, freedom of speech, sex education.

1987   *Teachers Pay and Conditions Act:* marked the ending of the Burnham Committee and the designation of 1,265 minimum hours per year for teachers.

1988   *Education Reform Act:* national curriculum and national testing; open enrolment; opting out; local management of schools; abolition of ILEA; abolition of university teachers' tenure; independence of polytechnics and colleges.

Bibliography

Addison, P. (1975) *The Road to 1945*, Cape

Ainley, P. (1988) *From School to YTS. Education and Training in England and Wales, 1944–1987*, Open University Press, Milton Keynes

Akenson, D.H. (1971) 'Patterns of English Educational Change: the Fisher and Butler Acts', *History of Education Quarterly*, Vol. 11, No. 2

Aldcroft, D.H. (1970) *The Inter-War Economy: Britain 1919–1939*, Batsford

Aldrich, R. and Leighton, P. (1985) *Education: Time for a New Act?* University of London Institute of Education

Alexander, R.J., Craft, M. and Lynch, J. (eds.) (1984) *Change in Teacher Education*, Holt, Rinehart & Winston

Allen, B.M. (1934) *Sir Robert Morant*, Macmillan

Allsobrook, D. (1986) *Schools for the Shires. The Reform of Middle-Class Education in mid-Victorian England*, Manchester University Press, Manchester

Andrews, L. (1976) *The Education Act, 1918*, Routledge & Kegan Paul

Annan, N. (1965) *J.F. Roxborough of Stowe*, Longman

Archer, R.L. (1921) *Secondary Education in the Nineteenth Century*, Cambridge University Press, Cambridge, reprinted Frank Cass, 1966

Argles, M. (1964) *South Kensington to Robbins*, Longman

Armytage, W.H.G. (1964, first edn.) *Four Hundred Years of English Education*, Cambridge University Press, Cambridge

Armytage, W.H.G. (1969) *The German Influence on English Education*, Routledge & Kegan Paul

Armytage, W.H.G. (1970) 'Battles for the Best: Some Educational Aspects of the Welfare–Warfare State in England', in P. Nash (ed.) *History and Education*, Random House, New York, USA

Armytage, W.H.G. (1978) 'Back up to Butler: the Biosocial Background of the Butler Act', *Westminster Studies in Education*, Vol. 1

Ashby, E. and Anderson, M. (1970) *The Rise of the Student Estate in Britain*, Macmillan

Ashby E. and Anderson, M. (1974) *Portrait of Haldane at Work on Education*, Macmillan

Assistant Masters Association (1955, 1958) *The A.M.A.*, Vol. 50, No. 1 and Vol. 53, No. 1

Ballard, P.B. (1936) 'The Special Place Examination', in Sadler M.E. (ed.), *International Institute Examinations Enquiry. Essays on Examinations*, Macmillan

Banks, O. (1955) *Parity and Prestige in English Secondary Education. A Study in Educational Sociology*, Routledge & Kegan Paul

Bantock, G.H. (1963) *Education in an Industrial Society*, Faber & Faber

Barker, B. (1986) *Rescuing the Comprehensive Experience*, Open University Press, Milton Keynes

Barker, R. (1972) *Education and Politics, 1900–1951: a Study of the Labour Party*, Clarendon, Oxford

Barker, T. and Drake, M. (eds.) (1982) *Population and Society in Britain 1850–1980*, Batsford

Baron, G. and Howell, D.A. (1968) *Royal Commission on Local Government. Research Studies 6, School Management and Government*, HMSO

Bates, A.W. (1984) *Broadcasting in Education*, Constable

Batley, R., O'Brien, O. and Parris, H. (1970) *Going Comprehensive: Educational Policy Making in two County Boroughs*, Routledge & Kegan Paul

Benn, C. and Simon, B. (1972) *Half Way There*, Penguin, Harmondsworth; (1970) McGraw Hill, Maidenhead

Benn, C. (1980) 'Comprehensive School Reform and the 1945 Labour Government', *History Workshop*, Vol. 10

Benn, T. (1987) *Out of the Wilderness. Diaries 1963–7*, Hutchinson

Bennett, T., Mercer, C. and Woollacott, J. (1986) *Popular Culture and Social Relations*, Open University Press, Milton Keynes

Berdahl, R. (1959) *British Universities and the State*, Columbia University Press, New York

Bernbaum, G. (1967) *Social Change and the Schools 1918–1944*, Routledge & Kegan Paul

Birchenough, C. (1938 edn.) *History of Elementary Education in England and Wales*, University Tutorial Press

Birrell, A. (1937) *Things Past Redress*, Faber & Faber

Bishop, A. (1971) *The Rise of a Central Authority for English Education*, Cambridge University Press, Cambridge

Black, C. (ed.) (1915) *Married Women's Work*, Bell & Son

Blackburn, F. (1954) *George Tomlinson*, Heinemann

Blackstone, T. (1971) *A Fair Start: the Provision of Pre-School Education*, Allen Lane

Blyth, W.A.L. and Derricott, R. (1977) *The Social Significance of Middle Schools*, Batsford

Board of Education (1905) *Report on Children under Five Years of Age in Public Elementary Schools*, HMSO

Board of Education (1906) *Report of the Consultative Committee Upon Questions Affecting the Higher Elementary School*, HMSO

Board of Education (1908) *Regulations for the Training of Secondary Schools*, Cd. 4184, HMSO

Board of Education (1911) *Report of the Consultative Committee on Examinations in Secondary Schools*, HMSO

Board of Education (1912) *The Training of Women Teachers for Secondary Schools. Educational Pamphlet No. 23*, HMSO

Board of Education (1912) *The Montessori System of Education. Educational Pamphlet No. 24*, HMSO

Board of Education (1913) *Annual Report 1912–13, History of the Training of Teachers for Elementary Schools*, HMSO

Board of Education (1922) Circular 1294, *Curriculum of Secondary Schools in England*, HMSO

Board of Education (1923) *Report of the Consultative Committee on Differentiation of the Curriculum for Boys and Girls in Secondary Schools*, HMSO

Board of Education (1926) *Report of the Consultative Committee on The Education of the Adolescent* (the Hadow Report), HMSO

Board of Education (1927) *Recent Development of Secondary Schools in England and Wales, Educational Pamphlet No. 50*, HMSO

Board of Education (1928) *The New Prospect in Education. Educational Pamphlet No. 60*, HMSO

Board of Education (1931) *Report of the Consultative Committee on the Primary School*, HMSO

Board of Education (1933) *Report of the Consultative Committee on Infant and Nursery Schools*, HMSO

Board of Education (1938) *Report of the Consultative Committee on Secondary Education* (the Spens Report), HMSO

Board of Education (1944) *Report of the Committee on the Public Schools and the General Educational System* (the Fleming Report), HMSO

Bogdanor, V. and Skidelsky, R. (eds.) (1970) *The Age of Affluence, 1951–1964*, Macmillan

Boothroyd, H.E. (1923) *A History of the Inspectorate*, Board of

Education Inspectors' Association

Boyle, A. (1972) *Only the Wind Will Listen. Reith of the BBC*, Hutchinson

Boyson, R. (1970) 'The Essential Conditions for the Success of a Comprehensive School', in Cox, C.B. and Dyson, A.E. *Black Paper 2*, Critical Quarterly Society

Bramwell, R.D. (1961) *Elementary School Work 1900–1925*, Institute of Education, University of Durham, Durham

Braybon, G. (1981) *Women Workers in the First World War*, Croom Helm

Brereton, J.L. (1944) *The Case For Examinations*, Cambridge University Press, Cambridge

Briggs, A. (1985) *The BBC: The First Fifty Years*, Oxford University Press, Oxford

Browne, J.D. (1979) *Teachers of Teachers. A History of the Association of Teachers in Colleges and Departments of Education*, Hodder & Stoughton

Burgess, R. (1983) *Experiencing Comprehensive Education, a Study of Bishop McGregor School*, Methuen

Burrows, J. (1978) *The Middle School*, Woburn Press

Burt, C. (1970) 'The Mental Differences between Children', in Cox, C.B. and Dyson, A.E. *Black Paper 2*, Critical Quarterly Society

Butler, R.A.B. (1982) *The Art of Memory*, Hodder & Stoughton

Calder, A. (1969) *The People's War: Britain 1939–45*, Cape

Callaghan, J. (1987) *Time and Chance*, Collins

Cantor, L. and Roberts, I. (1969) *Further Education in England and Wales*, Routledge & Kegan Paul

Carswell, J. (1985) *Government and the Universities in Britain. Programme and Performance 1960–80*, Cambridge University Press, Cambridge

Castle, B. (1980) *The Castle Diaries 1974–76*, Weidenfeld & Nicolson

Castle, B. (1984) *The Castle Diaries 1964–70*, Weidenfeld & Nicolson

Centre for Contemporary Cultural Studies (1981) *Unpopular Education*, Hutchinson

Chapman, J.V. (1985) *Professional Roots. The College of Preceptors in British Society*, Theydon Bois Publications, Epping

Charlton, M. (1983) *The Price of Victory*, BBC Publications

Chitty, C. (ed.) (1987) *Redefining the Comprehensive Experience*, University of London Institute of Education

Chitty, C. (1989) *Towards a New Education System: The Victory of the New Right?*, Falmer Press

Clark, Revd. A. (1985) *Echoes of the Great War: Diary of Revd.*

Andrew Clark 1914–19, Oxford University Press, Oxford

Clarke, F. (1940) *Education and Social Change. An English Interpretation*, Sheldon Press

Clarkson, M. (ed.) (1988) *Emerging Issues in Primary Education*, Falmer Press

Clegg, A. (ed.) (1972) *The Changing Primary School: its Problems and Priorities*, Chatto & Windus

Colville, Sir J. (1985) *The Fringes of Power. Downing Street Diaries, 1939–1955*, Hodder & Stoughton

Coote, A. and Campbell, B. (1982) *Sweet Freedom*, Pan

Corlett, J. (1929) *A Survey of the Financial Aspects of Elementary Education*, P.S. King and Son

Cotgrove, S. (1958) *Technical Education and Social Change*, Allen & Unwin

Cox, C.B. and Dyson, A.E. (1969–70) *The Black Papers*, Vols. 1–3, Critical Quarterly Society

Crosby, T.L. (1986) *The Impact of Civilian Evacuation in the Second World War*, Croom Helm

Crosland, C.A.R. (1956) *The Future of Socialism*, Cape

Crosland, S. (1982) *Tony Crosland*, Cape

Cross Commission (1888) *Report of the Royal Commission on the Elementary Acts*, HMSO

Crossman, R.H.S. (1975–7) *The Diaries of a Cabinet Minister* (ed. Janet Morgan), Hamilton/Cape (3 Vols.)

Crossman, R.H.S. (1981) *The Backbench Diaries of Richard Crossman* (ed. Janet Morgan), Hamilton/Cape

Cruickshank, M. (1963) *Church and State in English Education: 1870 to the Present Day*, Macmillan

Curran, J. and Porter, V. (1983) *British Cinema History*, Weidenfeld & Nicolson

Curran, J., Smith, A. and Wingate, P. (1987) *Impacts and Influences*, Methuen

Dancy, J. (1963) *The Public Schools and the Future*, Faber & Faber

Davies, M. Llewelyn (1915) *Maternity: Letters from Working Women Collected by the Women's Co-operative Guild*, Bell (Virago reprint, 1978)

Dawson, P. (1981) *Making a Comprehensive Work*, Blackwell, Oxford

Dean, D.W. (1970) 'H.A.L. Fisher, Reconstruction and the Development of the 1918 Education Act', *British Journal of Educational Studies*, Vol. 18, No. 3

Dean, D.W. (1986) 'Planning For a Postwar Generation. Ellen Wilkinson and George Tomlinson at the Ministry of Education,

1945–51', *History of Education*, Vol. 15, No. 2

Dent, H.C. (1968 edn.) *The Education Act 1944*, University of London Press

Dent, H.C. (1970) *1870–1970: Century of Growth in English Education*, Longman

Dent, H.C. (1977) *The Training of Teachers in England and Wales 1800–1975*, Hodder & Stoughton

Department of Education and Science, Circular 7/65, *The Education of Immigrant Children*, June 1965

Department of Education and Science, Circular 10/65, *The Organisation of Secondary Education*, July 1965

Department of Education and Science (1966, 1968) Annual Reports, HMSO

Department of Education and Science (1967) *Report of the Central Advisory Council for Education. Children and their Primary Schools* (the Plowden Report), Vol. 1, HMSO

Department of Education and Science (1970) *Towards the Middle School. Education Pamphlet No. 57*, HMSO

Department of Education and Science (1972) *Educational Priority. EPA Problems and Policies*, Vol. 1, HMSO

Department of Education and Science (1973) *Adult Education: A Plan for Development* (the Russell Report), HMSO

Department of Education and Science (1977) *Education in Schools: A Consultative Document*, HMSO

Department of Education and Science (1978) *Secondary School Examinations: A single system at 16 plus*, HMSO

Department of Education and Science (1978) *Comprehensive Education, Report of a DES Conference*, HMSO

Department of Education and Science (1979) *Curricular Differences For Boys and Girls. Education Survey 21*, HMSO

Department of Education and Science (1983) *Teaching Quality*, HMSO

Department of Education and Science (1984) *Education Observed 2. A review of published reports by HM Inspectors on primary schools and 11–16 and 12–16 comprehensive schools*, HMSO

Department of Education and Science (1985) *The Educational System of England and Wales*, HMSO

Devereux, W.A. (1982) *Adult Education in Inner London 1870–1980*, Shepheard-Walwyn with ILEA

Doherty, B. (1964) 'The Hadow Report, 1926', *Durham Research Review*, Vol. 4, No. 15

Donoughue, B. (1987) *Prime Minister. The Conduct of Policy under*

Harold Wilson and James Callaghan, Cape

Douglas, J.W.B. (1964) *The Home and the School. A Study of Ability and Attainment in the Primary School*, MacGibbon & Kee

Dyhouse, C. (1981) *Girls Growing Up in Late Victorian and Edwardian England*, Routledge & Kegan Paul

Eaglesham, E.J.R. (1956) *From School Board to Local Authority*, Routledge & Kegan Paul

Eaglesham, E.J.R. (1967) *The Foundations of Twentieth Century Education in England*, Routledge & Kegan Paul

Easton, W. et al. (1988) *Disorder and Discipline*, Temple Smith

Edwards, A.D. (1970) *The Changing Sixth Form in the Twentieth Century*, Routledge & Kegan Paul

Edwards, R. (1960) *The Secondary Technical School*, University of London Press

Elvin, L. (1987) *Encounters With Education*, University of London Institute of Education

Evans, K. (1985) *The Development and Structure of the English School System*, Hodder & Stoughton

Eysenck, H.J. (1970) 'The Rise of the Mediocracy', in Cox, C.B. and Dyson, A.E. *Black Paper 2*, Critical Quarterly Society

Fabian Society (1964) *The Public Schools*

Fairbairn, A.N. (ed.) (1980) *The Leicestershire Plan*, Heinemann

Fearn, E. and Simon, B. (eds.) (1980) *Education in the 1960s*, History of Education Society, Leicester

Fenwick, I.G.K. (1976) *The Comprehensive School 1944–1970*, Methuen

Fenwick, K. and McBride, P. (1981) *The Government of Education in Britain*, Martin Robertson, Oxford

Fenwick, K. (1985) 'Changing Roles in the Government of Education', *British Journal of Educational Studies*, Vol. 33, No. 2

Firmager, J. (1981) 'The Consultative Committee under the Chairmanship of Sir Henry Hadow: The Education of the Adolescent', *History of Education*, Vol. 10, No. 4

Fisher, P. (1982) *External Examinations in Secondary Schools in England and Wales 1944–1964*, Museum of the History of Education, University of Leeds, Leeds

Floud, J.E. (ed.), Halsey, A.H. and Martin, F.M. (1956) *Social Class and Educational Opportunity*, Heinemann

Ford, J. (1969) *Social Class and the Comprehensive School*, Routledge & Kegan Paul

Fraser, D. (1984 edn.) *The Evolution of the British Welfare State*, Macmillan

Galton, M., Simon, B. and Croll, P. (1980) *Inside the Primary Class-room*, Routledge & Kegan Paul

Gibbon, I.G. and Bell, R.W. (1939) *History of the London County Council 1889–1939*, Macmillan

Gilkes, A.N. (1957) *Independent Education: in Defence of Public Schools*, Gollancz

Gittins, D. (1982) *Fair Sex: Family Size and Structure 1900–39*, Hutchinson

Glass, D.V. (ed.) (1954) *Social Mobility in Britain*, Routledge & Kegan Paul

Goldthorpe, J.H. et al. (1980) *Social Mobility and Class Structure in Modern Britain*, Clarendon Press, Oxford

Goodson, I. (1983) *School Subjects and Curriculum Change*, Croom Helm

Gordon, P. (1980) *Selection for Secondary Education*, Woburn Press

Gordon, P. (ed.) (1985) *Is Teaching a Profession?*, University of London Institute of Education

Gordon, P. (1985) 'The Handbook of Suggestions for Teachers: its origins and evolution', *Journal of Educational Administration and History*, Vol. 17, No. 1

Gordon, P. (1986) 'Teaching as a Graduate Profession 1890–1970', *History of Education Society Proceedings of Annual Conference 'The Professional Teacher'*, Wilkes, J. (ed.), History of Education Society, Leicester

Gordon, P. (1988) 'Katharine Bathurst. A Controversial Woman Inspector', *History of Education*, Vol. 17, No. 3

Gordon, P. and Lawton, D. (1978) *Curriculum Change in the Nineteenth and Twentieth Centuries*, Hodder & Stoughton

Gosden, P.H.J.H. (1966) *The Development of Educational Administration in England and Wales*, Blackwell, Oxford

Gosden, P.H.J.H. (1972) *The Evolution of a Profession: a Study of the Contribution of Teachers' Associations to the Development of School Teaching as a Professional Occupation*, Blackwell, Oxford

Gosden, P.H.J.H. (1976) *Education in the Second World War*, Methuen

Gosden, P.H.J.H. (1983) *The Education System Since 1944*, Martin Robertson, Oxford

Gosden, P.H.J.H. 'The Role of Central Government and its Agencies, 1963–82', in Alexander, R.J., Craft, M. and Lynch, J. (eds.) *Change in Teacher Education*, Holt, Rinehart & Winston

Gosden, P.H.J.H. and Sharp, P.R. (1978) *The Development of an Education Service. The West Riding 1889–1974*, Martin Robertson,

Oxford

Grace, G. (1978) *Teachers, Ideology and Control*, Routledge & Kegan Paul

Gray, J. and Hannon, V. (1986) 'HMI's Interpretation of Schools' Examinations Results', *Journal of Educational Policy*, Vol. 1, No. 1

Gray, J.L. and Moshinsky, P. (1938) 'Ability and Opportunity in English Education', in Hogben, L. (ed.), *Political Arithmetic. A Symposium of Population Studies*, Allen & Unwin

Greene, G. (1984) *The Old School*, Oxford University Press, Oxford

Gretton, J. and Jackson, M. (1976) *William Tyndale: Collapse of a School – or a System?*, Allen & Unwin

Griffiths, A. (1971) *Secondary School Reorganization in England and Wales*, Routledge & Kegan Paul

Griggs, C. (1983) *The Trades Union Congress and the Struggle for Education, 1868–1925*, Falmer Press, Lewes

Griggs, C. (1985) *Private Education in Britain*, Falmer Press, Lewes

Halsey, A.H. (1986) *Change in British Society*, Oxford University Press, Oxford

Halsey, A.H., Heath, A.F. and Ridge, J.M. (1980) *Origins and Destinations*, Clarendon Press, Oxford

Hamilton, M.A. (1938) *Arthur Henderson*, Heinemann

Hargreaves, D.H. (1982) *The Challenge for the Comprehensive School*, Routledge & Kegan Paul

Harrison, J.F.C. (1961) *Learning and Living, 1790–1960*, Routledge & Kegan Paul

Harte, N. (1986) *The University of London 1836–1986*, Athlone Press

Haviland, J. (ed.) (1988) *Take Care, Mr Baker!*, Fourth Estate

Hearnden, A. (1984) *Red Robert, a Life of Robert Birley*, Hamish Hamilton

Heath, A. (1981) *Social Mobility*, Fontana

Heron, L. (1985) *Truth, Dare or Promise: Girls Growing Up in the 1950s*, Virago, 1985

Heward, C. (1988) *Making a Man of Him. Parents and Their Sons' Education at an English Public School 1929–1950*, Routledge

Hicks, D. (1974) 'The National Advisory Council on the Training and Supply of Teachers 1949–1965', *British Journal of Educational Studies*, Vol. 22, No. 3

Holmes, C. (1988) *John Bull's Island. Immigration and British Society 1871–1971*, Macmillan

Holmes, E.A.G. (1922) 'The Confessions and Hopes of an ex-Inspector of Schools', *Hibbert Journal*, Vol. 20

Honey, J.R. (1977) *Tom Brown's Universe*, Millington

House of Commons (1981), Education, Science and Arts Committee, *The Secondary School. Curriculum and Examinations*, HMSO

Howard, A. (1987) *Rab: the Life of R.A. Butler*, Cape

Howarth, T.E. (1978) *Cambridge Between Two Wars*, Collins

Hughes, B. (1979) 'In Defence of Ellen Wilkinson', *History Workshop*, Vol. 7

Humphreys, D.W. (1965) *The Relationship between the Training Colleges and the Universities before McNair*, Bristol University Institute of Education, Bristol

Hunt, F. (ed.) (1986) *Lessons for Life, the Schooling of Girls and Women, 1850–1950*, Blackwell, Oxford

Hurt, J. (1979) *Elementary Schooling and the Working Classes, 1860–1918*, Routledge & Kegan Paul

I.A.A.M. (1967) *Teaching in Comprehensive Schools*, Cambridge University Press

James, P.H. (1980) *The Reorganization of Secondary Education*, NFER, Windsor

Jarvis, P. (ed.) (1987) *Twentieth-Century Thinkers in Adult Education*, Croom Helm

Jay, D. (1980) *Change and Fortune*, Hutchinson

Jeffcoate, R. (1984) *Ethnic Minorities and Education*, Harper and Row

Jeffreys, K. (1984) 'R.A. Butler, the Board of Education and the 1944 Act', *History*, Vol. 69, No. 227

Jenkins, E.W. (1973) 'The Board of Education and the Reconstruction Committee, 1916–1918', *Journal of Educational Administration and History*, Vol. 5, No. 1

Johnson, D. (1987) *Private Schools and State Schools: Two Systems or One?* Open University Press, Milton Keynes

Johnson, L. (1979) *The Cultural Critics*, Routledge & Kegan Paul

Johnson, P. (1968) *Land Fit for Heroes*, University of Chicago, USA

Johnston, H.H. (1916) 'The Public Service and Education', *Nineteenth Century and After*, Vol. 80, No. 473

Jones, L.G.E. (1924) *The Training of Teachers in England and Wales. A Critical Survey*, Oxford University Press, Oxford

Jones, S.G. (1986) *Workers at Play: a Social and Economic History of Leisure 1918–39*, Routledge & Kegan Paul

Judge, H. (1984) *A Generation of Schooling. English Secondary Schools since 1944*, Oxford University Press, Oxford

Judges, A.V. (1954) 'The Comprehensive School', in *Studies in Education 6. The Problems of Secondary Education Today*, Evans

Kalton, G. (1966) *The Public Schools. A Factual Survey*, Longman

Kazamias, A. (1966) *Politics, Society and Secondary Education in*

England, University of Pennsylvania Press, Philadelphia, USA

Kelly, T. (1970) *A History of Adult Education in Great Britain*, Liverpool University Press, Liverpool

Kelly, T. (1981) *For Advancement of Learning: the University of Liverpool 1881–1981*, Liverpool University Press, Liverpool

Kilmuir, D. (1964) *Political Adventure*, Weidenfeld & Nicolson

Kogan, M. (1971) *The Politics of Education*, Penguin, Harmondsworth

Kogan, M. (1978) *The Politics of Educational Change*, Fontana

Kogan, M. and Kogan, D. (1983) *The Attack on Higher Education*, Kogan Page

Kogan, M. and Packwood, T. (1974) *Advisory Councils and Committees in Education*, Routledge & Kegan Paul

Lancaster, B. and Mason, T. (1987) *Life and Labour in a Twentieth-Century City: the Experience of Coventry*, Cryfield Press, Coventry

Langer, J.R. (1882) Presidential address, National Union of Teachers Conference 1882, National Union of Teachers

Lawn, M. (1987) *Servants of the State: the Contested Control of Teaching 1900–1930*, Falmer Press

Lawn, M. and Grace, G. (eds.) (1987) *Teachers: the Culture and Politics of Work*, Falmer Press

Lawton, D. (1980) *The Politics of the School Curriculum*, Routledge & Kegan Paul

Lawton, D. and Chitty, C. (eds.) (1988) *The National Curriculum*, University of London Institute of Education

Lawton, D. and Gordon, P. (1987) *HMI*, Routledge & Kegan Paul

Leese, J. (1950) *Personalities and Power in English Education*, Arnold

Legge, D. (1982) *The Education of Adults in Britain*, Open University Press, Milton Keynes

Leinster-Mackay, D. (1984) *The Rise of the English Prep School*, Falmer Press

Leonard, M. (1988) *The 1988 Education Act. A Tactical Guide for Schools*, Blackwell, Oxford

Lewis, J. (1984) *Women in England, 1870–1950*, Wheatsheaf, Brighton

Lewis, J. (ed.) (1986) *Labour and Love. Women's Experience of Home and Family 1850–1940*, Blackwell, Oxford

Lindsay, K. (1926) *Social Progress and Educational Waste: being a Study of the "Free Place" and Scholarship System*, Routledge

Lodge, P. and Blackstone, T. (1982) *Education Policy and Educational Inequality*, Martin Robertson, Oxford

Lomax, D.E. (ed.) (1973) *The Education of Teachers in Britain*, Wiley

Longmate, N. (ed.) (1981) *The Home Front*, Chatto & Windus

Low, R. (1979) *Documentary and Educational Films of the 1930s*, Allen & Unwin

Low, R. (1979) *Films of Comment and Persuasion of the 1930s*, Allen & Unwin

Lowe, R. (1984) 'Robert Morant and the Secondary School Regulations of 1904', *Journal of Educational Administration and History*, Vol. 16, No. 1

Lowe, R. (1987) 'Structural Change in English Higher Education 1870–1920', in Muller, D., Ringer, F. and Simon, B. (eds.) *The Rise of the Modern Educational System*, Cambridge University Press, Cambridge

Lowe, R. (1988) *Education in the Post-War Years: a Social History*, Routledge

Lowndes, G.A.N. (1937) *The Silent Social Revolution*, Oxford University Press, Oxford

Lynch, J. (1979) *The Reform of Teacher Education*, Society for Research into Higher Education, Guildford

Lynch, J. (1986) *Multicultural Education*, Routledge

McNay, I. and Ozga, J. (eds.) (1985) *Policy-making in Education: the Breakdown of Consensus: a Reader*, Pergamon

Maclure, S. (1970) *One Hundred Years of London Education, 1870–1970*, Allen Lane

Maclure, S. (1988) *Education Re-formed. A Guide to the Education Reform Act 1988*, Hodder & Stoughton

Macmillan, H. (1938) *The Middle Way*, Macmillan

Magnus, L. (1923) *The Jubilee Book of the Girls' Public Day School Trust 1873–1923*, Cambridge University Press, Cambridge

Mangan, J.A. (1981) *Athleticism in the Victorian and Edwardian Public School*, Cambridge University Press, Cambridge

Mann, J. (1985) 'Who Killed Schools Council?' in Plaskow, M. (ed.), *Life and Death of the Schools Council*, Falmer Press

Mansbridge, A. (1940) *The Trodden Road: Experience, Inspiration and Belief*, Dent

Manzer, R. (1970) *Teachers and Politics*, Manchester University Press, Manchester

Marsh, D.C. (1965) *The Changing Social Structure of England and Wales, 1871–1961*, Routledge & Kegan Paul

Marwick, A. (1965) *The Deluge. British Society and the First World War*, Bodley Head

Marwick, A. (1968) 'The Impact of the First World War on British Society', *Journal of Contemporary History*, Vol. 3, No. 1

Marwick, A. (1974) *War and Social Change in the Twentieth Century*,

Macmillan

Marwick, A. (1982) *British Society Since 1945*, Allen Lane

Masters, B. (1985) *The Swinging Sixties*, Constable

McCulloch, G., Jenkins, E. and Layton, D. (1985) *Technological Revolution? The Politics of School Science and Technology in England and Wales since 1945*, Falmer Press

Miles, M. (1968) *Comprehensive Schooling. Problems and Perspectives*, Longman

Ministry of Education (1947) *The New Secondary Education. Pamphlet No. 9*, HMSO

Ministry of Education (1958) *Secondary Education for All*, HMSO

Ministry of Education (1958, 1962, 1963) Annual Reports, HMSO

Ministry of Education (1959) *Report of the Consultative Committee on Fifteen to Eighteen* (the Crowther Report), HMSO

Ministry of Education (1963) *Central Advisory Council, Half our Future* (the Newsom Report), HMSO

Mitchell, W.F. and Beaulavon, G. (1936) 'The Training of Teachers', *Yearbook of Education*, Evans

Moberly, Sir W. (1949) *The Crisis in the University*, SCM Press

Montgomery, R.J. (1965) *Examinations*, Longman

Montgomery, R.J. (1978) *A New Examination of Examinations*, Routledge & Kegan Paul

Morgan, K.O. (1985) *Labour in Power 1945–51*, Oxford University Press, Oxford

Morris, A.J.A. (1977) *C.P. Trevelyan, 1870–1958. Portrait of a Radical*, Blackstaff Press, Belfast

Morris, H. (1924) *The Village College*, Cambridge University Press, Cambridge

Mortimore, P. et al. (1988) *School Matters: the Junior Years*, Open Books, Wells

Mowat, C.L. (1955) *Britain between the Wars, 1918–1940*, Methuen

Muller, D., Ringer, F. and Simon, B. (eds.) (1987) *The Rise of the Modern Educational System*, Cambridge University Press, Cambridge

Murphy, J. (1971) *Church, State and Schools in Britain, 1800–1970*, Routledge & Kegan Paul

Nash, P. (ed.) (1970) *History and Education*, Random House, New York

Niblett, W.R. et al. (1975) *The University Connection*, NFER, Windsor

Nicolson, N. (ed.) (1966–8) *Harold Nicolson. Diaries and Letters* (3 Vols.), Collins

Norwood, C. (1929) *The English Tradition of Education*, Murray

Ogren, G. (1953) *Trends in English Teachers' Training from 1800*, Stockholm, Sweden

Ozga, J. and Lawn, M. (1981) *Teachers, Professionalism and Class*, Falmer Press, Lewes

Padley, R. and Cole, M. (1940) *Evacuation Survey*, Routledge

Parker, P. (1987) *The Old Lie: the Great War and the Public School Ethos*, Constable

Parkhurst, H. (1922) *Education on the Dalton Plan*, Bell

Parkinson, M. (1970) *The Labour Party and the Organization of Secondary Education 1918–1965*, Routledge & Kegan Paul

Parliamentary Committee of Public Accounts (1967) *Higher Education*, HMSO

Paz, D.G. (1980) *The Politics of Working-Class Education in Britain 1830–50*, Manchester University Press, Manchester

Pedley, R. (1959) *The Comprehensive School*, Penguin, Harmondsworth

Pegg, M. (1983) *Broadcasting and Society 1918–1939*, Croom Helm

Pelling, H. (1984) *The Labour Governments 1945–51*, Macmillan

Percy, E. (1958) *Some Memories*, Eyre & Spottiswood

Perkin, H. (1969) *Key Profession. The History of the Association of University Teachers*, Routledge & Kegan Paul

Perry, G. (1985) *The Great British Picture Show*, Pavilion

Perry, W. (1976) *Open University: a Personal Account*, Open University Press, Milton Keynes

Petch, J.A. (1953) *Fifty Years of Examining. The Joint Matriculation Board 1903–1953*, Harrap

Peters, R.S. (ed.) (1969) *Perspectives on Plowden*, Routledge & Kegan Paul

Phillipson, N. (1983) *Universities, Society and the Future*, Edinburgh University Press, Edinburgh

Pile, Sir W. (1979) *The Department of Education and Science*, Allen & Unwin

Plaskow, M. (ed.) (1985) *Life and Death of the Schools Council*, Falmer Press

Public Schools Commission, *First Report* 1968, *Second Report* 1970, HMSO

Rae, J. (1981) *The Public School Revolution, Britain's Independent Schools, 1964–79*, Faber

Ranson, S. and Tomlinson, J. (eds.) (1986) *The Changing Government of Education*, Allen & Unwin

Redcliffe-Maud, J. (1982) *Experiences of an Optimist*, Hamish Hamilton

Rée, H. (1985) *Educator Extraordinary. The Life and Achievement of Henry Morris, 1889–1961*, Peter Owen

Reeder, D. (ed.) (1977) *Urban Education in the Nineteenth Century*, Taylor & Francis

Rees, D.B. (1982) *Preparation for Crisis: Adult Education 1945–80*, Hesketh, Ormskirk

Rhodes, G. (1981) *Inspectorates in British Government*, Allen & Unwin

Rich, R.W. (1933) *The Training of Teachers in England and Wales During the Nineteenth Century*, Cambridge University Press, reprinted Cedric Chivers, Bath, 1972

Richards, J. (1973) *Visions of Yesterday*, Routledge & Kegan Paul

Richards, J. (1984) *The Age of the Dream Palace*, Routledge & Kegan Paul

Richmond, W.K. (1978) *Education in Britain since 1944*, Methuen

Riley, D. (1983) *War in the Nursery*, Virago

Roach, J. (1971) *Public Examinations in England 1850–1900*, Cambridge University Press, Cambridge

Roach, J. (1979) 'Examinations and the Secondary Schools 1900–1945', *History of Education*, Vol. 8, No. 1

Robbins, Lord and Ford, B. (1965) 'Report on Robbins', *Universities Quarterly*, Vol. 20, No. 1

Roberts, E. (1984) *A Woman's Place*, Blackwell, Oxford

Robinson, E. (1968) *The New Polytechnics*, Penguin, Harmondsworth

Robinson, E. (1973) 'The Future of Teacher Education in the Polytechnics', in Lomax, D.E. (ed.), *The Education of Teachers in Britain*, Wiley

Rogers, R. (1980) *Crowther to Warnock. How Fourteen Reports Tried to Change Children's Lives*, Heinemann

Roy, W. (1983) *Teaching Under Attack*, Croom Helm

Rubens, L. (1970) 'The Ealing Case', in Cox, C.B. and Dyson, A.E. *Black Paper 2*, Critical Quarterly Society

Rubinstein, D. (1979) 'Ellen Wilkinson Re-considered', *History Workshop*, Vol. 7

Rubinstein, D. and Simon, B. (1973) *The Evolution of the Comprehensive School*, Routledge & Kegan Paul

Rudd, E. (1975) *The Highest Education*, Routledge

Rutter, M. et al. (1979) *Fifteen Thousand Hours. Secondary Schools and Their Effects on Children*, Open Books

Ryder, J. and Silver, H. (1985) *Modern English Society*, Methuen

Salter, B. and Tapper, T. (1981) *Education, Politics and the State*, Grant McIntyre

Salter, B. and Tapper, T. (1985) *Power and Policy in Education*, Falmer Press

Sampson, A. (1962) *Anatomy of Britain*, Hodder & Stoughton

Sampson, A. (1971) *The New Anatomy of Britain*, Hodder & Stoughton

Sampson, A. (1983) *The Changing Anatomy of Britain*, Hodder & Stoughton

Sanderson, M. (1972) *The Universities and British Industry, 1850–1970*, Routledge & Kegan Paul

Sanderson, M. (1987) *Educational Opportunity and Social Change in England*, Faber & Faber

Saran, R. (1973) *Policy-Making in Secondary Education*, Clarendon Press, Oxford

Schools Council (1965) *Change and Response. The First Year's Work 1964–65*, HMSO

Scott, P. (1984) *The Crisis of the University*, Croom Helm

Seaborne, M. (1968) 'William Brockington, Director of Education for Leicestershire 1903–1947', in Simon, B. (ed.) *Education in Leicestershire 1540–1940: a Regional Study*, Leicester University Press, Leicester

Seaborne, M. and Lowe, R. (1977) *The English School. Its Architecture and Organization, Vol. II 1870–1970*, Routledge & Kegan Paul

Searby, P. (1982) *The Training of Teachers in Cambridge University, 1879–1939*, Cambridge University Department of Education, Cambridge

Searle, G.R. (1971) *The Quest For National Efficiency*, Blackwell, Oxford

Seifert, R. (1987) *Teacher Militancy: a History of Teacher Strikes, 1896–1987*, Falmer Press

Selby-Bigge, L.A. (1927) *The Board of Education*, Putnam

Seldon, A. (1981) *Churchill's Indian Summer, the Conservative Government, 1951–55*, Hodder & Stoughton

Select Committee of the House of Lords on the Anti-Discrimination (No. 2) Bill (1972), HMSO

Selleck, R.J.W. (1972) *English Primary Education and the Progressives 1914–1939*, Routledge & Kegan Paul

Sendall, B. (1982) *Independent Television in Britain*, Vol. 1, Macmillan

Sharp, P.R. (1987) *The Creation of the Local Authority Sector of Higher Education*, Falmer Press

Shaw, B. (1983) *Comprehensive Schooling: the Impossible Dream?*, Blackwell, Oxford

Sherington, G. (1981) *English Education, Social Change and War, 1911–1920*, Manchester University Press, Manchester

Shinn, C.H. (1986) *Paying the Piper: the Development of the University Grants Committee 1919–46*, Falmer Press

Silver, H. (ed.) (1973) *Equal Opportunity in Education*, Methuen

Silver, H. (1975) *English Education and the Radicals, 1780–1850*, Routledge & Kegan Paul

Silver, H. (1980) *Education and the Social Condition*, Methuen

Simon, B. (1974a) *Education and the Labour Movement, 1870–1920*, Lawrence & Wishart

Simon, B. (1974b) *The Politics of Educational Reform, 1920–1940*, Lawrence & Wishart

Simon, B. (1981) 'Why no Pedagogy in England?' in Simon, B. and Taylor, W. (eds.), *Education in the Eighties*, Batsford

Simon, B. (1985) 'The Tory Government and Education 1951–60: Background to Breakout', *History of Education*, Vol. 14, No. 4

Simon, B. (1986) 'The 1944 Education Act: A Conservative Measure?', *History of Education*, Vol. 15, No. 1

Simon, B. (1988) *Bending the Rules. The Baker 'Reform' of Education*, Lawrence & Wishart

Simon, J. (1977) 'The Shaping of the Spens Report on Secondary Education 1933–38. An Inside View, Part I', *British Journal of Educational Studies*, Vol. 25, No. 1

Simon, J. (1977) 'The Shaping of the Spens Report on Secondary Education 1933–38. An Inside View, Part II', *British Journal of Educational Studies*, Vol. 25, No. 2

Simon, S.D. (1938) *A Century of City Government: Manchester 1838–1938*, Allen & Unwin

Simpson, L. (1984) 'Imperialism, National Efficiency and Education 1900–1905', *Journal of Educational Administration and History*, Vol. 16, No. 1

Smith, H.L. (ed.) (1986) *War and Social Change*, Manchester University Press, Manchester

Snow, G. (1959) *The Public School in the New Age*, Bles

Spender, S. (1945) *Citizens in War – and After*, Harrap

Stevenson, J. (1984) *British Society, 1914–45*, Penguin, Harmondsworth

Stewart, J. (1986) 'A Local Service: Strengthening the LEA', in Ranson, S. and Tomlinson, J. (eds.) *The Changing Government of Education*, Allen & Unwin

Stewart, W.A.C. (1989) *Higher Education in Postwar Britain*, Macmillan

Stubbs, W. (1986) 'The Metropolitan LEA', in Ranson, S. and Tomlinson, J. (eds.) *The Changing Government of Education*, Allen &

Unwin

Summerfield, P. (1984) *Women Workers in the Second World War*, Croom Helm

Sutherland, G. (1973) *Policy-Making in Elementary Education, 1870–1895*, Oxford University Press, Oxford

Sutherland, G. (1984) *Ability, Merit and Measurement. Mental Testing and English Education, 1880–1940*, Clarendon Press, Oxford

Symonds, R. (1986) *Oxford and Empire*, Macmillan

Szamuely, T. (1970) 'Comprehensive Inequality', in Cox, C.B. and Dyson, A.E. *Black Paper 2*, Critical Quarterly Society

Tawney, R.H. (1922) *Secondary Education for All*, Labour Party

Taylor, P.M. (ed.) (1988) *Britain and the Cinema in the Second World War*, Macmillan

Taylor, W. (1963) *The Secondary Modern School*, Faber

Taylor, W. (1984) 'The National Context 1972–82', in Alexander, R.J., Craft, M. and Lynch., J. (eds.) *Change in Teacher Education*, Wiley

Thompson, T. (ed.) (1987) *Dear Girl. The Diaries and Letters of Two Working Women (1897–1917)*, Women's Press

Thoms, D. (1980) *Policy-Making in Education: Robert Blair and the London County Council 1904–1924*, Museum of History of Education, Leeds

Tropp, A. (1957) *The School Teachers*, Heinemann

Truscot, B. (1945) *Redbrick University*, Penguin, Harmondsworth

T.U.C. Annual Conference Reports, 1922–1943

Tuck, J.P. (1973) 'From Day Training College to University Department of Education', in Lomax, D.E. (ed.) *The Education of Teachers in Britain*, Wiley

Valentine, C.W. (1932) *The Reliability of Examinations*, University of London Press

Vernon, B. (1982) *Ellen Wilkinson 1891–1947*, Croom Helm

Waddington, C.H. (1942) 'Science and Government', *The Political Quarterly*, Vol. 13, No. 1

Waites, B.A. (1976) 'The Effect of the First World War on Class and Status in England 1910–20', *Journal of Contemporary History*, Vol. 11, No. 1

Wallace, R.G. (1981) 'The Origins and Authorship of the 1944 Education Act', *History of Education*, Vol. 10, No. 4

Waller, R.D. (ed.) (1956) *A Design for Democracy*, Max Parrish

Walton, J. and Walvin, J. (eds.) (1983) *Leisure in Britain 1780–1939*, Manchester University Press, Manchester

Wardle, D. (1971) *Education and Society in Nineteenth-Century*

Bibliography

Nottingham, Cambridge University Press, Cambridge

Webb, S. (1916) 'The Coming Educational Revolution', *Contemporary Review*, Vol. 110

Weber, L. (1971) *The English Infant School and Informal Education*, Prentice-Hall, Englewood Cliffs, New Jersey, USA

Weeks, A. (1986) *Comprehensive Schools. Past, Present and Future*, Macmillan

Westall, R. (1985) *Children of the Blitz*, Viking, Harmondsworth

Whitbread, N. (1972) *The Evolution of the Nursery–Infant School 1800–1970*, Routledge & Kegan Paul

White, J.P. (1975) 'The End of the Compulsory Curriculum', in *The Curriculum*, The Doris Lee Lectures, University of London Institute of Education

Wiener, M.J. (1981) *English Culture and the Decline of the Industrial Spirit 1850–1980*, Cambridge University Press, Cambridge

Williams, W.E. (1942) 'Education in the Army', *The Political Quarterly*, Vol. 13, No. 3

Williams, G. 'The Leverhulme Programme ... Future Prospects', in Phillipson, N. (1983), *Universities, Society and the Future*, Edinburgh University Press

Wilson, E. (1980) *Only Halfway to Paradise. Women in Postwar Britain 1945–1968*, Tavistock Press

Wilson, H. (1971) *The Labour Government 1964–1970*, Weidenfeld & Nicolson

Wilson, H. (1979) *Final Term. The Labour Government 1974–1976*, Weidenfeld & Nicolson and Michael Joseph

Winter, J.M. (1986) *The Great War and the British People*, Macmillan

Wiseman, S. (1961) 'Examinations and the Primary School', in Wiseman, S. (ed.) *Examinations and English Education*, Manchester University Press, Manchester

Young, M. (1958) *The Rise of the Meritocracy, 1870–2033, An Essay on Education and Equality*, Thames & Hudson. 1961 edn., Penguin, Harmondsworth

Index